YOU SHALL KNOW THAT I AM YAHWEH

Bulletin for Biblical Research Supplements

Editor
RICHARD S. HESS, Denver Seminary

Associate Editor
CRAIG L. BLOMBERG, Denver Seminary

You Shall Know that I Am Yahweh

An Inner-Biblical Interpretation
of Ezekiel's Recognition Formula

JOHN F. EVANS

EISENBRAUNS | University Park, Pennsylvania

Library of Congress Cataloging-in-Publication Data

Names: Evans, John F. (John Frederick), author.
Title: You shall know that I am Yahweh : an inner-biblical interpretation of Ezekiel's
    recognition formula / John F. Evans.
Other titles: Bulletin for biblical research supplements.
Description: University Park, Pennsylvania : Eisenbrauns, [2019] | Series: Bulletin for
    biblical research supplement | Includes bibliographical references and index.
Summary: "An examination of the recognition formula 'you/they shall know that I
    am Yahweh' as a dominant feature of Ezekiel's prophecy. Reviews past scholarship,
    details of the refrain's usage, and the origin of the formula"—Provided by publisher.
Identifiers: LCCN 2019007730 | ISBN 9781575069869 (cloth : alk. paper)
Subjects: LCSH: Bible. Ezekiel—Criticism, interpretation, etc.
Classification: LCC BS1545.52.E93 2019 | DDC 224/.406—dc23
LC record available at https://lccn.loc.gov/2019007730

Eisenbrauns is an imprint of The Pennsylvania State University Press.

The Pennsylvania State University Press is a member of the Association of University
Presses.

It is the policy of The Pennsylvania State University Press to use acid-free paper. Pub-
lications on uncoated stock satisfy the minimum requirements of American National
Standard for Information Sciences—Permanence of Paper for Printed Library Material,
ANSI Z39.48-1992.

For My Family

CONTENTS

Figures

Tables

ACKNOWLEDGMENTS AND PREFACE

This work represents a thorough updating and revision of my 2006 DTh work, submitted to Stellenbosch University. Its publication has regrettably been delayed by five international moves. I express my gratitude to Professor Hendrik Bosman for providing patient, wise guidance as my promoter. I also thank my examiners, Professor Louis Jonker of Stellenbosch and Professor Daniel Block, now retired from Wheaton Graduate School. I will never forget Dan's warm-hearted compliments and his urging me on several occasions to get the study published; he also suggested submitting it to the BBR Supplement series. As editor of the BBR series, Professsor Richard Hess has offered most valuable guidance in the process of readying the manuscript for publication.

Having lived in Africa the last twenty years, I have come to appreciate more than before the value of community and the truth that "in an academic community everybody teaches everybody" (Nicholas Wolterstorff). It has been our privilege as a family to serve at the Theological College of Central Africa (Ndola, Zambia), Namibia Evangelical Theological Seminary (Windhoek), and Nairobi Evangelical Graduate School of Theology (Kenya). I owe more to my colleagues and past students than I could ever express. The same must be said for all our financial and prayer supporters, without whom we never could have worked overseas in theological education. I do not regard our mission work as a "sacrifice," but I gladly speak of theirs.

It would be remiss of me not to acknowledge the courtesies extended to me over the years by the library staff at the institutions where I have taught, as well as at Christian Theological Seminary in Indianapolis. Others deserving thanks are: my brother, Professor William B. Evans, who gave timely assistance in accessing articles unavailable to me in Africa; Dr. Andrew Mein of Westcott House, Cambridge, who read a draft of half my dissertation in 2005 with constructive criticism; and Dr. Bruce Winter and Dr. Peter Williams, successive wardens of Tyndale House, Cambridge, together with their staff, for providing me a superb study environment on a number of occasions. To one accustomed to "making do" with fewer library resources, Tyndale House is כגן עדן, "like the Garden of Eden" (Ezek 36:35).

I am deeply grateful to Maxine Elizabeth for the encouragement and love she gave me over the years as I worked on this project. She sacrificed countless evenings during my pastoral ministry and our missionary career so that I could be alone with my books and free from interruption. The very real sacrifices of our children, Martyn, Grace Elisabeth, and Daniel, are remembered too; I am enormously proud of them. This work is dedicated to my family members. Finally, I should acknowledge the prayer support of my mother and her friend Mrs. Gee-Gee Gerbig, who dedicated themselves years back to pray daily for this project.

Where English text versification differs from the Hebrew, it is placed in brackets. Unless otherwise noted, all Bible translations are my own.

General

√	root (of word; trilateral root of Hebrew verbs)
ANE	ancient Near East(ern)
E	Elohist source
EBH	Early Biblical Hebrew
ESV	English Standard Version (2001)
H	Holiness Code
J	Yahwist source
LBH	Late Biblical Hebrew
LXX	Septuagint
MS(S)	manuscript(s)
MT	Masoretic Text
n.	footnote or endnote
NIV	New International Version (1978, 1984, 2011)
NJB	New Jerusalem Bible
NJPS	*Tanakh: The Holy Scriptures: The New JPS Translation According to the Traditional Hebrew Text* (1985, 1999)
NRSV	New Revised Standard Version (1989)
P	Priestly source
RF	Recognition Formula
SPF	Self-Presentation Formula ("I am Yahweh")
Tg.	Targum
Vulg.	Vulgate

Reference Works

AB	Anchor Bible, or Anchor Yale Bible
ABD	*Anchor Bible Dictionary*. Edited by David Noel Freedman. 6 vols. New York: Doubleday, 1992.
ABRL	Anchor Bible Reference Library
ABRT	*Assyrian and Babylonian Religious Texts*. Edited by James A. Craig. 2 vols. Leipzig: Hinrichs, 1895–1897.
AnBib	Analecta Biblica
ANEM	Ancient Near East Monographs
ANET	*Ancient Near Eastern Texts Relating to the Old Testament*. Edited by James B. Pritchard. 3rd ed. Princeton: Princeton University Press, 1969.
ANETS	Ancient Near Eastern Texts and Studies
AOAT	Alter Orient und Altes Testament

ApOTC	Apollos Old Testament Commentary
ATANT	Abhandlung zur Theologie des Alten und Neuen Testaments
ATD	Das Alte Testament Deutsch
BA	*Biblical Archaeologist*
BAR	*Biblical Archaeology Review*
BASOR	*Bulletin of the American Schools of Oriental Research*
BBB	Bonner biblische Beiträge
BBR	*Bulletin for Biblical Research*
BBRSup	Bulletin for Biblical Research Supplements
BETL	Bibliotheca Ephemeridum Theologicarum Lovaniensium
BHK	*Biblia Hebraica*. Edited by R. Kittel. 7th ed. Stuttgart: Württembergische Bibelanstalt, 1973.
BHQ	*Biblia Hebraica quinta editione cum apparatu critic novis curis elaborato*. Edited by Robert Althann and Adrian Schenker. Stuttgart: Deutsche Bibelgesellschaft, 2004–. Fascicle 12: "Ezekiel" (forthcoming). Edited by Johan Lust.
BHS	*Biblia Hebraica Stuttgartensia*. Edited by Karl Elliger and Wilhelm Rudolph. Stuttgart: Deutsche Bibelgesellschaft, 1984.
BHT	Beiträge zur historischen Theologie
Bib	*Biblica*
BibInt	*Biblical Interpretation*
BibInt	Biblical Interpretation Series
BibOr	Biblica et Orientalia
BIOSCS	*Bulletin of the International Organization for Septuagint and Cognate Studies*
BJRL	*Bulletin of the John Rylands University Library of Manchester*
BKAT	Biblischer Kommentar Altes Testament
BN	*Biblische Notizen*
BWANT	Beiträge zur Wissenschaft vom Alten und Neuen Testament
BZ	*Biblische Zeitschrift*
BZAW	Beihefte zur Zeitschrift für die alttestamentliche Wissenschaft
CAD	*The Assyrian Dictionary of the Oriental Institute of the University of Chicago*. 21 vols. Chicago: The Oriental Institute, 1956–2006.
CahRB	Cahiers de la Revue Biblique
CBQ	*Catholic Biblical Quarterly*
CBSC	Cambridge Bible for Schools and Colleges
CC	Continental Commentaries
CHANE	Culture and History of the Ancient Near East
ConBOT	Coniectanea Biblica Old Testament
CTJ	*Calvin Theological Journal*
CurBR	*Currents in Biblical Research*
CurBS	*Currents in Research: Biblical Studies*
DCH	*The Dictionary of Classical Hebrew*. Edited by David J. A. Clines. 9 vols. Sheffield: Sheffield Phoenix, 1993–2016.
DDL	*Dictionary of Daily Life in Biblical & Post-Biblical Antiquity*. Edited by Edwin M. Yamauchi and Marvin R. Wilson. 4 vols. Peabody, MA: Hendrickson, 2014–2016.
DJD	Discoveries in the Judaean Desert

DNST	Dissertationes Neerlandicae: Series Theologica
DOTPr	*Dictionary of the Old Testament: Prophets.* Edited by Mark J. Boda and J. Gordon McConville. Downers Grove, IL: IVP Academic, 2012.
DSS	Dead Sea Scrolls
EdF	Erträge der Forschung
EHLL	*Encyclopedia of Hebrew Language and Linguistics.* Edited by Geoffrey Khan. 4 vols. Leiden: Brill, 2013.
EncJud	*Encyclopaedia Judaica.* 16 vols. Jerusalem: Keter, 1972.
ETL	*Ephemerides Theologicae Lovanienses*
EurHS	Europäische Hochschulschriften
EvT	*Evangelische Theologie*
FAT	Forschungen zum Alten Testament
FB	Forschung zur Bibel
FOTL	Forms of Old Testament Literature
FRLANT	Forschungen zur Religion und Literatur des Alten und Neuen Testaments
FS	Festschrift
GBS	Guides to Biblical Scholarship
GKC	*Gesenius' Hebrew Grammar.* Edited by Emil Kautzsch. Translated by A. E. Cowley. 2nd ed. Oxford: Clarendon, 1910.
HALOT	Ludwig Koehler, Walter Baumgartner, and Johann Jakob Stamm. *Hebrew and Aramaic Lexicon of the Old Testament.* Translated and edited under M. E. J. Richardson. 5 vols. Leiden: Brill, 1994–2000.
HAR	*Hebrew Annual Review*
HAT	Handbuch zum Alten Testament
HBM	Hebrew Bible Monographs
HBS	Herders Biblische Studien
HBT	*Horizons in Biblical Theology*
HCOT	Historical Commentary on the Old Testament
HeBAI	*Hebrew Bible and Ancient Israel*
HS	*Hebrew Studies*
HSM	Harvard Semitic Monographs
HTKAT	Herders theologischer Kommentar zum Alten Testament
HTR	*Harvard Theological Review*
HUB	Hebrew University Bible project
HUCA	*Hebrew Union College Annual*
IBHS	Bruce K. Waltke and M. O'Connor. *An Introduction to Biblical Hebrew Syntax.* Winona Lake, IN: Eisenbrauns, 1990.
ICC	International Critical Commentary
IDB	*Interpreter's Dictionary of the Bible*
IDBSup	*Interpreter's Dictionary of the Bible, Supplementary Volume*
Int	*Interpretation*
JANES	*Journal of the Ancient Near Eastern Society* (Columbia University)
JAOS	*Journal of the American Oriental Society*
JB	Jerusalem Bible (1966)
JBL	*Journal of Biblical Literature*
JBLMS	Journal of Biblical Literature Monograph Series
JBQ	*Jewish Bible Quarterly*

JBR	*Journal of Bible and Religion*
JETS	*Journal of the Evangelical Theological Society*
JITC	*Journal of the Interdenominational Theological Center*
JNES	*Journal of Near Eastern Studies*
JNSL	*Journal of Northwest Semitic Languages*
Joüon	P. Joüon and T. Muraoka. *A Grammar of Biblical Hebrew.* 2nd ed., with corrections. SubBi 27. Rome: Gregorian and Biblical Press, 2011.
JR	*Journal of Religion*
JSJSup	Supplements to the Journal for the Study of Judaism
JSNTSup	Journal for the Study of the New Testament Supplement Series
JSOT	*Journal for the Study of the Old Testament*
JSOTSup	Journal for the Study of the Old Testament Supplement Series
JSS	*Journal of Semitic Studies*
JTS	*Journal of Theological Studies*
KAT	Kommentar zum Alten Testament
KBL	Koehler, Ludwig, and Walter Baumgartner. *Lexicon in Veteris Testamenti libros.* 2nd ed. Leiden: Brill, 1958.
KEK	Kritisch-exegetischer Kommentar über das Neue Testament (Meyer-Kommentar)
LHBOTS	Library of Hebrew Bible/Old Testament Studies
LSAWS	Linguistic Studies in Ancient West Semitic
NAC	New American Commentary
NCBC	New Century Bible Commentary
NGTT	*Nederduitse Gereformeerde Teologiese Tydskrif*
NICOT	New International Commentary on the Old Testament
NIDOTTE	*New International Dictionary of Old Testament Theology and Exegesis.* Edited by Willem A. VanGemeren. 5 vols. Grand Rapids: Zondervan, 1997.
NSKAT	Neuer Stuttgarter Kommentar, Altes Testament
OAC	Orientis Antiqui Collectio
OBO	Orbis Biblicus et Orientalis
OBT	Overtures to Biblical Theology
OED	*Oxford English Dictionary*
OIAS	Oriental Institute of the University of Chicago Assyriological Studies
OLD	*Oxford Latin Dictionary*
OTE	*Old Testament Essays: Journal of the Old Testament Society of Southern Africa*
OTG	Old Testament Guides
OTL	Old Testament Library
OTM	Oxford Theological Monographs
OTP	*Old Testament Pseudepigrapha.* Edited by James H. Charlesworth. 2 vols. London: Darton, Longman & Todd, 1983–1985.
OTS	Old Testament Studies
OtSt	*Oudtestamentische Studiën*
ProEccl	*Pro Ecclesia*
PRR	*Presbyterian and Reformed Review*
PRSt	*Perspectives in Religious Studies*
PTMS	Princeton Theological Monograph Series

RB	*Revue Biblique*
RelSRev	*Religious Studies Review*
RevExp	*Review and Expositor*
RHR	*Revue de l'histoire des religions*
RSR	*Recherches de science religieuse*
SAA	State Archives of Assyria
SBB	Stuttgarter biblische Beiträge
SBL	Society of Biblical Literature
SBLDS	Society of Biblical Literature Dissertation Series
SBLSymS	Society of Biblical Literature Symposium Series
SBT	Studies in Biblical Theology
SComS	Septuagint Commentary Series
ScrHier	Scripta Hierosolymitana
SCS	Septuagint and Cognate Studies
SemeiaSt	Semeia Studies
SFACS	South Florida Academic Commentary Series
SHBC	Smyth & Helwys Bible Commentary
SJLA	Studies in Judaism in Late Antiquity
SJT	*Scottish Journal of Theology*
SSN	Studia Semitica Neerlandica
ST	*Studia Theologica*
StBibLit	Studies in Biblical Literature (Lang)
SubBi	Subsidia Biblica
TB	Theologische Bücherei: Neudrucke und Berichte aus dem 20.Jahrhundert
TBC	Torch Bible Commentary
TDOT	*Theological Dictionary of the Old Testament*. Edited by G. Johannes Botterweck, Helmer Ringgren, and Heinz-Josef Fabry. Translated by John T. Willis, Geoffrey W. Bromiley, and David E. Green. 15 vols. Grand Rapids: Eerdmans, 1974–2006.
THAT	*Theologisches Handwörterbuch zum Alten Testament*. Edited by Ernst Jenni and Claus Westermann. 2 vols. Munich: Kaiser; Zürich: Theologischer Verlag, 1971–1976.
ThTo	*Theology Today*
ThWAT	*Theologisches Wörterbuch zum Alten Testament*. Edited by G. Johannes Botterweck, Helmer Ringgren, and Heinz-Josef Fabry. 10 vols. Stuttgart: Kohlhammer, 1973–2000.
TICP	Travaux de l'Institut catholique de Paris
TJ	*Trinity Journal*
TNTT	Tilleggshefte Til Norsk Teologisk Tidsskrift
TOTC	Tyndale Old Testament Commentaries
TRu	*Theologische Rundschau*
TynBul	*Tyndale Bulletin*
UUA	Uppsala Universitetsårskrift
VT	*Vetus Testamentum*
VTSup	Supplements to Vetus Testamentum
WBC	Word Biblical Commentary
WMANT	Wissenschaftliche Monographien zum Alten und Neuen Testament

WO	*Die Welt des Orients*
WTJ	*Westminster Theological Journal*
WUNT	Wissenschaftliche Untersuchungen zum Neuen Testament
ZAW	*Zeitschrift für die alttestamentliche Wissenschaft*
ZTK	*Zeitschrift für Theologie und Kirche*

Introduction

It is surely one of the most striking literary phenomena in the entire Old Testament. Readers of Ezekiel find the phrase וידעתם כי־אני יהוה—"you shall know that I am Yahweh" (or one very similar to it)—repeated over seventy times. The refrain is so constant that interpreters are tempted to call it "monotonous"[1] and "stereotyped."[2] Certainly, it dominates the book. S. R. Driver, in his influential old introduction, agrees with this assessment and says, "It strikes the keynote of Ezek.'s prophecies."[3] More recently, Lawrence Boadt has spoken of the use of the refrain as "the most decisive characteristic of Ezekiel's theology."[4]

One would expect to find many monographs and articles treating at length the significance of the phrase, given its statistically remarkable usage and its importance as a key to understanding the message of this baffling Major Prophet. Surprisingly, however, this is not the case. With but three exceptions,[5] the only substantial essays that focus on the so-called recognition formula (hereafter, RF) in Ezekiel have come from Walther Zimmerli and were written over sixty years ago.[6]

More than a few volumes on the prophets (e.g., James Newsome and Brian Peckham) and in the field of Old Testament introduction (e.g., E. J. Young and Otto Eissfeldt) fail even to mention the phrase.[7] Many quote or mention the RF in passing and offer no probing discussion.[8] Others treat the subject, but only in a cursory and ancillary fashion, and in almost every case, these discussions are

1. Zimmerli, *I Am Yahweh*, 30.

2. Eichrodt, *Ezekiel*, 15. The most negative reaction is James Crenshaw's: "We hear the refrain ad nauseum" (*Prophetic Conflict*, 104).

3. Driver, *Introduction*, xxi; he speaks of "the proof saying that culminated in the recognition formula" as the keynote.

4. Boadt, *Ezekiel's Oracles against Egypt*, 170.

5. Lind, "A Political Alternative"; Strong, "Ezekiel's Use"; Callender, "The Recognition Formula." As discussed in ch. 2, even these articles do not have a singular focus on the RF.

6. Three Zimmerli essays that directly bear on the topic are collected in *Gottes Offenbarung* and translated for *I Am Yahweh*: "I Am Yahweh" (1–28) = "Ich bin Jahwe"; "Knowledge of God According to the Book of Ezekiel" (29–98) = *Erkenntnis Gottes nach dem Buche Ezechiel*; "The Word of Divine Self-manifestation (Proof-Saying): A Prophetic Genre" (99–110) = "Das Wort des göttlichen Selbsterweises (Erweiswort)."

7. Newsome, *The Hebrew Prophets*; Peckham, *History and Prophecy*; Young, *Introduction*; Eissfeldt, *The Old Testament*; Harrison, *Introduction*; Kaiser, *Einleitung*.

8. Representatives are: Sandmel, *Hebrew Scriptures*; Soggin, *Introduction*; Schmidt, *Introduction*; Brueggemann, *Introduction*; Collins, *Introduction*; and Sweeney, *TANAK*.

heavily dependent on Zimmerli's work. These weaknesses in the scholarship point to the need for further work in this crucial area of Ezekiel studies.

The scholarly neglect of the formula is all the more surprising in light of the explosion of interest in Ezekiel over the last forty years. Though many large-scale commentaries have been published,[9] including the English translation of Zimmerli's two-volume set,[10] though Ezekiel seminar groups have been established in organizations like SBL[11] and congresses devoted to Ezekiel studies,[12] and though doctoral dissertations on this once neglected prophet are multiplying, the RF has not received the attention it is due. It is hoped that, just as Zimmerli's research alerted scholarship to its significance and prompted good discussion in years gone by, the present study may contribute to a renewed discussion of the formula.[13]

I.1. Reasons for Undertaking this Study

Past scholarly neglect may be a compelling reason to undertake this exegetical and theological study, but there are additional grounds on which to pursue the research of the formula at this time. (1) In order to build wisely, one must test the foundation that has previously been laid. Up to this time, there has not been available a more thorough review of past scholarship on the refrain. This study helps fill this lacuna in Ezekiel scholarship—from 1900 to the present—on the way to providing a fresh research of the RF.

(2) Ezekiel scholars today have a keen interest in *theological* analysis, as well as in newer hermeneutical approaches, anthropology, ethics, metaphor, and gender studies. This is evidenced in part by the name chosen in 1996 for an SBL symposium that met annually from 1997 onward: "Seminar on Theological Perspectives on the Book of Ezekiel."[14] While the towering theological importance of the RF

---

9. Greenberg, *Ezekiel 1–20* and *Ezekiel 21–37*; Hals, *Ezekiel*; Allen, *Ezekiel 1–19* and *Ezekiel 20–48*; Pohlmann, *Buch des Propheten Hesekiel*; Block, *Ezekiel 1–24* and *Ezekiel 25–48*; Darr, "Book of Ezekiel"; Sedlmeier, *Ezechiel*; Hummel, *Ezekiel*; Odell, *Ezekiel*; Joyce, *Ezekiel*; Milgrom, *Ezekiel's Hope*.

10. Zimmerli, *Ezekiel 1*; Zimmerli, *Ezekiel 2*. These are translations of Zimmerli, *Ezechiel* (BKAT 13/1–2).

11. Two international meetings of SBL produced Tooman and Barter, *Ezekiel: Current Debates and Future Directions*. Regrettably I am yet to see it.

12. Worthy of mention are the OT section of the 35th Colloquium Biblicum Lovaniense (1985), the 1998 Congress of the Old Testament Society of South Africa, and the 2004 Oxford-Leiden Joint Seminar for Biblical Studies.

13. Scholars have already discussed my unpublished dissertation, "An Inner-Biblical Interpretation and Intertextual Reading of Ezekiel's Recognition Formulae with the Book of Exodus" (DTh diss., Stellenbosch University, 2006); see: Idestrom, "Echoes"; DeLapp, "Ezekiel as Moses"; Block, "The God Ezekiel Wants Us to Meet"; Wu, *Honor, Shame, and Guilt*, 94; Surls, *Making Sense of the Divine Name in Exodus*, 90, 106–7.

14. A portion of the seminar's work is published: Odell and Strong, *Book of Ezekiel*; Cook and Patton, *Ezekiel's Hierarchical World*; Mein and Joyce, *After Ezekiel*; Joyce and Rom-Shiloni, *The God Ezekiel Creates*; Rom-Shiloni and Carvalho, *Ezekiel in its Babylonian Context*.

should be beyond dispute among scholars, the present study still seeks to sub-
stantiate the claim that a failure to wrestle seriously with the "keynote" formula
hinders a full engagement with the theology of the prophecy.

(3) Another reason for attempting a new research of the refrain is the growing dissatisfaction with Zimmerli's older form-critical approach. More generally,
of course, *Formgeschichte* has gone into decline with regard to usage and importance.[15] But, more specifically here, Zimmerli's own form criticism has been challenged. Over the last thirty years, as Ezekiel studies have become something of a
"growth industry," scholars have called into question both Zimmerli's practice of
the form-critical method and the suitability of Ezekiel's prophecy for this type of
investigation.

Ellen Davis, in her Yale dissertation, argues that Zimmerli has subtly turned
aside from a classic form-critical methodology: "[He] cannot answer the form
critic's fundamental question about how these speeches functioned in their original oral settings. Instead of trying to coordinate the speech forms with social practice, . . . he traces their development through a purely literary process."[16] Could it
be that this change in critical method is necessary because Ezekiel's oracles are
fundamentally literary in character? Is there perhaps the tacit acceptance that
the search for substantial amounts of preliterary oral material in Ezekiel has, to a
great extent, been frustrated?[17] Did Zimmerli's adaptation of form-critical practice
anticipate recent developments in the methodology? The present study will return
to these questions later with further explanation of the criticisms leveled at Zimmerli and an exploration of possible refinements of form criticism for the study
of Ezekiel's RF. Clearly, more work is necessary.

(4) Yet another justification for undertaking this study is the shift from diachronic, historical-critical methods to synchronic or "holistic" methods.[18] Already
in 1986, Rolf Rendtorff told a congress of the International Organization for the
Study of the Old Testament:

> There is much discussion about a "change of paradigm." Certainly, the paradigm
> within which Old Testament scholarship has worked for more than a century,
> namely the old German *Literarkritik*, has lost its general acceptance. It is no longer
> possible to maintain that serious Old Testament scholarship has to be indispensably

15. For a discussion of what ails the form-critical enterprise and of potential remedies, see Sweeney and Ben Zvi, *Changing Face of Form Criticism*. Some repudiate older-style *Formgeschichte* in blunt
terms: veteran form-critic Antony Campbell says the exegetical method "has a future—if its past
is allowed a decent burial" ("Form Criticism's Future," 31). See also: Buss, *Changing Shape of Form
Criticism*; Toffelmire, "Form Criticism"; and Boda, Floyd, and Toffelmire, *The Book of the Twelve*.

16. Davis, *Swallowing the Scroll*, 16.

17. See the strong statement of Davis: "The very thing for which we lack evidence is the fundamental stratum of orally conceived preaching" (*Swallowing the Scroll*, 17).

18. For an early evaluation of the upheaval experienced in OT studies, with special focus on the
prophets, see Sawyer, "Change of Emphasis."

tied to this set of methodological principles. So far there is no alternative concept that has been generally accepted. According to Thomas Kuhn, one could say that there are different models used by certain groups of scholars, but none of them has won general acceptance. Old Testament scholarship now is in a stage of transition, and we cannot know whether there will be a new paradigm or if the near future will be characterized by a plurality of approaches and methods.[19]

And perhaps nowhere in Anglophone scholarship has this paradigm change been more in evidence than Ezekiel studies. Moshe Greenberg's commentary on Ezekiel 1–20, published the same year as the translation of Zimmerli's second volume in BKAT, has exerted wide influence among specialists, especially in the English-speaking world,[20] as an encouragement to use the method of "holistic interpretation." He urges scholars to seek coherence in the final form of the text and to exercise caution in labeling passages as secondary.[21] One need only consult the commentaries of Daniel Block and Katheryn Darr to recognize that a sea-change has taken place in Ezekiel studies since the 1960s and the publication of Zimmerli and Walther Eichrodt.[22] While it is true that some encourage a renewed, more radical diachrony (i.e., certain German redaction critics), even reasserting that the prophecy is a pseudepigraph,[23] that number does not dominate Ezekiel scholarship. The present study argues that newer synchronic hermeneutical approaches hold real promise for finding meaning in the refrain. Methods with such potential might be intertextuality, sociorhetorical interpretation,[24] speech-act theory,[25] and discourse analysis.

19. Rendtorff, "Between Historical Criticism and Holistic Interpretation," 302. Cf. Rendtorff, "Paradigm Is Changing."

20. Greenberg's influence in Germany has grown through the translation of his work for the Herder series, see *Ezechiel*, HTKAT (2001–2005).

21. Greenberg, "What Are Valid Criteria."

22. Block writes: "No scholar has had greater influence on my understanding of and approach to the book than Professor Greenberg" (*Ezekiel 25–48*, xiii). Darr likewise builds on Greenberg in focusing primarily on the text as it stands, rather than on a complex compositional history. She adds, however, a reader-oriented method that seeks "a late exilic reader's construal (understanding) of the book": "My reader does not bring to the text knowledge of the historical-critical methodologies developed especially in the nineteenth and twentieth centuries and of their goals" ("Book of Ezekiel," 1094).

23. See: Schulz, *Das Todesrecht*; Becker, "Erwägungen zur ezechielischen Frage"; Becker, "Ez 8–11 als einheitliche Komposition"; Schöpflin, *Theologie als Biographie*; Klein, *Schriftauslegung im Ezechielbuch*. Kaiser also favors the theory in *Einleitung*, 262–66. Udo Feist provides an account of the initial proposal by Leopold Zunz (1794–1886) in *Ezechiel*, 104–15. The best-known such proposal is in Torrey, *Pseudo-Ezekiel*.

24. See Robbins, *Exploring the Texture*, whose model blends literary/narrative analysis, sociology, rhetorical analysis, postmodern intertextuality, and ideological/theological criticism.

25. For OT research, see: White, *Speech Act Theory*; Houston, "What Did the Prophets Think They Were Doing?"; Briggs, *Words in Action*; Childs, "Speech-Act Theory." Excellent work has already been done in speech-act theory on the theological locus of revelation that is relevant to the study of

(5) It would be inaccurate, however, to say Greenberg has entirely rejected or bracketed diachronic concerns. As he pursues a more conservative final-form approach to Ezekiel, convinced of what Davis terms "the text's synchronic intelligibility,"[26] he shows keen interest in Ezekiel's indebtedness as a priest to Israel's traditions and Scriptures.[27] He takes pains to discover and elucidate the prophet's allusions to and interpretation of those Scriptures. Greenberg employs a type of inner-biblical interpretation that is more diachronic in nature, and his work shows the benefits of that method. He is one of those who, in the words of Brevard Childs, detect in Ezekiel's language and theological message "many signs of being influenced by a study of Israel's sacred writings."[28] If one follows Greenberg's lead, inner-biblical interpretation should be used as tool in studying the RF.

(6) The combination of synchronic and diachronic approaches,[29] though hard to accomplish, is a goal of this study. Exactly at that intersection will greater insight be gained and richer, more dynamic exegesis carried out. Additionally, the synchronic may serve as a control on the deficiencies or excesses of the diachronic, increasing the value of the latter. The converse is also true: the diachronic may act as a check on the deficiencies or excesses of the synchronic. The aim is to prove the wisdom of H. G. M. Williamson's observation, "The task of the interpreter is a struggle between the diachronic and the synchronic."[30] The question of balancing, merging, and/or separating the two must occupy our attention. What would a "balancing" look like, for example? Should one approach—say, the synchronic—be viewed as foundational? Eep Talstra is cited as encouraging readers to begin with synchronic analysis and, after running as far as possible with it, turn to diachronic questions.[31]

---

the RF; see Patrick, *Rhetoric of Revelation*. Some believe the theory should be applied more widely in biblical studies, and the approach is best suited to studying smaller, discrete units of text such as formulas, sentences, and dialogue (see Watts, review of Patrick, *Rhetoric of Revelation*). James Robson discusses Ezekiel from a speech-acts perspective in *Word and Spirit*, 71–79.

26. Davis, "Swallowing Hard," 219.

27. Greenberg, *Ezekiel 21–37*, 395.

28. Childs, *Introduction*, 364.

29. For a critique of the ways Saussure's famous distinction has been (mis)applied to biblical studies, see Deist, "On 'Synchronic' and 'Diachronic.'"

30. Williamson, review of Childs, *Isaiah*, 124. See also Joyce, "Synchronic and Diachronic Perspectives," who reminds us that Saussure himself placed the two in opposition, just as many contemporary biblical scholars are accustomed to doing, and that Saussure strongly discouraged such a "combination" of diachrony and synchrony (127). Joyce rejects Saussure's assertion that: "The contrast between the two points of view—synchronic and diachronic—is absolute and admits no compromise.... In studying a language from either point of view, it is of the utmost importance to assign each fact to its appropriate sphere, and not to confuse the two methods" (Saussure, *Course in General Linguistics*, 83, 98). For a critique of synchronic analysis, see Pohlmann, "Synchrone und diachrone Texterschließung."

31. He wrote, "Compositie gaat vóór de reconstructie van de tekst" (cited in Dubbink, "Story of Three Prophets," 13).

(7) The relationship between the Law and the Prophets has long been a prime concern of Ezekiel students, and theological and literary aspects of it deserve close attention. We note in passing that Zimmerli himself interrupted his Ezekiel project to address this relationship.[32] Building on the writings of Yehezkel Kaufmann, Avi Hurvitz, and Jacob Milgrom, several dissertations have researched the *literary* relation between Ezekiel and pentateuchal materials/sources, especially P and H, and conclude that the prophecy is later than P/H and bears marks of their influence. Worth mentioning in this respect are Mark Rooker, Risa Levitt Kohn, and Michael Lyons.[33] Their arguments and proposals deserve further exploration and testing, and the RF provides a restricted field for a manageable test. Given that the formula occurs nearly a dozen times in the book of Exodus, one should ponder the relationship between Ezekiel's RF and the Exodus scriptural "traditions" as a potential source.

(8) It is often remarked that Ezekiel's language and rhetorical habits are repetitious or stereotyped. For example, the characterization of idols as גלולים, perhaps "dung pellets" or "droppings" (KBL), occurs nearly forty times.[34] Also, Ezekiel's oracles are regularly introduced (49×) by the formulaic ויהי דבר־יהוה אלי לאמר ("and the word of Yahweh came to me saying").[35] Tyler D. Mayfield writes of the prophecy's "near-obsession with formulaic statements," noting that there are over 300. He gives as examples the prophetic utterance formula נאם־אדני יהוה ("utterance of Lord Yahweh"; 2× in Isaiah, 4× in Jeremiah, and 81× in Ezekiel) and the messenger formula כה אמר אדני יהוה ("thus says Lord Yahweh"; at least 120×).[36] The copious use of these formulas—mentioning as well the covenant formula, self-presentation formula (SPF), and RF—deserves further attention. Probably the best-known of all the repetitions in Ezekiel would be Yahweh's address to the prophet as בן־אדם ("son of man"; 93×). Why does the prophecy use a rhetorical strategy that, according to the testimony of some readers, may be tiresome and engender frustration? A more thorough, up-to-date research of the RF provides opportunity to illuminate Ezekiel's purposes in employing phrases and motifs in that repetitious manner.

(9) Another reason for undertaking this research would be the current lack of a systematic study of the relationships among the RFs in Ezekiel. Alongside

---

32. See Zimmerli, *The Law and the Prophets*.

33. Rooker, *Biblical Hebrew in Transition*; Levitt Kohn, *A New Heart and a New Soul*; and Lyons, *From Law to Prophecy*. See my review of Levitt Kohn in *OTE* 16 (2003): 538–40. Worth noting is that Julius Wellhausen partially based his argument that Ezekiel's played a transitional role from prophets to law on his linguistic studies into the historical development of the Hebrew language (see *Prolegomena*, 385–91).

34. See the discussion in Kutsko, *Between Heaven and Earth*, 25–47.

35. More complete listings of Ezekiel's frequently used vocabulary and formulas are found in Driver's *Introduction*, 297–98, and Tooman, *Gog of Magog*, 40–51.

36. Mayfield, "Re-Examination," 139–40.

better-known intertextuality, the literary critic today may ask questions about inner-textuality (or intra-textuality), the mutual relationships of texts within one corpus.[37] In seeking to interpret the RFs, one should look within the prophecy as well as outside it and evaluate possible interplay between formulas. How are the formulas to be heard together, as well as separately? Might Ezekiel be something of an echo chamber,[38] with attendant harmonies, dissonance, confusion, or amplification? How do the echoes work? Because no scholarship has been discovered that treats the interrelationships of the formulas, research is necessary.

(10) Finally, the benefits of a large-scale study of Ezekiel's RF extend beyond Ezekiel scholarship. The refrain appears in five other OT books, and similar related phrases can be traced in an additional nine. One finds the RF in the Apocrypha (Bar 2:31) and nonbiblical DSS documents (4Q385 2 I, 4; 4Q386 1 II, 1; 4Q388 7 6).[39] New Testament scholars note that certain passages (e.g., John 8:28; cf. 14:20; Rev 2:23) echo and refashion OT formulas related to the RF.[40] There are also examples of ANE literature employing phraseology comparable to Ezekiel's refrain. Correlating research across disciplines can shed more light on them all.

In many respects, there is now the need and opportunity for Ezekiel scholarship to attempt a fresh research of the RF. In this day, when the "assured results" of past scholarship no longer appear so assured, older hermeneutical models require reassessment, along with their conclusions, and newer methods should be explored in a complementary fashion.

I.2. The Plan of This Study

I.2.1. The Research Question, Argument, and Proposed Methodology

This study has a central concern: What is the literary and theological function of the RF in the book of Ezekiel? In pursuing the research question, I discuss

---

37. Examples of studies that ask such questions are: Beuken, "Servant and Herald"; Beuken, "Jesaja 33"; and van Ruiten, "Intertextual Relationship." Without using inter- or intra-textuality labels, other studies have engaged in close readings "between" similar texts in one prophetic book. See Clements, "Beyond Tradition-History"; Williamson, *Book Called Isaiah*; and Williamson, "Isaiah 62:4."

38. The metaphor of "echo" appears to be first used, and most elaborately used, in intertextual studies by John Hollander, *Figure of Echo*. Worth noting is that Hollander does not describe his approach as intertextuality. Biblical scholars are attracted to the terminology: Hays, *Echoes of Scripture in Paul*; Hays, *Conversion of the Imagination*.

39. Dimant, *Qumran Cave 4.XXI*, 23–24, 26, 62–63, 83.

40. They mention אני הוא and אני יהוה (the self-presentation formula). See Dodd, *Interpretation of the Fourth Gospel*, 93–96; Zimmermann, "Das absolute Ἐγώ εἰμι"; Feuillet, "Les *Ego Eimi* christologiques"; Ball, *"I Am" in John's Gospel*, 33–39; Charles, *Commentary on the Revelation of St. John*, 1:72. Drawing a parallel between Rev 2:23 and Ezekiel's RF are Beate Kowalski, *Rezeption des Propheten Ezechiel*, 98, and Satake, *Die Offenbarung des Johannes*, 173.

the formula with reference to the literary and theological relationship between the Law and the Prophets. In particular, this study argues that the seventy-odd RFs in Ezekiel mark a theological nexus and intertextuality between the prophecy and the book of Exodus and that those formulas are best interpreted alongside the numerous RFs in Exodus. Interpreted intertextually, Ezekiel's formula points readers of the oracles to know Yahweh as the God of the exodus, who still acts, in covenant, to judge and to deliver. (Here, *intertextual* is used in a broader sense, even including the phenomenon of inner-biblical interpretation.)[41] That intertextuality may be construed in two ways. First of all, in more diachronic fashion, it may be an intertextuality of production, in which a text can be written only in relationship to other texts. The interpreter who so construes the intertextuality will likely speak of sources, vectors of influence, conscious echoing, and authorial intention or rhetorical strategy. Secondly, according to a more synchronic reading of texts, it may be an intertextuality of reception,[42] in which a text can be read only in relationship to other texts.

With regard to proposed methodology, the approach of inner-biblical interpretation is well suited for exploring the text-production angle of intertextuality and the questions that emerge concerning the reading, reuse, and "re-presentation" (*Vergegenwärtigung*) of Exodus scriptural traditions in Ezekiel.[43] Also appropriate is a more synchronic intertextual approach that asks how the Exodus and Ezekiel texts, and in particular their RFs, may be read together today from the text-reception angle while bracketing most diachronic concerns. Taking the two approaches together provides means for researching and answering the research question of the literary and theological function of the RF in the book of Ezekiel. Used together, the two apporaches reveal a large number of parallels between Ezekiel and Exodus and indicate how well the RFs may be read alongside one another. Methodology is discussed more fully at the conclusion of chapter 1.

I.2.2. An Outline of the Study

With a proposal that the prophecy signals a dependence on earlier Scriptures, as the Childs quote above suggests (n. 28), one runs into debate over the compositional history of the Pentateuch and dating of the literary deposit of pentateuchal

---

41. Michael Fishbane regards his own approach to "inner-biblical interpretation/exegesis" as dove-tailing with "intertextuality." See my discussion of methodology in ch. 1.

42. I borrow "intertextuality of text production" and "intertextuality of text reception" from van Wolde, "Texts in Dialogue with Texts," 4.

43. It is understood that many scholars today are inclined to read the Pentateuch (in any recensional form) as a product of the Persian era and as possibly reflecting the influence of an exilic Ezekiel, instead of vice versa. Evidence that makes this alternative seem unlikely is presented in succeeding chapters.

traditions. Ever since Julius Wellhausen, Ezekiel has been considered a figure marking a transition in Israelite religion and the prophet's indebtedness to prophetic and priestly traditions and his literary relationship to pentateuchal materials (e.g., the Holiness Code) have been matters of debate. Chapter 1 briefly outlines the problem of the Law and the Prophets in historical criticism in preparation for discussing the presuppositions behind this study and strategies in approaching the RF.

Chapter 2 highlights the contributions of past scholarship and indicates both the points of controversy that require discussion, and points of confusion in the literature. (E.g., what is the true number of RFs in Ezekiel?) Additionally, the survey indicates how this study moves beyond previous work and offers a new perspective on the prophecy. Chapter 3 presents the results of basic exegetical spadework, cataloging occurrences of the formula and collecting details of its usage in Ezekiel. Because this study is concerned with intertextual links, the chapter also contains an appendix that lists all the RFs (and related phrases) in the OT, providing readers opportunity to compare and contrast the RFs and related phrases in different biblical books.

Chapter 4 examines the many parallels between Exodus and Ezekiel and argues that the evidence supports this study's theses that a "demonstrable relationship between texts"[44] does exist and that the RF is a marker of an intertextual relation. From a diachronic text-production angle, the evidence points to a repetition and (sometimes radical) transformation of Exodus texts and traditions in Ezekiel's oracles. The RF fits into this pattern. The present study queries specifically how Ezekiel takes up the formula, as an earlier text, to reuse, recontextualize, extend, reformulate, reinterpret, or transform it for an exilic audience.[45]

It was Gerhard von Rad's insight that the proper interpretation of a prophecy lies at the intersection of three lines: older theological tradition, the social and political situation of the prophet, and a new revelatory word from Yahweh.[46] Whereas chapter 4 explores the first in this triad, older theological "tradition" (now based in a text), chapter 5 of this study seeks to do justice to the second: the sociohistorical and religious context into which Ezekiel's oracles (with their RFs) were spoken. Research in this area points to two features of Ezekiel's theology that play in his use of the keynote formula: a distinguishing between the community in exile and those remaining in Judah after 597 and the defilement of the whole nation of Israel, which has never given up the idols of Egypt.

---

44. Van Wolde, "Texts in Dialogue with Texts," 4.

45. The scope of this study must be limited. A deep probing of each of the more general parallels of event, theme, and terminology according to inner-biblical interpretation (in order to discover the exegetical function of the repetition) is not feasible in this work.

46. Von Rad, *Old Testament Theology*, 2:130, cited in Tucker, "Prophecy," 328, 332.

Chapter 6 offers an interpretation of the RF, answering the research question and emphasizing that there is theologically both disjunction and conjunction between the formulas in Exodus and Ezekiel. From the standpoint of diachronic analysis, one could instead speak of "theological discontinuity and continuity" in Ezekiel's reuse of the formula. The study concludes in chapter 7 with a summary of the argument, followed by brief sections on the rhetorical strategy behind the persistent use of the RF and on defining its theological meaning in the prophecy.

CHAPTER 1

The Law and Prophets in Historical Criticism and Strategies for Approaching the Formula

Walther Zimmerli's *The Law and the Prophets* should not be regarded as some diversion from his commenting on Ezekiel (BKAT). That slim monograph takes up an issue of paramount importance for the study of individual prophetic books and for understanding the whole Old Testament. An Ezekiel specialist may even be bold enough to suggest that the relationship between the Law and the Prophets is more central in Ezekiel studies than anywhere else. It proves to be an overriding issue in this research of the RF.

1.1. The Law and the Prophets in Historical Criticism

Traditionally, church and synagogue agreed that Bible readers must "trace the Prophets to the Law, from which they derived their doctrine, like streams from a fountain; for they placed it before them as their rule, so that they may be justly held and declared to be its interpreters, who utter nothing but what is connected with the Law."[1] John Calvin's principle here typifies the so-called precritical view of the nature of divine prophecy and the relation between the Law and the Prophets. The written Torah, as God's prior self-revelation, formed the basis of the prophets' knowledge of Yahweh and his will for his covenant people.

As is well known, historical criticism discarded the traditional view, arguing that the Books of Moses merely purport to have come from the hand of the great lawgiver and provide an eyewitness account of the nation's origins. Critics denied the Mosaic authorship and literary integrity of the Pentateuch and set about reconstructing the history and religious development of Israel. The Law is not

---

1. Calvin, "Preface to the Prophet Isaiah," in *Commentary . . . Isaiah*, xxvi. Judaism held the same belief; the seventh of Maimonides's "Thirteen Fundamental Doctrines of the Jewish Religion" reads: "I believe with perfect faith, that the prophecy of Mosheh . . . has been true, and that he has been the father of all prophets." Rabbi Samuel states in the Babylonian Talmud that the prophets after Moses have no right to innovate in any way, but must stick to the Torah (Neusner, *Talmud of Babylonia*, b. Temurah 16A). See also Abraham Joshua Heschel: "Whatever a prophet was destined to prophesy was already uttered by Moses. The prophets were nothing but attendants to Moses, and they said nothing that they did not hear from others, in the name of Moses. It is as if inspiration is not the root of the prophetic utterance, but rather immersion in the teaching of Moses" (*Heavenly Torah*, 587).

the interpretive key to open up the whole OT; rather, it should be seen as a later development, at least in its final form. Antonius Gunneweg regards this as a fruit of critical scholarship: "the rediscovery of the fact that the law became predominant at a relatively late stage and that it is therefore *only of relative theological importance.*"[2]

The view was put forward that the prophets, in contrast to those who penned the legal traditions, were the truly original theologians. It was they who created, almost *de novo*, Israel's historical perspective as the people of God, the nation's social ethics, and an all-encompassing religious worldview with Yahweh at its center. Rather than their preaching being based on ancient covenant traditions in the Law,[3] the prophets themselves more or less originated those covenantal ideals that later came to be systematized in the Pentateuch.

The question arises of why this hermeneutical paradigm shift came about. I suggest the "theological problem of Old Testament legalism" as a primary force pushing forward this radical reinterpretation. Finding fault with a perceived legalism in the OT, many theologians came to believe not only that the two testaments cannot be placed on the same level but also that the OT must be discounted in the formulation of a truly Christian theology. Much of the OT seemed to present a lower religion that, to modern sensibilities, had to be set free from sacrificial ritual and other material elements and reestablished on a purely spiritual basis. Spirit must triumph over "letter." Law is not the goal of history, but rather freedom from all that trammels the human spirit.[4] In the nineteenth century, a Christian law–gospel dialectic was applied in such a way that OT religion as a whole, not just the legislation, was under suspicion as legalistic in essence. Some, like Friedrich Schleiermacher, would go so far as to reject the OT and warn against its seductive influence.[5] It is difficult today to imagine the extent of "the problem" for those who then wrestled with this Lutheran crux. German idealism,[6] the romanticism of their

2. Gunneweg, *Understanding the Old Testament*, 123–24 (emphasis added).
3. There has long been vigorous debate on the antiquity and significance of בְּרִית. Wellhausen argued it assumed a central position in Judah's religious thought around the time of Josiah (*Prolegomena*, 417–19). Important scholars challenged him on the late dating, such as Carl Steuernagel, Otto Procksch, Hugo Gressmann, and Walther Eichrodt, and by the mid-twentieth century, archaeological evidence for ANE covenants in the second millennium BC was taken by scholars such as George Mendenhall and Klaus Baltzer as undermining a late date. Wellhausen's view has been revitalized, however, since Lothar Perlitt's *Bundestheologie*. See also Nicholson, *God and His People*. For a critique of the late date, see McCarthy, *Treaty and Covenant*.
4. Georg Wilhelm Friedrich Hegel wrote: "Universal history exhibits the gradation in the development of that principle whose substantial purport is the consciousness of freedom" (*The Philosophy of Right/History*, 179).
5. Schleiermacher, *Christian Faith*, §132. Rudolf Bultmann expressed a similarly dismissive attitude toward the OT in the last century: "*To the Christian faith the Old Testament is no longer revelation* as it has been. . . . The events which meant something for Israel, which were God's Word, mean nothing more to us. . . . To the Christian faith the Old Testament is not in the true sense God's Word" ("Significance of the Old Testament," 31–32 [emphasis original]).
6. There was a dichotomy in historical criticism between what the critic calls "Israel's picture of her past" (i.e., the faith picture) and "what actually happened." Zimmerli wrote: "This divorce . . .

age that found the more severe themes of judgment in the OT repugnant, and Hegelian dialectics only served to put a sharper edge on the problem. A movement was afoot that regarded the OT as not merely pre-Christian, but actually opposed to the spirit of Christianity.[7]

1.1.1. Literary Criticism and Wellhausenism

Alongside the rejection of the OT as belonging to an alien religion, another attempt at resolving the problem was the literary criticism of Karl Heinrich Graf and Julius Wellhausen. It dawned on them that an altered perspective on the Law and the Prophets would yield a completely new reading of the OT. Their hypothesis that the law stood at the end of the history of Israel's religion, not the beginning, revolutionized views on the development of Israel's faith. The creatively original faith of the prophets, they argued, preceded a long period of decline into a moribund, legalistic religion that eventuated in the Pharisaism Jesus confronted. The Pentateuch is to be shifted to the "Jewish periphery of the canon." Wellhausen explains his excitement about this new historical approach in his *Prolegomena to the History of Israel* (1883):

> We cannot, then, peremptorily refuse to regard it as possible that what was the law of Judaism may also have been its product; and there are urgent reasons for taking the suggestion into very careful consideration.... In my early student days I was attracted to the stories of Saul and David, Ahab and Elijah; the discourses of Amos and Isaiah laid strong hold on me, and I read myself well into the prophetic and historical books of the Old Testament. Thanks to such aids as were accessible to me, I even considered that I understood them tolerably, but at the same time was troubled with a bad conscience, as if I were beginning with the roof instead of the foundation; for I had no thorough acquaintance with the Law, of which I was accustomed to be told that it was the basis and postulate of the whole literature. At last I took courage and made my way through Exodus, Leviticus, Numbers.... Yet so far from attaining clear conceptions, I only fell into deeper confusion.... At last, in the course of a casual visit in Göttingen in the summer of 1867, I learned through Ritschl that Karl Heinrich Graf placed the Law later than the Prophets, and, almost without knowing his reasons for the hypothesis, I was prepared to accept it;

---

of an intellectual 'doctrine' from its irrational historical 'superstructure'" was "influenced ultimately by idealist thought" ("History of Israelite Religion," 362).

7. Adolf von Harnack gave expression to the views of many when, in praise of Schleiermacher's "defense of the gospel," he wrote: "Die These, die im folgenden begründet werden soll, lautet: das AT im 2. Jahrhundert zu verwerfen, war ein Fehler, den die große Kirche mit Recht abgelehnt hat; es im 16. Jahrhundert beizubehalten, war ein Schicksal, dem sich die Reformation noch nicht zu entziehen vermochte; es aber seit dem 19. Jahrhundert als kanonische Urkunde im Protestantismus noch zu conservieren, ist die Folge einer religiösen und kirchlichen Lähmung" (*Marcion*, 248–49).

I readily acknowledged to myself the possibility of understanding Hebrew antiquity without the book of the Torah.[8]

Wellhausen was convinced the law was not the starting point for the faith of Israel, but for Judaism. With zeal, scholarship took up this revisionist thesis and began to work out the implications of the Graf-Wellhausen synthesis, which displaced the traditional view and the spectrum of earlier critical theories.[9] Doubtless, many of that era anticipated that the confusing historical data would neatly fall into place as the new hermeneutical key was applied, but their early, confident statements now seem naïve. Johannes Meinhold's assertion is representative: "Man kann wohl die Propheten ohne das Gesetz, das Gesetz aber nicht ohne die Propheten verstehen."[10]

In historical criticism, the prophet Ezekiel was disparaged because of his priestly heritage and priestly theological mindset. As the critics tended to mark a deep divide—some would speak of antithesis—between priest and prophet,[11] Ezekiel was reckoned as living on the wrong side of the divide. Wellhausen spoke of him unflatteringly as "the priest in prophet's mantle."[12]

We may call Jeremiah the last of the prophets; those who came after him were prophets only in name. Ezekiel had swallowed a book (iii. 1–3), and gave it out again. He also, like Zechariah, calls the pre-exilic prophets the old prophets, conscious that he himself belongs to the epigoni; he meditates on their words like Daniel and comments on them in his own prophecy (xxxviii. 17, xxxix. 8).[13]

When one reads all that the influential Wellhausen wrote about Ezekiel in his *Prolegomena*, it comes as little surprise that that prophecy was neglected, relative to Isaiah and Jeremiah, in critical scholarship over the following fifty years.

8. Wellhausen, *Prolegomena*, 3–4. Stephen B. Chapman has an important clarification: "For Wellhausen, the Torah was to be dated after the historical reality of prophecy, but before the prophetic writings and the other books. In his view, therefore, the Torah as a legally authoritative text still historically *preceded* the written Prophets, despite what the slogan *lex post prophetas* suggested" (*The Law and the Prophets*, 9).

9. Reviewing the development of pentateuchal criticism are: Rogerson, *Old Testament Criticism in the Nineteenth Century*; Knight, "The Pentateuch" (263–96 in Knight and Tucker, *Hebrew Bible and Its Modern Interpreters*); Whybray, *Making of the Pentateuch*; de Pury, *Le Pentateuque en Question*; Houtman, *Der Pentateuch*; Nicholson, *Pentateuch in the Twentieth Century*; Wenham, "Pondering the Pentateuch"; Weinfeld, *Place of the Law*; Dozeman and Schmid, *Farewell to the Yahwist?*; Dozeman, Schmid, and Schwartz, *The Pentateuch*; Gertz et al., *Formation of the Pentateuch*.

10. Meinhold, *Einführung*, 138.

11. This is true particularly of the latter OT period. "There is no fixed distinction in early times between the two offices," says Wellhausen (*Prolegomena*, 397).

12. Wellhausen, *Prolegomena*, 59.

13. Wellhausen, *Prolegomena*, 403.

The true prophets' experience, to Wellhausen's way of thinking, was to receive revelation that was at once personal, individual, intuitive, and immediate.[14] They were not bookish like Ezekiel the priest. Indeed, their oracles came by "free impulse" and can be sharply contrasted with Ezekiel's ways. "They do not preach on set texts; they speak out of the spirit which judges all things and itself is judged by no man. Where do they ever lean on any other authority than the truth of what they say; where do they rest on any other foundation than their own certainty?"[15] It is a mistake, then, to believe that the prophets were "the expounders of Moses." Wellhausen writes: "Their creed is not to be found in any book. It is barbarism, in dealing with such a phenomenon [prophecy] to distort its physiognomy by introducing the law. It is a vain imagination to suppose that the prophets expounded and applied the law."[16]

How did Wellhausen interpret the remarkable links between the book of Ezekiel and the Priestly Code, such as texts in Leviticus? He argued that there was literary borrowing, but in the opposite direction from what scholars had always assumed. Taking Lev 26 as a main text for discussion, Wellhausen argued that it bore an "Ezekielic colouring," together with preceding chapters.[17] Ezekiel has priority, and Leviticus builds upon the foundation laid by Ezekiel. As he moved to matters of detail, Wellhausen wrote: "The phrase *pine away in their iniquity* is repeated by Ezekiel as he heard it in the mouth of the people. He is its originator in literature; in Lev. xxvi it is borrowed."[18]

In his summary of Ezekiel's place in the development of Israel's religion, Wellhausen asserts that his role was pivotal:

> Ezekiel ... is the connecting link between the prophets and the law. He claims to be a prophet, and starts from prophetic ideas; but they are not his own ideas, they are those of his predecessors which he turns into dogmas. He is by nature a priest, and his particular merit is that he enclosed the soul of prophecy in the body of a community which was not political, but founded on the temple and the cultus.[19]

Wellhausen was confident and insistent about his thesis that the law follows the prophets. Later scholarship, however, would find it necessary to backtrack some distance and would begin, again, to speak of the prophets expounding the law.

---

14. Oddly enough, the ancient Israelite prophets know Romanticism's virtues of individualism (self-expression), spontaneity, primitivism, originality, and imagination.

15. Wellhausen, *Prolegomena*, 398.

16. Wellhausen, *Prolegomena*, 399.

17. Wellhausen, *Prolegomena*, 381.

18. Wellhausen, *Prolegomena*, 384.

19. Wellhausen, *Prolegomena*, 421.

1.1.2. Challenges to Wellhausenism

A newer method came to dominate the scene. Form criticism did not ignore the earlier source-critical method—in fact, it assumed source analysis as its ground-work—but it reoriented scholarship.[20] Because it undermined the "remarkable synthesis of literary analysis and historical reconstruction" that obtained in the late nineteenth century, form criticism has been termed not only a "modification" of, but "a revolt against Wellhausenism."[21] Whereas Wellhausen had outlined the Bible's compositional history almost solely in terms of written sources and editorial reworking, form critics dealt with the preliterary phase when traditions were passed down orally over generations. The focus was on smaller units of speech, the variety of fixed "forms" suited to and reflective of oral communication (oaths, curses, blessings, hymns, laments, parables, etc.).

Scholars could recognize old traditions and old laws common to both the prophetic writings and the books of the Law. The Pentateuch allegedly contained late material (P), but also pointed to complexes of much earlier traditions from which the prophets drew. For example, the form-critical work of Albrecht Alt, Alfred Jepsen, and others demonstrated the antiquity of law.[22] "By the middle of the twentieth century scholars were agreed that, when the so-called classical prophets began to emerge in the eighth century B.C.E., *many if not most of the narrative and legal traditions that constitute the Pentateuch already had taken shape.*"[23] It was necessary to rethink Wellhausen's understanding of the prophets and the relationship of law and prophecy.

Even more bracing challenges to Wellhausenism came from the field of tradition history engendered by form criticism. Scandinavians such as Ivan Engnell and Eduard Nielsen were antagonistic to the claims of literary critics[24] and insisted

---

20. This is truer of studies on the Prophets than of those on the Pentateuch. In 1985, Douglas Knight said the Graf/Wellhausen hypothesis of four sources "has for most scholars continued to represent the base point of Pentateuchal criticism" ("Pentateuch," 275). Defending the older *Literarkritik* in 1998, Nicholson agreed: "The work of Wellhausen, for all that it needs revision and development in detail, remains the securest basis for understanding the Pentateuch" (*Pentateuch*, vi). But a different evaluation must be given of Wellhausen's theory regarding the development of prophecy. Hans-Joachim Kraus concludes, "Daß die Propheten nicht im Sinne der Erklärungen Wellhausens als evolutionischer Aufbruch eines neuen Ethos zu verstehen sind, sondern daß sie vom altisraelitischen Recht und seiner Verkündigung herkommen" (*Die prophetische Verkündigung*, 29).

21. Anderson, "Hebrew Religion," 283.

22. Jepsen, *Untersuchung zum Bundesbuch*; Alt, *Die Ursprünge*.

23. Tucker, "Prophecy and the Prophetic Literature," 327 (emphasis added).

24. Ivan Engnell writes: "Does it really stand to reason that the typically time-bound literary criticism of the Wellhausen type and its obviously anachronistic method should be raised to everlasting dignity or endowed with eternal life? ... First I would like to state then, that the break with the literary-critical method must be radical; no compromise is possible. The old method must be replaced by a new one. And the only possible alternative is, as far as I can see, what is in Scandinavia called the traditio-historical method" ("Methodological Aspects," 21).

that oral tradition, with its ability to preserve and transform verbal materials over centuries until they were reduced to writing, best explains the development of the OT corpus. We interpreters should "free ourselves from the modern, anachronistic book-view," which is foreign to ancient Near Eastern cultural realities.[25]

In his *Oral Tradition*, Nielsen showed how the premises of tradition history, especially its emphasis on the role of oral tradition, undermine the source-critical enterprise's chronology of *documents*. But there is another casualty to be considered: tradition history collapses Wellhausen's notion of the evolution of "ethical monotheism" in ancient Israel, a theological reconstruction based on source criticism.

> If one admits that a written source, the literary age of which is three or four hundred years younger than that of another, contains features that are considerably older than the recension of the oldest written source, then one presupposes—as Gunkel does, too—that these written sources are the reduction to writing of century-old traditions, where the time of the reduction to writing in reality says nothing as to the age of the material, but at most something about its last revision. This is a very fruitful point of view, but at the same time it deprives literary criticism of one of its favourite criteria. For according to this view it is impossible as a matter of course to divide the *material* into three age groups and to distribute the three groups among J, E and P. For here indeed the youngest source has an element which is older than the present form of the oldest source. External criteria, such as the criterion of the name of the Deity and the stylistic criteria, remain, but in that case source criticism indisputably loses its charm, the charm which it possessed when literary critics were fully convinced that source distinction clarified the development of the Israelite religion in the times of the monarchy and the exile.[26]

This perspective on Pentateuchal traditions cannot help but promote a reevaluation of the prophets' indebtedness to those traditions.

Another revolutionary aspect of the traditio-historical method hinted in the Nielsen quote above is its dispute with Wellhausenism over the antiquity and value of the cultic traditions in the Pentateuch. Engnell found evidence of very old cultic traditions and wrote against an "anti-cultic" prejudice he found in many OT scholars.[27] Such prejudice, that cultic materials and sacral law must be placed late

---

25. Engnell, "The Traditio-Historical Method in Old Testament Research," in *Critical Essays*, 3.

26. Nielsen, *Oral Tradition*, 96–97.

27. In his essay, "Prophets and Prophetism," Engnell wrote: "Exegetes have unanimously placed strong emphasis on ethics as perhaps the most important factor which distinguishes 'genuine' prophetism from 'false' prophetism, which very indiscriminately is regarded as lacking ethical character and is characterized by its association with the cult. . . . According to this view, the prophets . . . come forth with an essentially anti-cultic proclamation. Their message is that righteousness should supplant the

in the devolution—not evolution—of the religion, long blinded scholarship from seeing the long-standing traditions behind the Law and recognizing the prophets' true relationship to ancient cultic traditions.

Outside of Scandinavia, traditio-historical research presents a somewhat more moderate face, especially in avoiding a sharp distinction between tradition as oral transmission ("living speech") and written presentation.[28] H. G. M. Williamson discusses how tradition history has taken a fresh tack in answering the question of how much the early prophets knew of the contents of the Pentateuch, Joshua, Judges, and Samuel. "Were they commentators on a received body of religious beliefs and practices, or were they innovators whose insights were later codified in other texts as well? And to what extent could the progress in prophecy through time be related to the growth in the other authoritative literature?" He explains:

> Von Rad sought to bypass the dilemma of the extent of inherited written historical material by appeal to what he called "tradition," that is to say, a body of inherited material, comprising both knowledge of past history and the formulation of certain basic and central religious concepts.... The attraction of von Rad's use of tradition was that it enabled scholars to read the prophets in a manner that was both somewhat more conventional than had become fashionable, and yet to do so with scholarly integrity on critical issues.[29]

A quote from Gerhard von Rad summarizes this well: "As we now see, they [the prophets] were in greater or lesser degree conditioned by old traditions which they re-interpreted and applied to their own times."[30] Zimmerli's interpretation of the RF largely derives from a tradition-history approach built on a form-critical base.

Certain circles reacted against tradition history because a strict focus on oral tradition was thought inadequate. Scholars sought to reexamine the literary process behind, and discern the redactional layers in, the final form of the Pentateuch and the Prophets.[31] The Marburg school centered on Otto Kaiser combined this

---

cult. As a result, the prophets create a new 'spiritual' form of religion which is 'without cult.' This understanding which is still predominant (at any rate, in popular expositions and text-books), is undoubtedly prompted by a Protestant tenet that cultic piety is of inferior power, a view inherited from the Age of Enlightenment and Rationalism. Advocates of this position operate on a purely anachronistic assumption that the prophets propagated a 'spiritual' religion which was independent of the cult. But, in reality, this is completely foreign to ancient Israel, including her prophets" (*Critical Essays*, 137.)

28. Helmer Ringgren urged that "oral and written transmission should not be played off against [one] another: they do not exclude each other, but may be regarded as complementary" ("Oral and Written Transmission," 34). Zimmerli takes the later written stages into account in "Das Gotteswort des Ezechiel."

29. Williamson, "History and Memory," 135.

30. Von Rad, *Old Testament Theology*, 2:4.

31. For the Pentateuch, I have in mind the creative role attributed to editors by John Van Seters's books and Whybray, *Making of the Pentateuch*.

redaction criticism with an instinct to date the entire written OT to the postexilic era,[32] and it has made radical proposals that bear on the RF. The Ezekiel research of Kaiser's students such as Hermann Schulz, Jörg Garscha, and Karl-Friedrich Pohlmann includes complex schemes of redactional layering;[33] they also show the influence of Wellhausen's grand theory of Israel's religious evolution. What principles may be used to distinguish the authentic material—if there is any—from the inauthentic, and how might one separate the earlier from the later in Ezekiel? Pohlmann and Garscha judge the more artful/poetic sections (parables) to be more prophetic in character, and therefore early.[34] But the more priestly "sacral law" layer is very late (ca. 300 BC), says Garscha. Prophets antedate law, and the two are kept separate. What bears the marks of oral communication (riddles and parables again) is more likely prophetic and early; whatever seems studied or literary is priestly and late. The RF and other repetitious features of the prophecy are discounted and relegated to the later strata.[35] The identity of Ezekiel as a priest-prophet disappears in some radical German scholarship.

Within the scholarship of the Marburg school, there is a markedly negative attitude toward oracles that are more literary in style or seem to have an affinity with and dependence on other texts or recorded traditions. Ezekiel the scholar, with his prophetic *Rückblick* to the "traditions" of Israel's founding, cannot be expected to fare well, as Kaiser asserts: "It can be demonstrated that the dependence of the prophets on tradition increases as the living force of prophecy flags, and finally gives way to scribalism and apocalyptic speculation, or falls into contempt (cf. Zech. 13.1 ff.)."[36] This postulate predisposes the reader to judge Ezekiel

32. This had earlier featured in some Scandinavians' work. E.g., H. S. Nyberg wrote: "The written O.T. is a creation of the Jewish community after the Exile; what preceded it was certainly only in small measure in fixed written form.... Only with the greatest reserve can we reckon ... with writers among the prophets.... We must reckon with circles, sometimes centres, of tradition, that preserved and handed on the material. It is self-evident that such a process of transmission could not continue without some change in the material handed on, but we have to do, not with textual corruption, but with active transformation.... For the rest, O.T. scholarship would do well to consider earnestly what possibility it can ever have of regaining the *ipsissima verba* of Old Testament personalities. We have nothing but the tradition of their sayings" (*Studien zum Hoseabuche,* cited in Eissfeldt, "Prophetic Literature," 128–29.)

33. Garscha claims to discover about eight layers (*Studien zum Ezechielbuch*).

34. This is in line with Otto Kaiser's dictum that "prophetic utterance as being divine utterance had to be made in exalted language," a fact that "assists in distinguishing between sayings of the prophets that were really uttered, and literary additions in the prophetic books" (*Introduction,* 212). This widely held notion of prophecy as properly issuing forth only in heightened language is reflected in many literary works, e.g.: Bridges, "Prometheus the Firegiver," lns. 433–35: "He may be mad and yet say true—maybe / The heat of prophecy like a strong wine / Shameth his reason with exultant speech."

35. According to Garscha, the RF belongs to a later stratum (early fourth-century): "Die Erkenntnisformel muß vielmehr in erster Linie als Kennzeichen der deuteroezechielischen Schicht angesehen werden" (*Studien zum Ezechielbuch,* 313–14).

36. Kaiser, *Introduction,* 215.

deficient and, unlike the "pure stream" of prophecy, unoriginal. It would seem that Kaiser's approach precludes any favorable consideration of the exilic prophet's theological relationship to the law or legal traditions.

This brand of redaction criticism faces strong opposition from inside Germany[37] and especially from outside. Ezekiel scholarship, generally speaking, has shifted away from a narrowly historical-critical program in which the text is "fractured into a historical succession of messages" and traditions.[38] This is apparent in the assumptions of important dissertations published over the last thirty years.[39] Resistance to that program is based in part, of course, on shifts in philosophical hermeneutics. However, there is also a strong conviction that the text itself, Ezekiel's prophecy, resists disassembly.

1.1.3. Canonical Criticism

There is a movement underway to read the OT with greater sensitivity to the traditional picture of ancient Israel and the development of her literature as presented by the OT itself. In a canonical focus, the tradition of Mosaic authorship of the Pentateuch has major theological implications for reading the canon.[40] There

37. Kraus states: "Angesichts der durch W. Zimmerli klar dargelegten Methodik tritt die extreme Situation, in welche die *verabsolutierte Redaktionskritik* hineingeraten ist, besonders kraß in Ersheinung. Vgl. J. Garscha, Studien zum Ezechielbuch. . . . Die herkömmlichen Grundsätze der Interpretation werden auf den Kopf gestellt" (*Geschichte der historisch-kritischen Erforschung*, 545–46). See Georg Fohrer's review of Garscha in *ZAW* and Zimmerli's evaluation in "Preface to the Second German Edition (1979)," in *Ezekiel 2*, xii–xiv.

38. This phrase is borrowed from Levenson, *Hebrew Bible*, 70.

39. Ellen Davis summarized the approach of her Yale dissertation: "The elegant architecture of the book grows more impressive with further study. Our investigations must be conducted with regard for the literary integrity of the text at every level, beginning with the earliest stages of composition. We are likely to render satisfactory interpretations only by proceeding on the assumption that the text was always intelligible in its synchronic dimensions, however its meanings may have been enriched and changed through diachronic evolution. It is wise to credit those who produced the text with the concern that it should be read" ("Swallowing Hard," 235). See also Stevenson, *Vision of Transformation*, esp. 125–42, and Kutsko's Harvard dissertation, published as *Between Heaven and Earth*. The latter writes: "Despite the lack of consensus on the form, unity, or redaction of the book of Ezekiel, scholars generally recognize that the book needs to be treated as a literary whole. Even when redaction is conspicuous, most passages resist precise divisions and classifications. Identifiable literary themes and recurrent phraseology suggest that approaching Ezekiel as a well-integrated, coherent text is warranted" (9).

40. Childs argues that higher critics and conservatives are so fixated on historicity—either denying or seeking to bolster the text's historical value—that both camps have failed to do "justice to the canonical understanding of Moses's relationship to the Pentateuch." There is need to interpret the Pentateuch and assess its function more as a unit, after which it will be clearer that it provides the foundation for the OT canon: "The fundamental theological understanding of God's redemptive work through law and grace, promise and fulfilment, election and obedience was once and for all established" (*Introduction*, 132). Canonically speaking: "The law, which derived from God's speaking to Moses, applies to every successive generation of Israel ([Deut] 31:11–13). It serves as a witness to

is unquestionably a tradition of the prophets building on a Mosaic foundation and viewing themselves as Moses's heirs. Practitioners of canonical criticism have shown great interest, therefore, in the topic of the Law and the Prophets as interrelated revelatory traditions and literary corpora.[41] Among those using a canonical approach and among literary critics reading the final form of the prophets, we find an increasing amount of scholarship on prophetic links to Moses and the Pentateuch.[42] (Ezekiel's prophecy figures prominently in this area.)[43] Did certain prophets understand themselves as fulfilling the role of a "new Moses"? What are we to make of the frequent parallels between the stories of the prophets' experiences and those of the Moses figure?

While appreciating the contribution of diachronic methods such as form criticism, Brevard Childs's canonical approach parts ways with them when drawing theological conclusions:

> To assume that the prophets can be understood only if each oracle is related to a specific historical event or located in its original cultural milieu is to introduce a major hermeneutical confusion into the discipline and to render an understanding of the canonical Scriptures virtually impossible. Rather, the true referent of the biblical witness can only be comprehended from within the biblical literature itself.[44]

Attentiveness to the canonical context requires interpreters to read the Prophets and the Law together, despite the fact that historical criticism discourages that endeavor with its dichotomy between Israel's "actual history" and "confessed history" and its scheme of dating compositions that, in certain cases at least, would

---

God's will (v. 28). The law of God has now been transmitted for the future generations in the written form of scripture. . . . Indeed, the original role of Moses as the unique prophet of God (34:10) will be performed by the book of the law in the future (31:26ff.). . . . In spite of the lack of historical evidence by which to trace the actual process, it would seem clear that the authorship of Moses did perform a normative role within a canonical context from a very early period The laws attributed to Moses were deemed authoritative, and conversely authoritative laws were attributed to Moses" (*Introduction*, 134).

41. See, e.g., Chapman's Yale dissertation, published as *The Law and the Prophets.*

42. Seitz, "The Prophet Moses"; O'Kane, "Isaiah." Two early articles by William Holladay cited by Seitz that researched this area were "Background of Jeremiah's Self-Understanding"; and "Jeremiah and Moses." See also Alonso Schökel "Jeremías como anti-Moisés," which explores the similarities and differences between the figures. On links between Exodus and Jeremiah, see Fischer, "Zurück nach Ägypten."

43. McKeating, "Ezekiel the 'Prophet Like Moses'?"; Patton, "I Myself Gave them Laws"; Levitt Kohn, "A Prophet like Moses?" Monographs that suggest the heuristic value of such links are: Levenson, *Theology of the Program*, and Kutsko, *Between Heaven and Earth.* Kutsko believes that "some of the traditions that are encountered in their final literary form in the Priestly sources of the Pentateuch were also available to Ezekiel in some form, oral or written" (13) and that "the prophet adapts Priestly traditions" (99). Here I leave aside for the moment the recent literature on inner-biblical interpretation, which has also made a contribution in this area.

44. Childs, "The Canonical Shape," 53.

rule out inner-biblical interpretation. In other words, the biblical relationship between the prophets and Moses's law is an intended result of the process of canonical shaping, and it must be reckoned with if we are to read the Bible as Scripture. Walter Brueggemann presses this very point and demonstrates how a canonical approach breaks with Wellhausenism:

> In addition to the Levites and these occasional mediators, the great prophets of Israel form a third group of practitioners of Torah mediation. The phenomenon of prophecy is rich and varied and largely ad hoc. The prophets derive from many traditions. In the canonical form of Israel's testimony, however, this disparate material has been largely ordered around themes of judgment and hope, which appear to be derived from Torah claims of blessing and curse.... In the Deuteronomic Torah, it is precisely disobedience to Torah that results in the catastrophe of 587 B.C.E., which plunges Israel into the fissure of exile. In canonical form, the prophets are informed by Torah and give accent to its invitation to life and its warning about death.[45]

1.1.4. Conclusion

Today there is no consensus regarding the relationship between the Law and the Prophets—the two considered either as canonical collections of texts or as theological traditions. The relationship has long been "one of the most contentious issues" and "has lost none of its edge" in scholarship.[46] On the one hand, many with diachronic interests dissent from Wellhausen's dictum that the prophets preceded the law. On the other hand, the critics claim not to have found much evidence of prophetic indictments being based on that juridical tradition. Moving away from historical-critical concerns, one must allow for an immensely meaningful theological relationship between the two.

The two traditions are obviously in tension in some ways, and scholars have wrestled with describing the tension. Von Rad posited elements of continuity between older legal traditions and the proclamation of the prophets, but he emphasized the discontinuities as the traditions were reinterpreted.[47] Zimmerli followed with his view that "the prophets brought something new, which needed

---

45. Brueggemann, *Theology of the Old Testament*, 588.

46. Blenkinsopp, "Prophecy and the Prophetic Books," 338. He claims one point of agreement among critics: the issue of the relationship "cannot be posed in a straightforward way in terms of relative priority."

47. Von Rad expresses the continuity thus: "[The prophets] are deeply rooted in the religious traditions of their nation; indeed, their whole preaching might almost be described as a unique dialogue with the tradition by means of which the latter was made to speak to their own day" (*Old Testament Theology*, 2:177). For discontinuity, see esp. *Old Testament Theology*, 2:176–87, and 1:66–68, 96–102. Von Rad said "the devastating force and finality of the prophetic pronouncement of judgment can never have had a cultic antecedent" (2:179). The dual aspects of continuity and discontinuity,

to be added to the law," and which superseded the law in the sense that "what the prophets proclaimed led to an inner crisis in the law."[48]

As this study proceeds, the relationship between the prophet Ezekiel and the Law will repeatedly occupy our attention. There will be exploration of both the continuities and the discontinuities. The tension created between the two in the prophecy is a creative one, provoked by tragedy and leading to profound theological reflection on Yahweh's purposes with his people.

1.2. Assumptions and Strategies for Approaching Ezekiel's Formula

As demonstrated in the following chapters, scholars bring a wide variety of hermeneutical commitments to bear on the topic of this study. Here I lay out my own perspective and methodology, acknowledging that "our presuppositions and methods shape the questions we bring to texts; and our questions inevitably influence the answers we discern there."[49] While maintaining an evangelical faith commitment and high respect for Scripture, I seek also to be critically engaged, not neglecting the research of those who do not share my faith.

1.2.1. General Assumptions Regarding Historical Critical Issues

Without necessarily denying the possibility of a complex, perhaps lengthy process of composition and redaction, more and more Ezekiel scholars are proceeding under the assumption that the final form is intelligible and the proper object of their study.[50] The orderly structure of the prophecy, the consistent use of certain characteristic phrases throughout the book, the pervasiveness of its theocentric orientation (both the theology and the dominance of direct divine speech), the elegant "halving" patterns that bind together large units of text, and so on all bear witness to the book's cohesiveness and unity. I do not count myself among those competent to discern what could or could not have been spoken/written by the prophet and what, if not, must therefore be credited to an editor.

While others carry on the discussion of such thorny issues as discriminating between the authentic and the inauthentic (or accretional)[51] or the text-critical

---

as von Rad defines them, may be the result of the conflicting theologies he finds throughout the OT. See further *Old Testament Theology*, 1:289–96.

48. Zimmerli, *The Law and the Prophets*, 13.

49. Darr, "Literary Perspectives," 131.

50. In addition to the dissertations quoted above (n. 39), see: Greenberg, "Valid Criteria"; Boadt, "Mythological Themes"; Galambush, "Ezekiel," who writes of a late-twentieth-century "profusion of studies that focus on the book's unity and explore its literary technique" (234).

51. Interpreters are poles apart. Kaiser's principle is "to view each text as a redactional creation until the contrary is proven" (cited in Zimmerli, *Ezekiel* 2, xiii). Greenberg, on the other hand,

problem of a shorter LXX,[52] this study will interpret the RFs as they appear in the Masoretic Text (*BHS*).[53] In the chapter below providing "Details of the Formula's Usage," the text-critical divergences between the LXX and MT will be listed and discussed at some length, but without any suggested alterations of the base text. There will also be a listing of RFs deemed secondary by Zimmerli; no attempt will be made to survey more broadly the differing redaction-critical conclusions of others.

Scholars take a strong interest in the origin of Ezekiel's RF, and this study squarely faces that historical critical question. All agree that the formula "is by no means an original coinage of Ezekiel himself."[54] Unless one is disposed to believe the prophecy shows not only an affinity with but also a distinguishable emulation of literature outside Israel,[55] the interpreter confronts *biblical* influences and "reactualized" biblical traditions, or the phenomenon of what Michael Fishbane, like Nahum Sarna before him, terms "inner-biblical interpretation." From where did the prophet derive this refrain that dominates his book? Addressing the question of the formula's origin should be a priority for research on Ezekiel's RF.

A conservative position regarding an earlier dating of the books of Moses,[56] including Exodus, may include the corollary interpretation that Ezekiel provides "commentary" on parts of Exodus.[57] Though this is thought to be at odds with

---

concludes that "Ezekiel's utterances were sacrosanct from the time they were written down" ("Valid Criteria," 135).

52. For orientation and bibliography, see Lange and Tov, *Hebrew Bible*, 557–85. Greenberg outlines a cautious approach in "Use of Ancient Versions."

53. DSS finds have not benefited text criticism of Ezekiel to any great extent, but see ch. 3 for discussion.

54. Zimmerli, *I Am Yahweh*, 41.

55. Some adduce evidence for strong nonbiblical, non-Hebrew influence on the language and structuring of Ezekiel's prophecy. Even more than *influence*, others judge there to be conscious modeling after non-Hebrew sources in the prophecy: Garfinkel, "Studies in Akkadian Influences"; Bodi, *Ezekiel and the Poem of Erra*; Sharon, "Biblical Parallel to a Sumerian Temple Hymn?"; Petter, *Ezekiel and Mesopotamian City Laments*. See also Odell, "Genre and Persona." In a later article, Odell seeks to answer possible criticism of her thesis that the prophecy, including ch. 1, achieved its coherence through "a sophisticated appropriation of the three-part Assyrian building inscription genre" ("Ezekiel Saw What He Saw," 162). There is no disputing that Ezekiel's prophecy should be read against its ANE background; such an approach is both necessary and illuminating (e.g., Block, "Divine Abandonment"). But a general and comprehensive emulation of obscure Assyrian, not Babylonian, building inscriptions (ca. 685 BC) or an Akkadian poem (*terminus ante quem* 750 BC) is to me unconvincing. (Note: Bodi argues the RF derives from the *Poem of Erra*; see *Ezekiel and the Poem of Erra*, 297–305.)

56. One evangelical textbook argues: "Moses' role in the production of the Pentateuch must be affirmed as highly formative although it is unlikely that Moses wrote the Pentateuch *as it exists in its final form*. The core of both the narrative framework and legislative material goes back to his literary instigation and authentically reflects both the circumstances and events there related" (LaSor, Hubbard, and Bush, *Old Testament Survey*, 9 [emphasis original].) See also: Harrison, *Introduction*; Longman and Dillard, *Introduction*; Hess, *Old Testament*, 24, 32–34.

57. Childs, *Exodus*, 113. See also n. 1 of this chapter.

critical orthodoxy on the formation of the Pentateuch, certain seasoned critics argue that there needs to be a reawakening to the canonical, theological, and literary importance of the Mosaic-authorship tradition.[58] Moreover, a portion of cutting-edge literary scholarship on the Pentateuch over several decades has been pushing back the date of the alleged Priestly Source to preexilic times, thus encouraging research on Ezekiel's possible dependence on pentateuchal materials, on Exodus in some recensional form. This study takes that encouragement. More needs to be said, however, about this revisionist scholarship.[59]

1.2.2. Revisionist Scholarship on "P" and Ezekiel

Scholars have long recognized a close relation between the Priestly Source—considered the latest—and Ezekiel, with their similarities in topics, themes, and phraseology. If Ezekiel comes from the priestly class and the "Priestly School" is thought to be responsible for P, how does one evaluate their interrelationship? Avi Hurvitz, who has done the most work on the relationship between P and Ezekiel, states: "Opinion is divided as to the appropriate interpretation of the literary proximity and phraseological similarities between these two compositions. Key questions in this discussion are *who depends on whom* (literarily) and *who precedes whom* (historically)."[60] Arguments over these questions can become devilishly complex. Some think both P and Ezekiel can be classified as a pastiche

---

58. John F. A. Sawyer writes: "Even today it can be argued that the tradition that Moses wrote the Pentateuch is more important, from a religious, theological and literary point of view, than the fact that he did not" (*Sacred Languages and Sacred Texts*, 102). See also Childs, *Introduction*, 132–35.

59. For the sake of argument, I occasionally cite alleged J/E, D, P, and H, though I disagree with source analysis and some assumptions of historical criticism as commonly practiced. Levenson writes: "I have argued that the price of recovering the *historical* context of sacred books has been the erosion of the largest *literary* contexts that undergird the traditions that claim to be based upon them.... Much of the polemics between religious traditionalists and historians over the past three centuries can be reduced to the issue of which context shall be normative. When historical critics assert, as they are wont to do, that the Hebrew Bible must not be taken 'out of context,' what they really mean is that the only context worthy of respect is the ancient Near Eastern world as it was at the time of composition of whatever text is under discussion. Religious traditionalists, however, are committed to another set of contexts, minimally the rest of scripture, however delimited, and maximally, the entire tradition, including their own religious experience" (*The Hebrew Bible*, 4–5).

60. Hurvitz, *Linguistic Study*, 10. His monograph builds on earlier articles: "Usage of שש and בוץ"; "Evidence of Language." Further research produced his "Language of the Priestly Source," "Dating the Priestly Source," and "Once Again." Hurvitz provides an explanation and defense of his method in "Can Biblical Texts Be Dated Linguistically?" and "Recent Debate on Late Biblical Hebrew." He says linguistic-philological considerations should outweigh the historical-chronological, the theological-ideological, and the literary-stylistic arguments when scholarship seeks "to determine the age of the source material preserved in the Hebrew Bible" ("Can Biblical Texts be Dated Linguistically?" 159). No one has approached his expertise in placing Ezekiel's prophecy on the continuum of the development of Biblical Hebrew. For further discussion of this branch of philology, see: Young, *Biblical Hebrew*; Miller-Naudé and Zevit, *Diachrony in Biblical Hebrew*; Kim, *Early Biblical Hebrew*.

of redactional layers and that perhaps the two were handled by the same redactors. In that case, how is one to draw any conclusions regarding precedence and literary dependence? Some hold that the RF is late redactional material in both.

But a surprising number of ranking biblical scholars, especially Jewish members of the guild, challenge the long-standing critical assumption that P is postexilic. They argue that it is not Late Biblical Hebrew (LBH). Rather, in the words of Hurvitz, "the Priestly source (in both its legal and narrative portions) falls within the compass of the classical corpora of the Bible," and the linguistic evidence points to the conclusion that "the 'formative' years which shaped the extant Priestly materials of the Pentateuch are those of the pre-exilic period."[61] Others besides Hurvitz who have advanced the scholarly discussion in this area are Yehezkel Kaufmann, Menaḥem Haran, Jacob Milgrom, and Ziony Zevit.[62] Though he has not published any substantial discussion of the issue, Moshe Greenberg apparently follows Kaufmann (whom he translated) regarding a preexilic P.[63] As could be expected, those committed to some version of the older *Literarkritik* challenge the shifting of the date of P earlier.[64]

Kaufmann's work especially has given impetus to this mediating position. He attacks both the exilic dating of P—"in every detail, P betrays its antiquity"[65]— and Wellhausenism:

Wellhausen's arguments complemented each other nicely, and offered what seemed to be a solid foundation upon which to build the house of biblical criticism. Since then, however, both the evidence and the arguments supporting the structure have been called into question and, to some extent, even rejected. Yet biblical scholarship,

61. Hurvitz, *Linguistic Study*, 7; Hurvitz, "Dating the Priestly Source," 99.

62. Kaufmann, *The Religion of Israel*; Kaufmann, *History of the Religion of Israel* 4; Abba, "Priests and Levites"; Haran, *Temples and Temple Service*; Haran, "Law Code"; Haran, "Behind the Scenes"; Haran, "Character of the Priestly Source"; Haran, "Ezekiel, P, and the Priestly School"; Zevit, "Converging Lines"; McConville, "Priests and Levites"; Propp, "Priestly Source Recovered Intact?"; Wenham, "Priority of P." Jacob Milgrom's commentaries assert an earlier date for P; see *Leviticus 1–16*, 3–13, which presents over a dozen reasons for a preexilic dating of P. One may also consult his collected essays in *Studies in Cultic Theology and Terminology*, his "Response to Rolf Rendtorff," and his "Priestly ('P') Source." Milgrom holds "that Ezekiel had all of P and most of H before him and, conversely, that there is not a single Priestly text that bears the influence of Ezekiel" ("Response to Rolf Rendtorff," 85). Further evidence is presented in Milgrom's "Leviticus 26 and Ezekiel" and "Case for the Pre-Exilic and Exilic Provenance."

63. Greenberg, *Ezekiel 1–20*, ix. See Greenberg's student Israel Knohl's *Sanctuary of Silence*: "I agree with Haran's identification of the reign of Ahaz and Hezekiah as a decisive period in the history of the Priestly writings" (201).

64. Levine, "Research in the Priestly Source"; Levine, "Late Language"; Levine, *Numbers 1–20*, 101–9; Davies, review of Hurvitz, *Linguistic Study*; Blenkinsopp, "Assessment of the Alleged Pre-Exilic Date." Seemingly without any personal commitment to source analysis is the linguistic critique of Mark Rooker et al. by J. A. Naudé in "Language of the Book of Ezekiel."

65. Kaufmann, *Religion of Israel*, 206.

while admitting that the grounds have crumbled away, nevertheless continues to adhere to the conclusions. The critique of Wellhausen's theory which began some forty years ago has not been consistently carried through to its end. Equally unable to accept the theory in its classical formulation and to return to the precritical views of tradition, biblical scholarship has entered upon a period of search for new foundations.[66]

In this connection, one should take note of Moshe Weinfeld's arguments that Deuteronomy, which he dates to the seventh century, cites and uses material from P but P does not cite Deuteronomy.[67]

Two dissertations make major contributions to the discussion. Mark Rooker's work at Brandeis University (since published) rates Ezekiel as the true transitional work between preexilic Early Biblical Hebrew (EBH) and LBH.[68] In a close comparison with Ezekiel's lexical features, P appears to be the earlier of the two. Rooker also treats the matter of possible use of sources and provides an abbreviated list of terminological connections he found between Ezekiel and texts in the Pentateuch. Led by Fishbane as his supervisor, Rooker suggests that the phenomenon of inner-biblical exegesis is in play at those points. In her work (also since published), Risa Levitt Kohn delves more deeply into the literary relationship of Ezekiel and P, providing a full catalog of shared terminology. Of particular interest for this study is her chapter, "Ezekiel and the Priestly Source Reconsidered," which analyzes the links in content and terminology and concludes that Ezekiel engages in inner-biblical exegesis:

> Ezekiel is familiar with the Priestly Source, but, clearly, his writing is more than just a product of its influence or tradition. The prophet appropriates P's terminology but feels comfortable situating it in new, different, and even contradictory contexts. . . . Ezekiel knows P, quotes P, but also modifies it at will, adding and deleting material as suits his personal agenda and the current circumstances of his audience.[69]

This is not the place to discuss at length the arguments over the dating of P; others have already helpfully reviewed them. Revisionists such as Hurvitz, Milgrom, and Levitt Kohn are not returning to an old conservative position on the Mosaic authorship of the vast body of material in the Pentateuch, but their work

---

66. Kaufmann, *Religion of Israel*, 1. Reviewing Kaufmann's work is Krapf, *Die Priesterschrift und die vorexilische Zeit*.

67. Weinfeld, "Pentateuch"; Weinfeld, *Deuteronomy and the Deuteronomic School*; and Weinfeld, *Place of the Law*. Kaufmann's work, cited above, also sets out to prove that P predated Deuteronomy.

68. Rooker, *Biblical Hebrew*, 53.

69. Levitt Kohn, *A New Heart*, 84–85. She also treats Ezekiel's literary relationship to Deuteronomy and the Deuteronomistic History.

encourages me to proceed more boldly in detailing Ezekiel's reuse of textual material in Exodus.[70] An increasing weight of evidence is being thrown behind the position that P/H is preexilic.[71] Regarding linguistic dating for the Five Books, I can agree with Jan Joosten of Oxford: "A first inference to be drawn from the diachronic framework is that the Pentateuch is to be regarded substantially as preexilic."[72]

Because the dating of P is "a tentative enterprise at best,"[73] I hope traditional source theories will not cause readers to balk either at the proposal of a preexilic P or at one of the central theses of this study, the position that Ezekiel draws on pentateuchal materials, including P texts. In view of the long-standing confusion in Pentateuch criticism,[74] Rolf Rendtorff cautions against a dogmatic position on a postexilic P:

> We really do not possess reliable criteria for dating the pentateuchal literature. Each dating of the pentateuchal "sources" relies on purely hypothetical assumptions which in the long run have their continued existence because of the consensus of scholars.... It must be said that the common dating of the "priestly" sections, be they narrative or legal, to the exilic or post exilic period, likewise rests on conjecture and the consensus of scholars, but not on unambiguous criteria.[75]

---

70. Gary Rendsburg believes the evidence for a much earlier dating of P is compelling: "In fact, typologically the entire Pentateuch may be considered a unified work and may be dated to a time earlier than the composition of Joshua, Judges and Samuel. This is not to say that writers of the Davidic period did not add such phrases as the boundaries given in Genesis 15:18, but as a whole the Pentateuch is ancient" ("Late Biblical Hebrew," 78).

71. Gordon Wenham writes: "A postexilic date ... is difficult to maintain in face of the abundant quotations in Ezekiel and of the linguistic evidence that P's vocabulary does not resemble that of late biblical Hebrew. A much earlier date is required by the evidence" (*Leviticus*, 13).

72. Joosten, "Diachronic Linguistics," 336. For the same reason, as well as others, in *A Prophet Like Moses*, Jeffrey Stackert believes the pentateuchal sources are preexilic. See also Hess, *Israelite Religions*, 46–59.

73. Childs, *Introduction*, 124.

74. Scholars have long expressed pessimism about the results of pentateuchal criticism. E.g., H. H. Rowley wrote in 1959 that we "find a more confused position today than at any time since the rise of criticism" (*Changing Pattern*, 11). Knight gave a description of the *statis quaestionis* in 1985: "Given these two factors—that the Pentateuch has so often served as the subject matter for innovative criticism throughout the history of biblical scholarship and that this literature is of crucial importance for our study of Israel's cultural history—it is all the more disconcerting to observe that uncertainties and disputes at very fundamental points are prevalent in current Pentateuchal studies" ("The Pentateuch," 264). Veteran scholar David Carr writes in 2016: "We know far less than we think we do about the formation of these texts. Put another way, I am ever more struck with just how fraught and difficult it is for us to know anything secure and detailed about the undocumented prehistory of any text. The field is littered with the carcasses of dead theories by once-prominent pentateuchal scholars, and I suspect that many theories advanced today will fare no better" ("Data to Inform Ongoing Debates," 106.)

75. Rendtorff, *The Problem*, 201–3.

1.2.3. A Diachronic Approach: Inner-Biblical Interpretation

It has been said that Scripture "is full of itself"[76] and that "the Bible is littered with self-referential allusions."[77] For some time, scholars have been exploring inner-biblical exegesis and intertextuality and paying more attention to the interpretation of the OT *within* the OT. The Scriptures themselves evidence the earliest stages of biblical exegesis. I am excited by approaches to reading OT texts in relation to other texts, many of the approaches having been developed within the humanities. In this section, I focus on inner-biblical exegesis or inner-biblical interpretation,[78] a phenomenon recognized by Jewish scholarship on the Bible and on midrash.

A century ago, nearly "all students of Hebrew literature assumed a wide and impassable chasm between the Bible and the literary products of post-canonical Judaism."[79] Research since in the fields of midrashic and haggadic interpretation and Qumran commentary (pesher) shows that similar modes of interpretation are to be found within the Hebrew Bible. Rather than a chasm, there is some continuity[80] from the rabbis back to the biblical writers who reflected on, cited, and interpreted earlier Scriptures (the earliest midrashic exegesis). Long before the rabbis offered commentary on Tanak, biblical writers engaged in exegesis. Thus, the Hebrew Bible should be read as an exegetical work in its own right and with an understanding that textual analysis and biblical interpretation were already being practiced in ancient Israel.

Though students of the OT have customarily thought of Scripture primarily as that on which exegesis and interpretation must be practiced, there is exegesis *within* the Hebrew Bible as well. Both canonical criticism and inner-biblical interpretation show a sensitivity to this reality and enrich scholarship by probing literary and theological relationships between authoritative texts. One quote from Childs' *Introduction to the Old Testament as Scripture* has been seminal for all of the research behind this study:

> Surely one of the most important aspects of Ezekiel's message was its dependence upon the activity of interpretation within the Bible itself. Not only was Ezekiel deeply immersed in the ancient *traditions* of Israel, but the prophet's message shows many signs of being influenced by a study of Israel's sacred *writings*. The impact of a collection of authoritative writings is strong throughout the book. Obviously, the

76. Sanders, review of Fishbane, *The Garments of Torah*, 433.
77. Eslinger, "Inner-biblical Exegesis and Inner-biblical Allusion," 47.
78. Both labels are widely used, with "inner-biblical interpretation" being the more general and probably more useful term.
79. Gordis, "Midrash and the Prophets."
80. See: Seeligmann, "Voraussetzungen der Midraschexegese"; Bloch, "Ezéchiel XVI"; Bloch, "Midrash"; Vermes, *Scripture and Tradition*; and Weingreen, *From Bible to Mishna*.

mediating of Israel's tradition through an authoritative written source represents a major canonical interest. The evidence that such activity was a major factor in the formulation of Ezekiel's original oracles would also account for the ease with which the canonical process adopted his oracles without great change.[81]

If the trailblazing theorists for inner-biblical interpretation were Kaufman, Sarna, Robert Gordis, Samuel Sandmel, and Jacob Weingreen,[82] then Fishbane is today's most experienced and methodologically savvy practitioner.[83] He has a sharp eye for changes in linguistic content and linguistic force as themes, words, phrases, and whole passages are "reused" by an ancient exegete. Fishbane questions how a writer takes up an earlier text to reuse, recontextualize, extend, reformulate, reinterpret or transform it. The *function* of echoing an earlier sacred utterance is also important to him. That function can vary: authoritative reference, reinterpretation, clarification, preservation of an authoritative memory, revitalization of what has perhaps become a "dead letter," and so forth.

Earlier on, this chapter discussed tradition history and its stress on oral tradition. While Fishbane shows an indebtedness to practitioners of the traditio-historical method,[84] he also makes a significant modification to the older method:

> Whereas the study of tradition-history moves back from the written sources to the oral traditions which make them up, inner-biblical exegesis starts with the received Scripture and moves forward to the interpretations based on it. In tradition-history, written formulations are the final of the many oral stages of *traditio* during which the traditions themselves become authoritative; by contrast, inner-biblical exegesis begins with an authoritative *traditum*.[85]

81. Childs, *Introduction*, 364 (emphasis added). He came to these conclusions by his study of Jewish postcanonical writings. One should, he says, trace "the development of the [midrashic] method back into the Old Testament period" ("Midrash and the Old Testament," 47).

82. Gordis, "Midrash and the Prophets"; Kaufmann, *The Religion of Israel*, and *History of the Religion of Israel*; Weingreen, "Rabbinic-Type Glosses"; Weingreen, "Exposition"; Sandmel, "Haggada within Scripture"; Sarna, "Psalm 89"; Wright, "Literary Genre Midrash."

83. Fishbane's more significant writings on inner-biblical interpretation are: "Torah and Tradition"; *Text and Texture*; "Revelation and Tradition"; *Biblical Interpretation*; *Garments of Torah*; "Inner-Biblical Exegesis"; *Exegetical Imagination*. Of special note in this study is Fishbane's identification of his approach as intertextual. He uses a broader definition of intertextuality in making this claim and is not at all pursuing postmodern intertextual study (see "Types of Biblical Intertextuality").

84. The debt is especially to Knight, from whom Fishbane develops the ideas of *traditio* (the handing down) and *traditum* (what was handed down) and how the former modifies the latter (see Knight, *Rediscovering the Traditions*). (Another scholar using *traditum* in a similar manner is Zimmerli; see his "Prophetic Proclamation and Reinterpretation.") Sanders's *Torah and Canon* must also be mentioned, as his method of "canonical criticism" (xi) and discussion of tradition history in relation to ancient Jewish midrash (xii–xx) apparently played a role in inspiring Fishbane's adaptation of traditio-historical research.

85. Fishbane, *Biblical Interpretation*, 7. His remarks about "the great methodological flaw of tradition-history" explain his adaptation to *written sources* as he seeks to escape the subjectivity and

Patrick Miller comments: "The distinction is an important one. Inner-biblical exegesis assumes an authoritative tradition and a 'stabilized literary formulation as its basis and point of departure.'"[86] These ideas shape my own approach to Ezekiel and the RF.

I argue that Ezekiel intentionally uses the book of Exodus to point the exiles back to the God of the exodus. The prophet seeks to point the people sorrowing in a foreign country back to Yahweh, who promises a fresh work of redemption in a "new exodus." The exiles have departed from covenant faithfulness to such an extent that they, like their idolatrous "fathers" in Egypt, need a new revelation of Yahweh. This is a profound thought, that the exile and the accompanying horrors may serve as a revelation of the same God who had delivered Israel from Egypt.

In exploring the influence of the RF's earlier usage, in pentateuchal material[87] and in the prophets, on Ezekiel's usage, I employ a type of diachronic method. It shows similarities to the traditio-historical, but pushes beyond tradition history to assert that there is a "hard text" here from which the prophet drew. The extensiveness of the parallels between Ezekiel and Exodus, I argue, indicates that the prophet is "citing an earlier text from a fixed literary base," rather than merely "using the formulae, word pairs, conventions and other lumber from the common literary storehouse"[88] stocked by earlier biblical writers.

Throughout, I work on more than one level regarding the premise that Exodus is, in some form, the literary precedent to Ezekiel. Having first argued for the credibility of that chronology and vector of influence with a review of scholarly literature on the dating of Exodus/P and Ezekiel, I secondly adduce evidence in support of the proposition that Ezekiel is broadly dependent on Exodus/P, and thirdly indicate how Ezekiel's RFs are most similar in style and use to those of Exodus. Fourthly, I press the point that Ezekiel's formulas are best interpreted in that light (i.e., as an allusion to Exodus). Yes, there may be some circularity in the reasoning, but it is not a vicious circularity. On the one hand, the RF is evidence supporting a broader argument for Ezekielian dependence on Exodus.

---

circularity that plague the method as practiced: "A *traditio* is inferred from a received *traditum*, and this 'recovered' *traditio* serves, in turn, as a principal means for isolating the components of that same *traditum*" (8–9). Sandmel earlier made a similar adaptation of tradition-history research; see his criticism of tradition-history researchers: "I sometimes have the feeling that some exponents of oral traditions so stress the oral that they forget that their pursuit is what lies behind documents which are written; and while one can overlook their scorn of literary critics, it seems a little more difficult to forgive their scorn of written documents.... And when the searcher for the sources forgets the particular document allegedly containing a source, the student has embarked on an egregious tangent. An oblivion to the text itself seems to me the greatest defect in present-day biblical scholarship" ("Haggada within Scripture," 108).

86. Miller, review of Fishbane, *Biblical Interpretation*, 378 (quote taken from Fishbane, 7).

87. As noted below, RFs appear in both J and P sections of Exodus. Thus, even a late dating of P does not preclude the influence of narrative material in Exodus on Ezekiel.

88. Miller, review of Fishbane, *Biblical Interpretation*, 380.

On the other, the formula as a more specific feature should be seen as derived from Exodus.

What controls can be used in evaluating disputable vectors of influence and the likelihood of borrowing? Drawing from scholars on both testaments,[89] especially Richard Hays, I follow a list of qualifications for legitimate allusions/echoes. The reader should look for: (1) credible chronological priority of the source text; (2) availability of a source to the author;[90] (3) availability of the source to the original audience, if there seems to be an expectation on the writer's part that they recognize the borrowing and find meaning in the literary relationship; and (4) "verbal and syntactical correspondence which goes beyond one key or uncommon term or even a series of commonly-occurring terms, also evaluating whether the expression is simply formulaic or idiomatic."[91] Additional clues for the reader would be: (5) the "volume of an echo," which Hays says "is determined primarily by the degree of explicit repetition of words or syntactical patterns," especially where "the precursor text within Scripture" is "distinctive or prominent";[92] (6) recurrent use of a smaller text unit that strengthens the cumulative case that the echoing is both intentional and of importance; and (7) evidence of widespread use of a particular literary corpus, such as H, which should alert the reader both to the possibility of finding additional allusions (even to other corpora) and to the legitimacy of terming it an allusion. Such widespread use could result in a clustering of affinities. Particularly strong is (8) "interpretive re-use" of another text.[93] It must be admitted that scholarship generally, both in the humanities and in biblical studies, finds this matter of proving influence difficult, especially in individual cases (does this text allude to that one?).

89. R. Hays, *Echoes of Scripture*; Porter, "Use of the Old Testament"; Sommer, *A Prophet Reads Scripture*; Carr, "Method"; Beetham, *Echoes of Scripture*; C. Hays, "Echoes of the Ancient Near East?"; Lyons, *From Law to Prophecy*, 47–75.

90. One could add, whether the author might be interested to read the source.

91. Schultz, "The Ties that Bind," 44.

92. R. Hays, *Echoes of Scripture*, 30. On "volume," see William Tooman's fine discussion of direction of dependence where a locution appears many times in one text but only once in another (*Gog of Magog*, 32–33).

93. Schultz, "The Ties that Bind," 44. Milgrom rigorously applies this principle of inner-biblical exegesis in "Leviticus 26 and Ezekiel." Investigation of "interpretive re-use" dominates Fishbane's *Biblical Interpretation*, in which he writes: "Aside from these few instances of *explicit* citation or referral, the vast majority of cases of aggadic exegesis in the Hebrew Bible involve *implicit* or virtual citations. In these cases, it is not by virtue of objective criteria that one may identify aggadic exegesis, but rather by a close comparison of the language of a given text with other, earlier Scriptural dicta or topoi. Where such a text (the putative *traditio*) is dominated by these dicta or topoi (the putative *traditum*), and uses them in new and transformed ways, the liklihood of aggadic exegesis is strong. In other words, the identification of aggadic exegesis where external objective criteria are lacking is proportionally increased to the extent that multiple and sustained lexical linkages between two texts can be recognized, and where the second text (the putative *traditio*) uses a segment of the first (the putative *traditum*) in a lexically reorganized and topically rethematized way" (285).

1.2.4. The Option of a Synchronic Approach: Intertextuality

When reflecting on the shape of historical criticism in biblical studies, literary critics in the humanities complain about text fragmentation,[94] implausible reconstructions of compositional history, lack of sympathy with the text, the exclusion of passages that do not comport with the critic's prejudgments, and a simple failure to elucidate the text. There is also an allegation that critics who attempt major reconstructions of biblical texts are interpreting nought but their own creations. Without agreement as to the base text to be interpreted, scholarship experiences frustration and diminished returns.[95] A turn toward final-form approaches seems to many a high, dry way out of a morass.

Among synchronic approaches, intertextual study seems well-suited for researching Ezekiel's RFs and their relation to others scattered over several biblical books. More theory than method, intertextuality explores how texts interpenetrate and interact with other texts. The term "intertextual" commonly denotes readings of related texts that are synchronic and seek to move beyond the literary-historical concerns that long dominated scholarship. Thaïs Morgan explains: "Intertextuality replaces the evolutionary model of literary history with a structural or synchronic model of literature as a sign system. The most salient effect of this strategic change is to free the literary text from psychological, sociological and historical determinisms, opening it up to an apparently infinite play of relationships."[96]

As developed by Julia Kristeva in the 1960s, *intertextualité* theorizes that: "Texts are interdependent and use each other. No text is an island."[97] Its perspective is that "every text is constrained by the literary system of which it is a part, and that every text is ultimately dialogical in that it cannot but record the traces of its contentions and doubling of earlier discourses."[98] In her essays,[99] Kristeva seeks to explain the poststructuralist ideas of Mikhail Bakhtin, who argued that "literary structure does not simply exist but is generated in relation to *another* text," and that "each word (text) is an intersection of word (texts) where at least one other word (text) can

---

94. Renowned English professor Northrop Frye judged much "higher" criticism of the Bible undeserving of its adjective: "Instead of emerging from lower criticism, or textual study, most of it dug itself into a still lower, or sub-basement, criticism in which disintegrating the text became an end in itself" (*Great Code*, xvii).

95. Note the lack of lasting results in pentateuchal (see n. 74) and prophets scholarship. Hans Barstad writes: "Evidently, most of the questions that were raised when the scientific study of biblical prophecy was first introduced upon the scholarly scene appear to remain as unanswered today as they were then" ("No Prophets?" 39).

96. Morgan, "Is There an Intertext in This Text?" 1–2.

97. Miscall, "Isaiah," 45.

98. Boyarin, *Intertextuality*, 14.

99. Kristeva, "Word, Dialogue and Novel," in *Kristeva Reader*, 34–61 (originally "Let mot, le dialogue et le roman," in *Séméiotiké: Recherches pour une sémanalyse* [Paris: Seuil, 1969], 143–73).

be read."[100] Kristeva coins and explains the term "intertextuality" as indicating how "any text is constructed as a mosaic of quotations; any text is the absorption and transformation of another."[101]

Texts should be understood as having an intertextuality regarding both their production and their reception. They can be written only in relationship to other texts, and they can be read only in relationship. These ideas have proved revolutionary and fruitful for many, both in the humanities[102] and in biblical studies. However, the theory of intertextuality is more far-reaching than any mere understanding of literature and literary relations; intertextuality also encompasses all of a culture's means of generating meaning or attaching meaning.[103]

Defining how intertextuality is understood in biblical studies is troublesome, since there can be a mixing of synchronic and diachronic concerns (often thought to be a corruption of the theory).[104] Even back in the 1980s, Sipke Draisma could write: "Exegetes differ about the way in which intertextuality should function as a model of inquiry when applied to biblical texts."[105] Some "purists" urge that intertextual studies be strictly synchronic and postmodern, avoiding questions of vectors of influence and literary borrowing.[106] Others use the language of

---

100. Kristeva, "Word, Dialogue and Novel," 37.

101. Kristeva, "Word, Dialogue and Novel," 37.

102. Early work on intertextuality, besides that of Kristeva and Barthes, includes: Plottel and Charney, *Intertextuality*; Culler, *Pursuit of Signs*; Jenny, "Strategy of Form"; Riffaterre, "Intertextual Representation"; Pfister, "Konzepte der Intertextualität"; Morgan, "Space of Intertextuality"; Worton and Still, *Intertextuality*; Clayton and Rothstein, *Influence and Intertextuality*. Note the survey in Bruce, "Bibliographie annotée." For current discussion, see Allen, *Intertextuality*.

103. See Culler, *The Pursuit of Signs*, 103: "'Intertextuality' thus has a double focus. On the one hand, it calls our attention to the importance of prior texts, insisting that the autonomy of texts is a misleading notion and that a work has the meaning it does only because certain things have previously been written. Yet in so far as it focuses on intelligibility, on meaning, 'intertextuality' leads us to consider prior texts as contributions to a code which makes possible the various effects of signification. Intertextuality thus becomes less a name for a work's relation to particular prior texts than a designation of its participation in the discursive space of a culture: the relationship between a text and the various languages or signifying practices of a culture and its relation to those texts which articulate for it the possibilities of that culture. The study of intertextuality is thus not the investigation of sources and influences as traditionally conceived; it casts its net wider to include anonymous discursive practices, codes whose origins are lost, that make possible the signifying practices of later texts. Barthes warns that from the perspective of intertextuality 'the quotations of which a text is made are anonymous, untraceable, and nevertheless *already read.*'"

104. For recent discussion, see: Miller, "Intertextuality in Old Testament Research"; Yoon, "Ideological Inception"; Barton, "*Déjà lu.*"

105. "Bas van Iersel," in Draisma, *Intertextuality*, 11. To follow the early debate, see: Fewell, *Reading Between Texts*; Exum and Clines, *New Literary Criticism*; Aichele and Phillips, *Intertextuality*.

106. They complain of those using literary theory to supply labels while continuing to practice traditional comparative studies. See van Wolde, "Trendy Intertextuality?" Note that van Wolde was anticipated by Kristeva herself, who in 1974 expressed displeasure at the development and even went to the extent of suggesting different terminology: "The term *intertextuality* denotes this transposition of one (or several) sign-system(s) into another; but since this term has often been understood in the

intertextuality as they examine how texts are utilized creatively in other texts, and especially the function of the inner-biblical quotations or allusions within their present canonical context. More historical questions of influence can thereby come to dominate. This is certainly the case with some prominent Jewish scholarship on inner-biblical interpretation and midrash. (Fishbane and others describe their work as intertextual in nature.[107]) It is true that intertextuality and the study of midrashic exegesis can deal in similar ways with, and ask similar questions about, the relationships between texts. As Robert Carroll writes, "biblical midrash is inevitably intertextual."[108] However, the mingling of approaches that come originally from very different sectors of the academy (postmodern French literary theory and the history of Jewish hermeneutics) is difficult to accomplish without altering both.

Kristeva's intertextuality has been modified and adapted by biblical scholars in varying degrees, and one can speak of distinct "schools" clustered around the theorists who follow a strategy more akin to Kristeva's or that of Roland Barthes, such as George Aichele, Tina Pippin, and Gary Phillips, and followers of a more restrained approach associated with Harold Bloom and especially with Hays, such as Kirsten Nielsen, Gail O'Day, Patricia Tull, and Robert Brawley.[109] The latter group, which now appears more numerous,[110] prefers to retain diachronic concerns about sources, precedence, influence, and borrowing, but "without making them the center of attention."[111]

---

banal sense of 'study of sources,' we prefer the term *transposition* because it specifies that the passage from one signifying system to another demands a new articulation of the thetic—of enunciative and denotive positionality. If one grants that every signifying practice is a field of transpositions of various signifying systems (an intertextuality), one then understands that its 'place' of enunciation and its denoted 'object' are never single, complete and identical to themselves, but always plural, shattered, capable of being tabulated. In this way polysemy can also be seen as the result of a semiotic polyvalence—an adherence to different sign-systems" ("Revolution in Poetic Language," in *Kristeva Reader*, 111). Is there some irony here in the fluidity of sign-systems, including her own terminology (as used by others), frustrating Kristeva and leading her to select a different "sign" with a more circumscribed "articulation," one she herself as an author circumscribes? She experiences "the plural" and "the shattered."

107. See n. 83 above, and see also: Hartman and Budick, *Midrash and Literature*; Neusner, *Canon and Connection*; and Boyarin, *Intertextuality*.

108. Carroll, "Intertextuality and the Book of Jeremiah," 70.

109. Important references are: Phillips, "Drawing the Other"; Aichele and Phillips, *Intertextuality and the Bible*; van Wolde, "Texts in Dialogue with Texts"; Pippin, *Apocalyptic Bodies*; Aichele, *Control of Biblical Meaning*. Examples of the more restrained are: Bloom, *Anxiety of Influence*; Hays, *Echoes of Scripture*; Tull [Willey], *Remember the Former Things*; Schultz, "Intertextuality, Canon, and 'Undecidability.'"

110. O'Day, "Intertextuality," 156: "In biblical studies, the narrower use of intertextuality—that is, patterns of literary borrowing among literary texts proper and textual relationships between specific literary corpora—is most prevalent. Intertextuality in the broader sense has been absorbed into general deconstructionist biblical interpretation."

111. Hays, *Echoes of Scripture*, 198.

I make use of more restrained intertextual research, steering clear of the Kristeva path for several reasons. There are deconstructionist underpinnings to postmodern intertextual theory that not only displace but also disparage the "author." Barthes famously even puts the author (and Author-God) to death.[112] According to those aligned with the Kristeva-Barthes strategy: "The basic force of intertextuality is to problematize, even spoil, textual boundaries—those lines of demarcation which allow a reader to talk about *the* meaning, subject, or origin of a writing. Such borders, intertextuality asserts, are never solid or stable. Texts are always spilling over into other texts."[113] Thus, the initial exegetical task of delimiting a text is problematic, and a text, to the extent that any single text can be discussed, is to be regarded as polyvalent and of indeterminate meaning. The French literary theory has also been criticized as having an anachronistic thrust, with the counterclaim that diachronic issues cannot be bracketed entirely.[114] By contrast, those in the Hays tradition characterize their intertextual studies as providing "a bridge between strictly diachronic and strictly synchronic approaches to biblical texts, challenging traditional notions of influence and causality while at the same time affirming that every biblical text must be read as part of a larger literary context."[115]

Literary connections between biblical texts are often demonstrable, but for those using the methods and assumptions of historical criticism, the issue of textual precedence can be far less clear. All acknowledge that the Bible is full of "mutual relationships," and where historical critics are uncertain about the vector of influence—and even where there is no uncertainty—a scholar pursuing intertextuality may proffer inner-biblical interpretations running in both directions.[116]

112. Barthes, "The Death of the Author." He attacks the author, and God as Author too: "To refuse to fix meaning is, in the end, to refuse God and his hypostases—reason, science, law" (147). In place of the so-called Author-God, he asserts the role of the reader: "We now know that the text is not a line of words releasing a single 'theological' meaning (the 'message' of an Author-God) but a multidimensional space in which a variety of writings, none of them original, blend and clash. The text is a tissue of quotations drawn from the innumerable centers of culture.... There is one place where this multiplicity is focused and that place is the reader, not, as was hitherto said, the author. The reader is the space on which all the quotations that make up a writing are inscribed without any of them being lost; a text's unity lies not in its origin but in its destination.... The birth of the reader must be at the cost of the death of the Author" (146, 148). For critical reaction to Barthes' proposal, especially by Michel Foucault, see Pease, "Author."

113. Beal, "Glossary," 22–23.

114. Reinhard Kuhn, a literary critic in the humanities, writes: "By abstracting a work from its cultural and temporal matrix an intertextual critic runs the risk of doing violence to history. The lack of constraints can lead to misreadings which totally distort the literary map. However, the intertextual approach need not be an anachronistic one" (*Corruption in Paradise*, 5).

115. O'Day, "Intertextuality," 157.

116. See, e.g., Dozeman, "Inner-biblical Interpretation." He does not describe his approach as intertextual (and shows concern for diachronic issues), but his reading in both directions is in line with intertextuality.

Ezekiel's prophecy in general and the RFs more specifically can be read intertextually as "language answering language" elsewhere.[117] "Reading between texts"
has the potential to enrich our literary and theological understanding of the formula in the several places or contexts where it is read (Exodus, Deuteronomy,
1 Kings, Isaiah, Joel). We may read in both directions: we are permitted to read
Exodus in light of Ezekiel as well as Ezekiel in light of Exodus. A summary of my
argument in its synchronic focus is: Ezekiel's RF is a marker of the whole prophecy's intertextual relation to Exodus, and the two books are best read together.
However, intertextual readings need not be restricted to Ezekiel and Exodus. For
instance, a reading between Ezekiel and Isaiah on the theme of profaning the
name is permissible, as also would be intertextual readings among Ezekiel and
extrabiblical writings from the ancient world down to today. Intertextual studies
encourage listening for *multiple* voices.[118] But there is need here to be more restric-
tive, considering the unbounded possibilities of intertextuality.[119]

Besides the questions raised by intertextuality about a "mutual relationship"
between books (Ezekiel and Exodus), intertextual study may additionally focus
on interactive texts *within* a unified work, such as the "parallel echoing" between
Ezek 36:27b and 37:24b.[120] A sensitivity to such intratextuality[121] can assist the
interpreter of Ezekiel's RFs: one may inquire as to how, and with what result,
individual formulas echo[122] each other throughout the prophecy. Even where one
does not know which text has literary priority in terms of composition, the order
provided by canonical context (succession of chapters and dating scheme) may

117. O'Donnell and Davis, "Introduction," in *Intertextuality and Contemporary American Fiction*,
xiii.

118. In a 1985 interview, Kristeva said that, in her conception of intertextuality, there is more than
Bakhtin's "dialogism"; there is a complex polyphony: "In the first place, there is the recognition that
a textual segment, sentence, utterance, or paragraph, is not simply the intersection of two voices in
direct or indirect discourse; rather, the segment is the result of the intersection of a number of voices,
of a number of textual interventions, which are combined in the semantic field, but also in the syntactic and phonic fields of the explicit utterance" (Waller, "Interview," 281).

119. Culler states this as one of the "dangers that beset the notion of intertextuality: it is a difficult
concept to use because of the vast and undefined discursive space it designates" (*The Pursuit of Signs*,
109). How does one deal with "an endless series of anonymous codes and citations" (111)? One reading, more limited in scope, is all that is manageable here.

120. Discussed briefly in Allen, "Structure, Tradition and Redaction." Cf. the linkage between
Ezek 13:1–16 and 13:17–23 detailed in my essay, "Death-Dealing Witchcraft in the Bible?"

121. "Intra-textuality" may be defined as "the complex *self*-referentiality by which (literary) texts
produce a rhetoric of meaningfulness" (Platter, review of Sharrock and Morales, *Intratextuality*).
Another definition is "internal dialogism"; this phrasing depends upon Bakhtin's thought and is used
by Tull in "Rhetorical Criticism and Intertextuality," 171.

122. The function of echoing an earlier/older sacred utterance, according to Fishbane, can be
quite varied: authoritative reference; reinterpretation; clarification; preservation of an authoritative
memory; revitalization of what has become a "dead letter," etc. Though Fishbane intends a diachronic
discussion, the same questions arise, framed a bit differently, in a consistently synchronic discussion.

suggest a priority for one's reading. For intratextuality, one may also choose to bracket these questions and read in both directions.

This study uses a simple, broad definition of intertextuality by a professor of English, Leland Ryken: "a situation in which the full meaning of a text depends on its interaction with another text."[123] The intertextual approach here (more theory than method)[124] builds less on the understanding of the nature of texts developed by Bakhtin and Kristeva and more on T. S. Eliot's essays "Tradition and the Individual Talent" (1919) and "The Function of Criticism" (1923).[125] My practice of intertextual reading downplays, rather than rebels against, diachrony and traditional ideas of the author, literary "genealogy," authorial intent, influence, and so on. It is an intertextuality that still seeks meaning in the texts, together, without deconstructing either the texts or the whole model of communication. Intertextuality as a postmodern polemic in semiotic theory is rejected.

This study examines mutual relationships (and dialogue) between texts while making use of a suggestive list of verbs produced by art historian Michael Baxandall

---

123. Ryken, *Words of Delight*, 361.

124. Tull makes this point lucidly: "Like many other concepts in biblical interpretation, intertextuality is more helpful in providing an angle of vision on the nature of biblical texts than in prescribing a precise set of procedures for producing an interpretation. Attention to intertextuality and rhetoric calls forth certain ways of posing questions, and benefits from both imagination and disciplined analytical skills" ("Rhetorical Criticism and Intertextuality," 166). Carol Newsom writes: "Bakhtin's approach is not a method to be applied so much as it is a perception about the nature of discourse and a provocative claim about what it takes to articulate the 'truth' of an idea. Its nonsystematic, nonabstract, nonreductive emphasis on unmerged voices in the text answers the biblical scholar's concern for respecting the variety and particularity of the Bible. The Bakhtinian emphasis on the *idea* in all its interactions challenges the tendency of biblical studies to let historical particularity isolate the text from substantive engagement with other discourses" ("Bakhtin, the Bible, and Dialogic Truth," 306).

125. Eliot, *Selected Essays*, 3–11 ("Tradition and the Individual Talent"; 1919) and 12–22 ("The Function of Criticism"; 1923). It is surprising how he anticipated many insights and concerns of intertextuality long before postmodernism. Eliot conceived of literature as "a living whole of all the poetry that has ever been written" (7), of which every writer and reader partakes. He wrote in 1923: "I thought of literature . . . of the literature of the world, of the literature of Europe, of the literature of a single country, not as a collection of the writings of individuals, but as 'organic wholes,' as systems in relation to which, and only in relation to which, individual works of literary art, and the works of individual artists, have their significance" (12–13).

Because every writer and reader partakes of one great tradition, Eliot writes: "No poet, no artist of any art, has his complete meaning alone. His significance, his appreciation is the appreciation of his relation to the dead poets and artists. You cannot value him alone; you must set him, for contrast and comparison, among the dead" (4). Past writers live on and assert themselves in the literary works of the one following after them. When we read the poetry of their successor, "we shall often find that not only the best, but the most individual parts of his work may be those in which the dead poets, his ancestors, assert their immortality most vigorously" (4). The individual is not to fight this relation to the tradition, but surrender: "What happens is a continual surrender of himself as he is at the moment to something which is more valuable. The progress of an artist is a continual self-sacrifice, a continual extinction of personality" (6–7). With regard to the whole tradition of literature, artists may be "conscious, not of what is dead, but of what is already living" (11). We may add that it lives in them and lives through them as they relate to it.

that may describe the relationships among works of art (either diachronically or synchronically):

> draw on, resort to, avail oneself of, appropriate from, have recourse to, adapt, misunderstand, refer to, pick up, take on, engage with, react to, quote, differentiate oneself from, assimilate oneself to, assimilate, align oneself with, copy, address, paraphrase, absorb, make a variation on, revive, continue, remodel, ape, emulate, travesty, parody, extract from, distort, attend to, resist, simplify, reconstitute, elaborate on, develop, face up to, master, subvert, perpetuate, reduce, promote, respond to, transform, tackle.[126]

Verbs I might add include "evoke" and "revoke," "convert" and "invert," "reinterpret" and "reapply," "recontextualize," and "reframe," and there are other textual relationships suggested by Fishbane and listed above (n. 122).

Alongside the assertion of traditionally styled exegesis that there is meaning in the text—discoverable meaning "authored" by the writer that requires the reader's interpretation—there is another common-sense assertion to make. Texts may generate still more meaning in their fuller canonical context, as they are read with other texts. The whole may properly be said to be greater than the sum of its parts. Just as more music is heard as various instruments of an orchestra play their parts, so much more is heard as texts interact. There are complexities and beautiful harmonies as one hears instruments or choir parts together. I think of counterpoint in J. S. Bach or the addition of descants in sacred choral music and draw analogies with "reading between texts." In the intertextual focus, I listen for what musicians call "consonances," which may seem "perfect" or "imperfect" (and needing perfect resolution).

I seek to avoid the pitfall of some intertextual research in which the selection of intertexts seems flippant and whimsical. This study assumes that a text may itself provide direction to the reader in selecting intertexts, that the text may include "specific signals" or "markers" that point "to the particular intertexts which the reader is expected to include when reading a book."[127] It is possible to investigate such markers and pursue these textual relations in a more text-centered than author-centered or reader-centered approach. From an evangelical and canonical perspective, one seeks the guidance of God's Spirit in selecting texts[128] and may happily read an earlier Scripture text in light of a later text.

126. Michael Baxandall, quoted in Clayton and Rothstein, "Figures in the Corpus," in *Influence and Intertextuality*, 6.

127. Nielsen, "Intertextuality and Hebrew Bible," 19. She writes further about "exegesis as a *response* to texts": "Responsible exegesis presumes that the exegete can point out the markers in the text on which the intertexts have been chosen" (31).

128. I honor "the role of the Holy Spirit in constantly bringing to fresh light the written scriptures as a divinely spoken Word" (Childs, "Canon in Recent Biblical Studies," 34).

Tull has urged that scholarship press beyond the initial question, "Is there, can there be, an echo of another text here?" There is need to ask what such a recollection of memory might be intended to convey. "What does it do? What does it mean to invoke previous speech, to recollect it, reformulate it, react against it, reinterpret it, and resurrect it as new speech? These are questions that begin to get at the heart of the significance of speech that is shared among writers of the Bible."[129] More synchronically, what does it mean that these texts can be read together? What does it mean to read them separately, and what might be lost as a consequence of separation? How do the texts interact and react? What do they do to each other? The goal of both the inner-biblical interpretation and the intertextual focus in this study of Ezekiel's formula is to press beyond the simple recognition of the phenomena (inner-biblical interpretation and intertextual relations) and assess how and why the texts speak together or to each other. Together with the questions of *dependence* brought forward by inner-biblical interpretation, I ask about a canonical *interdependence* of texts.

1.2.5. Mixing Diachrony with Synchrony and Defining Terms

In the background of this study's combination of the diachronic and synchronic is an exchange between Lyle Eslinger and Benjamin Sommer, who quarrel over the relative merits of "inner-biblical exegesis" (which treats questions of influence) and "inner-biblical allusion" (which, like intertextuality, is more consistently synchronic, in Eslinger's view).[130] Eslinger initially questioned Fishbane's approach in *Biblical Interpretation in Ancient Israel* and argued that all the uncertainties associated with causality vitiate inner-biblical exegesis. Precedence often cannot be demonstrated. He characterizes Fishbane as betraying a certain "literary naiveté" in his assumptions and method that is tied to a "reliance on historical-critical literary history." Eslinger urges greater caution, since "recent historical work on the Bible is increasingly pessimistic about using it as a source for writing about its own or ancient Israel's history." It is advisable, he says, to bracket historical concerns, which are "beyond verification."[131]

Sommer studied under Fishbane, has shown skill in inner-biblical interpretation,[132] and understandably wishes to defend it as a valid method.

---

129. Tull, "Rhetoric of Recollection," 78.

130. Eslinger, "Inner-biblical Exegesis and Inner-biblical Allusion"; Sommer, "Exegesis, Allusion and Intertextuality." As Eslinger notes, he wrote an earlier article using "inner biblical exegesis" but now repudiates the method (48).

131. Eslinger, "Inner-biblical Exegesis and Inner-biblical Allusion," 49, 51, 52, 58.

132. Sommer, *A Prophet Reads Scripture.* There is not necessarily any irony in his use of the term "allusion" (Eslinger's preference in 1992). Sommer fills the term with different meaning, and he points out that Eslinger, in reality, proposes an intertextual method. *Allusion* is normally used in literary criticism to denote an author's intention to recall to readers' minds an earlier text. It involves diachrony.

He responds along several lines. (1) Eslinger himself seems tied to a certain historical-critical orthodoxy (Wellhausen's dating of pentateuchal materials, the pessimism of "minimalist" historians, etc.) that leads him to disallow evidence in the text of, say, the prophets borrowing from P. (2) Inner-biblical interpretation is able to develop and apply criteria for distinguishing "between cases in which texts share vocabulary by coincidence or by their independent use of a literary tradition, on the one hand, and cases in which one author borrows vocabulary from an older text, on the other." (3) "The argument that an author alludes . . . is a cumulative one," as inner-biblical exegesis notes patterns of using and reinterpreting other texts. (4) "Allusion" is not so helpful a label for Eslinger's method, since the term, "as used by literary critics, does posit an earlier and a later text, so that the study of allusion necessarily involves a diachronic component."[133] (5) Eslinger's proposal that biblical scholars explore intertextuality is fine, but such a purely synchronic method has its own limitations and should not be used on its own. Diachronic approaches retain value and can be well-founded.

Rather than choose between the diachronic and synchronic (either/or), this study employs inner-biblical interpretation and intertextuality (both/and). In some sense, I am following up Sommer's suggestion that both are worth pursuing[134] and David Clines's proposal that scholarship move past the old oppositional thinking (Ferdinand de Saussure) to consider the diachronic and synchronic as "names for segments of a spectrum rather than the labels on the only two pigeonholes."[135]

Up to this point, this study has treated *allusion* and *echo* as synonyms. This raises the question of definitions. A failure to define terminology in inner-biblical interpretation would soon cause difficulty. While the *Oxford English Dictionary* defines "allusion," as employed in everyday language, to mean "a covert, implied or indirect reference,"[136] literary criticism uses the term differently, with a diachronic emphasis. *The New Princeton Encyclopedia of Poetry and Poetics* defines allusion as the "deliberate incorporation of *identifiable* elements from other sources, preceding or contemporaneous, textual or extratextual," differing "from parody and imitation in not being necessarily systematic," and "from source borrowing because it requires readers' knowledge of the original borrowed from."[137] It is clear, therefore, that *allusion* would be an unfit term to use in intertextual studies if explored, according to Eslinger's model, in a purely synchronic way without interest in authorial intent.

---

133. Sommer, "Exegesis, Allusion and Intertextuality," 483–84, 485, 486.
134. Another who urges that both be used is Schultz, "The Ties that Bind."
135. Clines, "Beyond Synchronic/Diachronic," 52.
136. *OED*, s.v. "allusion."
137. Miner, "Allusion" (emphasis added).

This study uses the terms *allusion* and *echo* in a nearly synonymous way. *Echo* may denote a less sustained, a slightly less distinct or distinguishable reference, and as used in this study, *echo* will normally refer to verbal parallels.[138] *Allusion* can also be broader than the term *echo* in this study. "The words of the alluding passage may establish a conceptual rather than a verbal connection with the passage or work alluded to."[139] As this study shifts from inner-biblical interpretation to intertextuality, the term *echo* will downplay the sense of intentionality, causality, or influence (i.e., B is an echo of an earlier voice A). This study rarely employs the term "quotation," for there are scarcely any examples in this literature to consider, especially if the stricter, modern concept of quotation controls our thinking (an explicit appeal to an earlier work, incorporating its wording, with formal citation of the source).[140] Perhaps in only two places could the term *quotation* be legitimately applied: this study argues that Ezek 20 informally "quotes" material in Exod 6 and 31. *Quotation* in these places would be defined, with Michael Fox, as "words taken from another source but used as the speaker's words."[141] Knowing the source in such cases is not absolutely necessary in order to make sense of the text (Fox contrasts this type with a second quotation-type represented in Ezek 12:22, 13:6, and 18:2).

This study will not follow Fishbane and Douglas Knight in their use of the terms *traditum* and *traditio*. James Kugel warns that the Latin terminology they use to differentiate between "the passing down" and "the tradition passed down" is not so distinct, dependable, or helpful.[142] When the noun *traditio* means both the process of "the handing down of knowledge" and "an item of traditional knowledge,"[143] how can it be distinguished from *traditum*, which may denote "that which is handed down"?

138. The definition of "echo" provided in a standard reference is: "A complex, subtle, and multifarious acoustic phenomenon involving a faint but perceptible repetition inside a work ('aged thrush' *echoes* 'ancient pulse' in both sound and meaning in Hardy's 'The Darkling Thrush') or between works (the 'low damp ground' in Eliot's *The Waste Land* may *echo* the 'old camp ground' of the sentimental tenting song)" (Holman and Harmon, *Handbook*, 158), But, in literary criticism, there is also such a thing as "obvious echo," which is not so easily distinguished from "allusion" (see "Allusion" in Holman and Harmon, *Handbook*).

139. Miner, "Allusion."

140. By the term "quotation," I do not refer to the narrative device of "quoted direct speech" within a single work (e.g., repetition in Gen 3:17 of the divine command in 2:16–17; or the retelling of the servant's experience in Gen 24). See Savran, *Telling and Retelling*.

141. Fox, "Identification of Quotations," 431.

142. Kugel, review of Fishbane, *Biblical Interpretation*. Kugel offers additional criticisms of Fishbane: "Identifying a specific kind of exegesis with its putative milieu or group" is overly speculative, and Fishbane inconsistently uses the terminology he selects.

143. *OLD*, s.v. *traditio*.

CHAPTER 2

Past Scholarship on Ezekiel's Formula

As mentioned in the introduction, scholarly discussion of Ezekiel's RF has typically been oblique, occasional, or subordinate to other interests. This chapter offers a four-part survey of scholarship, reviewing (2.1) select twentieth-century scholarship prior to Walther Zimmerli, (2.2) the contributions of Zimmerli in his essays and commentary, and (2.3) recent scholarship interacting with Zimmerli's work. A final section (2.4) draws out and analyzes the similarities and differences on certain key interpretive issues among the scholars examined. It will also indicate how this research of the RF builds on, and extends beyond, past scholarship. No attempt will be made to survey Ezekiel scholarship generally; others have capably done so already and can be consulted.[1]

2.1. Select Twentieth-Century Scholarship Prior to Zimmerli

2.1.1. "Hyper-Criticism" and Charles Cutler Torrey

Ezekiel scholarship throughout the 1800s had a more conservative cast than, say, Isaiah studies: the leading scholars viewed the book as unquestionably authentic, unified, and displaying a close familiarity with the Pentateuch.[2] With the dawn of

1. Irwin, *The Problem of Ezekiel*, 3–30; Gruenthaner, "Recent Theories"; Gordis, "Ezekiel in Contemporary Criticism"; Irwin, "Ezekiel Research Since 1943"; Rowley, "Ezekiel in Modern Study"; Kuhl, "Zum Stand" (citing his two earlier articles); Greenberg, Prolegomenon to Torrey, *Pseudo-Ezekiel*; Carley, *Ezekiel among the Prophets*; Childs, *Introduction*, 355–70; Zimmerli, *Ezekiel 1*, 3–8; Zimmerli, *Ezekiel 2*, xi–xviii; Lang, *Ezechiel*; Brownlee, *Ezekiel 1–19*, xix–xxiii; Joyce, *Divine Initiative*, 21–31; Boadt, "Ezekiel, Book of"; McKeating, *Ezekiel*; Darr, "Ezekiel among the Critics"; Feist, *Ezechiel*; Levitt Kohn, "Ezekiel at the Turn of the Century"; Galambush, "Ezekiel"; Pohlmann, "Forschung am Ezechielbuch"; Pohlmann, *Ezechiel: Der Stand der theologische Diskussion*; Joyce, *Ezekiel*, 3–60; Olley, "Trajectories"; Duguid, "Ezekiel: History of Interpretation"; Lyons, *Introduction*; and Mein, "Ezekiel: Structure, Themes, and Contested Issues."
2. S. R. Driver claimed that "no critical question arises in connection with the authorship of the book, the whole from beginning to end bearing unmistakably the stamp of a single mind" (*Introduction*, 279). Rudolf Smend warned against any criticism that would disintegrate the prophecy: "Man könnte kein Stück herausnehmen, ohne das ganze Ensemble zu zerstören.... Höchst wahrscheinlich ist das ganze Buch deshalb auch in einem Zuge niedergeschrieben" (*Ezechiel*, xxi–xxii). Heinrich Ewald represents the many who read Ezekiel as heavily dependent on the Pentateuch: Ezekiel "makes use of the Pentateuch as a matter of pure learning" and without "genuine prophetic originality and independence" (*Commentary on the Prophets*, 4:10). Karl Friedrich Keil believed Ezekiel's language

43

the twentieth century, Ezekiel scholarship took a fresh, more critical look at the prophecy. Johannes Herrmann (1908) proved to be the precursor of later radical scholarship with his position denying the complete literary unity of Ezekiel. Herrmann said that, while the prophecy was substantially the product of the sixth-century Ezekiel, there was also evidence of later editorial expansion.[3] The RF, thought to be easily detached from surrounding material, was often taken as an indicator of redactional activity. Herrmann especially excluded those formulas set in passages promising restoration, since he believed the original book included only prophecies of doom. It is accurate to say that he regarded a majority of the occurrences of the refrain to be secondary. From this time forward, a dismissive attitude toward the RF was a corollary of more radical literary criticism.

There followed after Herrmann a period characterized chiefly by the "unrestrained hyper-criticism" (*überstürzende Hyperkritik*)[4] of men like Gustav Hölscher and C. C. Torrey. It was little short of a revolution, by G. A. Cooke's reckoning.[5] In 1924, Hölscher proposed that "the authentic Ezekiel" was essentially a poet, fond of the 3+2 קינה rhythm, and that nearly all nonpoetic material ought not to be attributed to him.[6] Since little of the prophecy takes poetic form, Ezekiel is credited with fewer than 145 out of 1,273 total verses.[7] As might be predicted, all the passages that include the RF are clipped by Hölscher. There seemed little reason to search for meaning and purpose in accretionary material.

Torrey made the pseudepigraphic theory a more mainstream opinion in pre–World War II scholarship.[8] His monograph *Pseudo-Ezekiel and the Original Prophecy* (1930)[9] insisted that the original prophecy was very late, purporting to come

---

reveals great originality of mind, but that it "cannot hide the fact of its dependence on ancient models, especially on the language of the Pentateuch" (*Manual*, 1:356).

3. Herrmann, *Ezechielstudien*. Herrmann shifted over time toward a more severe criticism of Ezekiel's prophecy.

4. The phrase is that of Zimmerli in *Ezekiel 1*, 7 [*Ezechiel*, 1:11*].

5. G. A. Cooke writes: "In recent years the study of Ezekiel has undergone something of a revolution. . . . It is no longer possible to treat the Book as the product of a single mind and a single age" (*Critical and Exegetical Commentary*, v).

6. Hölscher, *Hesekiel*. This conclusion regarding Ezekiel's mode of communication is in line with his overall view of Hebrew prophecy as set forth in *Die Profeten*. He thought the prophets were given over to ecstasies, hypnotic visions, etc., resulting in the use of heightened language to declare their experiences of the paranormal.

7. The scholarship is divided on the exact count of verses, in whole or in part, Hölscher allowed Ezekiel. Zimmerli gives the number 144 from his reading of Hölscher (*Ezekiel 1*, 5), while Joyce reports a more generous 170 (*Divine Initiative*, 23). See also Eissfeldt, *Introduction*, 369. I calculated a few less than Zimmerli; the lower-end numbers appear more correct.

8. L. Seinecke earlier argued that the prophecy was best interpreted as a second-century pseudepigraph (*Geschichte*, 2:1–20), but Torrey reveals no acquaintance with Seinecke.

9. Indicative of the book's influence in the history of Ezekiel studies, though not its wide acceptance, is KTAV's 1970 reprint with a prolegomenon by Greenberg that includes the response of Shalom Spiegel in "Ezekiel or Pseudo-Ezekiel" and Torrey's rejoinder, "Certainly Pseudo-Ezekiel."

from the mid-seventh century (Manasseh's reign) but dating from the Hellenistic period. A redactor was responsible for reworking the prophecy into its present form, with a setting in the Babylonian exile.

Torrey's reasons for such a late dating are fascinating and bear on the argument of this study. He stamps the prophecy as one of the very latest of the OT writings because "the author of the work, as its interpreters have long observed, is a man of many books, one who *has at his disposal a library of sacred literature*, and habitually shows acquaintance with it."[10] Building on the doctoral work of his student, Millar Burrows, and cleverly using conservative scholarship to bolster his argument, Torrey states: "The plain fact, as one day will be generally recognized, is that the author of the book had before him the completed Pentateuch, in the very form in which it lies before us at the present day."[11] Ezekiel was always looking back to the "former days" (38:17), and, Torrey says, "in almost every case . . . in which the fact of borrowing can be surely demonstrated, it is evident that Ezekiel is the debtor."[12] Conservatives today are likely to contend that Torrey's appraisal of the situation of literary priority and borrowing was correct, but his explanation of it erroneous.[13]

One may summarize that the period of radical criticism during the first half of the last century tended to encourage a dismissive attitude toward the RF, and indeed, toward Ezekiel's prophecy as a whole. During the 1940s, however, two notable explanations of the formula appeared that served to spur on further work. Zimmerli would cite both.

The last word on the subject was Spiegel, "Toward Certainty in Ezekiel." Greenberg's interest in Torrey's theory, which he rejects, may be explained in part by appreciation for Torrey's arguments regarding Ezekielian use of earlier Scriptures. For the revival of the pseudepigraphal theory by Hermann Schulz, Joachim Becker, and others, see n. 23 in the introduction of the present volume. Schulz's and Becker's theories differ from Torrey's in their earlier, Persian-era dating. Zimmerli answered "pseudo" or "deutero" theories with a firm "Nein" in "Deutero-Ezechiel?"

10. Torrey, *Pseudo-Ezekiel*, 90 (emphasis added). Here Torrey echoes the conclusions of his student, Millar Burrows, who found evidence that Ezekiel is continually quoting or alluding to other Scriptures. There is borrowing not only from preexilic literature (J/E, Hosea, First Isaiah, and Jeremiah) but also from allegedly exilic or postexilic works such as H and P. Burrows writes: "His use of works of earlier authors is not confined to any one or two ways of using them; on the contrary, every conceivable form of literary dependence, short of downright transcription, can be illustrated from his pages" (*Literary Relations*, 13–14).

11. Torrey, *Pseudo-Ezekiel*, 91. Burrows holds that Ezekiel "knew the Pentateuch in approximately its present form" (*Literary Relations*, 68). In the context of his argument, Torrey cites Boyd, "Ezekiel and the Modern Dating." Boyd had argued that Ezekiel's widespread use of pentateuchal materials in the first quarter of the sixth century showed that the Books of Moses could not be as late as Wellhausen and other "negative critics" had proposed. The final form of the Pentateuch was not postexilic, but preexilic, and Ezekiel could prophesy under its influence. By contrast, Torrey would date the Pentateuch late (postexilic era) *and* argue for full pentateuchal influence on Ezekiel. In purporting to be exilic, therefore, the prophecy was inauthentic.

12. Torrey, *Pseudo-Ezekiel*, 93.

13. I thank my brother, Professor William B. Evans, for this characterization.

2.1.2. Sheldon H. Blank

In a lengthy article of 1940, Sheldon H. Blank treats both the Isaianic short statement of self-predication, "I am Yahweh," and the RF (Isa 45:3; 49:23, 26; 60:16).
Regarding the latter, he claims to be able to trace the "gradual growth of this
formula" in the writings of Deutero-Isaiah.[14] Blank places great emphasis on the
"counterpart to the formula" in Isa 41:23, where Yahweh challenges the gods of
the nations to prove themselves: "Declare to us the things to come, tell us what
the future holds, so that we may know that you are gods." Reflecting on this verse,
Blank says: "We could not ask for a more explicit clarification of the formula וידעו
כי אני יהוה."[15]

Also "most explicit as to the meaning of the formula" is Isa 40:28: "Do you not
know? Have you not heard? Yahweh is the everlasting God, the Creator of the ends
of the earth." These verses, among others, are evidence Blank adduces in explaining
the expression אני יהוה to mean "I am God" or "I am the sole deity." In brief, Blank
fits both the RF and the short statement אני יהוה into Isaiah's developed argument
for monotheism (based on Yahweh's unique ability to prophesy future events).
He makes valid points in exegeting those passages in which אלהים or אל seem to
be equivalent to and interchangeable with יהוה.

Blank is careful to note, however, that "the phrase אני יהוה also occurs in Deutero-Isaiah *without* monotheistic implications."[16] At points, "Yahweh" is clearly
used as a proper noun, as in 42:8, where the divine speaker is identifying himself
by name. (Blank associates such usage with both Exod 6 and Ezek 20.) This double
significance that the formula אני יהוה has in Deutero-Isaiah—meaning "I am God
alone" in some cases and "I am Yahweh" in others—does not invalidate his conclusions, Blank contends. Instead, the twofold usage "contributes to an understanding
of the full import of the argument from prophecy."[17] He writes:

> That Deutero-Isaiah identifies Him in whose name he speaks now as Yahveh, Israel's
> God, and now as God, the One, comports absolutely with that argument. The argu-
> ment is bent upon proving just this: that Yahveh is God—that Yahveh and God are
> identical. Deutero-Isaiah's universalism throughout is combined with the conten-
> tion that, between Israel and the one God, a special relationship exists. It is Israel's
> god, Yahveh, not the god addressed by any other nation, who is God—as Deutero-
> Isaiah proves to his satisfaction, with his argument through prophecy.[18]

14. Blank, "Studies in Deutero-Isaiah," 13.
15. Blank, "Studies in Deutero-Isaiah," 14.
16. Blank, "Studies in Deutero-Isaiah," 17 (emphasis original).
17. Blank, "Studies in Deutero-Isaiah," 18.
18. Blank, "Studies in Deutero-Isaiah," 18.

All this material, however, has to do with Isaiah. What is the significance of Blank's article for Ezekiel studies? In an eight-page appendix to his study, Blank examines the RF in Ezekiel and comes to the conclusion that "the words אני יהוה in the formula וידעו כי אני יהוה seem to have a meaning identical with that which they have in the Deutero-Isaianic formulation, and to mean: 'I am God.'"[19] This conclusion is supported with five arguments, as follows.

(1) There is a link between the RF and an expression that occurs twice in Ezekiel (2:5; 33:33): וידעו כי נביא היה בתוכם. Because the prophet's role was to speak for Yahweh, often prophesying future events, the credibility of the prophet and his God were of one piece. When the prophet announced an event in advance, it produced the conviction not only that Yahweh could reveal his intentions to his servants but also that Yahweh had the power to effect his will. Yahweh would do this because, as in Deutero-Isaiah's argument, he is God.

(2) Another common formula in Ezekiel—אני יהוה דברתי, "It is I, Yahweh, who have spoken"—is also connected to the RF and, Blank says, "is the basic formulation of which the formula וידעו כי אני יהוה is a development."[20] This formula, antecedent to the RF, is regarded as a divine seal, stamping the threat or promise to which it is connected as Yahweh's words. And if they are fulfilled, Yahweh is to be believed as God, the one true God. Thus, this formula "points to reasoning similar to that in Deutero-Isaiah's argument" for monotheism.[21]

(3) Blank is convinced that the combining of the RF with the formula אני יהוה דברתי in several places (6:10; 17:21, 24; 36:36; 37:14) strengthens the argument. The full meaning of the expanded formula with all its implications spelled out is: "They shall know that I (Yahveh, the speaker, the God of Israel, who make my intentions known in advance through my prophets) am God."[22] So, Blank contends, אני יהוה in Deutero-Isaiah and in Ezekiel has the same import.

(4) Since the nations are said to recognize Yahweh, and since the knowledge of *Yahweh as God of Israel* is too obvious a lesson to learn, Ezekiel's RF demands the interpretation that Yahweh will be acknowledged as the sole deity, the God the nations too must honor.

(5) In the final argument, which is rather tenuous and difficult to follow, Blank suggests that the למען שמו motif of Ezek 20 is closely connected to the RF and another idea: ונקדשתי . . . לעיני הגוים. The thought that Yahweh is jealous for his name and reputation among the nations "is scarcely to be distinguished from the thought of our formula."[23] Yahweh's acting for the sake of his name leads to

19. Blank, "Studies in Deutero-Isaiah," 35.
20. Blank, "Studies in Deutero-Isaiah," 36. Unfortunately, this important claim is left unsupported by the author.
21. Blank, "Studies in Deutero-Isaiah," 38.
22. Blank, "Studies in Deutero-Isaiah," 39.
23. Blank, "Studies in Deutero-Isaiah," 40.

their acknowledgment that he is God. Later in the twentieth century, John Strong would propose a similar linkage between שם למען and the RF and urge that the two refrains be read together for purposes of theological interpretation.

Blank's conclusion that Ezekiel is somehow dependent upon Deutero-Isaiah in his use of the RF has not won many adherents in the intervening years. (For arguments against literary dependence in this direction, see chapter 4.) Actually, Blank's conclusion is not worded to say Isaiah was Ezekiel's direct source or sole source for the RF. Rather, he writes: "The conclusion appears to me to be inescapable that *it is assumed by the author of the formula in Ezekiel that the reader is already acquainted with Deutero-Isaiah's reasoning and with his monotheistic construction of the name 'Yahveh.'"*[24]

Regarding other matters, Blank is noncommittal on the question of the refrain's authenticity (i.e., did it come from Ezekiel's hand or the hand of a subsequent editor?) and Ezekiel's source. After a detailed comparison of Exod 6:2–9 and Ezek 20:5–9, Blank tentatively suggests that "Ezekiel 20 appears to be dependent upon the whole of Exodus 6:2–9, including its secondary strata,"[25] but he declines to draw any firm conclusion on that issue. Later Jewish interpreters (e.g., Fishbane) would be bolder in their conclusions.

2.1.3. Herbert Haag

In a suggestive 1943 work known to Zimmerli, Herbert Haag proposes that the RF be viewed as originating in the Priestly document.[26] While drawing attention to the terminological and theological relationship between Ezekiel and Exodus, he argues that the RF in Ezekiel should be interpreted by reference to its use and meaning in the book of Exodus. Haag discusses the connection between the revelation of God's covenant name and the first occurrence of the RF (Exod 6), and he states that the other, later occurrences in the OT ought to be read in light of that early connection.

> Nun aber finden wir gerade in diesem priesterlichen Bericht über die Offenbarung des Jahve-Namens zum ersten Mal in der Bibel die Rede-Wendung: *"Ihr sollt erkennen, daß ich Jahve bin"* (Ex 6:7). Wir werden also gut tun, die Wendung zunächst aus diesem Zusammenhang heraus zu deuten. Daß diese Deutung die richtige ist, wird sich nachher aus der Prüfung der übrigen Stellen, in denen die Formel noch vorkommt, ergeben.[27]

---

24. Blank, "Studies in Deutero-Isaiah," 41 (emphasis original). Blank would later express a different conclusion regarding יהוה אני. He tentatively suggests that Second Isaiah "may have had help from Ezekiel" in developing the use of "Yahweh" as meaning "God" (*Prophetic Faith*, 68).

25. Blank, "Studies in Deutero-Isaiah," 45.

26. Haag, *Was lehrt die literarische Untersuchung?* 25–28.

27. Haag, *Was lehrt die literarische Untersuchung?* 27.

The conclusions Haag derives from his study prove by example that his approach in treating the refrain—that is, understanding the RF by reference to Exodus, especially Exod 6—leads to a clearer view of the covenantal significance of the formula. The theme of covenant comes out strongly in Haag's discussion. It is regrettable that Haag gave barely more than two pages to argue and explain his position, for Zimmerli would later sweep this work aside, stating that "the assumption of a direct dependence of Ezekiel on the Priestly writing inadmissibly oversimplifies the problem of tradition."[28] It is the argument of the present study that Haag's proposal not only deserves fuller review and reconsideration, but was steering scholarship in the right direction.

Old Testament studies took a conservative turn during the early 1950s, as the Albright school came into prominence and the "biblical theology" movement was launched. In the move away from the more extreme analyses of Hölscher and Torrey, Ezekiel scholarship received special impetus from C. G. Howie's cautious study of the compositional history of the book.[29] Also, British scholar H. H. Rowley exerted his considerable influence in urging greater respect for the text and its claims regarding authorship and setting.[30]

2.1.4. Herbert G. May

The 1956 commentary of Herbert G. May attempted something like a middle way between Hölscher and the newer, more conservative scholarship. As it is, May's work tends, shall we say, to fall between two stools. He tries to reflect the more cautious approach to the prophecy in his appreciation for Ezekiel's "considerable homogeneity,"[31] but at the same time, he dates the actual composition of the prophecy to the postexilic era, long after the prophet: "One person was largely responsible for the present form of the book.... We shall call this main redactor of the book the editor, even though he is both author and editor."[32] In short, May attributes much of the book, including the RF,[33] to the editor, whom he dates (with Hölscher) to the early fifth century. The exilic prophet himself, whose oracles are woven into the fabric of the book, had no hand in the actual composition of the book as we now have it.[34]

May follows Blank in attributing the formula's origin to Second Isaiah and interpreting its meaning in Ezekiel by Isaiah's monotheistic argument: "the meaning of

28. Zimmerli, *I Am Yahweh*, 146.

29. Howie, *Date and Composition*.

30. Rowley, "Ezekiel in Modern Study."

31. Herbert G. May, "Ezekiel," 45.

32. May, "Ezekiel," 45.

33. May, "Ezekiel," 62.

34. In May's view, "The problem of the book is the recovery of Ezekiel's own writings" ("Ezekiel," 45). Regarding Ezekielian materials, he says, "it has seemed impossible to isolate them with any certainty," and guesses "40 percent of the text ... should be ascribed to the editor" ("Ezekiel," 50).

the expression . . . is that he will be recognized as the one and only God."[35] According to May, there is theological discontinuity between the sixth-century prophet Ezekiel, who did not envision the salvation of the nations, and the later redactor, who used the RF and had a universalistic theology.[36]

2.1.5. Georg Fohrer (Postponed)

The work of Georg Fohrer is especially significant because he played an important role in the movement toward a reassessment of Ezekiel as a substantial unity, because he published important works on Ezekiel prior to Zimmerli,[37] and because he was among the first to critique Zimmerli's conclusions regarding the RF.[38] Fohrer's contribution to the discussion of the formula will be assessed after the review of Zimmerli's work. This is necessary because Zimmerli did what may be termed the ground-breaking work, and Fohrer's own views are set forth largely in discussion with, and in opposition to, Zimmerli's conclusions.

2.2. The Scholarly Contributions of Walther Zimmerli

There is no question that Zimmerli was the doyen among twentieth-century Ezekiel scholars: "[His commentary] is so full of knowledge and detail that it will not soon be replaced, even if the text-critical and redaction-critical methods on which it is based continue to decline in credibility. It remains a reference work of great value."[39] For research on Ezekiel's RF, Zimmerli's penetrating articles from the 1950s are just as valuable as his landmark *Biblischer Kommentar*. They draw what many consider to be definitive conclusions about the origin, function, and theological significance of the formula. Most recent commentators, including those like Greenberg who differ sharply with Zimmerli's hermeneutical approach,[40] are content to cite his work and assume the validity of those conclusions.

---

35. May, "Ezekiel," 97.

36. May, "Ezekiel," 62. Note also May's "Theological Universalism." He contends that, while the exilic Ezekiel did not propound universalism, some postexilic literature did, including the work of Ezekiel's editor. Harry M. Orlinsky challenges this in "Nationalism-Universalism and Internationalism." The debate is discussed in Strong, "Ezekiel's Use," 115–17. See also Weinfeld, "Universalism and Particularism."

37. Fohrer, *Die Hauptprobleme*; Fohrer and Galling, *Ezechiel*.

38. Fohrer, "Remarks," 310. See also Fohrer, *Introduction*, 409–10.

39. Levenson, "Perspective of Two Commentators," 217.

40. Greenberg, *Ezekiel 1–20*, 133; Block, *Ezekiel 1–24*, 36–39. Also merely citing Zimmerli's articles is Lindblom, *Prophecy in Ancient Israel*, 381. Carley's *Ezekiel Among the Prophets* bolsters and develops Zimmerli's main arguments.

Zimmerli refuses to follow those critics who regard the refrain as secondary, added by the hand of a later editor. Contrary to other commentators like Fohrer, Zimmerli declares that the RF is not easily detachable: "This recognition formula is connected in a characteristic way with the preceding context and represents part of the larger structure."[41] He regards it as redactional in a few texts, but even in those places, he still discusses the formula's meaning and purpose within the larger literary unit. There has been a general tendency among form critics studying the prophets to question the authenticity of passages promising hope and salvation. The prophet Ezekiel, some would lead us to believe, pronounced messages of unremitting doom.[42] Unfortunately, Zimmerli's work betrays a minor prejudice along these lines:

> That the form of the proof-saying is found relatively frequently in the somewhat later additions promising salvation (but certainly not only there, and not in chapters 40–48) can only be interpreted as showing that a stylized feature was provided by it, which could have been current particularly easily in the prosaic language of the school. However, in many places it clearly goes back to the prophet's own language and can in no way be denied to him.[43]

Zimmerli is not always clear as to which proof-sayings (with the RFs they contain) ought to be considered "somewhat later additions." He commonly speaks, almost without distinction, about a saying belonging "to the circle of Ezekiel and his school."[44] He categorized as secondary: 6:14; 11:12; 20:26; 22:16 (probable); 23:49; 28:24; and 38:16.

In an overview of Zimmerli's views on secondary expansions, one needs to examine his lengthy commentary appendix on the divine name in Ezekiel. All told, the name "Yahweh" occurs an astounding 434 times.[45] He finds that the expanded form of the divine name, אדני יהוה, makes up a full half of the cases (217 times). However, that expanded form is not distributed widely among occurrences of the RF, appearing only five times.[46] The contrast with the great majority of RFs that have the simple יהוה indicates to Zimmerli that the expanded formulas should be classed together, and "the formulation with אדני יהוה, form-critically at any rate,

---

41. Zimmerli, *Ezekiel 1*, 37.

42. Siegfried Herrmann, for example, contends that Ezekiel's prophecy originally contained no message of redemption and hope (*Die prophetischen Heilserwartungen*, 241–91).

43. Zimmerli, *Ezekiel 1*, 40.

44. Zimmerli, *Ezekiel 1*, 368.

45. Zimmerli, *Ezekiel 2*, 556. Through textual emendation at 21:14, Zimmerli comes to a tally of 435.

46. They are: 13:9; 23:49 (often discounted as redaction); 24:24; 28:24; 29:16.

[regarded] as a later degenerate form."[47] He suggests that, in these places, the text has been secondarily expanded.

Zimmerli was a rigorous practitioner of form criticism, and his interpretation of the RF exemplifies the strengths and weaknesses of his method. In his view, the formula consists of two parts, each of which has a different origin and *Sitz im Leben*. The verbal element "you will know" points to a fact—could be any word or deed—from which knowledge is to be gained. Taking Joseph's words to his brothers in Gen 42:34 as an early example of ידע being used in a process of proving and demonstrating, Zimmerli says, "the ידע-formulation . . . belongs to the sphere of legal examination in which a sign of truth was demanded."[48] Initially employed within a secular context, it also came to be used in a religious setting in which a person boldly requested signs from God so as to recognize the validity of the divine message (see Gen 15:8). The wisdom of Zimmerli's effort to establish an origin and *Sitz im Leben* for a solitary word, a much-used verb, ought to be questioned. Indeed, form-critical claims to discover the origins of various literary types are presently under attack.

Following the verbal assertion of recognition (*Erkenntnisaussage*) is the object clause כי אני יהוה ("that I am Yahweh"), which also is said to have a definite, discoverable setting in life. Ezekiel has a close connection theologically and terminologically to H, with its constant use of אני יהוה in legal stipulations, but Zimmerli traces the origin of Ezekiel's clause back to a formula of self-introduction (*Selbstvorstellungsformel*) "as we still find it quite fully set out in the Decalogue preamble, which is intentionally set at the head of the divine proclamations on Sinai."[49] In the essay "I Am Yahweh," he places this formula's *Sitz im Leben* in theophany accounts in which God appears and speaks while making covenants and giving the Law.[50] The "short form," which is also called the "pure form" and "basic form," is to be given form-critical priority, while expansions and amplifications (e.g. Lev 20:8: "I am Yahweh who makes you holy") constitute a "disintegration" of that original pure formula of self-introduction.

---

47. Zimmerli, *Ezekiel 2*, 556. On the combined "Adonai Yahweh," note also Fohrer, "Die Glossen," esp. 208. See ch. 3 of the present volume for discussion.

48. Zimmerli, *Ezekiel 1*, 37. Zimmerli further describes that test of veracity in "The Knowledge of God According to the Book of Ezekiel" (29–98 in *I am Yahweh*): "One person demands from another the offering of a specific, individual proof, a proof the first person is willing to accept as a sign of recognition of all the second person's statements. Recognition comes about by means of a critical testing before which the truth (אמת) of the word of whoever is tested must prove itself" (73). For a critique of Zimmerli's thesis regarding an original legal or prophetic setting in which a token of proof (*Zeichenbeweis*) is demanded, see Seeligmann, "Erkenntnis Gottes," esp. 416–20. Seeligmann treats a chain of OT texts in which the knowledge of God is more generally and commonly available through experiencing (hearing and seeing) evidence of God's power.

49. Zimmerli, *Ezekiel 1*, 37.

50. Zimmerli, *I Am Yahweh*, 22.

Self-introduction is said to be a kind of self-revelation of a person through the pronouncement of the name, and this formula may be used in the context of rein-troducing one already encountered.[51] The most important element of the clause "is the disclosure of Yahweh's personal name, a name containing the full richness and honor of the One naming himself."[52] So profound and basic is the formula of self-introduction that "everything Yahweh has to announce to his people appears as an amplification of the fundamental statement, 'I am Yahweh.'"[53] Zimmerli pays such close attention to that self-introductory statement because he believes that its "powerful content is supposed to resound in the statement of recognition."[54] He has that formula carry immense weight theologically.

Having dealt with the two constituent elements, Zimmerli can then speak of a combined formula (the recognition formula, or *Erkenntnisformel*) as the elements join to indicate the recognition of the person who freely introduces himself by name. That recognition is not mere passive observation, but rather involves acknowledgment of the person who reveals himself.

Often in Ezekiel's prophecy, that recognition of Yahweh is compelled (or nearly so) by proofs that he is who he claims to be in his name. The mention of facts and the prophecies of judgment and redemption all serve the function of proving what is said in the object clause. These prophecies of judgment and redemption are specifically to be fulfilled in divine acts. Using this interpretation, one gains a clearer understanding of the placement of the RF. Rhetorically, the formula is always connected with the account of an action of Yahweh. Yahweh is always the subject, even when his action is mediated through human beings. This frequently used, larger prophetic structure Zimmerli names "proof-saying" (*Erweiswort*).[55]

---

51. Zimmerli writes: "In the repetition of the self-introduction, the one who introduces himself actualizes his freedom afresh—even where it may recall an earlier knowledge and may recall fresh to the mind of the hearer this already known fact" (*Ezekiel 1*, 37–38).

52. Zimmerli, *I Am Yahweh*, 1–2.

53. Zimmerli, *I Am Yahweh*, 9.

54. Zimmerli, *I Am Yahweh*, 6.

55. Some are confused by his terminology in discussing the components of the RF and the larger "proof-saying" structure. They mistakenly use "proof-saying" as the synonym of "recognition formula" (e.g., Sweeney, "Ezekiel" [*Jewish Study Bible*], 1053). An equation can explain Zimmerli's terms:

ידע	+	אני יהוה	=	ידעתם כי־אני יהוה
assertion of recognition	+	formula of self-introduction	=	recognition formula
(*Erkenntnisaussage*)		(*Selbstvorstellungsformel*)		(*Erkenntnisformel*)

Where the RF stands at the conclusion of a prophetic announcement (*Zukunftswort*), that larger oracle pattern is termed a "proof-saying" (*Erweiswort*). Thus, the RF is but a part of the proof-saying, and those two terms are not synonymous. A final note of clarification: Zimmerli sometimes uses *Erkenntnisaussage* and *Erkenntnisformel* as nearly synonymous terms. Strictly speaking, the latter is a large subset of the former; see "Knowledge of God," §3.e.

In further analysis, Zimmerli explains that the proof-saying at its simplest is composed of a divine announcement (*Zukunftswort*) and the RF. In addition to this two-part proof-saying, Ezekiel employs a three-part form in which a "motivation" precedes the announcement of judgment.[56] Passages fitting this mold will begin with יען: "*Because* the Philistines acted vengefully . . . therefore (לכן) . . . I shall stretch out my hand against the Philistines. . . . Then they shall know that I am Yahweh" (25:15–17). In the developed proof-saying structure, the RF is normally positioned as the concluding target statement: recognition of Yahweh is the final goal and culmination of what is spoken in the preceding divine discourse.

Very helpful is Zimmerli's stress on Ezekiel's themes of divine sovereignty and initiative, which Paul Joyce has described as developing from the prophet's "radical theocentricity."[57] The RF is always connected to statements concerning a divine act. Yahweh is ever the author of the action through which recognition comes. Such recognition will not come about as the result of human speculation or reflection, but only in the face of Yahweh's acts, acts to which the prophet as proclaimer draws attention. Also, the formula always comes from the mouth of Yahweh himself. No formula refers to Yahweh in the third person: "you shall know that *he* is Yahweh."

Some err in thinking Zimmerli found the origin of the RF proper in Exodus because they see him tracing the origin of the self-introductory formula to the exodus tradition. Or more precisely, one can say he found that "formula of self-predication" (אני יהוה) lodged in the Decalogue preamble, thought to be quite early by tradition-history scholars. For Zimmerli, discovering the RF's origin was crucial for understanding the phrase and the doctrine of the knowledge of God in Ezekiel. Zimmerli rightly maintains that the RF must somewhere have had a life of its own, considering the tenacity with which it asserts itself in Ezekiel and the formula's marked tendency to allow variations only in a way clearly preserving the basic formulaic content and augmenting the sentence only at the end. What, then, is its origin?

The formula "is by no means an original coinage of Ezekiel himself."[58] Rather, its usage in Ezekiel is a relatively late witness to an "older tradition of prophetic discourse structure" manifested perhaps at its earliest in 1 Kgs 20. The account in Kings, he believes, is completely independent, classic in its diction (Early Biblical Hebrew), and was probably committed to writing shortly after the events transpired in the middle of the ninth century. In that account, said to be set in the context of the "holy war" tradition explained by Gerhard von Rad,[59] an unknown

---

56. Zimmerli, *Ezekiel 1*, 38–39.

57. Joyce, *Divine Initiative*, 89–105.

58. Zimmerli, *I Am Yahweh*, 41.

59. Von Rad, *Holy War*. Literature on the topic is surveyed in Ben Ollenburger's introduction to von Rad, *Holy War*; Niditch, *War in the Hebrew Bible*; and Trimm, "Recent Research on Warfare."

prophet announces Yahweh's help in the hour of enemy threat. King Ahab is twice told, "I will give this vast multitude into your hand, and you shall know that I am Yahweh" (1 Kgs 20:28; similarly 20:13). Zimmerli avers that 1 Kgs 20 represents the earliest occurrence of the prophetic form (*Erweiswort*) that includes the RF, but he goes on to question whether it might go back even further.[60]

Zimmerli also considers the employment of the formula as a traditional speech form in the Pentateuch. He seeks to discern the import of the RF in both the Priestly stratum (dated as postexilic) and the "older source-texts" of Exodus. He concludes that the Priestly writing, in its versions of the Moses story, "stands quite firmly in the force field of the older Moses tradition and is thus itself a branch of tradition that is independent of Ezekiel."[61] Though recognizing them, Zimmerli does not discuss at length the many similarities between the use of the RF in the Priestly passages of Exodus and its usage in Ezekiel. He states:

> Our overview shows that most of the Priestly passages employ the same strict for-
> mulation of the statement of recognition that we encountered in Ezekiel. They are
> integrated into a theologically sophisticated context in which Yahweh's initial deed
> on Israel's behalf—the leading out of Egypt mentioned in Israel's credo—plays
> a central role. It can be called both the means to knowledge as well as the actual
> content of knowledge (Exod. 6:7; 16:6).[62]

Considering these similarities, one begs to ask what the literary relationship between P (or traditions later recorded in P) and Ezekiel is.

At one point, Zimmerli appears to concede that the links between penta-teuchal materials or traditions (including P) and Ezekiel deserve greater atten-tion. He restates his conclusion regarding the refrain's origin, but then admits a difficulty remains:

> The passages in 1 Kgs 20 prompt us to view Ezekiel's use of the statement of recogni-
> tion within the context of an older prophetic tradition. On the other hand, *there can
> be no doubt that he has been strongly influenced by Priestly content;* cf. my analysis of

60. In "The Word of Divine Self-Manifestation (Proof-Saying)" (99–110 in *I am Yahweh*), Zim-merli presents a more lengthy exposition of 1 Kgs 20, which he terms "the earliest prophetic employ-ment of the proof-saying" (100).

61. Zimmerli, *I Am Yahweh*, 42. It appears that Zimmerli came to this position quite early. In his inaugural lecture at Göttingen, "Das Gotteswort des Ezechiel," he argued that a traditio-historical investigation of Ezek 20 reveals that Exod 6:2ff. is not as closely related as the literary affinities might indicate (253–54). Ezek 20 presents the exodus tradition without reference to the patriarchal tradition, while Exod 6 fuses them. Zimmerli wants to draw the conclusion that Ezekiel differs from the book of Exodus with regard to the exact formulation of the exodus tradition that influenced their composition.

62. Zimmerli, *I Am Yahweh*, 45–46. This is Zimmerli's major concession to the position taken in this study.

Ezekiel 14:1–11 in ZAW 66 (1954), pp. 1 ff. *The real tradition-critical problem as regards the prophecy of Ezekiel and the circle following him is the combination of priestly and prophetic influence.*[63]

When Zimmerli turns to examine the "pre-Priestly statements in the Moses tradition"—which may possibly be assigned to J, indicating that the tradition of the strict statement of recognition extends back to a time earlier than Ahab and 1 Kgs 20[64]—he confronts a stubborn problem. He normally designates "amplifications" and "expansions" of the strict form as a "degeneration" from that strict, theologically-terse form. The shorter formula is assumed to have form-critical priority. "Terse" and "pure" are adjectives that go together in Zimmerli's analyses.[65] However, again and again, Zimmerli discovers amplifications in the allegedly older pentateuchal sources, while the strict form is more characteristic of P. In fact, the data Zimmerli does not discuss stunning. Not only do "instances of a more freely formulated statement of recognition occur *more frequently* in the older textual sources,"[66] but the RFs found imbedded in the older sources are nearly all expansions! This seems like a glaring inconsistency. One wonders if it might indeed be fatal to a portion of Zimmerli's argument, since a primary reason for an early dating of the discourses and formulas in 1 Kgs 20 is "the almost classic terseness of their diction." After examining the formulas in likely J passages (outside what is, in the strict sense, prophetic literature), Zimmerli concludes that scholars are prevented from designating the RF as an exclusively prophetic form. Rather, "it seems to have been at home in a variety of circumstances from the very beginning."[67]

Clearly, this is not an altogether satisfactory answer to the questions of origin and *Sitz im Leben*. A form critic especially wishes to have a more certain answer to these questions before proceeding further. In "The Knowledge of God According to the Book of Ezekiel" (29–98 in *I am Yahweh*), Zimmerli discusses the RF's usage in Ezekiel and other OT books (30–63) and then gives closer scrutiny to the "roots" of the formula (71–91).

Zimmerli expounds on a number of his key insights. (1) Because the statement of recognition originally belonged in the context of symbolic events, it could not be exclusively limited to either the priestly or prophetic sphere. It could find a home anywhere decisions are made or ambiguous situations are clarified by means of symbolic events. Thus, the statement of recognition (ידע) does not originally belong, as one might initially assume, in the sphere of transmission of doctrine.

63. Zimmerli, *I Am Yahweh*, 146 (emphasis added).
64. Zimmerli, *I Am Yahweh*, 51.
65. Zimmerli, *I Am Yahweh*, 40.
66. Zimmerli, *I Am Yahweh*, 47 (emphasis added). The list of these freely formulated statements includes: Exod 7:17; 8:9, 20; 9:29; 11:7; Num 16:28–30.
67. Zimmerli, *I Am Yahweh*, 51.

It is not concerned with the knowing or learning of timelessly true propositions of some doctrinal system. (2) When the formula of self-introduction (in which Yahweh names himself) is joined to the recognition statement to form the RF, one is confronted by "ponderous and awkward phrasing." Why does Ezekiel, among others, insist on the statement "they will know that I am Yahweh," instead of the simpler "they will know me"? In a most probing section reminiscent of Karl Barth, Zimmerli explains:

> In the strict statement of recognition, ... the recognition content is not the simple, straightforward name of Yahweh that might be so easily inserted as the object (and you shall know Yahweh); rather, we encounter in its place Yahweh's self-introductory statement. ... Did this combination into the strict recognition formula not ultimately result from the disinclination to have Yahweh's name function as an object? Does the statement's awkward grammatical structure not express precisely that: even within the event of recognition—in which apparently the human is the subject with its action of recognition, and Yahweh the recognized object of this human action—Yahweh himself remains clearly and irreplaceably the subject. This incorporation of Yahweh's self-introductory formula into the statement of recognition within the context of symbolic events and divine judgment expresses the fact that Yahweh alone remains the subject of all recognition events—not only of those involving human recognition of divine action, but of human recognition and knowledge itself.[68]

(3) In addition, Zimmerli argues that, in the juxtaposition of the two elements in the RF (statement of recognition and self-introductory formula), both are given a new characteristic orientation.

> By incorporating Yahweh's self-introductory formula into itself, the statement of recognition is noticeably intensified into the sphere of finality. ... Something enduringly valid is being revealed here. ... It has attained the status of a central statement whose significance obtains in the middle of Yahweh's great historical acts on behalf of his people. On the other hand, however, this self-introductory formula has been expanded.[69]

The self-introductory formula steps outside its original liturgical setting in life, the theophanic event in the "limited sphere of solemn congregational celebration," to be employed in a prophetic setting.

Considering its usage in both the priestly and prophetic contexts, to which should one trace the origin of the RF? Zimmerli suggests that this question may

---

68. Zimmerli, *I Am Yahweh*, 84–85.
69. Zimmerli, *I Am Yahweh*, 85–86.

lead us back to an early period when a functional separation of priesthood and prophetic office did not yet apply. He says the early appearance of the strict statement
of recognition in the older Moses tradition and its later foothold in the prophetic
and priestly sphere would support this hypothesis. Note that, while this contention pushes the formula's origin back to an early time, this is not to say that Ezekiel
was influenced by the usage of the formula in that older Moses tradition. Just as
Zimmerli denies that Ezekiel is dependent at this point on older written prophecy,
he would deny a dependence on older written pentateuchal sources. "The book of
Ezekiel . . . stands in its tradition history on a completely different track. We can
follow the prophetic tradition from which it emerges through 1 Kings 20 back into
the northern Israelite national prophetic circles."[70]

After investigating the RF's origin, structure, and OT distribution along form-
critical lines, Zimmerli turns to a discussion of "the recognition event" or "the
concrete process of recognition"[71] to which the refrain points. All the evidence is
said to indicate that:

> The knowledge implied by the statement of recognition is not concerned with that
> part of Yahweh's being that transcends the world, though a superficial look at the
> strict formulation, "know that I am Yahweh," may tempt us to this conclusion. Such
> knowledge always takes place within the context of a very concrete history, a history
> embodied in concrete emissaries and coming to resolution in them. That history
> becomes a challenge and a claim in the proclaimer's words.[72]

This emphasis of Zimmerli on history is crucial to his explanation of the recognition event. "The knowledge implied by the statement of recognition can only be
described in connection with the actions of Yahweh that precede the recognition,
prompt it, and provide it with a basis."[73] Thus, the sequence of recognition is irre-
versible: first comes Yahweh's deed, then, secondly, there is human recognition.
Zimmerli urges that one guard against a mistaken sequential ordering that would
reverse this theological paradigm. He is entirely correct, and this insight may be
suggestive for further biblical-theological work in Ezekiel.

Zimmerli helpfully states that the statement of recognition has an imperative
thrust. The recognition of Yahweh is something expected of someone, something
demanded. But how is one to understand and respond to that demand unless
Yahweh acts? (The first condition for knowledge of Yahweh is that Yahweh
act.) Zimmerli implies that there is another obligation that stands alongside the

70. Zimmerli, *I Am Yahweh*, 88.
71. Zimmerli, *I Am Yahweh*, 63.
72. Zimmerli, *I Am Yahweh*, 63.
73. Zimmerli, *I Am Yahweh*, 64.

demand that Yahweh be recognized: "helpless supplication to Yahweh in the hour of decision,"[74] the humble request that Yahweh act.

Perhaps sensing that our terms "recognition" and "knowledge" will not necessarily communicate accurately that the formula's goal is higher than a correction of thinking or a lesson learned in the intellectual sphere,[75] Zimmerli presses the point that the recognition of Yahweh leads to a lasting decision for Yahweh. The consequences of recognition are typically confession, brokenness, and a yielding to the will of God. He says, "Recognition is not just the illumination of a new perspective; it is the process of acknowledgment that becomes concrete in confession and worship and leads directly to practical decisions."[76] It is apparent that Zimmerli equates the *recognition* in the RF with a transforming, saving knowledge of Yahweh, whether it is the covenant people, Israel, or the nations who come to "know."[77] This conclusion would prove controversial, and it merits full discussion.

Another of Zimmerli's observations regarding the recognition event is the potential for recognition to occur through not only an immediate divine act but also the recounting of Yahweh's acts from the past. This aspect is pregnant with significance for one studying Ezekiel's rehearsal of Israel's history (see especially chs. 16, 20, and 23). Zimmerli writes:

> According to the Old Testament faith, Yahweh's deeds do not occur merely in the given hour in which the people experience them and then sink from memory or lead a shadowy existence in a history that is directed toward the past. Again and again, the Old Testament paraenesis emphasizes the obligation to pass on the stories of Yahweh's deeds.... This [Yahweh's oracle in Exod 10:1–2] refers no doubt to the proclamation and witness of the congregation. However, if Yahweh's deeds do live in this proclamation, then it is self-evident that the recounting of Yahweh's deeds will also always demonstrate the hidden tendency to awaken recognition.[78]

This recounting of Yahweh's deeds "involves a full reactualization in which total—not merely secondary—recognition can be acquired once again." This being the case, the farewell speeches of Israelite leaders (Moses, Joshua, Samuel), the Passover rite, storytelling of Yahweh's acts in salvation history, and Scripture reading must have possessed tremendous power for good in the ongoing life of the covenant community.

---

74. Zimmerli, *I Am Yahweh*, 65.

75. Here we might alternatively speak of "truth stated in propositional terms."

76. Zimmerli, *I Am Yahweh*, 67.

77. Zimmerli has statements to this effect in several places. The fullest is probably a paragraph in "Knowledge of God" in which he speaks of "the worshipping confession" and "the adoration that kneels" (*I Am Yahweh*, 88).

78. Zimmerli, *I Am Yahweh*, 68–69. The theological influence of von Rad and his early "Credo" idea is evident here.

Zimmerli makes an excellent contribution to our understanding of Israel's religious life when he comments on the signs and observances through which Yahweh's actions live on:

> Yahweh's actions on behalf of his people live not only in the narrative proclamation of the people of God, but equally in the signs Yahweh has given his people as fixed observances, observances witnessing to his particular actions on behalf of this same people. Recognition and knowledge are revivified ever anew from the perspective of these signs and the people's encounter with them [So wird auch von diesen Zeichen und der Begegnung des Volkes mit ihnen her immer wieder neue Erkenntnis lebendig werden].[79]

The example of Sabbath should come to the mind of any reader of Ezekiel. Zimmerli helps us understand why the exiled prophet connects the Sabbath institution with Sinai rather than with creation. Ezekiel wished for Sabbath observance to be viewed in the context of Yahweh's historical acts on behalf of his people, "since in this case also recognition or knowledge of God is not acquired from some timeless, nonhistorical process." From this vantage point, the Sabbath is seen as nothing less than "the sacramental sign and warranty of a particular history from whose perspective Israel can recognize both its status as the elected people of God and Yahweh as the God who elects and sanctifies his people."[80]

In this present brief section, I have attempted the impossible. One cannot do justice in a dozen or so pages to Zimmerli's enormous learning and contribution to scholarly inquiry into the significance of the RF. It is with a certain sense of defeat that one must move on to consider how later scholars have critiqued and built upon Zimmerli's classic essays. A deep and strong foundation was laid by Zimmerli for all subsequent work. Surely all Ezekiel specialists can agree that, even where Zimmerli is not fully persuasive, he is instructive.

2.3. Scholarship Since Zimmerli

Since Zimmerli's comprehensive form-critical treatment of the RF in the 1950s, most who have worked in Ezekiel studies have contented themselves merely to cite Zimmerli's work and assume his conclusions, occasionally dissenting or attempting to fine-tune his analysis. The following discussion will focus more on those who have offered a contrasting viewpoint on the RF or who have treated that formula in a fuller, more probing way.

---

79. Zimmerli, *I Am Yahweh*, 70 (*Gottes Offenbarung*, 86).
80. Zimmerli, *I Am Yahweh*, 70.

2.3.1. Georg Fohrer

Quite soon after Zimmerli published his essays, Fohrer, who was already established as a noted Ezekiel scholar,[81] challenged his conclusions. Zimmerli's proposal that the prophet's use of the RF showed a dependence on the prophetic tradition that emerges in 1 Kgs 20 came in for pointed criticism. In two places,[82] Fohrer argues that the prophetic-discourse structure Zimmerli calls *Erweiswort* is quite late; it cannot be dated back three centuries. He asserts that "the occurrence of this formula twice in anecdotal prophetical utterances does not provide a broad enough basis for the assumption that centuries later Ezekiel made use of an early literary type."[83] Moreover, Zimmerli's selected texts in 1 Kings are best considered to be secondary interpolations that interrupt the flow of the narrative. Rather than a tradition behind 1 Kings providing Ezekiel with a prototype, these prophetical sayings "were instead given their present form by the last Deuteronomistic redactor of the books of Kings *on the basis of Ezekiel's words*."[84] Fohrer turns Zimmerli's interpretation of the formula's origin on its head, arguing that the final form of 1 Kings reveals a dependence on Ezekiel. The RF found in Kings is not an older literary type, but an "interpretive formula" easily appended to a text whose account of events, the redactors must have believed, needed authoritative explanation. While Fohrer is inclined to treat the formulas in 1 Kgs 20 as secondary accretions, his language at points indicates that he has retreated from his earlier position that the RFs in Ezekiel are secondary. Zimmerli's essays may have effected this change of mind.

What does Fohrer propose as the probable background, instead of prophetic traditions reflected in 1 Kings? He turns to the Yahwist source in Exodus, which includes the RF in the context of the plagues. Among other texts that might be cited, Exod 7:17 reads: "Thus says Yahweh, 'By this you shall know that I am Yahweh: see, with the staff that is in my hand I shall strike the water of the Nile, and it shall be turned to blood.'" Though Zimmerli and Fohrer disagree as to the precise background of the formula, they share common ground in their belief that it originated in oracles against the nations.[85] After the dialogue between Zimmerli and Fohrer, scholarship has viewed the prophetic tradition and exodus tradition (1 Kings and Exodus) as the two leading options to consider when facing the questions of the formula's origin and possible influences upon Ezekiel's usage.

What is the message communicated to the subject of the RF? What does it mean to "know that I am Yahweh"? And what is the function of the refrain? Fohrer goes to the first occurrences of what he terms the "interpretive formula" in the

---

81. Fohrer, *Die Hauptprobleme*, and Fohrer and Galling, *Ezechiel*.
82. Fohrer, "Remarks," 310, and *Introduction*, 409–10.
83. Fohrer, *Introduction*, 409.
84. Fohrer, *Introduction*, 409 (emphasis added).
85. This point is mentioned in Joyce, *Divine Initiative*, 93.

Yahwist material. Using the pentateuchal tradition as his guide, he says: "Its purpose is to provide a proper understanding of the event reported or announced, because every event needs interpretation. . . . It is intended to summon the listener to judge that it is Yahweh who has intervened or is about to intervene, with his wrath or with his aid."[86]

2.3.2. H. Graf Reventlow

H. Graf Reventlow does not draw much recent support from Ezekiel specialists for his claim that the prophet encourages hope that the nations will turn in allegiance to Yahweh, the covenant God of Israel.[87] In a 1959 article, Reventlow holds that the RF in speeches directed toward the nations indicates that there will ultimately be repentance. Yes, those formulas are set in the context of terrible judgment oracles, but Israel is also said to come to "know that I am Yahweh" through judgment. So, is it not possible that the nations might as well? Reventlow finds an affinity between Second Isaiah and Ezekiel in their use of formulas such as "before the eyes of the nations" and the RF. Despite these lines of argument, most scholars today are inclined to see the many RFs addressing the nations as a rhetorical device. In those passages, they say, "there are clear indications that the purpose is to highlight the revelation of Yahweh rather than to offer a positive vision of the role of that nation."[88] This debate is important for understanding the rhetorical purpose and the theological meaning of the RF in Ezekiel, and it will be discussed further in chapter 6.

2.3.3. Rolf Rendtorff

The issue of revelation in and through history has generated much work by theologians, especially since the 1950s, and Rolf Rendtorff's name figures prominently in the discussion. In a 1961 essay published in the controversial volume *Offenbarung als Geschichte* (published as *Revelation As History* in 1968), Rendtorff devotes quite a few pages to the formulas treated extensively by Zimmerli.[89] However, the formulas are discussed only insofar as they relate to his topic, "The Concept of Revelation in Ancient Israel." In other words, the discussion of the RF is subordinate to other concerns and questions.

---

86. Fohrer, *Introduction*, 410.

87. Reventlow, "Die Völker," esp. 35–36. The RF is one of several formulas he investigates.

88. Joyce, *Divine Initiative*, 94.

89. Rendtorff, "Offenbarungsvorstellungen," 21–41 (translation in "Concept of Revelation," 25–53). Zimmerli responded in "'Offenbarung,'" and Rendtorff made a rejoinder in "Geschichte und Wort."

Rendtorff takes issue with Zimmerli's conviction that the short refrain אני יהוה is the original formulation of the self-introductory statement. Rather, he argues, "it appears as an abbreviation of the statement in an expression of the most intense meaning."[90] Specifically, Zimmerli's short form represents "the strictly cultic style of the later priestly texts in the Pentateuch and Ezekiel,"[91] and it is a reduction of such expressions in older texts as: "I am Yahweh, the God of your fathers," "I am Yahweh, who has brought you out of Egypt," or "I am Yahweh your God." He interprets the use of the name יהוה as a claim to power, to unique power over other gods: "The short form presents the final pregnant coalescence of Jahweh's titles of power."[92]

Rendtorff goes a step further and claims that, even in priestly texts, the short form is not the original, basing his reasoning on the presence of the well-developed form in Exod 20: "I am Yahweh your God, who brought you out of the land of Egypt, out of the house of bondage." This reasoning overturns the interpretation of the formula as one of "self-introduction." Instead, it is an assertion of authority, reinforcing the laws to which it was originally attached: "The name יהוה must be here presupposed as known and carrying weight that commands emanating from this God have an authority that is unambiguously binding."[93]

Turning to the RF, Rendtorff agrees with a number of Zimmerli's lines of interpretation, while disagreeing once again over the issue of which form ought to be considered original. He draws attention to the very objection raised earlier in the summary of Zimmerli's work. The so-called older sources of the Pentateuch rarely ever have the shorter expression כי אני יהוה, but the expanded forms abound (cf. Exod 8:10; 9:14, 29). Thus, Rendtorff contends that אני יהוה ought to be understood as an abbreviation for fuller, more "theologically pregnant" statements, such as אנכי יהוה אלהיך ("I am Yahweh your God") in Exod 20:2.[94] With this in mind, Rendtorff declares: "The name itself is not the object of understanding, but the claim of power supported by it. The short formula must also be understood as a technical expression summing up this activity."[95] Through Yahweh's act accompanied by the formula, the witnesses would acknowledge his power and superiority and that he alone is God. Appropriate to this interpretation is the translation of

90. Rendtorff, "Concept of Revelation," 40.
91. Rendtorff, "Concept of Revelation," 40.
92. Rendtorff, "Concept of Revelation," 40.
93. Rendtorff, "Concept of Revelation," 41.
94. Here Rendtorff builds on Karl Elliger's research into the formula, done apparently in preparation for the latter's BKAT volume, *Deuterojesaja*. See Elliger, "Ich bin der Herr—euer Gott" and "Das Gesetz Leviticus 18." Elliger offered a few criticisms of Zimmerli's work in passing. He urged that אנכי יהוה not be viewed as an originally independent element later merged with אלהיכם. Also we should understand the name *Yahweh* as possessing overtones of older statements: "I am Yahweh, the God of your fathers," or "I am Yahweh who brought you out of Egypt."
95. Rendtorff, "Concept of Revelation," 42.

Erkenntnisformel used throughout his article: "the formula of acknowledgment." He construes it as such, and not as a *recognition* of one newly introduced.

When evaluating the RF as employed in the prophetic sphere, Rendtorff is inclined to follow Zimmerli in tracing the tradition back to 1 Kgs 20, but he also takes time to discuss "the expressions of knowledge" (RFs) found in Exodus.[96] Once again, he uncovers evidence that he believes supports his contention that אני יהוה is virtually an abbreviation. When the RF is reused later in Ezekiel and Second Isaiah, it is transformed and redirected toward the self-vindication of Yahweh. Rather than stating Yahweh's intention to intervene on behalf of Israel (as in 1 Kgs 20), "the formula [in Ezekiel] is exclusively connected with words of judgment."[97] These claims will be tested later in this study.

Rendtorff uses these observations as a springboard for his main point regarding the problem of revelation. The knowledge of Yahweh in his deity is intended not only for Israel, but for other nations as well. He points to the formulaic passages in Exodus as indicating that Pharaoh and the Egyptians "ought" to have acknowledged God. He draws parallels with Ezekiel's statement that "all flesh" (21:4, 10 [20:48; 21:5]) ought to confess. Rendtorff writes: "It is always Jahweh's demonstration of power that is observable and understandable to all the peoples and all the world."

> All peoples, "all flesh," the ends of the world, see what happened, and its meaning as the self-vindication of God is accessible to them all. History is not here understood as the "aimed" activity of God, at least not in the sense that it is only "aimed" at Israel. It is not something penultimate which has only a subservient function in relation to the self-manifestation of Jahweh. On the contrary, it has its fundamental meaning *as* a happening because in it God himself is manifested. This has only to be acknowledged by anyone who saw and experienced what happened.[98]

Thus, acknowledgment does not come about through the isolated word of proclamation, but by the activity that the word proclaims. What is decisive is not the divine word or the proclamation of the name Yahweh.[99] This is thought by some to be an extreme position.

96. With regard to the Exodus formulas, Rendtorff makes the key observation that the expressions of knowledge involving the Egyptians use the simple אני יהוה (Exod 7:5; 14:4, 18), while those addressed to Israel read אני יהוה אלהיכם (Exod 6:7; 16:12; 29:46). In ch. 4 of this study, that claim by Rendtorff will be tested and the Exodus formulas will be compared with patterns of Ezekiel's RFs.

97. Rendtorff, "Concept of Revelation," 44. This is an odd assertion, since he himself quotes, within the next few lines, a passage with the RF promising restoration (37:12–13).

98. Rendtorff, "Concept of Revelation," 46.

99. G. Johannes Botterweck cites the following in his entry for ידע in *ThWAT*, 3:482. Rendtorff claims, "das Geschehen selbst kann und soll ja in dem, der es sieht und es in seinem Zusammenhang als Handeln JHWHs versteht, Erkenntnis JHWHs wirken" ("Offenbarungsvorstellungen," 40), and

An acute, self-critical thinker, Rendtorff has repeatedly revisited some of the same theological and literary questions taken up in 1961, writing on the topic of revelation and history and discussing the RF and related texts where the verb ידע is found.[100] In his essays, fascinatingly, he reveals an affinity for Greenberg's "holistic interpretation," and he offers criticism of the form-critical approach in which he was trained. Regarding *Formgeschichte*, he contends that: (1) "It can easily lead to the isolating of individual text units from one another, the consequence being an atomization of the text." (2) Texts need to be read as a whole, without all their smaller sub-units being set apart form-critically; they "have actually been formulated with an eye to a wider context," and we must therefore assay a redefinition of our form categories and, in places, perhaps substitute "prophetic book" for "prophetic saying."[101] (3) Form criticism must be supplemented by final-form methods. These points of critique may apply to Zimmerli. Finally, Rendtorff faults his own early work on the RF for failing to note how ידע "points back to a self-revelation of God which has already taken place."[102]

2.3.4. *Walther Eichrodt*

The views of Walther Eichrodt are of interest because of his sensitivity to the theology of Ezekiel. The approach of his worthy commentary for Das Alte Testament Deutsch in 1959–1966[103] is in the mainstream of critical opinion, though he is faulted somewhat for frequent emendations in favor of the shorter LXX, particularly with regard to the dual-designation אדני יהוה.[104] He occasionally resists this tendency in his interpretation of the RF (e.g., at Ezek 20:26). Eichrodt regards the text of Ezekiel achieved by critical research "as being in the main that committed to writing by Ezekiel himself,"[105] and this more conservative perspective accepts the formula as part of the original prophecy in most instances.

Because Eichrodt views the RF as being in line with certain priestly emphases, his analysis of Ezekiel's priestly style and method of argument deserves some

---

Zimmerli counters, "die Geschichte gegenüber dem Selbsterweis Jahwes nur dienende Funktion, denn das den Menschen anredende 'Ich bin Jahwe' ist das eigentlich Gemeinte" ("Offenbarung," 30). Fair summaries of the debate are Knierim, "Offenbarung," and Preuss, *Theologie*, 1:228–58.

100. Among Rendtorff's essays, see especially two in *Canon and Theology*: "Revelation and History: Particularism and Universalism in Israel's View of Revelation" (114–24) and "Ezekiel 20 and 36:16ff. in the Framework of the Composition of the Book" (190–95). See also his *Covenant Formula*.

101. Rendtorff, *Canon and Theology*, 194–95 ("Ezekiel 20 and 36:16ff.").

102. Rendtorff, *Canon and Theology*, 117–18 ("Revelation and History").

103. Eichrodt, *Der Prophet Hesekiel*. (English in *Ezekiel*, trans. Cosslet Quin)

104. Eichrodt, *Ezekiel*, 12.

105. Eichrodt, *Ezekiel*, 13. Of course, the critical research undertaken views the final form as "the result of a complicated process of remodelling, elaborating, and supplementing" (21). Eichrodt is not always confident that the redactors are true and faithful interpreters of the prophet's line of thinking (see 41–43).

attention. That analysis has several profound insights, one of which points to Ezekiel's probable intellectual training while preparing for a career in the Zion priesthood. The education resulted in a thorough acquaintance with the history of Israel
and its sacred literature.

> He grew up amid the proud traditions of a priesthood where a unique conception
> of history was combined with a conception of God of a deeply spiritual character
> full of inner greatness and other-worldly sublimity. . . . The exercise of pronouncing
> and interpreting the law had trained him to express his ideas with extreme pre-
> cision of thought and terminology, and had also taught him to present his views
> in an architectonic construction and to give full consideration to all their various
> aspects. In expressing his thoughts he likes to make use of the scholastic lecture,
> enumerating each different case and the conclusions resulting from it, which gives
> his manner of speech the slow repetitive flow of the pedagogue and educationalist,
> but also the carefully chosen terms and weighty formulations of attained results.
> This intellectualist training had been combined with the acquiring of great learning,
> which shows an acquaintance not only with the past history of his own nation, its
> literature and the problems of its government and political development, but also
> such understanding of the life of surrounding nations as made it possible for him to
> criticize both their religious beliefs and their political activities.[106]

In expressing himself with "extreme precision of thought and terminology,"
Ezekiel made use of "an astonishingly rich variety of forms."[107] The RF deserves
special mention among all those forms because of its prominence. Eichrodt says
that that "stereotyped form" points to the objective of God's actions, "which is to
confer a new knowledge of himself." What is the essence of this knowledge, according to Eichrodt? He describes it as a "recognition of the all-prevailing almighty
power and the exclusive rights of the divine Lord, but [which] also points to obedience to his will." He will speak of Yahweh acting "to prove his own existence to a
humanity estranged from him."[108] Generally, Eichrodt is dependent on Zimmerli's
essays, and he emphasizes many of the same themes: the recognition is always connected to and has its source in some historical action by Yahweh by means of which
he wills to make himself known. Though not discussing the origin of the formula,
Eichrodt refers to Zimmerli's finding that it is a feature found in earlier prophecy
(1 Kgs 20:13, 28). He is comfortable using Zimmerli's terminology (specifically
Erweiswort), but he develops his own as well, such as the designation "statement
of design" (*die Zweckangabe*) for the RF.[109]

---

106. Eichrodt, *Ezekiel*, 22.
107. Eichrodt, *Ezekiel*, 15.
108. Eichrodt, *Ezekiel*, 15.
109. Eichrodt, *Ezekiel*, 38 (*Hesekiel*, 30*).

Eichrodt is among the several who, like Reventlow and Peter Ackroyd,[110] perceive a missionary purpose in the oracles of judgment against the nations. Eichrodt believes that there will be a positive recognition of Yahweh among the nations through his acts in history.

> The aim of Ezekiel's commission to preach is seen to be the revelation of God by word and deed, leading to the knowledge "that I am Yahweh," i.e. a will to universal lordship aiming at world-recognition of his lordship. Such a divine declaration belongs to a dimension different from all contemplative ways of representing God, and from all metaphysical statements regarding his nature; it is the statement of a fact demanding recognition and surrender. By going beyond Israel and including the Gentiles, it frees God's act of revelation from being imprisoned within a dogma of election tying him indissolubly to a single nation, obliging him to give it the first place among the nations and to impart himself to it alone.[111]

Whether there is sufficient cause to interpret the formulas spoken to the nations in so positive a light will be discussed in chapter 6.

Those familiar with Eichrodt's *Theology of the Old Testament* would expect from the commentary a stress on the theme of covenant, and they are not disappointed. In my opinion much of the commentary's value and insight derives from his covenantal approach. He explores Ezekiel with that topic in mind and masterfully draws out the theology of the prophecy. He repeatedly shows that "only the unfathomable patience of God, who keeps faith with a nation which has faithlessly broken his covenant, makes it possible to discern within the history of corruption a history of salvation, which celebrates the praise of the compassionate Lord of the covenant."[112]

Though Eichrodt does not speak of the RF as a covenantal formula, he does interpret it by reference to covenant. He leaves no doubt that it dominates the prophecy:

> The purpose of God's dealings with Israel and the nations which dominates Ezekiel's whole message . . . finds its proper expression in the objective explicitly stated in the statement of design, 'they shall know that I am Yahweh.' The phrase 'I am Yahweh' which is used to describe the content of this knowledge is a formula which points back to a cultic event, God's own affirmation of the incomparableness of his own nature, *as he makes himself known in concluding the covenant.*[113]

---

110. Ackroyd, *Exile and Restoration*, 115.
111. Eichrodt, *Ezekiel*, 44.
112. Eichrodt, *Ezekiel*, 45.
113. Eichrodt, *Ezekiel*, 38 (emphasis added).

2.3.5. Frank Lothar Hossfeld

Following after Fohrer, who urged caution among fellow *Alttestamentler* in proposing new literary types (*Gattungen*),[114] Frank Lothar Hossfeld (1977, 1983)[115] subjects Zimmerli's proposal of a "proof-saying" *Gattung* to a thorough critique. Even as he respects Zimmerli's diligent work and appreciates his intent to elucidate the usage and meaning of the RF within Ezekiel, Hossfeld finds fault with his approach at several points, mainly in the areas of syntactical analysis and conclusions regarding the structure of the *Erweiswort*. First of all, he alleges that, as Zimmerli discusses the positioning of the RF within the proof-saying, he fails to indicate his criteria when separating the prophetic speech-material into categories. He merely gives examples of positioning and is not sufficiently analytical in drawing his conclusions about the "normal order" of elements in the proof-saying's structure: "Für diese Einteilung nennt Zimmerli keine genauen Kriterien noch gibt er die Belege an. Die Bewertung "Normalanordnung" preßt die Statistik allzu schnell in einen vorgefertigten Rahmen und setzt eine Interpretation des Kontextes voraus."[116]

The second point of disagreement concerns Zimmerli's main conclusion that the RFs "normally" come "at the end of a line of thought within a cohesive speech unit" (*am Ende einer Gedankenreihe innerhalb des Redezusammenhangs*) and function as a "final syntactic construction," or *Schlußsyntagma*. Hossfeld proceeds to do a painstaking study of the positioning of the RFs within discrete speech units, and he concludes that, out of eighty formulas,[117] only twenty-five serve as a "reliable concluding announcement" (*verläßlicher Schlußanzeiger*). These are mostly the shortest and simplest formulation, "you/they shall know that I am Yahweh." Discerning the position of the RF within speech units is more difficult where it is expanded. Expansions, then, require greater attention.

> Schwieriger und damit unsicher wird es, die Position der Erkenntnisformel zu bestimmen, wenn die Erkenntnisformel erweitert wird; denn durch die Erweiterungen kann sich die Erkenntnisformel unmerklich von der End- in die Kontextposition verlagern. Das gerade bei der Erkenntnisformel zu beobachtende Phänomen der Erweiterung hängt mit die Variabilität des Erkenntnisinhaltes zusammen.

---

114. Fohrer, "Remarks," 310. After mentioning a proposal of his own and Zimmerli's essay on a new *Gattung* (*Erweiswort*), Fohrer says here: "It is necessary, however, to exercise caution in the discovery of new literary types."

115. Hossfeld, *Untersuchungen*, 40–46.

116. Hossfeld, *Untersuchungen*, 40.

117. See my data collected in ch. 3, where I count seventy-two more carefully defined "recognition formulas" and an additional eight "closely related phrases" in Ezekiel. There is debate about the true tally of RFs.

Hossfeld's analysis of the syntactical positioning of the RFs—his main interest—will long be valuable to scholarship.

The third point of critique stems from Hossfeld's syntactical analysis and his conclusion that Ezekiel's RF, in its variability and flexibility, does not easily fit within the bounds of the proof-saying as defined by Zimmerli. Other scholars have pointed out that even Zimmerli himself frankly admits the seriousness of the problem here.[118] Too frequently, he must speak of a "breakup of the original structure" (*Auflösungserscheinung der ursprünglichen Wortstruktur*), or "this later breakup of the form" (*diese junge Zersetzung der Form*), or "the awkward formulation of the statement, deviating so strongly from what is normal" (*die ungelenke, von üblichen stark abweichende Formulierung der Aussage*).[119] In considering the problems associated with Zimmerli's proposal, it may be wise for scholarship to be more guarded about this *Gattung*. As for Hossfeld, he declares that he doubts the existence of such a literary type and contends that the RF should be interpreted "only as a formula" and not within an alleged *Erweiswort*:

> Unter der Hand haben wir die Erkenntnisformel nur als Formel betrachtet und nicht so sehr als Gattungsweiser einer von Zimmerli beschriebenen Gattung "Erweiswort." Die Variabilität ihrer Funktionen unterstützt die Meinung Fohrers, in ihr nur eine "deutende Formel" zu sehen und nicht ein Merkmal, das eine ganze Gattung konstituiert; zumal diese Gattung nach Zimmerli selbst schon in ihren vermeintlich ältesten Exemplaren 1 Kön 20,13.28 unter einer "anhebenden Erweichung des Stils" leidet, und im Ezechielbuch eine "starke Zersetzung der Redeform, ja ein gelegentlich völliges Zerfließen derselben im größeren Redezusammenhang fest[zu]stellen ist."[120]

2.3.6. Philip Harner

Philip Harner's 1988 monograph on Isaiah's use of the divine self-predication "I am Yahweh" relates "two complexes of thought: the meaning and function of the formula 'I am Yahweh,' on the one hand, and the analysis of the themes of grace and law in II Isaiah, on the other."[121] Because Harner's procedure is first "to examine the meaning of the self-predication . . . in Old Testament tradition, apart from II Isaiah, and then argue that the phrase retained its traditional connotations as II Isaiah himself used it,"[122] he includes an examination of the RF in Ezekiel. That

118. E.g., Mosis, "Ez 14,1–11," 184.
119. Zimmerli, *Ezekiel 1*, 39 (*Ezechiel*, 1:59*); Zimmerli, "Knowledge of God," 36 (*Erkenntnis Gottes*, 10, and *Gottes Offenbarung*, 50).
120. Hossfeld, *Untersuchungen*, 45–46.
121. Harner, *Grace and Law*, vi.
122. Harner, *Grace and Law*, vii.

examination is sufficiently detailed and insightful to command the attention of Ezekiel scholars.

Harner chooses not to distinguish between the use of יהוה אני as a formula of self-predication and יהוה אני as a constituent part of the RF. Instances of both usages are lumped together. This decision may be objected to at the outset. Correctly, and in agreement with Zimmerli's approach, he posits no difference between the short form and expansions such as "I am the Lord Yahweh" and "I am Yahweh your God."

He believes "the original setting for the divine self-predication 'I am Yahweh' was God's revelation of himself to Moses."[123] The early narrative sources indicate an "original setting in the time of Moses," and the later sources are said to confirm it. The exodus narratives also signal God's intent to reveal himself more widely. "Yahweh's revelation to Moses, as important as it was in itself, was closely corre- lated with his working through historical events to make himself known, in ever widening circles, to his own people and also to others."[124]

Establishing the original setting of the form in both the exodus event and the giving of the law allows Harner to underscore the theological point of his book:

> The self-predication, from the very beginning, was associated with the themes of grace and law together. It introduced Yahweh as the God who freely took the initia- tive to deliver his people from bondage, and it also presented him as the God who asked his people to live according to his laws within the covenant relationship that he had established. The self-predication in the covenant at Sinai illustrates this close connection between the themes of grace and law: "I am Yahweh your God, who brought you out of the land of Egypt, out of the house of bondage. You shall have no other gods before me ..." (Exod. 20:2 ff.).[125]

This point is well taken, and the stress on covenant is suggestive: grace precedes law; grace forms the theological basis for the expectations Yahweh places upon his covenant people; grace and law are securely linked together in the covenant.

Harner also traces the introductory statement,[126] "you/they shall know that...," to the early narrative sources of the Pentateuch. He parts ways with Zim- merli and states, "Ezekiel received this introductory statement from the [J/E] tra- dition available to him and evidently found it so meaningful that he used it much more often than any previous writer."[127] Harner suggests that the introductory

---

123. Harner, *Grace and Law*, 12.
124. Harner, *Grace and Law*, 12.
125. Harner, *Grace and Law*, 13.
126. This is what Zimmerli terms the "statement of recognition."
127. Harner, *Grace and Law*, 34. The tradition cited in not 1 Kgs 20, but J/E, "composed some centuries before the time of Ezekiel himself."

statement and formula of self-predication may have been combined "in the context of liturgical celebrations."[128]

According to Harner, Ezekiel, like Second Isaiah, associates the self-predication with the themes of both grace and law.

> When God introduces himself as Yahweh, he promises to bring the Israelites out of Egypt into a new land, and he also commands them not to give their loyalty to other gods or to worship idols. In all these respects Ezekiel faithfully reflects the structure of earlier tradition, since a number of other sources, as we have seen, also associate the formula "I am Yahweh" with a theophany to Moses or Israel that takes place in Egypt, embraces the themes of grace and law, and initiates a relationship in which God will deal with Israel throughout the course of her history.[129]

This may be construed as a more traditional approach to the prophets. Harner is proposing that covenant, with its themes of grace and law, is the basis and theological background for all the phrases of self-predication, going all the way back to the time of Moses and Israel's earliest oral and literary traditions. This study contends that Harner's traditio-historical conclusions, marking out a closer connection between Exodus and Ezekiel's formulas than did Zimmerli's, are more in line with the evidence.

Taking up the twentieth chapter of Ezekiel, which is all-important for understanding the prophecy's RF, Harner says that Ezekiel used the divine self-predication itself as a way of reinforcing the parallels between the exodus/wilderness period and Ezekiel's own time.

> Yahweh addressed the Israelites with his self-predication when he gave them statutes and ordinances in the wilderness (Ezek. 20:12, 19, 20, 26). He will address them in a similar way when he brings them out of exile, judges them once again in the "wilderness," and restores them to their own land (Ezek. 20:38, 42, 44). On a literary level this use of the divine self-predication highlights the similarities between the two periods and gives a sense of unity to the structure of thought in the chapter. On a theological level it enables Ezekiel to remind his fellow exiles that Yahweh is still a God of grace and law, as he was when he first began to work in the history of Israel. As a God of grace, Yahweh seeks to deliver his people; as a God of law, he must enter into judgment against them. His grace will prevail because he will act for the sake of his "name," just as he originally acted toward the wilderness generation.[130]

---

128. Harner, *Grace and Law*, 36. Zimmerli said they combined in a holy-war context.
129. Harner, *Grace and Law*, 37.
130. Harner, *Grace and Law*, 38. Relating the revealed God of grace to the revealed God of holy law is among Ezekiel's central theological concerns.

That Ezekiel made self-conscious use of the language of the exodus tradition in order to draw parallels between Israel "in the days of her youth" and in the exile is also the interpretation proposed by Haag and Fohrer, and the present study moves in a similar direction, highlighting how the RF is best understood as a part of the exodus tradition.

2.3.7. Paul M. Joyce

One of the more fruitful dissertations on Ezekiel published over the last thirty years is Paul Joyce's 1989 *Divine Initiative and Human Response in Ezekiel*. He investigates not only the RF in Ezekiel, but the full range of formulas, and he concludes that all highlight the extent to which the focus of the book is on Yahweh himself. He terms this orientation "the radical theocentricity of Ezekiel" (title of his ch. 6) and finds it difficult to parallel anywhere else in the OT.

Joyce begins his investigation of the RF with a summary of its varied usage. He also includes a most helpful table showing the distribution of formulas into categories: Who will recognize? In the context of what divine act? That table is modified[131] and presented as Table 1, as it will prove useful later for comparing Ezekiel's RFs with those in other OT books.

In agreement with a majority of anglophone Ezekiel specialists, Joyce regards the bulk of the occurrences of the formula as primary. The RF is best interpreted as integrally related to the contexts in which it occurs—not easily detachable— and as a core, distinctive feature of the style and theology of the prophet. Joyce must be correct in his view that, since the formula of self-predication occurs in so many different parts of the OT, "it would seem inappropriate to attempt to relate Ezekiel's use of the particular words 'I am Yahweh' exclusively to any one background."[132] Also attractive are his recommendations to consider the origin of the RF as a whole and to pass over Zimmerli's attempts to establish separate and distinct settings in life for the formula's two parts.

Joyce declines to take sides in the Zimmerli–Fohrer debate over whether Ezekiel's RFs show a dependence on a prophetic tradition exemplified in 1 Kgs 20 or on the Mosaic tradition (older pentateuchal sources). He only goes so far as to suggest that important, but slim, evidence "points in favour of a background in

---

131. Joyce, *Divine Initiative*, 91. Note that, for two of the RFs, Joyce provides a dual classification: 39:28 is said to be both "G" and "H," while 28:26 is found in "E" and "H." I have *not* simply reproduced Joyce's table here, as two modifications seemed necessary. First of all, he has not included all the RFs. I added the following to his category "G": 13:14; 15:7; 20:38; 21:10[5]; 22:22; and 33:29. His category "H" needed 37:14. The RF in 20:12 is missing on Joyce's list, but that refrain does not easily fit any of his eight categories and is therefore omitted. The second problem is his inclusion of 25:14 ("they shall know my vengeance"), which is not a proper RF. (Note: corrections are in non-bold italics.)

132. Joyce, *Divine Initiative*, 92.

Table 1. Joyce's Categories of Recognition Formulas in Ezekiel (Modified) (Corrections in italics)

The Nations Will Know That 'I Am Yahweh' When . . .

(A) Yahweh punishes the nations 25:5, 7, 11, 17; 26:6; 28:22, 23; 29:6, 9, 16; 30:8, 19, 25, 26; 32:15; 35:4, 9, 15; 38:23; 39:6 [Variations = 'Expansions': 25:14; 35:12]	(B) Yahweh delivers the nations
(C) Yahweh punishes Israel	(D) Yahweh delivers Israel 36:23; 39:7 [Expansions: 17:24; 36:36; 37:28]

Israel Will Know That 'I Am Yahweh' When . . .

(E) Yahweh punishes the nations 28:26b; 39:22	(F) Yahweh delivers the nations
(G) Yahweh punishes Israel 6:7, 10, 13, 14; 7:4, 27; 11:10, 12; 12:15, 16, 20; *13:14; 15:7;* 20:26, *38; 21:10[5];* 22:16, 22; 23:49; 24:24, 27; *33:29;* 39:28a	(H) Yahweh delivers Israel 16:62; 20:42, 44; 28:24, 26a; 29:21; 34:27; 36:11, 38; 37:6, 13, *14;* 39:28b [Expansions: 20:20; 34:30]
[Expansions: 5:13; 7:9; 13:9, 21, 23; 14:8; 17:21]	

NOT CLASSIFIED: 20:12

Exodus."[133] His 2009 commentary hints at an explanation for his reluctance to choose sides:

> One needs to discriminate between a range of possibilities: literary dependence; oral dependence; joint access to shared tradition, written or oral; broader, more diffuse affinities and even coincidental independent developments, albeit within a shared cultural setting. Then there is the possibility of the redaction of Ezekiel by hands associated with other books of the Hebrew Bible, and conversely the influence of the book of Ezekiel on the redaction of other books. Clearly there is much in this area that cannot be known with confidence.[134]

Any who wrestle with Ezekiel admit that the prophet's RF speaks a "cryptic message" when presented as it is normally, without elaboration. Joyce asserts that its style of presentation "gives the formula a certain aura of mystery, which

133. Joyce, *Divine Initiative*, 155n27. Cf. Joyce, *Ezekiel*, 34.
134. Joyce, *Ezekiel*, 35.

serves to highlight the theocentricity of Ezekiel's presentation."[135] He observes that
the mystery can even involve ambiguity in the reader's mind about who is being
addressed in a specific RF.

> The concern that it should be known that "I am Yahweh" is at times so pressing that the
> specific recipients of this revelation fade into relative obscurity and it becomes unclear
> precisely who is being addressed—in such cases we are forcefully reminded that the
> focus is upon the God who is known rather than upon those by whom he is known.[136]

Joyce denies that Ezekiel reveals any hope that foreign nations will turn in
allegiance to God. Using his table, he shows that no text says that the nations will
"know "that I am Yahweh" when God delivers them. Nor do they come to that recognition when they observe Israel's punishment. There is no evidence in Ezekiel
that the nations are to turn in repentance and faith to Israel's God. With regard to
the few passages where the nations come to "know" through Israel's deliverance,
Joyce notes that Israel's deliverance always means (or relates to) judgment upon
the nations. The RF is to be taken as "a rhetorical device, serving to highlight the
central concern, which is the revelation of Yahweh."[137]

2.3.8. Millard C. Lind

In a little-noticed 1990 essay for a Mennonite publisher,[138] Millard Lind offers a
unique "political alternative" to other interpretations of the RF. Ezekiel, he says,
faults Zedekiah's court for rebelling "against Yahweh's political leadership" (theo-
politics) and engaging in ANE power politics (realpolitik). Lind refers to the
diplomacy of the era and says Israel has "been seduced to harlotry by attraction
to military power."[139] Yahweh takes action against this treason so that he may be
recognized "as political leader." The RF, then, "is concerned ultimately with the
establishment of a Yahwistic governmental structure" in the world. Put another
way, it conveys the "concept of the universal recognition of another kind of political existence, the rule of Yahweh's word as demonstrated by a prince who in the
midst of the nations functions under Yahweh's covenant."[140]

---

135. Joyce, *Divine Initiative*, 94. In *Ezekiel*, Joyce calls the RF "the most characteristic expression
of the radical theocentricity ... of this prophet" (27; see also 91).
136. Joyce, *Divine Initiative*, 94.
137. Joyce, *Divine Initiative*, 95.
138. Lind, "A Political Alternative."
139. Lind, "A Political Alternative," 265. He explains here that the deities "of the NE empires were
power oriented gods; alliance with these military powers is synonymous with trust in these gods ...
which is incompatible with Yahwistic politics (cf. Lang [*Kein Aufstand*] 1978, pp. 183–186)."
140. Lind, "A Political Alternative," 266.

In oracles against the nations (esp. Ezek 38–39), according to Lind, "the nations will recognize Yahweh as universal political leader who opposes imperialistic militarism." God's actions also have the positive aim of attracting "Israel's historical enemies [that they] might participate with Israel in acknowledgment of the politics of quietness and confidence."[141] No doubt, Lind makes a contribution to discussion of the RF, and the political aspect deserves attention. One wonders, however, if his thick political lens distorts Ezekiel's message at points. Is the SPF ("I am Yahweh") within the formula receding from view, to be replaced by "acknowledgment ... of an alternative politics to the realpolitik of the Near East"? Has Lind colored the *knowing* to become political repentance: "The nations will perceive (*wĕrāʾû*) that autonomous, violent politics end in the death of the international community"?[142] My critique is that he is reductionistic, making Israel's idolatry fundamentally political. Ezekiel's view, rather, is that the root problem is religious (an idolatrous "heart"), and the nation's faithlessness comes to expression variously in politics, economic oppression, sexual immorality, bloodshed, and so on.

2.3.9. John Strong

In 1995, while a member of the "SBL Ezekiel Consultation Steering Committee," John T. Strong published an article noteworthy as the first discussion since Zimmerli to focus on Ezekiel's RF.[143] His argument is not chiefly concerned with the formula per se, but rather seeks to establish that Ezekiel's theological use of it "is fully nationalistic and does not envision the eventual inclusion of the foreign nations in the covenant with Yahweh."[144]

Strong joins the longstanding debate in biblical theology and OT interpretation over nationalism and theological universalism in the Scriptures. As seen already in this chapter, the issue has repeatedly been taken up by Ezekiel specialists. Strong posits that an evaluation of Ezekiel's theology regarding universalism must deal directly with the RFs, which do speak of the nations coming to "know that I am Yahweh" (e.g., 25:5, 7, 11, 17). Is this *knowing* the same as Israel's when she comes to "know that I am Yahweh" in her salvation (e.g., 34:27; 37:14)?

Because Zimmerli has written the "definitive study of the recognition formula,"[145] Strong begins with his interpretation, that the RF speaks of "an *experiential, confessional knowledge* of Yahweh on the part of the subject."[146] He shows

141. Lind, "A Political Alternative," 267, 268.
142. Lind, "A Political Alternative," 260, 269–70.
143. Strong, "Ezekiel's Use." Strong's 1993 doctoral dissertation at Union Theological Seminary in Virginia had been "Ezekiel's Oracles Against the Nations Within the Context of His Message."
144. Strong, "Ezekiel's Use," 133.
145. Strong, "Ezekiel's Use," 118.
146. Strong, "Ezekiel's Use," 118 (emphasis original).

that Zimmerli understood this knowledge as "coming about in the worshipping confession, Yahweh is God."[147] Therefore, Ezekiel's theology is, in this one respect, comparable to Deutero-Isaiah's. Strong dissents from Zimmerli's tentative conclusion and urges interpreters to consider Ezekiel's RF as pointing to two different types of confession.

Strong takes Ezek 36:22–23 as a key text for unlocking the meaning of the RF as Ezekiel directs it toward the nations. It is key for two reasons. First of all, the formula is used "with the foreign nations as the subject . . . outside of a foreign nation oracle."[148] Secondly, the recognition or acknowledgment of the nations is said to come when Yahweh acts למען שם "for the sake of [my] name." When one understands the significance of that name, Yahweh, and the meaning of the phrase למען שם, then the way is open "to understand what kind of knowledge of Yahweh Ezekiel intended when he placed the foreign nations as the subject of the recognition formula."

Much of Strong's article (nearly ten pages [120–29]) expounds the meaning of למען שם, rather than the RF, because he views it as foundational for his thesis that Israel was not only given Yahweh's name, but "called to be Yahweh's name, that is, his testimony to the nations of his power."[149] Because Israel had failed to guard the honor of the name, Yahweh himself is moved to act so as to reestablish the testimony that he is the creator God who rules over chaos and also the Divine Warrior who triumphs over his enemies.[150] Ultimately, Yahweh's powerful actions, through which he is recognized by the nations, are both "for the sake of my name" and for the sake of Israel, who bears the name. Yahweh's actions are not for the sake of the nations. Rather, the nations will be brought to submission when they hear of Yahweh's victory over chaos on behalf of Israel. "If Israel is defeated, then the knowledge that Yahweh has power over chaos will have been lost. Again, the basic issue is not the conversion of the nations, but power."[151] Ezekiel's RFs, thus interpreted, do not teach that the nations will come to worship Yahweh or be blessed in covenant with Yahweh.

How does Israel's apparent defeat in the exile provide a testimony to Yahweh's power? Does exiled Israel continue in her role as testimony? To answer these questions, Strong guides the reader through Ezek 20 and its tripartite historical

147. Zimmerli, *I Am Yahweh*, 88.

148. Strong, "Ezekiel's Use," 120.

149. Strong, "Ezekiel's Use," 127. Strong builds on the Harvard research of S. Dean McBride ("The Deuteronomic Name Theology," 1969) and Frank Moore Cross ("The Religion of Canaan and the God of Israel," in *Canaanite Myth and Hebrew Epic*). For a critique of the exegetical basis for the "name theology," see Wilson, *Out of the Midst of the Fire*.

150. Strong combines a creation theology with the Divine Warrior motif, though the exegetical basis in Ezekiel for a creation theology is not made clear. When expounding a creation theology, he uses texts in Genesis and Exodus in which the theology is undoubtedly present.

151. Strong, "Ezekiel's Use," 124.

retrospective. Just as Yahweh once acted to create a nation as a testimony for his name by redeeming Israel out of Egypt, so he is acting again to re-create the nation as a testimony to his power. The phrase למען שם explains Yahweh's purpose in the exodus and in the exile. The covenant God who determined to redeem a people living among the nations as a testimony will once again redeem. The covenant God who withheld destruction from his disobedient people and determined to bring them into a promised land will keep his promise. "According to Ezekiel, the exile is not the destruction of Israel, but rather a fresh beginning."[152]

Strong argues that the nations will know Yahweh as the deity who controls chaos and works to restore Israel as his testimony. As the surrounding nations such as Egypt, Ammon, Moab, and Edom oppose Israel and the Divine Warrior's purposes with Israel, they are punished. They are stopped so Yahweh may "continue what he began with the exodus"[153] and finally settle his covenant people in the land. The RF is not used in the oracles against Tyre, Strong contends, because that sea-faring city-state was not aligned against Israel. "The nationalistic content of the recognition formula seems only to have been appropriate in the context of battle between Yahweh and his enemies."[154]

In the article, there are helpful links made to other Scripture texts, though Strong regularly speaks of *traditions* instead of *texts*. When arguing his case that the "knowledge" of Yahweh spoken of in the RF does not have the deliverance or covenant blessing of the nations in view, Strong appropriately turns to the use of the formula against Egypt in the exodus narrative. Ezekiel's formula, it seems, should be interpreted in line with the RFs in Exodus.

> The events culminating in the creation of Israel are orchestrated to bring Pharaoh and Egypt to a knowledge of Yahweh's power as Creator. Yet Egypt is not depicted as worshipping Yahweh or joining Yahweh's nation. Rather, Israel, in its creation, testifies to Yahweh's power over Chaos, and Egypt is merely intended to accept this testimony submissively.[155]

This is a helpful approach and an example of intertextual analysis.

Readers may suggest one weakness in Strong's article. He repeatedly makes claims that Yahweh's actions למען שם, "for the sake of [my] name," are also for the sake of, or on behalf of, Israel. Yet Ezekiel does not establish this tie. Has Strong

---

152. Strong, "Ezekiel's Use," 128.

153. Strong, "Ezekiel's Use," 130.

154. Strong, "Ezekiel's Use," 132. Strong here is influenced by Eichrodt and Zimmerli in his decision to treat the RF against Tyre in 26:6 as secondary. Recent commentators, including Greenberg and Block, do not. Some may regard it as a weakness of the article to base a lengthy argument regarding Tyre on a debatable redaction-critical decision.

155. Strong, "Ezekiel's Use," 123–24.

not taken into account the related texts in chapter 36 that incline the reader to a radically theocentric interpretation of שם למען and that explicitly deny the tie he seeks to make? "Thus says the Lord Yahweh, 'It is *not for your sake*, O house of Israel, that I am about to act, but for the sake of my holy name, which you profaned among the nations where you went" (36:22; cf. 36:32).

Strong also causes much weight of meaning to rest on the phrase שם למען in his interpretation of the RFs as used against the nations. Surely it is problematic for his line of argument that שם למען does not appear in any of the oracles addressed to the nations. Nowhere do we read that Yahweh is acting to punish the nations "for the sake of my name." That phrasing is located exclusively in oracles addressed to Israel.

Another problem is the lack of explanation of how the nations will "know that I am Yahweh" through their punishment. Strong places emphasis on the nations' acknowledgment of Yahweh in his actions on behalf of Israel. It is difficult to see, in the years immediately following the destruction of Jerusalem, how the punishment of Ammon serves the interests of Israel or promotes Israel's restoration as a testimony to God's power. Can the nations "know that I am Yahweh," without reference to Israel, in their own experience of Yahweh's dreadful judgment? A comparison of Joyce's category "A" and category "D" is instructive at this point (see Table 1). There is a much higher frequency of RFs that associate the nations' acknowledgment of Yahweh with their punishment than associate it with Israel's deliverance.

If Zimmerli were alive, he might offer a critique of Strong where the latter attempts to define the Name. Strong fills "Yahweh" with a certain content. For the nations to "know that I am Yahweh" is for them to know him as the Divine Warrior who initially, as creator, brought order out of chaos, and they come to know him as the God of Israel who fights on behalf of his people. Clearly, Strong has shifted away from Zimmerli's position that Yahweh's personal self-introduction is at the heart of the RF. Self-introduction, Zimmerli insists, is "precisely that which it [the formula] intends," and that is why the formula always has the wording אני יהוה and never reads "You shall know Yahweh" or "You shall know that he is Yahweh." Zimmerli's critique could apply to Strong:

> Yahweh's personal self-introduction ... can only occur from his mouth. Thus any attempt to understand the strict statement of recognition in Ezekiel and elsewhere from the perspective of a meaning of the name disclosed by Exodus 3:14 is falsely directed from the very beginning; such attempts fail to recognize the mystery that cannot be reduced to a definition—and the irreversible direction of the process of self-introduction.[156]

156. Zimmerli, *I Am Yahweh*, 153.

The best, most compelling case to be made for a wholly negative usage of the RF in Ezekiel with reference to the nations would require an exegetical examination of all the formula's occurrences. This Strong does not attempt, perhaps for reason of article length. Regrettably, there is scarcely any discussion in the article about the origin of the formula, its varied usage, or its rhetorical purpose. Whatever the small deficiencies of his article, Strong is successful in making his argument regarding the nationalistic use of the formula *against* the nations, and scholars must take account of his findings.

2.3.10. Daniel I. Block

The 1997–1998 evangelical commentary of Daniel Block is a high point of late-twentieth-century Ezekiel scholarship. Building on Zimmerli, Leslie Allen's *Ezekiel 20–48*, and especially Greenberg's *Ezekiel 1–20*, Block has produced an encyclopedic two-volume work. Here I concern myself only with summarizing his conclusions regarding the "profound" RFs, which he says number seventy-two[157] and dominate the prophecies.[158]

Block shows his indebtedness to Zimmerli's mid-century essays, following him closely in several aspects of interpretation. First of all, Block believes the proper line of interpretation is to emphasize the significance of אני יהוה ("I am Yahweh") within the structure of the RF. Self-introduction is crucial in the larger formula. He writes that Zimmerli "observes correctly that where the self-introduction formula is incorporated into the recognition formula, the real intention of an oracle is not to announce an event but rather to refer *through* the pronouncement to Yahweh's historical self-manifestation in his action, a manifestation that all observers are to recognize and acknowledge."[159]

The self-introductory formula is of such importance to Block that he rejects the common appositional rendering of אני יהוה דברתי as "I, Yahweh, have spoken."[160] It should instead be translated so as to preserve, not obscure, the self-introductory aspect: "I am Yahweh, I have spoken." This policy also holds where Ezekiel brings this formula and the RF together: וידעתם כי אני יהוה דברתי; "Then you shall know that I am Yahweh, I have spoken" (17:21). At this point, Block goes beyond Zimmerli, who was open to the appositional rendering.

---

157. Block, *Ezekiel 1–24*, 39. Elsewhere he speaks of "87 occurrences of the recognition formula" (763n204), citing Zimmerli's appendix (*Ezekiel 2*, 556). The question of Zimmerli's true tally of formulas is discussed in ch. 3.

158. Block, *Ezekiel 1–24*, 36.

159. Block, *Ezekiel 1–24*, 38n89 (emphasis original).

160. Block, *Ezekiel 1–24*, 37–38. Zimmerli terms this the "formula for the conclusion of a divine saying" (*Ezekiel 1–24*, 26), or "Schlußformel des Gotteswortes" (*Ezechiel*, 1:40*).

A second continuity with Zimmerli is Block's form-critical approach, though moving in a more conservative direction.[161] Perhaps one may regard it as a "chastened" form criticism, used alongside more synchronic methods.[162] Block regularly uses Zimmerli's form-critical categories such as "word-event formula" and "proof-saying," occasionally employing alternate terminology such as "demonstration oracle." (One adjustment or refinement one could wish Block had made is the avoidance of the designation "pure form" for the shortest form of the RF.) He follows Zimmerli in his understanding of the RF within the proof-saying structure as a concluding statement[163] and as clueing the reader to the rhetorical intention of whole oracles—the acknowledgment of Yahweh.

Block parts with Zimmerli over the derivation of the RF. Whereas Zimmerli looks to a northern Israelite prophetic tradition, reflected in 1 Kgs 20 (holy-war setting), as the influence on Ezekiel, Block views the exodus narratives as the source from which the formula is drawn.[164] He also uses those narratives to help interpret Ezekiel's formulas. Even where he differs with Zimmerli, there yet remain strong elements of continuity, as Block stresses the idea of divine self-manifestation, the form-critical "proof-saying," and the fact that the revelation comes by the divine word within history.

> Drawing on the exodus narratives (cf. Exod. 6:6–9; 7:1, 5, 17), this formula transforms Yahweh's oracles from mere announcements of coming events into announcements of Yahweh's self-manifestation. They become prophetic proof-sayings, according to which the actions of God are designed to bring the observer to the recognition of Yahweh's person and his sovereign involvement in human experience. Ezekiel will offer no doctrinal speeches, no descriptions of Yahweh's nature. It is in the narrative of history that his character is proclaimed. This refrain calls on the hearer of Ezekiel's oracles to stand back and watch Yahweh act, whether it be in judgment or salvation, and then draw the obvious theological conclusions. Just as the deliverance of his people from Egypt centuries earlier had been intended to impress the Israelites, the Egyptians, and the world with the presence and character of Yahweh, so too will his acts of judgment on a rebellious people.[165]

---

161. E.g., Block, "Ezekiel's Boiling Cauldron."

162. All benefit from Block's discussion of chiasms, panels, and other final-form features. E.g., he displays the balanced structure of the oracles against the nations in *Ezekiel 25–48*, 4–5.

163. Block says, "this formula usually signals the end of a demonstration oracle/proof saying in Ezekiel" (*Ezekiel 25–48*, 131).

164. Block has reaffirmed this conclusion recently. See "The God Ezekiel Wants Us to Meet," 169–70, where he reexamines the RF to argue that the prophecy, despite an emphasis on divine fury, is not "graceless."

165. Block, *Ezekiel 1–24*, 39. It is worth highlighting that Block speaks of the "exodus narratives," rather than a more amorphous exodus tradition.

Block's position that "underlying Ezekiel's usage is a keen awareness of the traditional exodus narratives"[166] is similar to the position of Haag, Fohrer, and Harner.

Block joins a growing chorus of contemporary Ezekiel specialists in denying
that the prophecy foresees a positive, saving recognition of Yahweh among the
nations. He says Ezekiel does not share Isaiah's "universalism and cosmic interest,"
which rather "stand in sharpest contrast to the parochialism of Ezekiel."[167] What
attention Ezekiel does pay to the nations is explained by their relationship to Israel;
they are the *surrounding* nations, having had direct dealings with the covenant
people.

> The oracles against the nations (chs. 25–32) leave no doubt about Yahweh's sover-
> eignty over all, but the rise and fall of foreign powers have historical significance
> primarily to the extent that these events touch the fate of Yahweh's people (28:24–
> 26).... He is indeed concerned that all the world recognize his person and his pres-
> ence in their affairs, but his agenda is always focused on Israel.[168]

Block reminds readers that Ezekiel's vision of a fully restored Israel provides room
for non-Israelites, but only through "their incorporation into the new order,"
through their "adaptation to and integration into what is clearly Israelite society
and culture."[169]

What does he suggest is the meaning of the RF in the oracles against the
nations? How should we define the verb "know" in such texts as Ezek 39:7, which
says, וידעו הגוים כי אני יהוה קדוש בישראל ("then the nations shall know that I am
Yahweh, holy in Israel")? Block seems to prefer "acknowledge" as a rendering of
ידע in these RFs. Yahweh's intended goal is that even the proud pagans acknowledge him "as the sovereign Lord of their own history." The nations "must submit
to the Lord of history" and be brought to "acknowledge him as supreme." For the
nations, as well as for Israel, he is "the One behind all these events as the sovereign
Yahweh."[170]

The single text that gives Block pause is 29:13–16, where Egypt is said to "know
that I am Yahweh" when it is regathered from captivity and resettled in its land
of origin. This sounds remarkably like the prophecies of deliverance and blessing
delivered to Israel (e.g., 20:41–42). Block identifies this text as "a modified restoration oracle."[171] In doing so, however, he does not revise his considered opinion

---

166. Block, *Ezekiel 1–24*, 38.
167. Block, "Ezekiel, Theology of," in *NIDOTTE*, 4:618.
168. Block, *Ezekiel 1–24*, 47.
169. Block, *Ezekiel 1–24*, 47n3.
170. These phrases are taken from Block, *Ezekiel 25–48*, 125, 128, 139, 144.
171. Block, *Ezekiel 1–24*, 144. Greenberg's exegesis of ch. 29 reaches much the same conclusion,
though neither commentator apparently had opportunity to consult the other prior to publication.

that hope for the nations does not feature in Ezekiel. In view of the other bracing judgment oracles against Egypt, one may say that 29:13–16 reads as a moderation of judgment, rather than as a true salvation oracle. They are "restored" to become a "lowly kingdom," one that will never recover its lost glory and power of long ago. Even what seems like a gracious reestablishment of the Egyptian nation is for Israel's benefit, that she might have a living reminder (a continuing, diminished Egypt) of her misplaced trust and faithlessness. Block makes a good argument that Egypt's "preferential treatment," in comparison to the severe messages of destruction delivered to other neighbors, may be based on the less serious charges Egypt faces. She had only failed to deliver Israel. "Whatever its motives, Egypt had tried to prevent the collapse of Judah,"[172] while Ammon, Edom, and others had tried to hasten it. The *Schadenfreude* of the latter nations (25:2–3, 6)—not forgetting also their opportunistic attacks on the Jews (25:12, 15)—was an affront to Yahweh and deemed to be deserving of severe judgment.[173]

2.3.11. Jacqueline E. Lapsley

Jacqueline E. Lapsley's 2000 dissertation at Emory is distinguished by its relating the knowledge of God and the RF to issues of human moral identity and transformation.[174] The chief concern of her work is the crisis point in Ezekiel's anthropology and theology where "make yourselves a new heart" (18:31) is juxtaposed to "I will give you a new heart" (36:26; cf. 11:19). How is the moral self to be transformed? Lapsley chooses to address the tension not by asking the old *theological* questions, but rather new ones:[175] "What is going on in Ezekiel's anthropology? Reflecting theologically is, after all, inherently connected to thinking about anthropology. To know God is to know self, and vice versa."[176] Her fresh approach is to examine how the text reflects a tension between repentance and determinism.[177]

Greenberg makes mention of Walter Vogels's "Restauration de l'Égypt" (*Ezekiel 21–37*, 611). In his own interpretation, Greenberg shies away from a universalistic reading (*pace* Vogels) and says the oracle "expresses a deliberate judgment that takes Egypt's lesser guilt into consideration."

172. Block, *Ezekiel 25–48*, 145.

173. Block, *Ezekiel 25–48*, 17.

174. Lapsley, *Can These Bones Live?*

175. Interpreters have tended to focus on the tension (a) between divine initiative and human responsibility, or (b) between the individual and collective levels of responsibibiltiy.

176. Lapsley, *Can These Bones Live?* 41.

177. Lapsley, *Can These Bones Live?* 26: "In Ezekiel it is not the *unit* of responsibility but the *possibility* of human responsibility *at all* that is brought into question by such a starkly sovereign portrait of God. The ethical tensions evident in the book suggest that Ezekiel may be attempting to work out a solution. . . . In other words, *theological* questions have tended to dominate the scholarly discussion so far described, but they obscure equally important *anthropological* questions, the answers to which may clarify why Ezekiel's portraits of God and of human beings take the form they do."

According to Lapsley, Ezekiel's readers can detect "a dual shift in the understanding of human beings as moral persons," a shift away from what predominates in the Hebrew Bible. Instead of the *origin* of virtuous moral selfhood existing inherently in persons (capable to will and act), it exists "in God as a potential gift to humanity." The second shift involves the *form* of moral selfhood, no longer centered on acting rightly and keeping laws: "In much of Ezekiel, action recedes as the primary element in moral identity; rather, the moral selfhood given by God focuses on *knowledge* (knowledge of God and knowledge of self), ... with moral action flowing out of that knowledge as an important, but derivative consequence." Lapsley is careful to nuance her thesis, adding that this dual shift is not "so definitive" or "complete" that "the previously dominant view" disappears. No, that view is reasserted in Ezekiel, and this generates the tension she explores. She prefers to speak of "a movement *toward* a new way of thinking about human beings."[178]

Prior to treating the RF, she makes two strong claims about the literary character Ezekiel being a sign, more than a messenger, and a prototype for the people in his moral identity. Both of these roles tie into the knowledge of God. First, she argues on the basis of 24:24 that "he himself is a *sign* [מופת] to the people which will bring them new knowledge about who Yahweh is."[179] Secondly, she argues that Ezekiel is a *model* for Israel not so much in his actions, but in the knowledge of Yahweh he has received, "which constitutes the core of his moral self."[180] The prophet is "embodying the knowledge he seeks to convey."[181]

Lapsley leans heavily on Zimmerli's research of the RF as she discusses what constitutes the knowledge of God and how it is aquired. While agreeing that "not recognizing Yahweh is tantamount to disobedience," she also believes Israel is "portrayed as incapable of obeying an imperative concealed in the recognition formula."[182] It is here that she stakes out her position. Israel is presently devoid of a true knowledge of Yahweh, but in the future, they will surely receive that knowledge that "ultimately entails certain behavioral modifications": "In short, the new knowledge of Yahweh will lead inexorably to walking in the statutes and

---

178. Lapsley, *Can These Bones Live?* 6–7 (emphasis original).

179. Lapsley, *Can These Bones Live?* 115 (emphasis original). This claim may overreach in that Ezekiel seems especially a sign/suffer for what Israel will do: bear/suffer for sin; eating siege-rations; be burned, struck with a sword, and scattered (like Ezekiel's hair); pack belongings for exile and carry them off; tremble in eating/drinking; fail to mourn. Is it not "the divine acts themselves that will bring about knowledge of Yahweh" (122)? Is it the case that Ezekiel-as-sign brings a knowledge of the identity of Yahweh "designed to be absorbed in such a way that the self is transformed by this new knowledge"? My preference is to link the sign-acts with knowing Ezekiel is Yahweh's prophet (2:5): God has commanded the sign-acts and he fulfills his promises to judge, as enacted by his prophet.

180. Lapsley, *Can These Bones Live?* 116. However, does the prophecy give any prominence to *Ezekiel's* own knowledge of Yahweh or his own moral self?

181. Lapsley, *Can These Bones Live?* 121.

182. Lapsley, *Can These Bones Live?* 123.

observing the ordinances, but this will be a direct consequence of divine, not human, action."[183]

There is much to commend in Lapsley, but her presentation of the knowledge of Yahweh as including an exclusive relationship with him and moral transformation prompts questions. Can one say that such knowledge "concerns at heart an orientation to existence that shapes human identity and action"? Are all who receive this knowledge "changed at the core of their own identity" and "empowered to choose morally appropriate actions and carry them out"?[184] Does this *knowing* always involve modified behavior?[185] Does her idea of "knowing" as internal transformation work well in the context of terrible judgment oracles (where the majority of RFs occur)? Why do few other interpreters stress a moral/ethical strand of knowing in Ezekiel? While putting such questions, one should not miss Lapsley's intent. Her thesis mainly takes account of RFs in restoration oracles to Israel (28% of the total); what she labels a shift of moral identity applies only to the Israel addressed in the "salvation" chapters, not to the nations.

2.3.12. Dexter Callender Jr.

In a 2015 essay, "The Recognition Formula and Ezekiel's Conception of God," Dexter Callender calls the RF "one of the more difficult aspects of the book," adding that the formula is "virtually unique to Ezekiel,"[186] which is a puzzling assertion. Callender treats the RF in some measure, but he seems most interested in exploring "problematic aspects that Ezekiel presents in his conception of the deity"[187] and how the philosophical, linguistic, and psychoanalytical thought of Jacques Lacan may be brought into the discussion. He believes the RF "addresses the problematic nature of the network of signifiers around which human subjectivity is constituted" and focuses on three features: Yahweh's name and subjectivity according to Lacanian "symbolic order"; "the radical ambiguity of the symbolic order"; and "a situational orientation within the order of the symbolic" whereby "knowledge results from violent or traumatic acts." Callender concludes that the RF "is used by Ezekiel and his editors to exceed onto-theological speculation, and instead approach a self-orienting reflection on radical subjective contingency."[188]

---

183. Lapsley, *Can These Bones Live?* 124.

184. Lapsley, *Can These Bones Live?* 125.

185. This seems pertinent because Lapsley admits the RF, as used in oracles against the nations, does not envision covenant blessings for them (*Can These Bones Live?* 122).

186. Callender, "Recognition Formula," 72. He lists but five texts outside Ezekiel containing the RF: Exod 14:4, 18; 1 Kgs 20:28; Isa 49:23; Joel 3:17. Another puzzle is that he later also has two incoherent references to "the covenant formula 'I am Yahweh your God'" (77).

187. Callender, "Recognition Formula," 85.

188. Callender, "Recognition Formula," 72. In my opinion, Callender's essay is least useful where he reads a Lacanian perspective back into the ancient world: "The language of the book of Ezekiel

Beyond the obscure psychoanalytical theory and structuralism, Callender makes salient points about the covenant orientation of "Yahweh" as a name[189] and Jan Assmann's research on the ANE idea of the deity being manifested in the name's recitation. He examines Exod 6 to demonstrate that "the literary background of the recognition formula lies in covenant language,"[190] and he is impressed that, in 6:7, the covenant formula combines with the RF. He then turns to Ezek 20 and mentions that the opening of the chapter (vv. 5–7) "associates the recognition formula with the imagery of covenant in part by an allusion to the tradition preserved in Exod 6." Furthermore, chapter 20 "emphasizes covenant by reference to the signs of the covenant: statutes and ordinances (vv. 11–12, 18–20, 28–31) along with reference to the Sabbath, given in language reminiscent of Exod 31:12–17."[191] He here appears to accept the research of Risa Levitt Kohn (cited) regarding the prophet's reusing Torah materials.[192]

In keeping with Callender's interest in how a subject is mediated by language, especially in this case by the one name constantly repeated in the RF, he includes good discussion of Yahweh guarding "my holy name" (שֵׁם קָדְשִׁי). He shows the development of the theme as: first, the danger of profaning (חלל) the name is realized when the people defile/profane (טמא) themselves (20:7, 18, 30, 31); then, secondly, in chapter 36 the land is defiled (טמא; vv. 17–18) through Israel's idols; and finally, Yahweh is discredited in the sight of the nations as Israel is dispersed/exiled (vv. 19–20). Callender's fine insight is that all three stages of profanation are reflected "in the revealed attitude of the nations: 'These are the people of Yahweh yet they had to go out of their land' (v. 20)."[193] In a manner comparable to Yahweh's jealousy for his name when he led Israel out of Egypt and when Israel fell into idolatry at Sinai (20:9, 14, 22; cf. Exod 32:12), Yahweh would act in future days "to show myself holy" (20:41), or act "for the sake of my name" (20:44; 36:22–23a) so that it would not be profaned in the sight of the nations. Callender stresses, as few others have, that "the people signify Yahweh's holiness, leading the nations to knowledge of the covenant: 'and the nations shall know that I am Yahweh,

suggests that the prophet and his editors held a view of human subjectivity that embraced such an understanding of the nature of language as carrying within it a sort of Lacanian negation" (74). In this reconstrual of the prophet's thought-world, Ezekiel can be said to cast Yahweh's statutes "as pure signification, with no necessary connection to life and death" (86). Does Callender also mean to raise doubts in his final paragraph that the "I" of the RF has a meaningful, real referent? He writes here: "The speaking 'I' of Ezekiel's Yahweh appears to be anything but onto-theological. The prophet and his editors go beyond mapping a fixed ego-subject onto the deity, and construct instead an image out of complex human subjectivity, constituted in the symbolic order."

189. Callender writes: "In the context of Ezekiel's use of the recognition formula, Yahweh's name participates in the same semantic field as the notion of covenant" ("Recognition Formula," 77).

190. Callender, "Recognition Formula," 75.

191. Callender, "Recognition Formula," 76–77.

192. See Levitt Kohn, "'Mighty Hand and an Outstretched Arm.'"

193. Callender, "Recognition Formula," 79.

says the Lord Yahweh, when I establish my holiness *through you* before their eyes
(בהקדשי בכם לעינים [36:23]).”[194] He says the land is also a signifier as a cleansed
people are restored to their homeland, and he points to God's intention in 36:30
to address the nations' derision: "I will make the fruit of the tree and the produce
of the field abundant, so that you may never again suffer the disgrace (חרפה)
of *famine among the nations*."[195]

In another suggestive passage, Callender argues that "the Gog oracle presents
a reversal that entails a permanent *end to the profaning of the Name*," both for Israel
and for the nations.[196] He draws attention to 39:7, where God declares, "My holy
name I will make known (אודיע) among my people Israel; and I will not let my
holy name be profaned any more; and the nations shall know that I am Yahweh, the
Holy One of Israel." One might add, however, that such language is not restricted
to the Gog oracles (see 20:39, 41). Reflecting on his argument and these Ezekiel
texts, I believe they provide at least a partial answer to the question of why the
RF does not appear in chapters 40–48. The promises of salvation and restoration
indicate a new age when the holiness of Yahweh's name will be acknowledged and
properly guarded; no longer will there be need for the deity to speak and act so
as to judge, remove profanation, and cleanse his people in order for all to "know
that I am Yahweh." Callender summarizes:

> The notion of the sign figures prominently in the calculus of the recognition for-
> mula, but this also functions within a broader context according to which the people
> and land are signs to the nations. The name, the people, and the land, all stand for
> the subject Yahweh and become sacred or profane as signs of the complex subjec-
> tivity of Yahweh.[197]

2.3.13. Related Studies on Exodus and Isaiah

Parallel to the past research of Ezekiel's RF, there have been studies of the formula as it occurs in the book of Exodus and elsewhere in the OT. A few of the
more recent of these are worth noting in passing. One written by Marc Vervenne
deserves special mention because of its highly detailed nature and its ancillary
discussion of the RF in Ezekiel.

---

194. Callender, "Recognition Formula," 79n32, helpfully ties in Ezek 20:41, "where Yahweh's
holiness is manifested *in the sight of the nations,* . . . immediately followed in v. 42 by the recognition
formula which is further clarified through a covenantal allusion ('You shall know that I am Yahweh,
when I bring you into the land of Israel, the country that I swore to give to your ancestors')."
195. Callender, "Recognition Formula," 80 (emphasis original).
196. Callender, "Recognition Formula," 80 (emphasis original).
197. Callender, "Recognition Formula," 80.

First of all, an article by Randall Bailey on the book of Exodus, though it includes the wording of the formula in its title, may be quickly passed over, since the RF is scarcely discussed and the thesis is muddled.[198] Secondly, Lyle Eslinger has contributed two studies to the discussion of the formula in Exodus. His initial article ("Freedom or Knowledge") argues that the number of occurrences of the RF indicates that the theme of "knowing Yahweh" is more central to the exodus narrative than is the theme of liberation. Redemption out of the house of bondage has as its goal Israel's true knowledge of Yahweh and their freedom to worship him. Liberation is the means to an end.[199] Eslinger's later article ("Knowing Yahweh") briefly reviews the work of Zimmerli on the RF, but focuses primarily on the crux of Exod 6:3 and the much-discussed solution of R. W. L. Moberly.[200] In Eslinger's proposed reworking of Moberly's thesis, the wording in Exod 6:3—"by my name Yahweh I was not known"—is best read as a RF variant. Eslinger says we must pay closer attention to the "collocation" *ydʿ* + *Yahweh*. Further, as we realize "the technical nature of the phrase 'knowing Yahweh' in Exodus and especially Ezekiel,"[201] we cannot assume that "knowing Yahweh" means the same as "calling on the name of Yahweh." If one asks Eslinger what the "technical nature of the phrase" is, he contends that God is not claiming in Exod 6:3 that the name had not been used previously, but that "no one had ever known him by the name Yahweh" through experiencing "his awesome interventions in human affairs."[202] In other words, the collocation makes sense only as a description of revelation received in the context of historical interventions such as the exodus.

Because Eslinger associates the RF in Ezekiel with its use in Exodus, there is the implication that the exile/return and the exodus are events of the same order

198. Bailey, "And they shall know that I am YHWH!" Bailey argues there was an unsuccessful attempt by P to replace the liberation theme that was the thrust of earlier sources (J, E) in the "plague narratives" (nomenclature Bailey rejects). In P's recasting, what is stressed is a competition between YHWH and the gods of Egypt and a related call to piety (to know YHWH). He considers the RF a marker of the Priestly school's "desire to supplant liberation thought" (17). What seems to have escaped Bailey's notice is that, according to traditional source criticism, the formula is just as prominent in J as in P. This overthrows both his general argument regarding the theological thrust of Exodus and his specific interpretation of the RF's meaning and function in the narrative.

199. Eslinger, "Freedom or Knowledge?" A contrasting study of the exodus narratives, not mentioned by Eslinger, is Miranda, *Marx and the Bible*, 44–53, 78–88. Miranda discusses the RF, especially in Exodus, and emphasizes the liberation theme.

200. Eslinger, "Knowing Yahweh." The work by Moberly is *The Old Testament of the Old Testament*. The latter argues that Exod 6:3 should be read in a straightforward fashion. The patriarchs and other characters in the biblical story prior to Moses did not know the name Yahweh at all. The use of the divine name in the speech of characters in Genesis (4:1, 26, etc.) is anachronistic and "conveys the perspective of the Yahwistic storytellers, who are retelling originally non-Yahwistic traditions in a Yahwistic context" (70). Thus, a source-critical solution or a harmonization strategy (e.g., the patriarchs knew the name but not its significance) is unnecessary.

201. Eslinger, "Knowing Yahweh," 193.

202. Eslinger, "Knowing Yahweh," 194.

or class. Yahweh is intervening in awesome historical acts of judgment and deliverance, and in this context, he will make himself known. Further, one can "know
that I am Yahweh" only when that is the deity's announced intention and when
the deity acts in history. Where Yahweh proclaims his name in explicit association
with the prophesied events, there and only there can one *know*. One may speak
the name *Yahweh* without knowing:

> Might not humans who can use the name reasonably be said to "know Yahweh"?
> Well Pharaoh certainly uses the name in Exod 5:2, but his is an ironic disclaimer of
> such knowledge in the same breath with which he utters the name. To use the name
> is not necessarily to know "I am Yahweh" according to the theological conventions at
> work here. The collocation *yd* + *Yahweh* has, in biblical literature, an inflexible refer-
> ence. It describes a unique cognitive state born of a particular experience derived
> from special intervention by Yahweh in human affairs. So the statement made by
> Yahweh seems true for the patriarchal period that he describes in Exod 6:3.
>   Unfortunately, for divine purposes, the same truth persists for the remainder of
> biblical history (cf. Ezek 20).[203]

Another one of Eslinger's most important points is a distinction between "salvation" and the "knowledge of Yahweh." He argues that "the salvation of Israel was not
his [Yahweh's] primary purpose. The logic of the divine intervention is that knowledge of Yahweh comes before liberation from Egypt, both in fact and in priority."[204]

The above-mentioned essay by Vervenne concerns "The Phraseology of 'Knowing YHWH' in the Hebrew Bible."[205] It gives special attention to Isaiah but also
provides data on other OT books, Exodus and Ezekiel included. The strengths of
the work are less theological and more syntactical analysis, and Vervenne supplies
a wealth of technical information for comparing language in different books. He is
interested in all texts that speak of knowing Yahweh, not just the RF.[206] With regard
to the RF, Vervenne follows the procedure established by Zimmerli of dividing the

203. Eslinger, "Knowing Yahweh," 196.
204. Eslinger, "Knowing Yahweh," 195. One can argue with this claim, for the narrative appears
to connect the full recognition of Yahweh's power and authority, by both the Egyptians and Israelites,
with the parting of the Red Sea and the drowning of the Egyptian army (see Exod 14:4–5, 11, 18, 25,
30–31).
205. Vervenne, "Phraseology of 'Knowing YHWH.'" Perhaps it was too ambitious to attempt
in a single article to compile and synthesize all the OT material on this topic. Vervenne's data on
Ezekiel is slightly confusing at two or three points. E.g., he says, the "recognition formula in the strict
sense of the word appears most frequently in the book of Ezekiel (69×)" (474), but in the very next
sentence, Vervenne tallies the formulas as follows: chs. 1–24 = 36×; chs. 25–32 = 19×; chs. 33–39 =
22×; making the total 77×, not 69×.
206. Therefore, he discusses such passages as Elijah's prayer in 1 Kgs 18:36–37: "O Yahweh, God of
Abraham, Isaac and Israel, let it be known today that you are God in Israel . . . answer me, O Yahweh,
answer me, that these people may know that you, O Yahweh, are God."

refrain into two parts: "the expression of the act of knowing" (ידע כי), which he prefers to call *Erkenntnisaussage* with Zimmerli, and "the expression of the content of knowing" (though variable, commonly אני יהוה), which he terms *Erkenntnisinhalt*. Vervenne has strengthened the foundation laid by Zimmerli and others,[207] so future scholars may build well.

2.4. Conclusion

In concluding this review, I briefly note some more important points of controversy or confusion in the literature and analyze the similarities and differences among scholars on key interpretive issues. In addition, I indicate how this study moves beyond work previously done and offers a fresh perspective on the literary and theological function of the RFs in Ezekiel.

There have been encouraging developments in the course of scholarship on Ezekiel's RF, especially over the last sixty years. Prior to Zimmerli's essays, especially in post–World War I scholarship, the formula was frequently rejected as part of the original prophecy (Herrmann, Hölscher, Fohrer, and May), with the result that little attention was paid to it. It was an accretion to be recognized and deleted, rather than a meaningful refrain to be interpreted in the prophet's theology. Since Zimmerli's foundational essays, most Ezekiel scholars have recognized the RF as both authentic and integral to the prophetic oracles, even if they have respectfully quarreled with a number of Zimmerli's conclusions regarding the source influencing Ezekiel's usage and the *Erweiswort* idea (Fohrer). Zimmerli sparked debate on many interpretive issues, and his voice continues to stand out in today's debates.

Among the points of controversy or confusion in past scholarship, the following deserve special mention. (1) Further exegetical research is required regarding the exact number of occurrences of the formula in Ezekiel, as there are wild discrepancies in scholars' data. Margaret Odell estimates that the RF "occurs some fifty-five times throughout the book," and Greenberg speaks of "some sixty occurrences," while Bernhard Lang says it is "etwa achtzig Mal" that the formula appears.[208] Several agree on eighty-six as the correct tally of formulas.[209] Even those who

---

207. E.g., Floss, *Jahwe Dienen—Göttern Dienen*. For general studies on the theme of the knowledge of God in the OT (besides Vervenne, Floss, and others previously cited), see also: Hänel, *Erkennen Gottes*; Mowinckel, *Erkenntnis Gottes*; Botterweck, *"Gott erkennen"*; Wolff, "'Wissen um Gott'"; Wolff, "Erkenntnis Gottes"; Baumann, "'Wissen um Gott'"; Gaboriau, "La connaissance de Dieu"; Dentan, *Knowledge of God*; Seeligmann, "Erkenntnis Gottes"; Vall, "Epistemology of Faith"; Carew, "To Know or Not to Know"; and articles on דעת/ידע in the theological lexicons.

208. Odell, *Ezekiel*, 81; Greenberg, *Ezekiel 1–20*, 133; Lang, *Ezechiel*, 92.

209. Towner, *Daniel*, 176; Hanson, *People Called*, 217. This tally of eighty-six represents the occurrences of ידע in the Qal stem within the prophecy, but fourteen of those have no association with the RF (e.g., 10:20: "I knew that they were cherubim").

have done the most careful work on this topic offer different counts. Joyce says the formula "occurs fifty-four times in its basic form and over twenty more times with minor variations."[210] Strong provides a list of seventy-three.[211] William Tooman's well-received dissertation claims the RF appears sixty-nine times, but in another essay, he gives the total as fifty-eight.[212] Zimmerli catalogs seventy-two formulas in his 1954 booklet *Erkenntnis Gottes nach dem Buche Ezechiel*, but strangely he makes reference to ninety-two RFs in the first appendix of his work in the BKAT series. Other individuals offering disparate counts are Block (see n. 157 above) and Vervenne (see n. 205). There is need, then, to clear away confusion at this point.

(2) Another contentious point is the source of Ezekiel's RF. Prior to Zimmerli, some proposed that Ezekiel (or a later redactor) drew the refrain from Deutero-Isaiah and that its meaning is consistent between the two prophets (Blank, May). Others believed that all of Ezekiel's RFs (Haag) or portions of Ezekiel employing the RF such as chapter 20 (Blank again) reveal a dependence on P. It was Zimmerli who first posited that the "proof-saying," an old prophetic *Gattung* used in oracles against the nations and exemplified in 1 Kgs 20, was the original context for the formula and that Ezekiel has been influenced by that prophetic tradition. Many have followed closely in Zimmerli's steps (Carley, Hals, and Strong) or cited his conclusions without evident dissent (Greenberg and Allen). Other have expressed a mild (Rendtorff and Joyce) or strong preference for the view that Ezekiel's RF is drawn from the exodus "narratives" or the "priestly traditions" now reflected in Exodus (Fohrer, Harner, Joseph Blenkinsopp, Eslinger, and Block). This point of debate will be taken up in chapter 4.

(3) Scholars are sharply divided over certain matters of theological interpretation. Where Ezekiel's RF is addressed to the nations, does the phrasing "know that I am Yahweh" indicate God's missionary purpose to reveal himself to foreign nations in salvation and covenant blessing? Does the RF indicate that the nations will participate in salvation? While some aver that it does (Reventlow, von Rad, Eichrodt, and Ackroyd), others claim it does not (Cooke, Yehezkel Kaufmann, Katheryn Darr, Strong, and Block). More work is needed to discern what it means to *know* and also what is meant by the object clause "I am Yahweh" in the context of oracles against the nations. Is the meaning of the RF in those oracles similar to the meaning of the formula when spoken to Israel? How does the message of the RF in oracles of judgment compare with the message of the formula in oracles of deliverance or restoration?

---

210. Joyce, *Divine Initiative*, 89.

211. Strong, "Egypt's Shameful Death," 481. He includes 25:9.

212. In *Gog of Magog*, Tooman writes: "Variations on the recognition formula are very common in Ezekiel, appearing seventy-eight times. Most common is the expression ידע + כי־אני יהוה (69 times)" (41). However, he states elsewhere that the RF occurs fifty-eight times in Ezekiel ("Transformation," 52).

(4) How is the phrase אני יהוה to be understood? Yes, there are certain more literary issues here that scholars debate: (a) whether to separate it out as a part of the RF with a distinct *Sitz im Leben* (Zimmerli) or not (Joyce); and (b) whether it functions as a formula of divine self-introduction (Zimmerli)[213] or as an assertion of authority (Rendtorff). Perhaps it could be read instead as a formula of "self-manifestation" (Odell) or a "self-declaratory statement" (Catrin Williams)? Others have spoken of a *Hoheitsformel* (Karl Elliger), *Imponierformel* (Lang), *Ausschließlichkeitsformel* (Sedlmeier), or *Autoritätsformel* (Joachim Becker).[214]

But, alongside the literary issues, there are also theological questions about the meaning of אני יהוה as a component within the RF; those beg for attention in this study too. May one properly interpret the name Yahweh as carrying certain theological freight? Emphasizing the holy-war context, Strong understands *Yahweh* to carry the meaning of "Divine Warrior" within the RF. As mentioned, this is in opposition to Zimmerli, who insists that the formula always has self-introduction at its heart and that the name represents "the mystery that cannot be reduced to a definition." Should the "self-predication statement" be read as a self-introduction, as self-presentation, as self-assertion? Such questions call for discussion.

Eichrodt, Greenberg, Block, Brevard Childs, Lawrence Boadt, and others have noted that the prophet Ezekiel shows an acquaintance with Israel's sacred literature. The present study seeks answers to many of the questions posed above by exploring the literary relationship between Ezekiel and Exodus and moves beyond existing scholarship (especially since Zimmerli) in two respects: (1) its concentration on the RF, with the unanswered questions about it, and (2) an argument that the literary and theological function of the formula in Ezekiel is best illumined by identifying and interpreting the intertextual relationship between Ezekiel and Exodus.

---

213. Zimmerli's term *Selbstvorstellung* is best translated "self-introduction" but can also carry the idea of self-presentation. His classification is supported by Anja Angela Diesel in *"Ich bin Jahwe"* (107). She adds, however, that *Selbstvorstellung* is a rarer usage, alongside *Selbstidentifikation* and what she terms *Selbstvergegenwärtigung* (God making himself present).

214. Odell, "'Are You He?'" 130; Williams, *I Am He*, 23; Elliger, *Deuterojesaja*, 462; Lang, *Ezechiel*, 95; Sedlmeier, *Studien*, 308; Becker, "Zur 'Ich bin'-Formel," 46. Karin Schöpflin lists still more options and critiques Zimmerli's *Selbstvorstellung* proposal in *Theologie als Biographie*, 114–16.

CHAPTER 3

Details of the Formula's Usage in Ezekiel

In his essay "The Knowledge of God according to the Book of Ezekiel," Zimmerli aptly refers to the "tenacious reoccurrence" (*hartnäckige Wiederholung*)[1] of the formula, "you (or they) shall know that I am Yahweh." The verb ידע appears in Qal more frequently in Ezekiel than any other Bible book.[2] Of the eighty-six occurrences there, the vast majority (seventy-two) are some variation of the "exceedingly important"[3] RF. There are only fourteen occurrences of ידע in Qal in Ezekiel apart from the RF.[4]

Clearly, from the list on the following pages, Ezekiel contains a remarkable variety of RFs. They are not so "stereotyped" as some think. This study is restricted to those employing ידע with the clause כי אני יהוה.[5] Those occurrences that have just the verb and the three-word clause are known as the "strict form," to be discussed in this chapter. Other RFs are expansions on that shorter form, and these too merit attention. At the bottom of the list are added sections of "Other ידע Phrases Similar to the Formula," and "Other Phrases without ידע Similar to the Formula." Though these are not strictly within the purview of this research, they are noted as bearing some relation to the RF proper.

1. Zimmerli, *I Am Yahweh*, 30 [*Gottes Offenbarung*, 42].
2. *New Concordance to the Old Testament* (Even-Shoshan) indicates that 1–2 Sam has the next highest count (seventy-seven), and there are 821 total occurrences of ידע in Qal in the Hebrew Bible.
3. Hals, *Ezekiel*, 32.
4. 2:5; 10:20; 11:5; 14:23; 17:12; 19:7; 25:14; 28:19; 32:9; 33:33; 37:3; 38:14, 16; 39:23. A few of these strongly resemble the RF (2:5; 14:23; 25:14; 33:33; 38:16), and one appears to develop from and tie in with an immediately preceding formula (39:23). In the remainder, the subjects are: Ezekiel (10:20); Yahweh (11:5; 37:3); the people of Israel (17:12); the king of Judah, or second princely lion cub (19:7); international observers of Tyre's downfall (28:19); Pharaoh (32:9); and Gog (38:14).
5. There is one exception. I include 20:26, the one occurrence in which the conj. כי is replaced by אשר, but this is not considered as a true "strict form."

3.1. List of Ezekiel's Recognition Formulas and Related Phrases

3.1.1. The "Strict" Recognition Formula and Expansions—Second Person

וידעתם כי־אני יהוה

(A) And/then you (pl.) shall know that I am Yahweh
19×: 6:7, 13;[6] 7:4; 11:10, 12; 12:20; 13:14, 21, 23 (vv. 21 and 23 have וידעתן); 14:8; 15:7; 20:38, 42, 44; 25:5; 35:9; 36:11; 37:6, 13

וידעת כי־אני יהוה

(B) And/then you (sg.) shall know that I am Yahweh
4×: 16:62; 22:16; 25:7; 35:4

וידעתם כי אני אדני יהוה

(C) And/then you shall know that I am Lord Yahweh
3×: 13:9; 23:49; 24:24

לדעת כי אני יהוה אלהיכם

(D) So that you will know that I am Yahweh your God
1×: 20:20 (with inf. const.)

וידעתם כי אני יהוה דברתי

(E) And/then you shall know that I am Yahweh, I have spoken (or: that I, Yahweh, have spoken)
2×: 17:21; 37:14; cf. 5:13

וידעתם כי אני יהוה מכה

(F) And/then you shall know that I am Yahweh, who smites (or: [it is] I, Yahweh, who smites)
1×: 7:9

וידעתם כי־אני יהוה שפכתי חמתי עליכם

(G) And/then you shall know that I am Yahweh, I have poured out my wrath upon you (or: that I, Yahweh, have poured)
1×: 22:22

---

6. The NIV (1978, 1984, 2011) renders 6:13 as a third-person plural.

וידעת כי־אני יהוה שמעתי את־כל־נאצותיך אשר אמרת

(H) And/then you (sg.) shall know that I am Yahweh, I have heard all the contemptible things you have said (or: I, Yahweh, have heard all the contemptible things ...)
1×: 35:12

3.1.2. The "Strict" Recognition Formula and Expansions—Third Person

וידעו כי־אני יהוה

(I) And/then they shall know that I am Yahweh
23×: 6:14; 7:27; 12:15, 16; 24:27; 25:11, 17; 26:6; 28:22, 23; 29:9, 21; 30:8, 19, 25, 26; 32:15; 33:29; 34:27; 35:15; 36:38; 38:23; 39:6

למען אשר ידעו אשר אני יהוה

(J) So that they would know that I am Yahweh
1×: 20:26 (with Qal impf. and אשר instead of כי)[7]

וידעו כי־אני יהוה לא אל־חנם דברתי לעשות להם הרעה הזאת

(K) And/then they shall know that I am Yahweh; I did not speak in vain about bringing this disaster on them (or: They shall know that I, Yahweh, did not speak in vain about bringing this disaster on them)
1×: 6:10

וידעו כי אני אדני יהוה

(L) And/then they shall know that I am Lord Yahweh
2×: 28:24; 29:16

וידעו כי אני יהוה אלהיהם

(M) And/then they shall know that I am Yahweh their God
2×: 28:26; 39:28

וידעו בית ישראל כי אני יהוה אלהיהם

(N) And/then the house of Israel shall know that I am Yahweh their God
1×: 39:22

וידעו כל־ישבי מצרים כי אני יהוה

(O) And all that live in Egypt shall know that I am Yahweh
1×: 29:6

7. Note the discussion below of this formula's absence in the LXX and the questions raised by scholars about it being secondary.

וידעו הגוים כי־אני יהוה

(P) And/then the nations shall know that I am Yahweh

1×: 36:23

וידעו הגוים כי אני יהוה מקדש את־ישראל

(Q) And the nations shall know that I am Yahweh, I make Israel holy (or: that I, Yahweh, make Israel holy)

1×: 37:28

וידעו הגוים כי־אני יהוה קדוש בישראל

(R) And/then the nations shall know that I am Yahweh, the Holy One in Israel (or: that I, Yahweh, am the Holy One in Israel)

1×: 39:7

וידעו הגוים אשר ישארו סביבותיכם כי אני יהוה בניתי

(S) And/then the nations that remain around you shall know that I am Yahweh, I have rebuilt (or: that I, Yahweh, have rebuilt)

1×: 36:36

וידעו כי־אני יהוה דברתי בקנאתי בכלותי חמתי בם

(T) And/then they shall know that I am Yahweh, I have spoken in my rage when I spend my wrath against them (or: that I, Yahweh, have spoken in my rage . . .)

1×: 5:13

וידעו כי אני יהוה אלהיהם אתם

(U) And they shall know that I am Yahweh their God, I am with them (or: that I, Yahweh their God, am with them)

1×: 34:30

לדעת כי אני יהוה מקדשם

(V) So they would know that I am Yahweh, who makes them holy (or: that I, Yahweh, made/make them holy)

1×: 20:12 (with inf. const.)

וידעו כל־עצי השדה כי אני יהוה השפלתי עץ גבה

(W) And all the trees of the field shall know that I am Yahweh; I bring down the tall tree (or: . . . that I, Yahweh, bring down the tall tree)

1×: 17:24

וידעו כל־בשר כי אני יהוה הוצאתי חרבי מתערה

(X) And all flesh shall know that I am Yahweh, I have drawn my sword from its scabbard (or: that I, Yahweh, have drawn my sword from its scabbard)
1×: 21:10[5]

3.1.3. Other ידע Phrases Similar to the Recognition Formula

וידעו כי נביא היה בתוכם

And they shall know that a prophet has been among them
2×: 2:5; 33:33

וידעתם כי לא חנם עשיתי את כל־אשר־עשיתי בה נאם אדני יהוה

And you shall know that I have not done without cause all that I have done in her [Jerusalem], declares the Lord Yahweh
1×: 14:23

וידעו את־נקמתי נאם אדני יהוה

And they shall know my vengeance, declares the Lord Yahweh
1×: 25:14

לא למענכם אני־עשה נאם אדני יהוה יודע לכם

Not for your sake will I do [this], declares the Lord Yahweh, let it be known to you
1×: 36:32[8]

למען דעת הגוים אתי בהקדשי בך

So that the nations may know me when I demonstrate my holiness through you
1×: 38:16 (with inf. const.)

וידעו הגוים כי בעונם גלו בית־ישראל

And the nations shall know that the house of Israel went into exile for their iniquity
1×: 39:23

3.1.4. Other Phrases Without ידע Similar to the Formula

וראו כל־בשר כי אני יהוה בערתיה לא תכבה

All flesh shall see that I am Yahweh, I have kindled it, it shall not be quenched (or: that I, Yahweh, have kindled it; it will not be quenched)
1×: 21:4 [20:48]

---

8. Moshe Greenberg terms this "a skewed recognition formula" (*Ezekiel 21–37*, 734).

וראו כל־הגוים את־משפטי אשר עשיתי ואת־ידי אשר־שמתי בהם

And all nations shall see my judgment which I execute and my hand which I lay upon them.

1×: 39:21

3.2. Analysis of the Formula's Usage

3.2.1. *The Shorter "Strict Form" and the "Expansions"*

The RFs are usually divided as to usage into several categories, with special attention given to the "basic form"[9] or "formally strict version" (*festen formalen Geprägtheit*).[10] It seems best to follow that pattern here. Besides the basic form, there are numerous longer or expanded formulas. Use of the term "expanded" is meant to be phenomenological, descriptive only of its enlarged form and not indicating derivation from the strict form. From this vantage point, the longer forms may be categorized as expansions *on* the basic form without stipulating that they are expansions *of* the basic form in a genetic sense.

Most important to interpreters is the shorter form,[11] "and you/they shall know that I am Yahweh" (categories A, B, and I above). Compared with the expanded forms, the shorter "strict form" predominates with forty-six[12] out of seventy-two total RFs.[13] That simple, shorter refrain is evenly divided between occurrences having second-person verbs (twenty-three) and those with third-person verbs (also twenty-three). When one takes into account the entire range of RFs, thirty-one verbs are second person and thirty-nine are in the third person.[14]

9. Joyce, *Divine Initiative*, 89.

10. Zimmerli, *I Am Yahweh*, 100 [*Gottes Offenbarung*, 121]. Hossfeld chooses to use the adjective *streng* (*Untersuchungen*, 41).

11. The designation "short form" (*Kurzform*) is used by Hans Ferdinand Fuhs in *Ezechiel 1–24*, 41. One also discovers it in the *TDOT* article on ידע by G. Botterweck (*TDOT*, 5:471). This designation would be excellent because it is simply descriptive and does not—as with "pure form" (*reiner Form*; Zimmerli, *Ezechiel*, 1:57*)—beg the question with regard to issues of origin and development. The prime difficulty in using "short form" is Zimmerli's application of the term to the "formula of self-introduction" (אני יהוה). The terms "shorter form" and "strict form" are, instead, employed in this study.

12. Zimmerli identifies fifty-four RFs as the "pure form" (*Ezekiel 1*, 38), to be distinguished from expanded forms. What explains his larger number than the forty-six reported here? He employs a broader definition of "pure/shorter form" and includes categories (C, J, L, O, P above) not allowed in this study's definition (ידע Qal pf., *waw*-conj. + כי אני יהוה). E.g., Zimmerli includes refrains that expand the object clause with the very common "double designation of God" as אדני יהוה (*Ezekiel* 2, 558).

13. For a list of Ezekiel's RFs in consecutive order, see Table 6.

14. In addition to these seventy, two RFs employ the Qal inf. const.: 20:12 (third-person, understood from context) and 20:20 (second-person, understood).

Among the twenty-six formulas that differ from the strict "shorter form" and
that show a range of permutations, nine are verbally expanded (e.g., "they shall
know that I, Yahweh, did not threaten in vain").[15] In a larger total of fifteen cases
the RF is expanded nominally.[16] These may be expansions either of the subject
who recognizes (e.g., "*all who live in Egypt* shall know . . .") or of the divine predicate who is recognized (e.g., ". . . that I am Yahweh *their God*"). The formula is
expanded with a predicate participle in three places (e.g., ". . . know that I, Yahweh,
strike").[17] Some individual RFs are expanded in a couple ways; for example, the RF
in 17:24 (sole example in category W above) has both verbal and nominal expansion. Two other formulas differ from the shorter refrain in unique ways: 34:30
forms the predicate with a prepositional phrase,[18] and 20:26[19] replaces the conjunction כי with אשר, which is less frequently used in introducing the subordinate
object clause throughout the OT.[20] (This study discusses below the text-critical
problem of 20:26.)

3.2.2. Confirming the Total Number of Formulas in Ezekiel

Regrettably, at the conclusion of his commentary, Zimmerli brings confusion
with regard to the tally of RFs. That confusion needs to be cleared away. Earlier,
in his essays of the 1950s and in his commentary introduction, he carefully delin-
eated seventy-two refrains and cataloged the various formulations (strict form
and expansions). He also discussed related texts such as 21:4[20:48], which reads
ראה instead of ידע.[21] That research informs, and is also confirmed in, the present
study, although with a few refinements. However, in an appendix (late 1968) to his

---

15. Ezek 5:13; 6:10; 17:21, 24 (also nominally expanded); 21:10[5] (also nominally expanded);
22:22; 35:12; 36:36; 37:14. (These comprise categories E, G, H, K, S, T, W, and X above.)

16. Ezek 13:9; 17:24 (also verbally expanded); 20:20; 21:10[5] (also verbally expanded); 23:49;
24:24; 28:24; 28:26; 29:6; 29:16; 34:30; 36:23; 39:7 (also adjectivally expanded); 39:22; 39:28. (These
comprise categories C, D, L, M, N, O, P, R, U, W, and X above.)

17. Ezek 7:9; 20:12; 37:28. (These comprise categories F, Q, and V above.)

18. Category U above.

19. Category J above.

20. GKC, §157a; IBHS, §38.8.d.

21. Zimmerli comes close to regarding this text as a true RF: "Unusual in the recognition formula
is not only the variation of the customary ידע to ראה . . ." (*Ezekiel* 1, 424). In listing all the formulas,
however, he excludes 21:4[20:48] and arrives at the same number recognized by this study: seventy-
two. See "The Knowledge of God According to the Book of Ezekiel," esp. 30–31 and nn. 5–9. "In order
to be thorough, we need to *include within the context of this form of speech* one or perhaps two passages
in which the verb *ydʿ* is replaced by *rʾh* (to see), a term frequently used as its parallel" (31; emphasis
added). Zimmerli ultimately concludes that the phrases with ראה are "analogous formations" (31).
HALOT (s.v. ידע) lists several texts in which the two verbs are used together in a synonymous fashion:
1 Sam 12:17; 24:12; 1 Kgs 20:7; 2 Kgs 5:7; Jer 2:19. One may add to this list Isa 5:19. For discussion of ידע
and ראה as frequent "synonymous readings" that are best read together, see Talmon, "Synonymous
Readings."

commentary, he discusses the "dual designation of God" and makes a surprising reference to "the *five* cases of אדני יהוה in some recognition formulae in the proof saying (13:9; 23:49; 24:24; 28:24; 29:16)" and the "overwhelming majority of *eighty-seven* (including 20:5, 7, 19) recognition formulae which have simple יהוה."[22]

There are several problems arising from Zimmerli's appendix and the quote above. (1) The reader is surprised at the much larger number of ninety-two total RFs in Ezekiel (eighty-seven instances with simply יהוה plus five with אדני יהוה). What explains the discrepancy between Zimmerli's earlier count of seventy-two and the later tally of ninety-two? There certainly was no typographical error (mistyped "87"instead of "67"; as 67+5 = 72), which we know for two reasons: (a) later in that appendix, there is another reference to the eighty-seven RFs "without the addition of אדני"; and (b) the passages he includes in the high count of eighty-seven (Ezek 20:5, 7, 19) are never listed among those texts that earlier totalled his sixty-seven formulas without אדני. (2) Though the discrepancy in Zimmerli's writings on this point is obvious, he never explains it. Also, he gives no clues how he may have redefined *Erkenntnisformel* more broadly so as to expand the range of phrases he includes in his tally. (3) Even by including all the phrases in Ezekiel that are similar to the RF, as defined in both Zimmerli's early essays and in this study, the reader still cannot find ninety-two formulas that contain the divine name. Even when including all the previously defined *Erkenntnisformeln*, all the related phrases that contain the divine name יהוה, and all the other texts in Ezekiel that contain "knowing Yahweh" language, one falls short of even eighty occurrences. (4) It appears impossible to reconcile Zimmerli's earlier and later figures.

Zimmerli's initial work, which was far more detailed, complete, and focused, should be reckoned as his true position and as providing his most reliable conclusions. (That work is also the most cited in discussions of the RF.) I urge that the data and the conclusions based on it, established in 120 pages of Zimmerli's programmatic work,[23] should not be overturned by a pair of puzzling references

22. Zimmerli, *Ezekiel 2*, 556 (emphasis added). There is grammatical ambiguity in the translation: does the subordinate clause, "which have simple יהוה," have "majority" or "recognition formulae" as its antecedent? There is quite a difference between saying, "the majority (greater portion) of 87 formulae which contain simple יהוה," and saying, "the 87 formulae which contain simple יהוה." The German is clearer, and a fuller citation is in order: "Man möchte danach fragen, ob auch die 5 Fällen von אדני יהוה in einigen Erkenntnisformeln des Erweiswortes (13:9; 23:49; 24:24; 28:24; 29:16) als geschlossene Gruppe zusammenzunehmen seien. Ihnen steht aber eine überwältigende Mehrzahl von (mit Einrechnung von 20:5, 7, 19) 87 Erkenntnisformeln gegenüber, die einfaches יהוה enthalten" (*Ezechiel*, 2:1250–51). Zimmerli here specifies that the eighty-seven formulas with simple יהוה must be added to the five with אדני יהוה, resulting in a total of ninety-two RFs in Ezekiel.

23. Zimmerli, "The Knowledge of God According to the Book of Ezekiel" (29–98 in *I am Yahweh*) "Word of Divine Self-Manifestation (Proof-Saying), A Prophetic Genre" (99–110 in *I am Yahweh*) and "Introduction" in *Ezekiel 1*, 36–41 [*Ezechiel*, 1:55*–62*].

in an appendix. At this point, it is also important to take note that many scholars have not been so strict about the final tally of seventy-two. Zimmerli himself occasionally names as *Erkenntnisformeln* some among those eight texts that are related to the RF but do not exactly fit his definition of the formula (see 3.1.3–4. above). For example, when he comes to exegete 2:5 in his commentary, he writes: "Zum erstenmal begegnet hier eine der für das Buch Ez in besonderer Weise charakteristischen Erkenntnis-formulierungen."[24] I also mention in this regard Bernhard Lang, who follows Frank Lothar Hossfeld in adding the eight "related phrases" to the standard seventy-two formulas to reach a count of eighty.[25]

3.2.3. *Text-Critical and Redaction-Critical Issues*

As previously noted, the Septuagintal text of Ezekiel (esp. Papyrus 967, ca. AD 200) is considerably shorter than the Masoretic text, and the LXX also contains certain transpositions (esp. in 7:1–11). Some older scholars, Gustav Jahn and Walther Eichrodt among them, as well as leading text critic Johan Lust,[26] have expressed strong confidence in the value of the LXX Ezekiel as "a witness to an earlier 'canonical' Hebrew text"[27] notably shorter than the MT. However, recent studies on the Hebrew manuscripts from Qumran and especially Masada—predating Pap967 by over two centuries—indicates "a broadly proto-Masoretic text, which contains sections absent in the pre-Hexaplaric Greek versions."[28] Our concern here is only with the RF. Might one expect that the shorter LXX would contain fewer occurrences of the refrain? As it turns out, the Göttingen edition[29] shows that the Septuagint includes all the RFs found in the Hebrew with one exception.[30] The refrain in 20:26 is missing in the LXX. An additional discrepancy between the two traditions is a displacement of oracular material in chapter 7 that affects the

24. *Ezechiel*, 1:73. See also his discussion of 21:4[20:48] in *Ezekiel 1*, 315, 424 (*Ezechiel*, 1:322, 466), and of 39:21 in *Ezekiel 2*, 319 (*Ezechiel*, 2:968).

25. Lang speaks of the RF occurring "etwa achtzig Mal" (*Ezechiel*, 92). See also Hossfeld, *Untersuchungen*, 40–46, and Odell, "Are You He?" 126–63.

26. Jahn, *Ezechiel*; Lust, "Ezekiel 36–40." See also Pierre-Maurice Bogaert, "Le deux rédactions conservées."

27. Lust, "Major Divergences," 92. Reaching a similar conclusion are Klein, *Schriftauslegung*, 60–65, and Lilly, *Two Books of Ezekiel*. Leading commentators, however, are dubious: Zimmerli, *Ezekiel 2*, 245; Greenberg, *Ezekiel 21–37*, 739; Block, *Ezekiel 25–48*, 338–43; Joyce, *Ezekiel*, 205–6.

28. Hector M. Patmore, "The Shorter and Longer Texts," 231. See Talmon, Newsom, and Yadin, *Masada VI*, 59–75. For further discussion and bibliography, see Lange, "Ancient Hebrew Texts." Johan Lust continues to hold that the three longer "minuses" in LXX "are witnesses to an earlier Hebrew text in which these sections were not yet added" ("Ezekiel Text," 161). One must now take account of the thorough research of Ashley S. Crane (*Israel's Restoration*) and Timothy P. Mackie (*Expanding Ezekiel*).

29. Ziegler, *Ezechiel*. In the shorter Pap967, there are an additional two RFs missing (36:36, 38) with the major "minuses" of 12:26–28, 32:25–26, and 36:23b–38.

30. Observe that Vaticanus omits 11:11–12 (RF in v. 12); Alexandrinus does not.

formulas we are studying. The RF in MT 7:4 is located at LXX 7:8, while the one in MT 7:9 is located at LXX 7:6, a reversal in order of appearance.

The text-critical problem of 20:26 deserves consideration. Because the RF and its introduction (למען ידעו אשר אני יהוה) are missing in the Septuagint's rendering and in certain other ancient witnesses,[31] some are inclined to treat the text as secondary.[32] They believe the wisdom of their decision is confirmed by internal evidence, noting that no other formula in Ezekiel has either the introductory phrase למען אשר or אשר in place of כי within the object clause. Finally, the imperfect sets this RF apart as unique and as a likely insertion by a later hand that did not conform to the usual pattern of use (*perfectum consecutivum*). More recent commentators, though, in line with contemporary final-form interests, are reluctant to excise it. Leslie Allen believes the formula fits neatly into a "complex chiastic jigsaw of [vv.] 3–31" and could be integral "to an early stage of the redacted text."[33] Daniel Block mentions the text-critical issue but interprets the Hebrew text as we have it.[34] It is fair to say that the refrain at 20:26 is suspicious, but it is not deleted from the list considered in this study.[35]

I note in passing that the research behind this study tends to confirm the conclusions of earlier Septuagint scholarship (esp. Henry St. John Thackeray[36]) that the Greek translation was not done by a single hand but falls into three recognizable sections: chapters 1–27 and 40–48 belong to a first translator, and 28–39 belong to a second. RFs within 1–27 are normally rendered with verbless object clauses (without εἰμι). For example, 6:7 reads, καὶ ἐπιγνώσεσθε ὅτι ἐγὼ κύριος. In chapters 28–39, one regularly finds the verb included in the object clause, such as in καὶ γνώσονται ὅτι ἐγώ εἰμι κύριος (38:23). Out of seventy-one total refrains, the only occurrences not following this pattern are 7:9 (LXX 7:6) in the first

31. The other ancient versions and witnesses are: a couple of Old Latin manuscripts (Constance, Fragmenta Sangallensia), Coptic (Sahidica), Justin Martyr, and Jerome. However, the Targum has the formula.

32. The team of Ezekiel scholars taking this position is impressive: Cooke, *Ezekiel*, 219; Wevers, *Ezekiel*, 118; Eichrodt, *Ezekiel*, 272–73; and Zimmerli, who says that the absence of the RF in ancient versions, the introduction of the formula with למען אשר, and the replacement of כי with אשר all indicate its secondary character (*Ezekiel 1*, 401).

33. Allen, *Ezekiel 20–48*, 4. See also Allen, "Structuring."

34. Block, *Ezekiel 1–24*, 634–40. Greenberg takes notice of the LXX lacking a portion of 20:22 but mentions neither this text-critical problem nor the missing RF in v. 26 (*Ezekiel 1–20*, 361, 368–70); he treats the MT as it stands. The same is true of Darr's commentary ("Book of Ezekiel," 1284) and the study by Scott Walker Hahn and John Sietze Bergsma ("What Laws Were 'Not Good'?").

35. As more and more scholars treat the MT and LXX as reflections of different redactional stages, with each text tradition allegedly experiencing its own processes of literary growth, the importance of the LXX as a witness to the earliest Hebrew text of Ezekiel may decline.

36. Thackeray, "Greek Translators" and *Septuagint and Jewish Worship*. For updated discussion, see Lust, "Multiple Translators?" Lust believes there was a single translator who varied his style ("Ezéchiel dans la Septante").

section and 36:36 and 38[37] and 37:14 in the second. One wonders if the variations may be the result of a final editing. My conclusions regarding the LXX are closely similar to those of Leslie John McGregor.[38]

The dual designation of God as אדני יהוה is another text-critical issue arising from the comparison of the MT and LXX. Though very common in the MT of Ezekiel, appearing a total of 217 times,[39] the dual designation is rare in the Septuagint.[40] Because the LXX normally renders יהוה by κύριος, a redundancy (κύριος κύριος) was understandably often avoided by the translators.[41] Moshe Greenberg gives good reasons for distrusting past scholarship—see Karl Elliger's apparatus in *BHS*—which urged the deletion of a portion of the occurrences of אדני to bring the MT more into line with the LXX.[42] I consider plausible a McGregor suggestion that the LXX translators originally rendered the dual designation with κύριος joined to a Greek transliteration of the name יהוה but that later editors commonly replaced the combined *kurios yhwh* with simple *kurios*. If such alterations did take place, then text-critical deletion of instances of אדני in the MT would clearly be destructive.

Zimmerli's redaction-critical conclusions, as they touch on the RFs, deserve mention because of the influence of his essays and commentary. He rejects the older literary-critical view (Rudolf Smend, etc.) that Ezekiel was "a scribe who

---

37. Lust asserts that the omission of 36:23c–38 in Pap967, "the earliest witness of the pre-hexaplaric Septuagint of Ezekiel," is not accidental (the result of *parablepsis*). That passage was not in the earliest forms of the LXX, he contends, nor in the Hebrew *Vorlage*, but rather was composed and inserted as a transition between chs. 36 and 37 ("Ezekiel 36–40"). This may help to explain the evidence of different translation habits with regard to the RFs in this passage. Lust is supported by Tov, "Recensional Differences." The case for accidental omission is made in Filson, "Omission," and Wevers, *Ezekiel*, 273.

38. McGregor, *Greek Text of Ezekiel*. An earlier study was Turner, "Septuagint Version."

39. Zimmerli, *Ezekiel 2*, 556.

40. It appears that the most thorough analysis of the distribution of various forms of the divine name in the LXX witnesses was done by McGregor, *Greek Text of Ezekiel*, 223–57 (appendix B).

41. There are occurrences of the doublet κύριος κύριος in Codex Vaticanus (12:10; 13:20; 14:6; and 43× in 20:38–39:29), and even the transliteration ἀδωναι κύριος (36:33, 37). John W. Olley offers a succinct discussion of both the dual designation and the RF in the LXX in *Ezekiel*, 28–31.

42. Greenberg, *Ezekiel 1–20*, 64–65. Zimmerli discusses the matter in an appendix, and while he does not necessarily delete אדני on text-critical grounds, he does class all five dual designations within RFs (categories C and L above) as "a later degenerate form" in his redaction criticism (*Ezekiel 2*, 556). Note that Zimmerli became more conservative toward the MT later in life and urged readers not to follow his decision in the commentary to bracket אדני where it occurs in the "complaint to Yahweh" form, the "introductory messenger formula," and "the formula for a divine saying" (*Ezekiel 2*, 562). The fullest discussion of the dual designation in Ezekiel is probably Hamilton, "Theological Implications." Olley argues that LXX Ezekiel's simple κύριος where the MT reads אדני יהוה need not be understood as evidence of a shorter *Vorlage*, but may reflect the translation convention at the time ("Divine Name and Paragraphing"). Also supporting the dual designation as original is Lust, "אדני יהוה in Ezekiel," who notes elsewhere that the Masada fragments preserve the double name ("Divine Titles," 143). However, Lust regards the five occurrences of אדני יהוה within the RF (13:9; 23:49; 24:24; 28:24; 29:16) as "the work of late glossators or copyists" ("Divine Titles," 143).

composed the whole book,"[43] proposing instead that the prophecy experienced editorial activity of long duration. "Aus der Hand der 'Schule' Ezechiels stammt dann ohne Zweifel das heute vorliegende Ezechielbuch."[44] This "school" added to the original oracles, and there was also the "updating of tradition"[45] (*Fortschreibung*) at numerous points. Zimmerli wonders if chapters 1–39 and 40–48 were originally separate complexes,[46] and he regards a number of sections of the prophecy as redactional (but not to be dismissed in exegesis). The listing of RFs in passages Zimmerli termed redactional "insertions" (*Einschübe*) must be somewhat tentative, since he himself expresses different levels of certainty in his redaction-critical evaluations. Also, he believes the prophet may have played a leading role in the editing.[47] The earliest edition of the book, he suggests, included: 1:1–3:16a; 3:22–17:24; 19:1–24:27; and 33:21–39:29. The following formulas are doubted to be original, at least in the sense of belonging to the first book, before the "school" (with Ezekiel?) began its editing work: 6:13–14;[48] 11:10, 12;[49] 22:16;[50] 25:5, 7, 11, 17; 26:6; 28:22, 23, 24, 26; 29:6, 9, 16, 21; 30:8, 19, 25, 26; 32:15.[51] One RF (20:26) is rejected outright as not belonging to the book until centuries later; Zimmerli believes it was absent from the *Vorlage* of the LXX. The unique form in 38:16, where the object clause usually containing the SPF (אני יהוה) is replaced by the accusative with the first-person pronoun, למען דעת הגוים אתי, "belongs to a later addition."[52]

43. Zimmerli, *Ezekiel 1*, 75 (*Ezechiel*, 1:113*).

44. Zimmerli, *Ezechiel*, 1:109*.

45. Zimmerli, *Ezekiel 1*, 73.

46. Zimmerly mentions in passing (*Ezekiel 1*, 73) the comment of Josephus that Ezekiel had left two books to posterity (*Ant.* 10.5.1.).

47. Contra more recent redaction critics, many of whom trained at Marburg and who mark a hard author–editor distinction, Zimmerli cautions: "In individual cases *it is often not possible to define the borders at which the prophet's own work passes over into that of the school.* The possibility that a great part of the transmission in the 'school' and the 'updating of tradition' of many oracles took place in Ezekiel's house by the prophet himself is not to be dismissed out of hand. That the prophet himself knew something of school instruction, which is phenomenologically very different from the older prophetic preaching in public, is made very clear by passages such as chapter 18; 33:1–9, 10–20. Thus besides the oral proclamation of rhythmically composed sayings, which continued the manner of preaching of the earlier prophets, *we must reckon that the prophet himself undertook the secondary work of learned commentary upon and further elaboration of his prophecies,* i.e., with a kind of 'school activity'" (*Ezekiel 1*, 71 [emphasis added]). Greenberg would later second this proposal of authorial editing while critiquing the "school" hypothesis (*Ezekiel 21–37*, 396).

48. Zimmerli, *Ezekiel 1*, 39. Zimmerli believes "a certain pretentious fullness of expression is intended where a second recognition formula follows on an earlier one," and in 6:13–14, it is redactional.

49. Zimmerli, *Ezekiel 1*, 40.

50. Zimmerli, *Ezekiel 1*, 40.

51. Most of these RFs occur in the oracles against the nations, portions of which, in Zimmerli's view, existed as independent collections. According to his reconstruction, "the narrative of 33:21f must once have followed directly on 24:15 in an earlier redaction phase" (*Ezekiel 1*, 71).

52. Zimmerli, *Ezekiel 1*, 39. Cf. Jer 24:7 ("... to know me, that I am Yahweh").

The foregoing discussion of his redaction criticism may leave a wrong impression, and a final word may reassure those who inquire about statistics of the RFs appearing in the final form (MT). When Zimmerli records the statistics of the formula's appearances, he does *not* base his data or conclusions on a reconstructed text. Even where he is most certain of his text-critical and redaction-critical research, such as in rejecting 20:26, Zimmerli still includes the doubtful formula in his total of seventy-two (with an additional eight texts "in the wider circle").[53]

3.2.4. The Subjects Who Come to "Know that I Am Yahweh"

Which subjects are said to "know that I am Yahweh" in Ezekiel? In answering this, one again confronts the great variety in the RF formulations. In the majority of occurrences (forty-six of seventy-two), Israel is the implied subject of the verb ידע. To clarify, however, the name *Israel* occurs only once (39:22) as the explicit subject of the verb. Israel is denoted in different ways within oracles that include the RF: "children of Israel,"[54] the "house of Israel,"[55] the "land of Israel,"[56] or "the people of the land."[57] ("Judah" appears fifteen times, but never in conjunction with the RF as the implied subject.) Jerusalem and its environs are singled out in some oracles,[58] or there may be a joint reference to Jerusalem and the rest of the population of the land: "those living in Jerusalem and in the land of Israel" (12:19). Both the exiled Jews (24:24) and those who had remained in the land (33:27–29)—only to be judged later—would come to know Yahweh. Certain individuals or special classes in Israel receive judgment oracles with attached RFs, such as the "foolish prophets" and "the daughters of your people who prophesy out of their imagination" (מלבהן) in chapter 13 and "the prince in Jerusalem" in 12:10–16. The generation who left Egypt under Moses is the subject in 20:12, 20, and 26. Metaphorical subjects who *know* include: "Oholah and Oholibah" (23:49); "the mountains of Israel" (36:8–12); the "dry bones" (37:6, 13); and "all the trees of the field" (17:24). The last of these is almost certainly a reference to the surrounding nations (cf. ch. 31), who will "know that I am Yahweh" as God acts to plant or bring down a "tree" in the community of nations.

Scholars count twenty-six RFs in Ezekiel that speak of other nations knowing Yahweh through his actions (Table 2). In several places, "the nations" (הגוים) in general are said to come to know,[59] but there is also a rather full list of named

53. Zimmerli, *Ezekiel 1*, 38.
54. Children/sons of Israel: 6:5.
55. The house of Israel: 11:5–12; 14:6–8; 22:17–22; 24:21–24; 36:37–38; 39:22.
56. The land: 7:1–9.
57. Inhabitants of the land: 7:7; the people of the land: 7:27; 12:19–20; etc.
58. For Jerusalem, see 5:8–13, 15:6–7, 22:16; see also references to the city in 11:2–12 and 16:2.
59. See 36:23, 36; 37:28; 38:23; 39:7; cf. 38:16 and 39:23.

Table 2. Nations Addressed by Recognition Formulas in Ezekiel

"All the trees"	1×
Amon	2×
Moab	1×
Philistia	1×
Tyre	1×
Sidon	2×
Egypt/Cush	8×
Mount Seir/Edom	4×
"Nations" (generic)	5×
Magog	1×

countries who recognize Yahweh.[60] The oracles against the nations mention individuals such as Pharaoh (thirteen times),[61] the leader (נגיד) of Tyre (28:2), and
the mysterious Gog (גוג נשיא ראש משך ותבל). But no formula reads, "and *he* shall
know that I am Yahweh" (cf. Jer 9:23). In one or two texts, there is uncertainty as
to whether the refrain has the nations or Israel as the subject who recognizes (see
28:26, which I argue below is spoken to Israel).

Various experiences lead to the recognition of Yahweh. Those in Israel who
know may be the slain (6:7), or they may be those who observe the judgment
of death on others but who apparently survive (14:8), perhaps in exile (6:8–10;
12:16). They may be Jews already in exile, hearing news of Jerusalem's destruction
(24:24). Those who recognize Yahweh may also be those who finally experience
a new exodus out of the nations where they are scattered (20:42), though some
of these—like the generation that left Egypt in Num 14:23?—will not be allowed
entry into the land of Israel (20:38). Those who do enter (39:28) will be delivered
from malicious neighbors and wild beasts (28:24; 34:25–31). The experiences of
the nations that lead to recognition of Yahweh are likewise quite varied. They
could be ghastly events: plague (28:23); destruction of cities (25:5); obliteration
of the memory of the nation (25:10); or slaughter (26:6). On the other hand, the
nations could also come to recognize Yahweh by his gracious restoration of Israel
(36:36) and Israel's sanctification (37:28).

Reviewing all the RFs, both simple and expanded, one finds that verbs taking a
singular subject are found a total of five times (16:62; 22:16; 25:7; 35:4; 35:12). These
verbs are all second-person (וידעת), and all refer to nation-states. The first two

60. The nations (and texts) are: Ammon (25:5, 7); Moab (25:11); Philistia (25:17); Tyre (26:6);
Sidon (28:22, 23); Egypt (29:6, 9, 16; 30:8, 19, 25, 26; 32:15); Mount Seir/Edom (35:4, 9, 12, 15); the
nations (36:23, 36; 37:28; 38:23; 39:7); Magog (39:6). The occurrence of the formula in the oracle
against Tyre is disputed by some; see, e.g., Strong, "Ezekiel's Use," 119, and Zimmerli, *Ezekiel* 2, 33.

61. 29:2–3; 30:21–22, 24–25; 31:2, 18; 32:2, 31 (2×), 32; cf. 17:17 (not an oracle against the nations).

occurrences are the shorter form of the refrain. With only three exceptions—all in chapter 20 (vv. 12, 20, and 26)—the RF is always found in the Qal perfect with *waw*-conjunctive.[62] The two refrains with infinitive constructs (20:12 and 20) stand apart from the rest of the formulas because they do not prophesy a future recognition, but rather look back and interpret redemptive history.

3.2.5. Literary Context, Genre, and Syntactical Analysis

Without exception, Ezekiel's RF occurs in divine utterances announcing God's acts on the plane of history. His intervention in human affairs declares, "I am Yahweh." Though other OT books refashion the refrain with the result that it loses its character as direct divine speech,[63] Ezekiel does not. He never reports, "Yahweh will do X, and they will know *he* is Yahweh." We never read in Ezekiel, "then you will know Yahweh" (Hos 2:22[20]).

Readers of Ezekiel's prophecy also observe that the formula and the "proof-saying" of which it is said to be a part may be found in poetic as well as prosaic passages. Scholars, however, disagree over the amount of poetry in Ezekiel and the number of RFs in a poetic context.[64] This may be because, as Zimmerli says: "We may reckon at many points in Ezekiel with an elevated prose, which does not move in a rough meter, but allows free variation. It has some metrical features, aiming to run in double twos and double threes."[65] The number of RFs found in a poetic context is limited because poetry was not this prophet's usual style. The reader finds far less poetry than in the other Major Prophets, especially Isaiah.

Leading scholars regard Ezekiel's fifteen chronological markers as the most important structuring device on the macro-level.[66] This raises the question of where among the oracles, chronologically, we find the RF appearing. Is it used more frequently in prophecies dated prior to the commencement of Jerusalem's siege and destruction (see 24:1) or in those dated after that? One may question whether all the oracles and sign-acts following a certain date citation are contemporaneous

---

62. For categorization of the RF as usually a relative *waw* perfect (consequential *wqtl*) in the telic sense, see *IBHS*, §32.2.1.d.

63. Compare Deut 4:35 and Isa 19:21.

64. The editors of *BHS* regard six RFs as being set in a poetic context (7:4, 9, 27; 29:6; 32:15; 35:4). Zimmerli's commentary counts three formulas in a poetic style (7:4, 9, 27), while *BHK* has discerned four (28:23; 30:8; 30:19; 32:15). There is not even a single formula for which the three parties all agree on it being set in poetry. As a matter of policy, the HUB prints the prophetic corpus in prose format, "as it appears to the eye" in the Aleppo Codex. The Ezekiel fascicle in *BHQ* is scheduled for release in 2020.

65. Zimmerli, *Ezekiel 1*, 40. Considering the lack of poetic material, he says "Ezekiel belongs to a later phase of prophecy, which is no longer determined throughout by the spoken word, delivered publicly" (41).

66. Childs, *Introduction*, 365; Mayfield, *Literary Structure*, 84–117; Lyons, *Introduction*, 77–80.

Table 3. Dating of Recognition Formulas in Ezekiel

RFs to Israel Prior to Jerusalem's Siege (ca. 588 BC)	30
RFs to Nations Prior to Siege/Destruction	1
RFs to Nations After Siege/Destruction	25
RFs to Israel After Siege/Destruction	16

(e.g., chs. 4–7, following the date in 3:16).[67] However, in Table 3 (cf. Table 5), it is assumed, without hard evidence one way or the other, that they are.

To trace the overall structure of the book, Zimmerli delineates individual oracles by the appearance of "the personal narrative form,"[68] or prophetic word formula (וַיְהִי דְבַר־יְהוָה אֵלַי). This works well, but Tyler Mayfield convincingly argues that, if the chronological markers are combined with the prophetic word formulas, the macrostructure of the prophecy becomes much clearer.[69] The distribution of the RF within this refined macrostructure is worth examining (see Table 6).

Though the book is extraordinarily focused on God, with direct divine speech dominating chapters 2–39, readers properly give attention to rhetorical form and the genius of the prophetic messenger, noting that Ezekiel adopts various compositional styles. He delivers visions (chs. 1–3; 8:1–11:4; 37:1–14; chs. 40–48), lengthy allegories (chs. 16 and 23), and parables (chs. 17 and 24). He sings laments (ch. 19), and he records disputation speeches (ch. 18 and 33:1–20) and "street theatre" symbolic actions (chs. 4, 5, 12, and 24 and 37:15–28).[70] Generally speaking, one seldom finds the RF in these sections (see Figure 2 and Table 6). One noticeable exception would be the vision of the valley of dry bones (37:1–14), which includes a high concentration (three times). Where the RF is found in these visions, allegories, and sign-act passages, it usually comes at the conclusion without interrupting the vision, allegory, or fable as a speech-unit (e.g., 16:62). Wherever it occurs, it normally appears at the conclusion of an oracle segment. Only sixteen times does the distinct literary unit in which an RF is found continue beyond that target statement: 6:10, 13; 11:12; 12:15; 13:14; 15:7; 16:62; 20:42; 30:8, 25; 34:27, 30; 35:12; 36:36;

---

67. One text in which this is especially questionable is 30:1. Should one read that oracle as a resumption of that begun in 29:1? (The date at 30:20 may incline us to think so.) Or should the reader understand 30:1 as continuing the oracle of judgment against Egypt in 29:19–20, given that the preceding oracle ended on a more positive note that Egyptians would be restored to their land (29:13–16)? I conclude that 30:1–19 is best read as both resumptive of 29:1–16 and building on the much later oracle of 29:17–21 because of all the literary ties. Block speaks of the subsequent oracle as "completing the picture of Egypt's doom as outlined in ch. 29: vv. 1–4, 6–8 link with 29:8–16; vv. 10–12 with 29:17–21; vv. 13–19 with 29:10–11" (*Ezekiel 25–48*, 155).

68. Zimmerli, *Ezekiel 1*, 24.

69. Mayfield, "Re-Examination."

70. Zimmerli observes that the visions in Ezekiel "are always followed by a section which speaks of sign-actions" (*Ezekiel 1*, 73). The exception to this rule would be chs. 40–48.

37:13; 39:28. Ezekiel may extend the oracle beyond the RF with an infinitive clause introduced by the ב preposition (6:13; 12:15; 15:7; 20:42, etc.).

Two details of the formula's usage stand out. First, It does not appear even once in the final vision. Is this fact best explained by the eschatological nature of the vision, which looks forward to God's plan of restoration for his people, who presumably have already come to "know that I am Yahweh"? Is the absence of the formula in 40–48 perhaps to be explained by the pronounced shift away from prophecies of Yahweh's intervention in history? Is it missing because of the shift in genre? The second surprising detail is Babylon's absence in the list of nations recognizing Yahweh through judgment. Why, considering the brutality of Babylon's army (2 Kgs 25) and the sorrows visited upon God's people through the exile (Pss 79 and 137), is that nation excluded from the list? One answer could be Babylon's place in providence as God's sword of judgment, as explained by this prophetic book;[71] see chapter 21 and 30:25: ‏וידעו כי־אני יהוה בתתי חרבי ביד מלך־ ‏בבל. Other suggestions are that Babylon is, in fact, obliquely mentioned, if readers identify Nebuchadnezzar II as Gog[72] or identify the judgment in 21:35–37[30–32] as against the "sword," not Ammon.[73]

Many have commented on Ezekiel's use of numerous "stereotyped" phrases besides the familiar RF.[74] The prophet will occasionally join the formula with another of his characteristic phrases to form interesting compounds. To cite but one example, the parable of the two eagles and the transplanted vine concludes with the declaration, "I, Yahweh, have spoken, and I will do it" (17:24). But a few lines earlier, in 17:21, this common asseveration[75] is combined with the RF: "And you shall know that I am Yahweh, I have spoken." The reader finds much the same expansion in 5:13 and 37:14.

Most of the RFs (fifty-two) are found in passages announcing Yahweh's judgment. One should take special note that only in Ezekiel is the RF used in a message of judgment against Israel. No other OT book has this phenomenon. The remaining twenty RFs in Ezekiel promise deliverance or covenant blessing, and these blessings, interestingly, are to be shown only to Israel.[76] In a few of these twenty

---

71. See: Zimmerli, *Ezekiel 2*, 304; Block, *Ezekiel 25–48*, 434; Joyce, *Ezekiel*, 214.

72. McKeating, *Ezekiel*, 121–22; Galambush, "Necessary Enemies." As Cooke notes (*Ezekiel*, 408), this theory had currency in the nineteenth and early twentieth centuries (e.g., Heinrich Ewald and A. Meinhold).

73. Zimmerli, *Ezekiel 1*, 449–50; Greenberg, *Ezekiel 21–37*, 448; Block, *Ezekiel 1–24*, 697–98; Lyons, *Introduction*, 30; contra Cooke, *Ezekiel*, 236.

74. See Driver, *Introduction*, 297–98, and Tooman, *Gog of Magog*, 40–51, for lists of these oft-repeated phrases. Among them are: "son of man," "disperse among the nations," "pour out my fury upon," and "see, I am against you."

75. The phrase "I, Yahweh, have spoken" is found in: 5:17; 21:22[17], 37[32]; 22:14; 24:14; 26:14; 30:12; 34:24; 36:36.

76. Ezek 16:62; 20:12, 20, 42, 44; 28:24, 26; 29:21; 34:27, 30; 36:11, 23, 36, 38; 37:6, 13, 14, 28; 39:7, 28.

occurrences, the nations are said to "know that I am Yahweh," but the recognition will come as the *gôyîm* observe how Yahweh deals graciously with his own people and how he has acted to sanctify his name.

The judgment oracles have two other remarkable features. First, they contain all of those phrases related to the RF that replace אני יהוה with another object clause (see 3.1.3 above). An example would be 25:14: "And they shall know my vengeance, declares the Lord Yahweh." Secondly, the oracles of judgment, whether spoken to Israel or the nations, never include an RF addressed to the judged[77] that reads, ". . . shall know that I am Yahweh your/their God." The expansion of the RF with the additional "your God" or "their God" occurs only in oracles of deliverance addressed to Israel.[78]

The phrase אני יהוה, often termed the *Selbstvorstellungsformel*, or "self-introductory formula" (better "self-presentation formula" [SPF][79]), is prevalent in the OT (approx. 110 times outside the RF).[80] There is also evidence for its use throughout the ANE in the mouths of deities and kings.[81] Elliger and Zimmerli[82] have shown that both the short form and the longer form (אני יהוה אלהיך) of the formula frequently follow a law or series of laws in Leviticus (esp. chs. 18–26), almost as a divine signature. On occasion, it can function as a preamble to a series of laws, such as in Exod 20:2, Lev 18:2, and Deut 5:6 (the two Decalogue passages have אנכי). But the SPF also finds a place in prophetic oracles as an assurance that Yahweh will fulfill his promises (see Exod 6). Examining the book of Ezekiel, one finds scarcely any use of the SPF independent of the RF, or the echo of the formula using a different verb

77. This is an important qualification because Israel in two places (28:26 and 39:22) is said to "know that I am Yahweh their God" when Yahweh punishes the nations (which may be reckoned a deliverance for Israel).

78. Found in the related categories E and H in Joyce's table. See: 20:20; 28:26; 34:30; 39:22, 28.

79. Another proposal is *Offenbarungsformel* (see Zimmermann, "Das absolute Ἐγώ εἰμι"). I choose to use the terminology "self-presentation" rather than "self-introduction," though there is good reason to understand אני יהוה in some contexts as a "divine self-assertion" instead of "self-presentation." The idea of "self-introduction" does not seem to be present in Ezekiel's use of אני יהוה in the few places it appears on its own. As K. Günther writes, "Jahwe tritt nicht als Unbekannter auf, sondern verweist im Zusammenhang mit der Kundgabe seines Namens auf schon Bekanntes und früher Geschehens (Gen 15,7; 26,24; 28,13; 31,13; Ex 3,6; auch: Hos 12,10; 13,4). Die angeschlossene Verheißungsrede stellt das zukünftige Handeln Gottes in desen geschichlichen Zusammenhang" ("אני *'anî* ich," *THAT*, 1:220).

80. See Diesel, "*Ich bin Jahwe*," 10–11.

81. Among the more important studies of the "I-statement," most relating ANE religious texts to so-called Second Isaiah, see: Poebel, *Das appositionell bestimmte Pronomen*; Dion, "Le genre littéraire sumérien"; Bergman, *Ich bin Isis*; Ringgren, "הוא *hû'*; אני *'anî*; אנכי *'ānōkhî*," in *TDOT*, 3:341–52 (esp. 346–48); Dijkstra, *Gods Voorstelling*, 17–35, 85–221; Harner, *Grace and Law*, 3–10, 145–47; Michel, "Nur ich bin Jahwe"; Becker, "Zur 'Ich bin'-Formel"; Manfred Weippert, "'Ich bin Jahwe'—'Ich bin Ištar von Arbela'"; Diesel, "*Ich bin Jahwe*."

82. Elliger, "Ich bin der Herr—euer Gott"; Zimmerli, "Ich bin Jahwe." Elliger's arguments that the short form ("I am Yahweh"; *Hoheitsformel*) and the longer form ("I am Yahweh, your God"; *Huldformel*) have distinctly different theological import (228–30), may be rejected.

of perception (ראה in 21:4 [20:48]), or the conclusion formula for divine speech (*Schlußformel eines Gottesspruchs*), אני יהוה דברתי (21:37[32]). The only use of אני יהוה independent of the RFs and conclusion formulas is found in Ezek 20 (vv. 5, 7, 19), where God recounts the redemption out of Egypt and the giving of the law (avoidance of idols).[83] This "I am Yahweh" (SPF), though it also serves as a component part of the RF, should be interpreted as a separate formula with a distinct use, function, and theological import of its own.[84] Considered together, the SPF and the full RF exemplify and lend emphasis to the first-person style of the prophecy.

Grammarians have devoted much research to the verbless (or nominal) clause, including the SPF, אני יהוה.[85] Today, there is broad agreement that, after a verb of perception such as ידע, a verbless כ object clause "should express simultaneity."[86] In chapter 2, I noted a chief problem in translating the SPF within the verbally expanded RF. Should אני יהוה be translated appositionally[87] ("you shall know that I, Yahweh, have spoken") or not ("you shall know that I am Yahweh, I have spoken")? There are compelling arguments against the appositional rendering[88] because it tends to obscure the self-presenting or self-revelatory aspect of the verbless clause אני יהוה, not only in the RFs but also in texts such as 22:14 and 24:14 ("I am Yahweh. I have spoken. It shall happen"). It is desirable to preserve the element of insistent self-declaration, certifying both that the one revealing himself in the Name is acting and that the one acting is revealed by asserting the Name.[89]

The RF does not appear everywhere Ezekiel's oracles describe Yahweh's action to judge or to bless. That is to say, Ezekiel may prophesy divine intervention without employing the formula. However, where it does appear (outside the retrospective of ch. 20), it occurs only in oracles proclaiming divine action. Scholars struggle to understand the function of the RFs in their literary context, and some urge that further research be undertaken. Marc Vervenne writes:

> It is clearly of primary importance that we examine the way in which the pKY [phraseology of "knowing YHWH"] is syntactically related to its context. As a matter of fact, its syntactic relationship with what precedes is determinative of the

---

83. The phrase regularly appears in the context of recalling the exodus event and identifying Yahweh as God of the exodus; see Exod 20:2 (אנכי); 29:46; Lev 11:45; 18:2–5 (3×); 19:36; 22:31–33 (3×); 23:43; 25:38, 55; 26:13, 44–45 (3×); Num 3:13; 15:41; Deut 5:1–6; Ps 81:11[10]; Hos 13:4.

84. See also the brief interpretive section in 6.2.5 in ch. 6 of the present volume.

85. Earlier works were Andersen, *Hebrew Verbless Clause*, and Hoftijzer, "Nominal Clause Reconsidered." For current discussion, see: *IBHS*, §8.4; Joüon, *Grammar*, §154 (for nom. clause אני יהוה, esp. §154.j); Miller, *Verbless Clause*; and Zewi, "Nominal Clause."

86. De Regt, "Macrosyntactic Functions," 288.

87. In recent studies, the traditional term "apposition" is replaced by "rear-dislocation" (or "left-dislocation," in the study of Hebrew); see Niccacci, "Types and Functions," 245–48.

88. To clarify, I speak of the RF. Certain texts with the SPF (אני יהוה) apart from the RF (e.g., 14:4, 7, 9) require an appositional rendering.

89. Along similar lines, see: Zimmerli, *I Am Yahweh*, 102–103, 139; Block, *Ezekiel 1–24*, 36–39.

function of the pKY. The pKY is normally seen as a motif of purpose: deeds of YHWH in history intended to let him be known/recognised.[90]

Therefore, the content of the verb ידע is less that "Yahweh has done thus and such" and more that "I am Yahweh."[91] Through the proclamation of the Name in association with the prophesied intervention, Yahweh personally is recognized; this is the thrust of the related phrase "so that the nations would know me" (38:16).

Vervenne also notes some scholars who take a different view, denying that the formula is a purposive construction, such as Fohrer, who says that the RF "is intended to summon the listener to judge that it is Yahweh who has intervened or is about to intervene, with his wrath or with his aid."[92] There is not necessarily, then, a *Vorstellung* or self-presentation; nor is the one who says, "I am Yahweh," proving himself (*Erweiswort* idea). "It is an explanatory formula which indicates how the announced or narrated intervention of YHWH should be correctly understood, namely as an action *of* YHWH."[93] On these disputed points, the present study finds, first, that the RF does indicate the purpose or goal of the prophesied action (the idea that it is merely an explanatory formula seems weak and inadequate) and, secondly, that Yahweh is manifesting and proving himself (or proving the truth of his word, which has been ignored). There is an aspect of *Erweiswort*, though the *Gattung* structure Zimmerli sought to outline frequently breaks down.[94]

Vervenne's syntactical analysis indicates that the pKY can have an "explicit purposive construction."[95] He mentions first of all the למען "particle of purpose" found repeatedly in Exodus, Isaiah, and Ezekiel.[96] Secondly, the ל-*qetol* infinitive form one reads in some "knowing Yahweh" texts[97] can properly be "considered a purposive construction, since it is apparent from the syntax that it is connected as such to a preceding clause."[98] It must be admitted, however, that grammarians face difficulty in distinguishing purpose and result, since "the notions of purpose and result are often expressed by the same means"[99] in Hebrew.

---

90. Vervenne, "Phraseology," 481. He notes the important scholars who think the formula indicates purpose: Zimmerli ("Knowledge of God"), Schoors (*I Am God Your Saviour*, 119, cf. 88–90), and J. P. Floss (*Jahwe Dienen*, 299).

91. So says Schoors, *I Am God Your Saviour*, 113.

92. Fohrer, *Introduction*, 409–10. Vervenne cites others challenging Zimmerli's position at this point: Hossfeld, *Untersuchungen*, 40–46; Lang, *Ezechiel*, 95–97.

93. Vervenne, "Phraseology," 482 (emphasis original).

94. As noted by Hossfeld, *Untersuchungen*, 40–46.

95. Vervenne, "Phraseology," 483.

96. See Exod 8:6[10], 18[22]; 9:29; 11:7; Isa 41:20; 43:10; 45:3, 6; Ezek 11:20; 20:26; 38:16. Cf. 2 Chr 6:33.

97. E.g., Exod 31:13; Deut 4:35; 1 Kgs 8:43; Jer 24:7; and Ezek 20:12, 20.

98. Vervenne, "Phraseology," 484.

99. Joüon, *Grammar*, §169.i.

Another syntactical observation is that Ezekiel not uncommonly places the RF (*weqaltí* -x) in a series of *weqaltí* forms, and as Vervenne notes, the refrain is not always in the final position in such stringing.[100] Vervenne does not consider the *weqaltí* pKY to be a purposive form. "It can, however, indicate succession or more precisely consecution and ought to be translated as follows: 'so', 'thus', 'then.'"[101] Approximately half of Ezekiel's RFs could be translated to reflect consecution ("as a consequence thereof...").

One advance over previous scholarship is Greenberg's explanation of a "halving pattern" in Ezekiel's oracles and a sometimes associated "afterwave effect in oracle-closure."[102] As he examines passages and their features—articulation, opening and closing formulas, "distinctive homogenous linguistic and poetic textures"— he discovers their larger structures, their "design and ... integrating elements." The "most important" structure is the "halving pattern and repetition," described as follows: "a theme, A, is propounded in the first, usually longest, part of the oracle; it is followed by a second theme, B, which is somehow related to the first theme (by skewing or development of an aspect of it); B characteristically ends, or is followed by a coda, with elements of A and B intermingled."[103]

The RF can play a key part in the halving pattern and serve as a signpost, indicating the conclusion of sections.[104] The formula serves this function well in the very first halving pattern, located in Ezek 6, which also contains the "afterwave." There, Greenberg points out, the main oracle of verses 3–7 closes with the RF and is followed by an afterwave in 8–10 that also closes with the formula. The second oracle is characteristically shorter, verses 11–13aα, and has a concluding RF. Its afterwave, 13aβ–14, is said to begin with the infinitive (בהיות) and to close with the RF.[105] The use of the keynote formula within such carefully designed structures makes it seem more integrated into the oracles, not an accretion, and also more purposeful from a rhetorical and theological standpoint.

3.2.6. *Clusters and Concentrations of the Formula*

There is a clustering phenomenon with Ezekiel's RFs. Readers discover that several chapters may pass between appearances of the formula. None appear in the opening

---

100. Examples in Ezekiel provided by Vervenne would be: 5:13; 6:6–7, 8–9, 12–13, 14; 13:14, 23; 14:8; 16:62; 20:41–42, 43–44; 22:16; 24:27; 25:7, 14, 17; 28:22–23; 29:9; 30:19, 26; 33:29; 34:27; 36:11, 23, 35–36; 37:6, 12–13, 14; 38:23; 39:6, 21–22, 29–30. We can compare: Exod 6:6–8 (an excellent example indeed); 7:4–5; 29:46; 1 Kgs 20:28.

101. Vervenne, "Phraseology," 485.

102. Greenberg, *Ezekiel 1–20*, 25–26.

103. Greenberg, *Ezekiel 1–20*, 25.

104. The RF often appears in the "halving" device, but not always (e.g., 38:1–4a // 39:1–2a; see Milgrom, *Ezekiel's Hope*, 4–5, for discussion).

105. Greenberg, *Ezekiel 1–20*, 137.

Table 4. Greatest Concentrations of Recognition Formulas in Ezekiel

6:1–14	Oracle against "the mountains of Israel"	4×
12:8–20	Oracle explaining the sign-act in chapter 12	3×
13:1–23	Oracle against the false prophets	4×
20:1–44	Historical retrospective and oracle	6×
28:20–26	Oracle against Sidon	4×
29:2–16	Oracle against Pharaoh and against all Egypt	3×
35:1–15	Oracle against Mount Seir/Edom	4×
36:8–38	Oracle of blessing upon trampled Israel	4×
37:1–14	Vision of the valley of dry bones, resurrection	3×

vision and the immediately following sign-acts (1:1–5:4), in the first temple vision (8:1–11:4), in the disputation and lament in chapters 18–19, or in the final temple vision (chs. 40–48). Where it does appear, there are sometimes high concentrations. A list of "clusters" is provided in Table 4. The greatest concentration of RFs in a single cluster would be the prophecy against Sidon in 28:20–26. Within that oracle, only 119 words in the Hebrew, the refrain appears four times. Those four, however, are split between a judgment oracle addressed to Sidon (vv. 20–24) and an associated prophecy of Yahweh's blessing upon Israel (vv. 25–26), possibly still addressed to Sidon.[106] Higher concentrations in clusters can indicate the presence of the "after-wave" phenomenon and what might be termed a "doublet arrangement," where a second RF closely follows on another at the conclusion of a divine speech.[107]

3.3. Conclusion

This chapter, with its catalog of the RF in all its variations, will prove useful later, when Ezekiel's formulas will be compared with those from other Bible books. In inner-biblical interpretation, it may be supposed that Ezekiel's use of the RF will likely be most similar to that portion of Scripture from which it is derived. Patterns of use in Ezekiel may mirror patterns found elsewhere. For intertextual and intratextual studies, the data will help to focus readers' attention on similarities of language where echoes are heard. To aid readers in the comparison, this chapter includes a chart (Figure 1) categorizing all the RFs in the OT and an appendix that lists all those formulas, together with a large assortment of related phrases.

106. Zimmerli says 28:25–26 "are not to be considered as an independent oracle" (*Ezekiel* 2, 100). However, he also thinks the oracle comes from a later hand.

107. These seem to be a unique characteristic of Ezekiel's prophecy, as my research has not discovered them elsewhere. See: 6:13–14; 11:11–12; 12:15–16 (note also v. 20); 20:42–44; 25:5–7; 28:22–26 (4×); 30:25–26; 34:27–30; 37:13–14. Ezekiel 39:22–23 might be considered a close relation of this. Ezekiel 35:12 and 15 are not in this category because they are divided by the formula כה אמר אדני יהוה.

Figure 1. Recognition Formulas in Books of the Old Testament

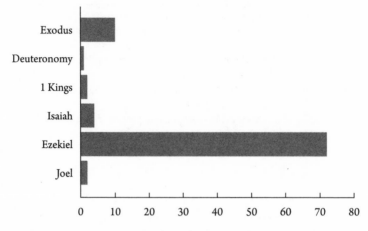

Books	Total	Strict	Expanded	Israel	Nations	+/−
Exodus	10	2	8	5	5	4/6
Deuteronomy	1	—	1	1	—	1/0
1 Kings	2	2	—	2	—	2/0
Isaiah	4	1	3	2	2	4/0
Ezekiel	72	46	26	46	26	20/52
Joel	2	—	2	2	—	2/0

The symbol +/− above indicates formulas in oracles of salvation/judgment

Figure 2. Distribution of Ezekiel's Recognition Formulas According to Chapter

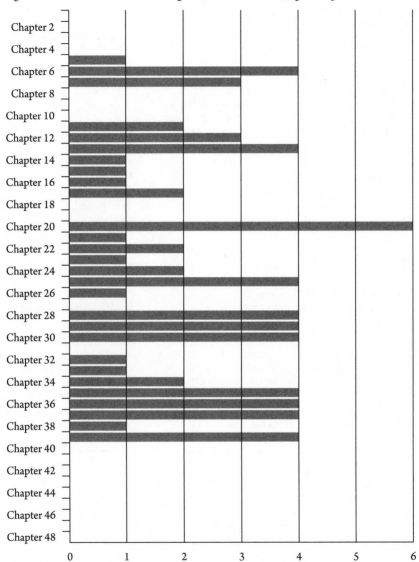

Table 5. Distribution of Ezekiel's Recognition Formulas According to Chronological Framework (Date Formulas)

Texts	Dates	Formulas	Time of Recognition
1:1–3:15	July 593	2:5 (rel.)	Post-586/5?
3:16–7:27	July 593	5:13; 6:7, 10, 13, 14; 7:4, 9, 27	Post-586/5
8:1–19:14	Sept. 592	11:10, 12; 12:15, 16, 20; 13:9, 14, 21, 23; 14:8, 23 (rel.); 15:7; 16:62; 17:21, 24	Post-586/5?
20:1–23:49	Aug. 591	20:12, 20, 26, 38, 42, 44; 21:4[20:48] (rel.), 10[5]; 22:16, 22; 23:49	Past history (20:12, 20, 26); Post-538 (20:38, 42, 44); Post-586/5 (the rest)
24:1–25:17	Jan. 588	24:24, 27; 25:5, 7, 11, 14 (rel.), 17	Post 586/5 (24:24, 27); Neighbors' fall (the rest)
26:1–28:26	586?	26:6; 28:22, 23, 24, 26	Tyre attacked; Sidon judged; Jews' relief from neighbors
29:1–16	Jan. 587	29:6, 9, 16	Egypt punished; Jews see Egypt humbled
29:17–21	Apr. 571	29:21	Jews strengthened and Ezekiel's mouth opened
30:1–19	Apr. 571?	30:8, 19	Egypt punished
30:20–26	Apr. 587	30:25, 26	Egypt punished/scattered
31:1–18	June 587	—	—
32:1–16	Mar. 585	32:15	Egyptians struck down
32:17–33:20	Mar. 585?	—	—
33:21–39:29	Jan. 585	33:29, 33 (rel.); 34:27, 30; 35:4, 9, 12, 15; 36:11, 23, 36, 38; 37:6, 13, 14, 28; 38:16 (rel.), 23; 39:6, 7, 21 (rel.), 22, 23 (rel.), 28	Post-586/5 (ch. 33); Jews' rescue from false shepherds; Edom's desolation; Jews' return to the land; Israel's resurrection; rescue from Gog
40:1–48:35	573	—	—

(rel.) = related to the RF proper

Table 6. Distribution of Ezekiel's Recognition Formulas Within the Macrostructure of the Prophecy

Unit	Text	Recognition Formulas
Vision of Chariot-Throne, Ezekiel's Call; Judgment Oracles Against Israel		
1.	1:1–3:15	— cf. 2:5
2.	3:16b; 3:22–5:17	1×: 5:13
3.	6:1–14	4×: 6:7, 10, 13, 14
4.	7:1–27	3×: 7:4, 9, 27
Vision of Yahweh's Glory Departing Jerusalem; More Judgment Oracles Against Israel		
5.	8:1–10:22; 11:22–25	—
6.	11:1–13	2×: 11:10, 12
7.	11:14–21	—
8.	12:1–16	2×: 12:15, 16
9.	12:17–20	1×: 12:20
10.	12:21–25	—
11.	12:26–28	—
12.	13:1–23	4×: 13:9, 14, 21, 23
13.	14:1–11	1×: 14:8
14.	14:12–23	— cf. 14:23
15.	15:1–8	1×: 15:7
16.	16:1–63	1×: 16:62
17.	17:1–24	2×: 17:21, 24
18.	18:1–32	—
19.	19:1–14	—
Confrontation over Salvation History; More Judgment Oracles Against Israel		
20.	20:1–44	6×: 20:12, 20, 26, 38, 42, 44
21.	21:1–12 [20:45–21:7]	1×: 21:10[5]; cf. 21:4 [20:48]
22.	21:13–22[8–17]	—
23.	21:23–37[18–32]	—
24.	22:1–16	1×: 22:16
25.	22:17–22	1×: 22:22
26.	22:23–31	—
27.	23:1–49	1×: 23:49
Oracles Concerning Jerusalem's Siege and Against Hostile Surrounding Nations		
28.	24:1–14	—
29.	24:15–27	2×: 24:24, 27
30.	25:1–17	4×: 25:5, 7, 11, 17; cf. 25:14

Table 6. (*cont'd*)

Unit	Text	Recognition Formulas
Judgment Oracles Against Tyre and Sidon		
31.	26:1–21	1×: 26:6
32.	27:1–36	—
33.	28:1–10	—
34.	28:11–19	—
35.	28:20–26	4×: 28:22, 23, 24, 26
Judgment Oracles Against Egypt		
36.	29:1–16	3×: 29:6, 9, 16
Oracles Declaring Egypt's Fate; Lament for Egypt		
37.	29:17–21	1×: 29:21
38.	30:1–19	2×: 30:8, 19
Judgment Oracle Against Pharaoh; Defeat by Babylon		
39.	30:20–26	2×: 30:25, 26
Judgment Oracle Against Pharaoh (Lesson of Assyria's Devastation)		
40.	31:1–18	—
Lament over Pharaoh		
41.	32:1–16	1×: 32:15
Judgment Oracle Against Pharaoh/Egypt (Consigned to the Pit); Ezekiel a Watchman		
42.	32:17–32	—
43.	33:1–20	—
Report of City's Fall; Oracles About Jerusalemites, Israel's Shepherds, Deliverance, and Gog		
44.	33:21–22	—
45.	33:23–33	1×: 33:29; cf. 33:33
46.	34:1–31	2×: 34:27, 30
47.	35:1–36:15	5×: 35:4, 9, 12, 15; 36:11
48.	36:16–38	3×: 36:23, 36, 38
49.	37:1–14	3×: 37:6, 13, 14
50.	37:15–28	1×: 37:28
51.	38:1–39:29	5×: 38:23; 39:6, 7, 22, 28; cf. 38:16; 39:23
Vision of a New Temple and Israel's Restoration		
52.	40:1–48:35	—

Note: The date formulas demarcate thirteen sections, and the prophetic-word formulas introduce the fifty-two individual oracles.

APPENDIX: LIST OF RECOGNITION FORMULAS AND RELATED PHRASES OUTSIDE EZEKIEL

A. Exodus

A.1. The "Strict" Recognition Formula and Expansions

וידעתם כי אני יהוה אלהיכם

And you shall know that I am Yahweh your God
Exodus 6:7; 16:12

וידעו מצרים כי־אני יהוה

And the Egyptians shall know that I am Yahweh
Exodus 7:5; 14:4, 18

בזאת תדע כי אני יהוה

By this you (singular) shall know that I am Yahweh
Exodus 7:17 (Qal impf.)

למען תדע כי אני יהוה בקרב הארץ

So that you (singular) shall know that I, Yahweh, am in this land
Exodus 8:18[22] (Qal impf.)

וידעתם כי־אני יהוה

And that you may know that I am Yahweh
Exodus 10:2

וידעו כי אני יהוה אלהיהם

And they shall know that I am Yahweh their God
Exodus 29:46

לדעת כי אני יהוה מקדשכם

So you may know that I am Yahweh, who makes you holy
Exodus 31:13 (with inf. const.)

A.2. Phrases Related to the Recognition Formula

למען תדע כי־אין כיהוה אלהינו

So that you may know that there is no one like Yahweh our God
Exodus 8:6[10]

בעבור תדע כי אין כמני בכל־הארץ

So you may know that there is no one like me in all the earth/land
Exodus 9:14

למען תדע כי ליהוה הארץ

So that you may know that the earth/land belongs to Yahweh
Exodus 9:29

למען תדעון אשר יפלה יהוה בין מצרים ובין ישראל

So that you may know that Yahweh distinguishes between Egypt and Israel
Exodus 11:7

וידעתם כי יהוה הוציא אתכם מארץ מצרים

And you shall know that Yahweh brought you out of the land of Egypt
Exodus 16:6

B. Leviticus
Phrase Related to the Recognition Formula

למען ידעו דרתיכם כי בסכות הושבתי את־בני ישראל בהוציאי אותם מארץ מצרים
אני יהוה אלהיכם

That your generations may know that I made the children of Israel live in booths
when I brought them out of the land of Egypt; I am Yahweh your God
Leviticus 23:43

C. Numbers
Phrase Related to the Recognition Formula

ואמר משה בזאת תדעון כי־יהוה שלחני לעשות את כל־המעשים האלה

And Moses said, "By this you shall know that Yahweh has sent me to do all these
works"
Numbers 16:28

D. Deuteronomy
D.1. The Expanded Recognition Formula

למען תדעו כי אני יהוה אלהיכם

So that you would know that I am Yahweh your God
Deuteronomy 29:5[6]

D.2. Phrases Related to the Recognition Formula

אתה הראת לדעת כי יהוה הוא האלהים אין עוד מלבדו

You were shown this so you might know that Yahweh he is God; there is none
besides him
Deuteronomy 4:35

וידעת היום והשבת אל־לבבך כי יהוה הוא האלהים

Know then this day and keep in [your] heart that Yahweh he is God
Deuteronomy 4:39

וידעת כי־יהוה אלהיך הוא האלהים

Know that Yahweh your God, he is God
Deuteronomy 7:9

E. Joshua

Phrases Related to the Recognition Formula

היום הזה אחל גדלך בעיני כל־ישראל אשר ידעון כי כאשר הייתי עם־משה אהיה עמך

This day I shall begin to make you great in the eyes of all Israel that they may know that as I was with Moses, so I am with you
Joshua 3:7

בזאת תדעון כי אל חי בקרבכם

By this you shall know that the living God is among you
Joshua 3:10

למען דעת כל־עמי הארץ את־יד יהוה כי חזקה היא למען יראתם את־יהוה אלהיכם כל־הימים

So that all peoples of the earth might know the hand of Yahweh, that it is strong, and so that you might fear Yahweh your God perpetually
Joshua 4:24

F. 1 Samuel

Phrase Related to the Recognition Formula

וידעו כל־הארץ כי יש אלהים לישראל

Then all the world shall know that there is a God of/for Israel
1 Samuel 17:46

G. 1–2 Kings

G.1. The "Strict" Recognition Formula

וידעת כי־אני יהוה

And you (sg.) shall know that I am Yahweh
1 Kings 20:13

וידעתם כי־אני יהוה

And you (pl.) shall know that I am Yahweh
1 Kings 20:28

G.2. Phrases Related to the Recognition Formula

למען ידעון כל־עמי הארץ את־שמך ליראה אתך

So that all peoples of the earth may know your name and fear you
1 Kings 8:43

למען דעת כל־עמי הארץ כי יהוה הוא האלהים אין עוד

So that all peoples of the earth may know that Yahweh he is God; there is no other
1 Kings 8:60

וידעו העם הזה כי־אתה יהוה האלהים

So this people may know that you, Yahweh, are God
1 Kings 18:37

וידעו כל־ממלכות הארץ כי אתה יהוה אלהים לבדך

So all kingdoms on earth may know that you alone, O Yahweh, are God
2 Kings 19:19 (cf. Isa 37:20)[108]

H. Isaiah

H.1. The "Strict" Recognition Formula and Expansions

למען תדע כי־אני יהוה הקורא בשמך אלהי ישראל

So that you shall know that I am Yahweh, who calls you by name, the God of Israel
Isaiah 45:3

וידעת כי־אני יהוה אשר לא־יבשו קוי

And you shall know that I am Yahweh, those who wait for me shall not be put to
shame
Isaiah 49:23

וידעו כל־בשׂר כי אני יהוה מושיעך וגאלך אביר יעקב

And all flesh shall know that I am Yahweh, your Savior and your Redeemer, the
Mighty One of Jacob
Isaiah 49:26

וידעת כי אני יהוה מושיעך וגאלך אביר יעקב

And you shall know that I am Yahweh, your Savior and your Redeemer, the Mighty
One of Jacob
Isaiah 60:16

H.2. Phrases Related to the Recognition Formula

ונודע יהוה למצרים וידעו מצרים את־יהוה ביום ההוא

And Yahweh will make himself known to the Egyptians, and the Egyptians shall
know Yahweh in that day
Isaiah 19:21

---

108. Aarnoud van der Deijl speaks of 1 Kgs 18:37 and 2 Kgs 19:19 as appearances of the "recognition
formula" (*Protest or Propaganda*, 288–89). There is arguably some imprecision here, as he asserts the
formula has the following structure: "This has happened/is happening/will happen, so that you/they
know that YHWH alone is God/that there is a God in Israel/a prophet in Israel."

וידעו כל־ממלכות הארץ כי־אתה יהוה לבדך

So all the kingdoms of the earth may know that you are Yahweh, you alone
(or : . . . that you, Yahweh, are [God] alone)
Isaiah 37:20[109]

למען יראו וידעו וישימו וישכילו יחדו כי יד־יהוה עשתה זאת

So that they may see and know, may put [it before them] and consider together,
that the hand of Yahweh has done this
Isaiah 41:20

ונדעה כי אלהים אתם

So we may know that you are gods
Isaiah 41:23

למען תדעו ותאמינו לי ותבינו כי־אני הוא

So that you may know and believe me, may understand that I am he
Isaiah 43:10

למען ידעו ממזרח־שמש וממערבה כי־אפס בלעדי אני יהוה ואין עוד

So they may know, from the rising of the sun and [to] its setting, that there is none
apart from me. I am Yahweh and there is no other
Isaiah 45:6

לכן ידע עמי שמי לכן ביום ההוא כי־אני־הוא המדבר הנני

Therefore my people will know my name; therefore in that day [they will know]
that I am he, who speaks; behold me
Isaiah 52:6

I. Jeremiah

Phrases Related to the Recognition Formula

כי אם־בזאת יתהלל המתהלל השכל וידע אותי כי אני יהוה

But let the one who boasts boast of this: that he understands and knows me, that
I am Yahweh
Jeremiah 9:23[24][110]

---

109. At the end of 37:20, 1QIsaᵃ reads יהוה אלוהים לבדכה, instead of יהוה בדך (Ulrich and Flint, *Qumran Cave 1, II*, 60). Some believe this DSS should be followed (Blenkinsopp, *Isaiah 1–39*, 468; Wildberger, *Isaiah 28–39*, 411), but others retain the difficult MT reading without אלוהים, which is bolstered by the Vulg. and Tg. (Beuken, *Isaiah II/2*, 334). The preference of J. J. M. Roberts is unclear (*First Isaiah*, 461–63). Adding אל[ו]הים, the formula in Isa 37:20 reads as in 2 Kgs 19:19. Because the Great Isaiah Scroll tends to be expansive (according to Kutscher, *Language and Linguistic Background of the Isaiah Scroll*), I prefer the *lectio difficilior*.

110. Though Jer 9:23[24] and 24:7 include the verb ידע and the clause כי אני יהוה (thus fitting the definition of an RF), there is both an interruption of the expected phrasing with a personal pronoun

וידעו כי־שמי יהוה

And they shall know that my name is Yahweh
Jeremiah 16:21[111]

ונתתי להם לב לדעת אתי כי אני יהוה והיו־לי לעם ואנכי אהיה להם לאלהים

And I will give them a heart to know me, that I am Yahweh, and they will be my
people and I will be their God
Jeremiah 24:7[112]

למען תדעו כי קום יקומו דברי עליכם לרעה

So that you will know that my words of calamity against you will surely stand
Jeremiah 44:29 (cf. 44:28)

J. Hosea
Phrases Related to the Recognition Formula

והיא לא ידעה כי אנכי נתתי לה הדגן

And she did not know that I gave her the grain
Hosea 2:10[8]

וידעת את־יהוה

And you shall know Yahweh
Hosea 2:22[20]

ואנכי יהוה אלהיך מארץ מצרים ואלהים זולתי לא תדע

I am Yahweh your God [since you came] from the land of Egypt, you know no
God but me.
Hosea 13:4

K. Joel
Expanded Recognition Formulas

וידעתם כי בקרב ישראל אני ואני יהוה אלהיכם ואין עוד

as object and a different rhetorical point. The formulaic language no longer indicates a "knowing"
that results from observing prophesied divine action. Some contend that the clause כי אני יהוה is
secondary in the two texts; see Holladay, *Jeremiah 1*, 658. For Jack Lundbom, these passages do not
give the content to be known—"that I am Yahweh"—but should be understood with the particle כי
being rendered as "for" (*Jeremiah 1–20*, 232–33).

111. In his commentary, Rabbi Kimchi considers this sentence equivalent to what we term the
RF (Cohen, *Jeremiah*, 106).

112. The RSV, NRSV, and ESV obscure the interruption of the RF structure in the Hebrew:
"I will give them a heart to know that I am the LORD." Again, I see no sense in deleting כי אני יהוה as
secondary with Holladay (*Jeremiah 1*, 654).

And you shall know that I am in Israel, and that I am Yahweh your God, and there is no other
Joel 2:27

וידעתם כי אני יהוה אלהיכם שכן בציון הר־קדשי

And you shall know that I am Yahweh your God, dwelling in Zion, my holy mountain
Joel 4:17[3:17]

L. Zechariah
Phrases Related to the Recognition Formula

וידעתם כי־יהוה צבאות שלחני

And you shall know that Yahweh Sebaoth sent me
Zechariah 2:13[9]

וידעת כי־יהוה צבאות שלחני אליך

And you shall know that Yahweh Sebaoth sent me to you
Zechariah 2:15[11]

וידעת כי־יהוה צבאות שלחני אליכם

And you[113] shall know that Yahweh Sebaoth sent me to you
Zechariah 4:9

וידעתם כי־יהוה צבאות שלחני אליכם

And you shall know that Yahweh Sebaoth sent me to you
Zechariah 6:15

M. Malachi
Phrase Related to the Recognition Formula

וידעתם כי שלחתי אליכם את המצוה הזאת להיות בריתי את־לוי אמר יהוה צבאות

You shall know that I have sent you this admonition so my covenant with Levi may stand, says Yahweh Sebaoth[114]
Malachi 2:4

---

113. MT and LXX have a 2ms subject, but some commentators note that "Peshiṭta, Targums, Vulgate, and some medieval Hebrew manuscripts have a 2mp," and the final word of the clause "reveals that a 2mp audience is clearly in view" (Boda, *Zechariah*, 299). Others hold that the singular verb addresses Zerubbabel (Hanhart, *Sacharja 1–8*, 250–51; Wolters, *Zechariah*, 134–35).

114. Termed an RF in Weyde, *Prophecy and Teaching*, 173–76.

N. Psalms
Phrases Related to the Recognition Formula

הרפו ודעו כי־אנכי אלהים

Be still and know that I am God
Psalm 46:11[10]

וידעו כי־אלהים משל ביעקב לאפסי הארץ

That they may know that God rules over Jacob to the ends of the earth
Psalm 59:14[13]

דעו כי־יהוה הוא אלהים

Know that Yahweh, he is God
Psalm 100:3

וידעו כי־ידך זאת אתה יהוה עשיתה

Let them know that this is your hand, that you, Yahweh, have done it
Psalm 109:27[26]

כי אני ידעתי כי־גדול יהוה ואדנינו מכל־אלהים

For I know that Yahweh is great, and our Lord is greater than all gods
Psalm 135:5

O. 2 Chronicles
Phrase Related to the Recognition Formula

וידעו מנשה כי יהוה הוא האלהים

And Manasseh knew that Yahweh, he is God
2 Chronicles 33:13

CHAPTER 4

The Origin of Ezekiel's Formula and Questions of Inner-Biblical Exegesis

"All things are known through comparison"

—Leon Battista Alberti (1404–1472)[1]

In his seminal *Old Testament Theology*, Gerhard von Rad remarks on the close correspondence between Jer 31–32 and Ezek 36 when they speak of God's saving activity including his granting Israel a "new heart," upon which Yahweh's law is written that they might obey. Von Rad comments: "There are striking parallels with Jer. XXXI. 31ff.; *one feels that Ezekiel must somehow have had Jeremiah's prophecies in front of him* (in particular, Jer. XXXII. 37ff.)."[2] His instinct here is likely the correct one,[3] and he draws the conclusion that "there is nothing surprising in the fact that Ezekiel was *au fait* with all that went on in the homeland, even in detail, for this is how exiles have behaved down through the ages."[4]

If von Rad may make such an assertion concerning literary dependence based on a few close parallels between the two prophecies, then the *many* parallels adduced and the examples of inner-biblical exegesis in this chapter justify the assertion of Ezekiel's literary dependence on the book of Exodus. This chapter will present evidence and argue that Ezekiel drew from Exodus as an authoritative "hard text" (in some recensional form). There are serious difficulties with the standard critical view that Ezekiel drew from a growing, rather nebulous body of "tradition" made up of teachings, formulas, and freely formulated history telling,

---

1. Alberti, *On Painting*, 54.
2. Von Rad, *Old Testament Theology*, 2:235 (emphasis added).
3. There is no serious difficulty in believing that a copy of some of Jeremiah's later prophecies made its way to Babylon. At least one letter (Jer 29) was reportedly sent to Babylon in a continuation of efforts to disseminate his prophecies, just as earlier oracles were already being distributed years before the exile of the young priest Ezekiel in the year 597 (see Jer 36). Also, Ezekiel's prophecy makes mention both of traffic (24:26) and of news filtering back (11:15) from the west to the community in exile.
4. Von Rad, *Old Testament Theology*, 2:221. In addition to von Rad's observation regarding the typical behavior of exiles in gathering news from the homeland, the common priestly background of Jeremiah and Ezekiel increases the likelihood of literary borrowing. For further evidence, see Holladay, *Jeremiah 2*, 81–84. Dalit Rom-Shiloni seeks to explain the "silence" between the two figures ("Ezekiel and Jeremiah").

to be (re)interpreted however the community of faith chose.[5] The close, detailed correspondence between Exodus and Ezekiel at so many points does not, in my view, comport well with critical theories regarding the free handling of sources and traditions. There is a contradiction between the notion of a "free handling of tradition" and the sort of strict, exact use that Ezekiel makes of materials now found in the final form of the Pentateuch.

In this chapter, evidence is presented in support of two claims: (1) that Ezekiel's prophecy as a whole betrays a broad dependence on the book of Exodus, and (2) that Ezekiel's use of the RF was inspired by and had its source in Exodus. These two theses are interrelated, and the cumulative evidence adduced in support of the first serves to strengthen the second.

4.1. The Broad Dependence of Ezekiel on the Book of Exodus

Research on inner-biblical interpretation suggests that much scholarly work remains to be done on the prophetic books to understand the role of Scripture—Torah, psalmody, previous prophets—in shaping the prophets' messages. To what extent has Ezekiel the prophet been "influenced by a study of Israel's sacred writings"?[6] May we properly speak, as Brevard Childs does, of a "preoccupation with scripture on the part of Ezekiel"?[7] Yes, the broad dependence of Ezekiel on the Pentateuch (as a literary deposit in some recension), particularly Exodus, may be seen in (1) the many linguistic and terminological parallels and the examples of inner-biblical exegesis, (2) the similarities of themes, events, and theology, that seem to direct one to read Ezekiel and Exodus together, and (3) Ezekiel's reuse of "scriptural traditions" in a recontextualizing and sometimes sharply revisionary way.

4.1.1. Linguistic and Terminological Parallels

The most striking observation of Ezekielian dependence on Exodus comes from close examination of the prophet's reuse of Exod 6. He makes repeated use of

---

5. Daniel Block urges more weighing of evidence that even the earliest writing prophets called attention to a written law and the people's deviation from it: "Hosea knew a written body of divine תורה ('instructions'; 8:12)" ("In Search of Theological Meaning," 233). Block also points here to Deut 31:9–13 and 33:10, which charge priests with the responsibilities of teaching "your ordinances to Jacob and your torah to Israel" (33:10) and of preserving copies of the law that it might be passed on to a new generation of leadership (17:18), making them what Block calls "custodians of a written torah." He also here mentions Ezek 22:26 and its reference to the priests doing violence to "my law." How may Ezekiel have understood his ministry, in priestly terms, as one of upholding the integrity of the law and teaching it? See Betts, *Ezekiel the Priest*.
6. Childs, *Introduction*, 364.
7. Childs, *Introduction*, 364.

what Walther Zimmerli calls the two-sided covenant formula[8]—"you will be my people and I will be your God"[9]—which first appears in Exod 6:7 (P), immediately adjacent to the first RF. This profound promise/decree of engagement appears in Ezek 11:20, 14:11, 34:24, 36:28, 37:23, and 37:27. Ezekiel modifies the statement in 34:30–31 by merging it with the RF and then quickly repeating the sense of it: "You, my sheep, ... are people, and I am your God." With this parallel, one glimpses Ezekiel's pattern of selecting a theme or formula from Exodus and multiplying its usage in his prophecy. He does more than "borrow" a formula, he appropriates it as his own and employs it with something bordering on extravagance.

Michael Fishbane states that Ezek 20:4–11 and 33–36 "withstands a point-by-point comparison with the language of Exodus 6:2–9," and he finds a distinct purpose in the prophet's borrowing: "Indeed, it is just by virtue of this terminological relationship to Exodus 6:2–9 that the power and paradox of Ezekiel's midrashic reinterpretation—of a 'new' exodus done in wrath against Israel—are accentuated."[10] Prior to Fishbane, Sheldon Blank and Herbert Haag offered a close comparison of Exod 6 and Ezek 20.[11] Table 7 draws from their work and adds further parallels. Especially worth noting first is that Ezekiel's style of reinterpretation shows a strong tendency to repeat terms and phrases several times. Where he borrows phraseology, he will use and reuse the material. This pattern also shows up, of course, in Ezekiel's multiplication of the RF. Secondly, the two texts demonstrate the same rhetorical development with three features: (a) *repeated* use of the SPF ("I am Yahweh") by itself, combined with (b) the verb ידע in the Niphal first-person singular ("I revealed myself"), leading to (c) the appearance of the RF. No other books, or even chapters, in the Hebrew Bible exhibit these three together. Finally, both chapters include retrospectives.

Table 7 includes persuasive parallels, but when readers proceed further in Ezek 20 and compare verses 33–42 with Exod 6, the effect is little short of breathtaking. Ezekiel uses the precise language of God's compressed speech to Moses, and chapter 20 becomes remarkably like a phrase-by-phrase exposition of Exod 6. The reader is thus provided with two separate examples within a single chapter (Ezek 20:5–26 and 33–42) of Ezekiel's inner-biblical interpretation of one Torah text (Exod 6:1–9). Recognizing one case helps readers find the other. Fishbane shows

8. Zimmerli, *Ezekiel 1*, 309.

9. From a redemptive historical perspective, this covenant refrain is best understood as a reaffirmation of the basic covenant promise made to Abraham: "I shall establish my covenant between me and you and your seed after you, as an everlasting covenant over their generations, to be God to you and to your seed after you. ... I will be their God" (Gen 17:7–8; allegedly P).

10. Fishbane, "Torah and Tradition," 276–77.

11. Blank, "Studies in Deutero-Isaiah," 44–45; Haag, *Was lehrt die literarische Untersuchung?* 24–27; Fishbane, *Text and Texture*, 132.

Table 7. The First Reuse of Exodus 6 in Ezekiel 20

Exodus 6		Ezekiel 20
נודעתי (v. 3)	"I revealed myself"	נודעתי (v. 9); ואודע (v. 5)
נשאתי את־ידי (v. 8)	"I lifted my hand" (in an oath)	ואשא ידי (2× in v. 5) / נשאתי ידי (v. 6) / אני נשאתי ידי (v. 15) / אני נשאתי את־ידי (v. 23)
אני יהוה (vv. 2, 6, 8)	"I am Yahweh"	לאמר אני יהוה אלהיכם (v. 5) / אני יהוה אלהיכם (v. 7)
וידעתם כי אני יהוה אלהיכם (v. 7) "You shall know that I am Yahweh your God"		לדעת כי אני יהוה (v. 12) / לדעת כי אני יהוה אלהיכם (v. 20) / ידעו אשר אני יהוה (v. 26)
והוצאתי אתכם מתחת סבלת מצרים (v. 6) "I will bring you out from under the yokes of the Egyptians"		להוציאם מארץ מצרים (v. 6) "Bring them out from the Land of Egypt"
ולא שמעו אל־משה (v. 9) "But they did not listen to Moses"		ולא אבו לשמע אלי (v. 8) "But they would not listen to me"

the relationship between texts by means of a table[12] that is reproduced in slightly modified form at Table 8.

Fishbane concludes: "Because of the intentional reuse of Exodus 6:6–8, Ezekiel's oracle takes on a heightened effect. Its sarcasm and bitterness were undoubtedly not lost on his first audience."[13] A case can well be made that it was not only the prophet who was familiar with these motifs and quotations; Childs surmises that the exiled people likely recognized Ezekiel's prophecy recorded in chapter 20 as a "commentary on Ex. 6."[14] There was a common literary heritage from which Ezekiel could draw. The function of the echoing was to evoke the exiles' memory of the exodus event with the familiar language of that narrative, retelling the story in a most negative fashion as an "unholy-history" of the nation.

12. Fishbane, *Text and Texture*, 132.
13. Fishbane, *Text and Texture*, 132. More recently, Fishbane writes: "This recognition motif is a signature feature of the prophet Ezekiel and echoes a formula first found in the Book of Exodus" (*Haftarot*, 88).
14. Childs, *Exodus*, 113.

Table 8. The Second Reuse of Exodus 6 in Ezekiel 20

Exodus 6:6–8		Ezekiel 20:33–42
והוצאתי	"I will take [you] out"	והוצאתי
בזרוע נטויה	"with an outstretched arm"	בזרוע נטויה
ובשפטים	"and with judgments" / "I will judge"	ונשפטתי
וידעתם כי אני יהוה	RF (exactly the same version)	וידעתם כי אני יהוה
והבאתי אתכם	"and I will bring you" / "when I bring you"	בהביאי אתכם
אל־הארץ	"to the land" / "to the land of Israel"	אל־אדמת ישראל
אשר נשאתי את־ידי	"which I swore" (lit. raised my hand)	אשר נשאתי את־ידי
לתת אתה	"to give it"	לתת אתה
לאברהם ליצחק וליעקב	"to Abraham, Isaac and Jacob" / "to your forefathers"	לאבותיכם

Risa Levitt Kohn notes an additional parallel between Exod 6 and Ezek 20,[15] and the shared terminology is of special interest in this study because of the close proximity of an RF in the Ezek 20 text (same verse).

(Exod 6:4) ארץ מגריהם   "the land of their sojourn"   ארץ מגוריהם (Ezek 20:38)

According to her research: "This expression occurs five times in P (Gen. 17:8; 28:4; 36:7; 37:1; Exod. 6:4) and once in Ezekiel (20:38). It is not found elsewhere in the HB."

If, as I propose, Ezekiel made a special study of Exod 6 and its wording, readers may expect to find other terms or phrases from Exod 6 used in the prophecy. The theological term "possession" or "heritage" (מורשה), used in Exod 6:8 (allegedly P) to denote the promised land, is a good first example. Ezekiel is the only other book to use the term in this sense,[16] and uses it repeatedly (11:15; 25:4, 10; 33:24; 36:2–5) in a manner that fits its literary style. Another term in Exod 6 widely used in Ezekiel is "acts of judgment" (שפטים),[17] often with "great/mighty" (גדל). It occurs in Exod 6:6, 7:4, and 12:12 (all P), and then ten times in Ezekiel (5:10, 15; 11:9; 14:21; 16:41; 25:11; 28:22, 26; 30:14, 19). Other appearances are Num 33:4 (P), Prov 19:29, and 2 Chr 24:24. Among these last three, the Numbers text confirms how שפטים is especially associated with the exodus narrative. The Proverbs text is unrelated theologically to Ezekiel's usage, and the Chronicles text, judged to be much later by its linguistic profile, could not have exerted any influence on Ezekiel's use of the term. If the prophecy is indeed recalling the language of the exodus story at this

---

15. Levitt Kohn, *New Heart*, 39. The spelling varies, with Exod 6:4 lacking a *waw* in מגוריהם.

16. Deut 33:4 employs the word to describe "the law which Moses gave us."

17. *HALOT* gives an alternate definition of "penalty."

point, the book would be signaling one of its prime theological emphases: Yahweh, a God of great *judgments* in Egypt, intends to effect similar judgments again.

A clear pattern emerges in comparing Exodus texts with Ezekiel: the latter seems to take up numerous locutions found in the former and reemploy them in an elaborate, repetitious manner. Still another expression from Exod 6, לכן אמר, is reused in Ezekiel following this remarkable pattern. This "therefore say" introduces a divine oracle to be delivered to God's people by Moses (Exod 6:6; Num 25:12—both P) or by the prophet Ezekiel (11:16, 17; 12:23, 28; 14:6; 20:30; 33:25; 36:22). It occurs nowhere else in the OT.[18]

Seven more examples of linguistic and terminological parallels will complete this brief listing. More could be adduced, but these examples must suffice. Anyone examining Exod 31:13 (P) with Ezek 20:12 and 20 even in translation sees the correspondence between them.[19] The similarities between the Hebrew texts are perhaps even more noticeable, and some of these, though not all, will be discussed below.[20]

(Exodus 31:13)

אך את־שבתתי תשמרו כי אות הוא ביני וביניכם לדרתיכם לדעת כי אני יהוה מקדשכם:

(Ezekiel 20:12, 20)

וגם את־שבתותי נתתי להם להיות לאות ביני וביניהם לדעת כי אני יהוה מקדשם:

ואת־שבתותי קדשו והיו לאות ביני וביניכם לדעת כי אני יהוה אלהיכם:

So close is the similarity between the passages that Walther Eichrodt dismisses the Ezekiel verses as secondary. He believes they come from a later "priestly redactor of the prophetic text who slavishly copied the phraseology of Exodus 31."[21] In a Princeton Seminary dissertation, Joon Surh Park argues the opposite, that Exod 31 is dependent on Ezek 20.[22] Though Park is correct in assuming a relationship of literary dependence, it is something of an oddity for him to assert the priority of Ezekiel.[23] Such an argument is out of the mainstream of Ezekiel scholarship,[24] and

18. The observation and statistics come from Levitt Kohn, *New Heart*, 75.

19. Exod 31:13 reads: "You shall keep my Sabbaths. This will be a sign between me and you for the generations to come, so that you may know that I am Yahweh, who makes you holy." Ezek 20:12 and 20 have similar language: "I also gave them my Sabbaths as a sign between us, so they would know that I am Yahweh, who made them holy.... Keep my Sabbaths holy, that they may be a sign between us. Then you shall know that I am Yahweh your God."

20. See 4.2.2 below. Levitt Kohn also discusses these parallel texts (*New Heart*, 33).

21. Eichrodt, *Ezekiel*, 264 (see also his "Der Sabbat bei Hezekiel").

22. Park, "Theological Traditions," 78–80.

23. There is now a strong trend in some circles to date almost all OT literature to the postexilic era. To such scholars, Park's conclusions are more acceptable.

24. Prior to Zimmerli's time, G. A. Cooke writes of Ezek 20:12: "the present verse is merely a quotation from Ex. 31:13 P from H; the same may be said of v. 20." Probably on account of his late

it is undercut by recent studies arguing that Ezekiel's language is closer than P to Late Biblical Hebrew (see ch. 1), and by the evidence that Ezekiel shows a pattern of borrowing from, and often radical revision of, earlier traditions/texts. For his part, Zimmerli resists the idea that there must be dependence running in either direction: "The close connection of the sabbath motivation of 20:12 with Exodus 31:13 must not be explained by a literary-critical reduction of the text in various ways, but by reference to Ezekiel's origin in the priestly legal tradition with its fixed language."[25] I doubt, however, that the number and range of parallels between the final form of Exodus and Ezekiel can be adequately explained by reference to *tradition*. There must be a "hard text" behind all of Ezekiel's parallels and allusions to materials now found in the final form of Exodus.

The preceding arguments and data in this section, showing how Ezek 20 used Exodus, indicate that the prophet is almost certainly copying earlier phraseology. Eichrodt's instinct was correct, though he need not have dated the materials as he did or denied the authenticity of the Sabbath reference (with all other Sabbath references in Ezekiel).

Moses and Ezekiel have parallel experiences in the latter parts of the books of Exodus and Ezekiel, experiences in which they meet with Yahweh on top of mountains[26] and receive visions and detailed building plans for the dwelling place of God: the tabernacle in Moses's case (Exod 25–27 [P]) and a postexilic temple in Ezekiel's vision (esp. Ezek 40–44). Set in these similar contexts, there are texts that relate how both priest-prophets observe the descent of the glory of Yahweh upon his dwelling place. The Hebrew texts of Exod 40:35 and Ezek 43:5 suggest that the prophet's description has been influenced by Exodus. Setting them alongside each other allows readers to appreciate more fully the relationship.

(Exodus 40:34 and 35)	(Ezekiel 43:5)
וכבוד יהוה מלא את־המשכן	והנה מלא כבוד־יהוה הבית
"And the glory of Yahweh filled the Tabernacle"	"See, the glory of Yahweh filled the Temple"

---

dating of P, Cooke regards the Sabbath texts in Ezekiel as secondary, "the handiwork of a later scribe, zealous for the Law" (*Ezekiel*, 217). Moshe Greenberg calls the Ezekiel texts "a virtual citation of Exod. 31:13" (*Ezekiel 1–20*, 366). Leslie Allen says of chapter 20 that "Ezekiel now follows traditional strands of the pentateuchal narratives in his depiction of the Exodus and of lawgiving and lawbreaking in the wilderness" (*Ezekiel 20–48*, 10). Joseph Blenkinsopp's perspective on many elements of ch. 20, including the Sabbath references, is that "Ezekiel follows priestly tradition" (*Ezekiel*, 88).

25. Zimmerli, *Ezekiel 1*, 410. The same sort of conclusion is drawn by Henning Graf Reventlow in comparing H with Ezekiel; see *Wächter über Israel*, which views similarities as resulting from shared priestly tradition.

26. Jon Levenson says the mountain of Ezekiel's vision can be interpreted as both Zion and Mount Sinai (*Theology of the Program*, 7–24, 37–53). The first is "literal," while the second is "typo-logical" (41).

The contention that Ezekiel was not only aware of but also influenced by the Exodus account of Moses receiving detailed building plans for Yahweh's sanctuary is strengthened by the observation that the term "span" or "hand's-breadth" (טפח) occurs twice in the alleged Priestly Source of Exodus (25:25; 37:12) and three times in Ezekiel's measurements (40:5, 43; 43:13), without appearing anywhere else in the OT.[27]

The third parallel between Exodus and Ezekiel is almost exact in its vocabulary. In the first extended passage in Ezekiel to include the RF, chapter 6, the reader finds the expression דברתי לעשות להם הרעה, "I said I would do evil to them" (v. 10). Exod 32, which records the Golden Calf incident, also speaks of disaster that Yahweh threatened to bring upon the people: הרעה אשר דבר לעשות לעמו (v. 14). According to Moshe Greenberg, this expression occurs only in these two passages throughout the Hebrew Bible.[28]

A fourth example of shared terminology is the phrase נטה את־ידי ("stretch out my hand/forearm"), which Levitt Kohn notes as appearing four times in Exodus (all P) and five times in Ezekiel.[29] (Additionally, it is found in Jer 6:12.) Out of the four occurrences in Exodus, the single text that has Yahweh as the subject of נטה (7:5) also contains a RF: "Then the Egyptians shall know that I am Yahweh when I stretch out my hand." In Ezekiel, too, the verb נטה is used with Yahweh as the subject (all five times), and one text includes an attached RF. Levitt Kohn writes: "In Ezek. 6:14, Yahweh's purpose echoes Exod. 7:5: '... so they will know that I am Yahweh.'"[30] There is an ironic twist in language, however. Ezekiel reuses a phrase that once referred to Yahweh's activity in saving his people at the time of the exodus, but the God of Israel now stretches out his hand *against* Israel to make himself known.

Examine a fifth example. Both men received peculiar visions of God in his glory—outside the promised land, one might add—when they were commissioned, and the spectacle of the כבוד יהוה is a leading motif in both Exodus and Ezekiel. The glory visions included the aspects of storm clouds (ענן) and fire/lightning (אש) (Exod 19:16 [E]; 24:15–18 [P]; Ezek 1:4), a clear pavement or "fixed platform"[31] under the feet of God (Exod 24:10 [J]; Ezek 1:22, 26), and objects beneath the deity that appeared like "sapphire" (ספיר), probably what is today

---

27. Levitt Kohn, *New Heart*, 54.

28. Greenberg, *Ezekiel 1–20*, 135.

29. Those texts are: Exod 7:5, 19; 14:16, 26; Ezek 6:14; 14:9, 13; 25:13; 35:3.

30. Levitt Kohn, *New Heart*, 33.

31. Zimmerli, *Ezekiel 1*, 130. The terminology referring to the platform differs (because of perspective?): Exodus speaks of a pavement (כמעשה לבנת) under the feet of Yahweh, while Ezekiel looks at it from below and speaks of an expanse or "firmament" above the heads of the four living creatures (רקיע אשר על־ראשם). Use of "firmament" may tie this Ezekiel text to Gen 1 (allegedly P), which contains six occurrences of רקיע. Other than Gen 1 and Ezekiel's five occurrences (1:22, 23, 25, 26; 10:1), it rarely appears (Pss 19:2; 150:1; Dan 12:3).

called lapis lazuli (Exod 24:10 [J]; Ezek 1:26; 10:1).[32] Nowhere else in the OT is there a text that associates ספיר with God's locale.

In another parallel, Ezek 8 tells of a vision of gross idolatry being practiced on the temple grounds by "seventy elders of the house of Israel" (8:7–13). This should be tied to the Exodus account of the "seventy elders of Israel" approaching Yahweh at Sinai (Exod 24:9–11 [J]). In the whole of the OT, only one other passage refers to seventy elders (Num 11 [J/E]). Childs goes so far as to say that Ezekiel's vision "is not understood unless this cultic abuse is seen in the light of the covenant ceremony in Exod. 24:9ff."[33] The contrast between idolatrous elders and the earlier elders worshipping before Yahweh is stinging. Once again, there is a shock for readers of Ezekiel's oracles who know the narratives in Exodus.

Mention of "the firstborn" prompts specialists to think of the notorious difficulties with Ezek 20:26. Aside from the theology there, the link between that text's phrasing (כל־פטר רחם; "every first issue which opens a womb") and the consecration of the firstborn (כל־פטר רחם again) in Exod 13:12 and 15 and 34:19 [all J/E] deserves attention. The connection between Exod 13:12 and Ezek 20:26 is even clearer with the adjacent Hiphil forms of עבר (inf. const. in Ezek; pf. in Exod). There is one other occurrence of the phrase כל־פטר רחם in the entire Bible (Num 18:15 [P]), and it is without an accompanying עבר verb. Daniel Block is surely right to say of the Ezekiel text that "the form of the ... statement is influenced by the traditional rite of redemption of the firstborn" in Exod 13.[34]

The evidence mounts that the stories, themes, catch-phrases, and formulas of Exodus were recognizable to the people and *saturated* the mind of the prophet. Because Exodus was part of the literary heritage shared by Ezekiel and his contemporaries, historical references, allusions, and even quotations could be used to considerable rhetorical effect, especially where familiar language was "skewed"[35] to deliver a reproach. The situation among the exiles made supreme demands on the preacher-prophet's rhetorical skills, for the people would not listen (Ezek 2:3–8).

The oracles of Ezekiel would seem to lose a measure of their coherence and power if there were not a common record of their historical past available to the

---

32. Some scholars take ספיר in Ezek 10:1 to describe Yahweh's throne (NIV; NRSV), as in 1:26, while others understand Ezekiel to speak of a lapis lazuli platform that parallels Exod 24:10 (NJPS; Greenberg, *Ezekiel 1–20*, 179–80; Block, *Ezekiel 1–24*, 319). True "sapphire" or "corundum" seems to have been unknown in the ANE (see *HALOT*, 764, and Sarna, *Exodus*, 153).

33. Childs, *Introduction*, 364. See the similar comments in Duguid, *Ezekiel and the Leaders*, 113, Allen, *Ezekiel 1–19*, 143, and Block, *Ezekiel 1–24*, 289–90.

34. Block, *Ezekiel 1–24*, 636.

35. Greenberg, *Ezekiel 1–20*, 372. He also writes further here: "We conclude that Ezekiel characteristically utilizes a traditional phrase with a shocking twist: in the new Exodus the ferocity that tradition asserted was unleashed upon Egypt in the old one will be turned against rebellious Israel in order to force it finally to accept what it never had before—God's kingship over it in the land he chose for it."

people. How else could Ezekiel repeatedly reproach the nation for its lack of historical memory? "You did not remember the days of your youth" (16:22, 43). Without that common record to which Ezekiel might appeal, the six references to Egypt in 23:1–27 would be rhetorically irrelevant.

This seems to be an instance in which Occam's razor cuts through the complexity of many arguments. It stands to reason that Exodus was available at that time in a literary form similar to what exists today if one considers that: (1) Ezek 20 reminds the people of their deliverance from Egypt, as Hosea had done earlier; (2) that "reminder" indicates that the nation knew the story of her past (which could be scandalously retold in chs. 16 and 23); (3) Ezek 20 recalls the nation's historical experience using some of the exact language set down in the final form of Exodus; and (4) the rhetorical punch of the prophetic retelling would seem to require the audience's familiarity with and recognition of both the story and the wording that Ezek 20 uses.

Zimmerli disagrees with this assessment and offers a markedly different perspective on Ezekiel's revisionist history in chapter 20 and elsewhere. He seeks to understand those texts using von Rad's ideas regarding the "short historical credo."[36] The credo idea proves useful to Zimmerli for explaining the strict, structured way in which Ezekiel retold Israel's history.

> G. von Rad has shown that Israel, at a very early period, formulated certain credo-like summaries of its account of its original encounter with Yahweh, which could not easily be expanded by its subsequent historical experience. Ezekiel 20 can only be understood, in its traditio-historical background, when we see how the prophet takes up here the sacred core of the credo formulation which he had received and retells Israel's history on the basis of it.[37]

How had Ezekiel received this credo formulation? Zimmerli believes it was tradition conveyed in part by "priestly theology." Indeed, "the similarity of the formulations [i.e., the content of the historical recounting in Ezek 20] to those of Ex 6 suggests that Ezekiel was following a priestly theology in this."[38] Elsewhere, he explains that the "saving history," which included events and their theological interpretation, was "memorized in the credo."[39]

Building on von Rad, Zimmerli set the pace in Ezekiel scholarship for two generations. He stressed the importance of traditio-historical research, and his influence is seen in many contemporary scholars' constant reference to *tradition*—traditions encapsulated in priestly theology, in prophetic formulations, in legal

36. Von Rad develops the historical credo idea in "Form-critical Problem" and in vol. 1 of his *Old Testament Theology*.
37. Zimmerli, *Ezekiel 1*, 405.
38. Zimmerli, *Ezekiel 1*, 407.
39. Zimmerli, *Ezekiel 1*, 412.

formulations, and so on. However, can scholarship really understand the relationship between, say, Exod 6 and Ezek 20 by making reference to the *traditions* and theology of Ezekiel's priestly heritage? Were the prophet merely carrying on an academic discussion with fellow priests, Zimmerli's approach might be more convincing. Allusion is a social phenomenon, and according to the testimony of the prophecy, Ezekiel is invoking the historical memory *of the people*, not only the heirs of a priestly theology and its traditions. Certainly, the oracles are highly intellectual, but the prophet's commission was to "go and speak to the house of Israel" (3:1; cf. vv. 4–11, 17), to all the exiles (אל־הגולה אל־בני עמך 3:11). He wrote for the whole community (כל־בית ישראל 3:7), not a select few. And the fact that Ezekiel employs a form of parody indicates the availability to his audience of the original material that he twists into a different shape. What is not well known cannot sensibly be "parodied" before an audience.[40]

When one bears in mind the audience and/or readership of Ezekiel's oracles, scholars' attempts to settle the issue of parallels by constant recourse to the notion of tradition alone appear artificial.[41] It is not enough to say: "As both prophet and priest, Ezekiel had access to a wide variety of *traditional* forms of speech. He made full use of the prophetic speech formulae."[42] It is not enough for senior evangelicals to cite Zimmerli's critical conclusions regarding tradition, rather than to rethink the questions raised by the RF as it appears in various OT books.[43] To say merely that Ezekiel's characteristic formulas are "rooted in the *tradition* of the Exodus and conquest"[44] is to fight shy of the evidence of text quotation and inner-biblical interpretation produced in this chapter. One must take account of the "multiple and sustained" linkages between the two texts and of Ezekiel's reuse of Exodus material "in a lexically reorganized and topically rethematized way."[45] I choose to speak of "texts," or at least "*scriptural* traditions."

40. See Block, *Ezekiel 1–24*, 613, and Lust, "Ez., XX, 4–26 une parodie." Ezekiel's whole argument in several places (esp. chs. 16, 20, and 23) falls to the ground unless the people have some agreed-upon history that the prophet can reference. If one seeks to interpret ch. 20 by taking seriously an exilic date and context, one seems driven to this conclusion. Of course, those who date the final form of pentateuchal books late could force Ezekiel to fit their scheme with complex redaction criticism (ranging far into the postexilic period) or with a Deutero-Ezekiel theory.

41. E.g., Henry McKeating writes: "The Mosaic traditions which influenced the compilers of the book of Ezekiel were not necessarily those of our finished Pentateuch, but *the partially formed traditions* which were its raw material.... *There are practically no echoes of the Pentateuch's language*" ("Ezekiel the 'Prophet like Moses'?" 108 [emphasis added]). The evidence presented in this study contradicts McKeating's assertion.

42. Blenkinsopp, *Ezekiel*, 7.

43. Allen, *Joel, Obadiah, Jonah and Micah*, 96; Hubbard, *Joel and Amos*, 80.

44. VanGemeren, *Interpreting the Prophetic Word*, 329. One may add Allen, who allows that the prophecy demonstrates a "use of Exod 6:6–8" (*Ezekiel 20–48*, 8) but then writes, "*from priestly tradition* concerning Israel's experience in Egypt the prophet borrows the motifs of God's self-disclosure by name and of his sworn promise of the land (cf. Exod 6:3, 6–8)" (9; emphasis added).

45. Fishbane, *Biblical Interpretation*, 285. He here states a criterion for recognizing inner-biblical interpretation. My use of Fishbane's phrasing is not meant to suggest that, on this specific point,

After researching the parallels adduced in this section, I can heartily agree with Childs's conviction:

> Surely one of the most important aspects of Ezekiel's message was its dependence upon the activity of interpretation within the Bible itself. Not only was Ezekiel deeply immersed in the ancient traditions of Israel, but the prophet's message shows many signs of being influenced by a study of Israel's sacred writings. The impact of a collection of authoritative writings is strong throughout the book. Obviously, the mediating of Israel's tradition through an authoritative written source represents a major canonical interest. The evidence that such activity was a major factor in the formulation of Ezekiel's original oracles would also account for the ease with which the canonical process adopted his oracles without great change.[46]

Again, to quote Childs: "This preoccupation with scripture on the part of Ezekiel should come as no surprise since the importance of the 'scroll' which is eaten is stressed right from the start (3.1ff.)."[47] There is a turning-on-its-head of the usual scholarly expectation with the prophetic literature: instead of writing down what has been orally delivered, Ezekiel speaks out the word of God that was written on a scroll.

It is not the argument of this chapter that Ezekiel was influenced *exclusively* by Exodus in some authoritative recension. The prophecy shows evidence of knowing other pentateuchal narratives and laws, drawing from them as well.[48] Scholars have long studied the many links between Ezekiel and the Holiness Code (Lev 17–26),[49] and they are of huge theological and literary import.[50] There are also connections

---

he himself would disavow critical conclusions regarding *tradition*. He readily employs the terminology and methodology of tradition history (with modifications mentioned above in ch. 1).

46. Childs, *Introduction*, 364.

47. Childs, *Introduction*, 364.

48. Greenberg makes this point in "Influence of Tradition." See also Levitt Kohn, *New Heart*, Lyons, *From Law to Prophecy*, and Gile, "Deuteronomy and Ezekiel's Theology," 287–306.

49. Early works are: Klostermann, "Ezechiel und das Heiligkeitsgesetz" [1877]; Horst, *Leviticus xvii–xxvi und Hezekiel*; and Paton, "Holiness Code." As Zimmerli notes (*Ezekiel 1*, 46), the relation between the two is so close that some old interpreters thought Ezekiel was either the author of H (Graf) or its redactor (Horst). Paton concludes that "the only theory which will explain all the facts of the relation of Ez. to Lev. xvii–xxvi is that Ez. had this legislation before him as a written code" (115). Since then, some have proposed other alternatives: Ezekiel and H must have drawn from a common source (Fohrer, *Hauptprobleme*, 144–48); Ezekiel is dependent on a preexilic H that had edited an even earlier P (Milgrom, "Leviticus 26 and Ezekiel," 57–62); and proposals of influence in either direction are simplistic (Zimmerli). Allen provides an in-depth comparison of Lev 26 with Ezekiel in *Ezekiel 1–19*, 92–96 ("Excursus: The Relation between Leviticus 26 and Ezekiel 4–6") and comes to conclusions similar to Paton's, as does Lyons in *From Law to Prophecy*. For the view that H depends on Ezekiel, see Müller, "Prophetic View."

50. Many have cataloged the parallels. Among the more impressive ones detailed by Levitt Kohn are the following. Only in Ezekiel and so-called H do we read the phrase ונתתי גשם בעתם/בעתם נתתי גשם

between Ezekiel and the books of Genesis[51] and Numbers,[52] links clear enough to have impressed Levitt Kohn, Stephen Cook, and others as examples of inner-biblical interpretation.[53] One might ask what "Scriptures" existed in Ezekiel's day. Many Ezekiel scholars like Ellen Davis, impressed by this evidence, are led to conclude that "there must have existed before the fall [of Jerusalem] some form of Scripture, probably comprising the basic elements of the Torah and much of the Prophets."[54] Though a few excellent studies have been done in the past,[55] the task remains for someone to investigate in a more exhaustive manner Ezekiel's complex literary relationships to other Scriptures.

4.1.2. Similarities of Theme, Events, and Theology

The above linguistic and terminological parallels between Exodus and Ezekiel establish that the latter drew from the former. There is a clear pattern of reference back not only to exodus events in the prophet's historical retrospectives, nor only to a theological exodus tradition, but also to Exodus texts. In short, I have demonstrated a textual relationship and a dependency or "intertextuality of text production." If one grants this conclusion, arrived at inductively through research of specific examples, it may serve as a deductive "warrant" to read the many similarities of theme, events, and theology in Exodus and Ezekiel as further support for

---

("provision of rain in its season"; (Lev 26:4; Ezek 34:26), דמיהם בם/דמו בו ("his/their blood [be] upon him/them"; Lev 20:9, 11, 12, 13, 16; Ezek 18:13; 33:5), or רדה בפרך ("ruling with harshness"; Lev 25:43, 46, 53; Ezek 34:4). Most impressive of all are the "sword" phrases found only in Lev 26 and Ezekiel. How can there not be a genetic relationship when all of these phrases are reused in combination? They are: הביא חרב עליכם ("bring the sword against you"; Lev 26:25; Ezek 5:17; 6:3; 11:8; 14:17); הריק אחריכם חרב ("unsheathe the sword against you"; Lev 26:33; Ezek 5:2, 12; 12:14); and חרב תעבר בארץ ("a sword passing through the land"; Lev 26:6; Ezek 14:17). Discussing these shared locutions and literary dependence are Levitt Kohn, *New Heart*, 39, 47, 67, and 74, and Lyons, *From Law to Prophecy*. Preston Sprinkle presents further evidence of borrowing in "Law and Life."

51. J. Oscar Boyd treats Ezekiel's use of P in "Ezekiel and the Modern Dating," 35–42, while W. L. Moran discusses Ezekiel's reworking of J material in "Gen 49,10."

52. See, e.g.: (1) the expression יום לשנה יום לשנה ("a day for a year"), found nowhere else in the OT but Num 14:34 and Ezek 4:6; (2) the sharp response שמעו־נא ("hear now!"), which occurs in Num 16:8 and 20:10 and Ezek 18:25 but nowhere else in the OT; and (3) the idiom רב־לכם ("enough!"), which is found in P texts associated with rebellion (Num 16:3, 7) and in Ezek 44:6 and 45:9. These examples are listed by Levitt Kohn in *New Heart*, 67–69. Especially convincing is Boyd's close comparative reading of Num 14:34 (P) and Ezek 4:5–6, in which he shows that there are linked phrases beyond the expression "a day for a year" ("Ezekiel and the Modern Dating," 44–48). We read in so-called P, "for the number of days . . . forty days, a day for its year, a day for its year . . . you shall bear your iniquities." In Ezekiel, we read, "according to the number of days . . . forty days, a day for its year, a day for its year . . . you shall bear the iniquity of the house of Judah."

53. See Cook, "Innerbiblical Interpretation," and Levitt Kohn, *New Heart*, 67–69.

54. Davis, *Swallowing the Scroll*, 30.

55. Burrows, *Literary Relations*; Hurvitz, *Linguistic Study*; Levitt Kohn, *New Heart*.

the claim that Ezekiel's prophecy is dependent on Exodus and that an intertextual relationship exists that is fruitful to explore.

Though he may not have viewed himself as a second Moses, Ezekiel may well have understood his calling as similar in some fashion to that of Moses.[56] Both came from the tribe of Levi, and according to the biblical story, Moses necessarily had much to do with the establishment of the priesthood to which Ezekiel was heir so many centuries later. (It is commonplace in Ezekiel scholarship to note the personal tragedy in the fact that the exiled son of Buzi was unable to enter the priesthood to assume official duties.) The account of Moses's life does not tell of his performing the regular priestly duties in the Tabernacle, but he did take on certain priestly functions, particularly intercessory prayer for the sinful people and mediation on their behalf before Yahweh (Exod 32:11–13; possibly 17:11; cf. Num 14:13–19). It was the function of the priest to enter God's presence as a representative of the people and to act as God's representative to the people in proclaiming the law (Exod 24:3–7 [E?]; Ezek 7:26; cf. Ezra 7:10; Neh 8). Priests were charged with the duty of imparting, not perverting, the knowledge of God (Deut 31:9–13; Jer 2:8; Hos 4:1–9; Mal 2:7), especially in "teaching the children of Israel all the statutes that Yahweh has spoken to them by Moses" (Lev 10:11; cf. Ezek 7:26 [ותורה תאבד מכהן]). Certainly, the Pentateuch indicates that Moses eminently performed these functions. He also offered sacrifices (Exod 40:29) and sanctified the people by sprinkling blood upon them (Exod 24:8 [E?]). Besides his priestly ministry, Moses is also presented in Exodus as a prophetic figure[57] and regarded in biblical literature as a prophet without equal (Num 12:6–8; Deut 34:10; cf. Hos 12:14[13]). The merging of priestly and prophetic roles in Moses may well have been a profound idea to Ezekiel, the priest-prophet; it is certainly a topic of much debate in current Ezekiel scholarship, especially the relative prominence of each role and the possible tension between them.[58]

Moses and Ezekiel are also linked by similar life events recorded in Exodus and Ezekiel. Both are commissioned by God to go to a people steeped in idolatry and held captive in a foreign land, and they act as mediators to reintroduce Yahweh to his chastened people. As Moses was the prophetic agent of Yahweh certified by signs that portend judgment (Exod 4:9 [J]), so is Ezekiel (Ezek 4; 12; and

---

56. McKeating argues that Ezekiel regarded himself as a "second Moses" figure, or if we decide not to speak of the prophet himself (McKeating's own inclination, on second thought), that the compiler(s) "chose to present him" as such, as "one who repeats Moses' work in a new setting, and, be it noted, *repeats it with more success than Moses himself*" ("Ezekiel the 'Prophet Like Moses'?" 104 [emphasis original]).

57. See Di Pede, "'C'est par un prophète.'"

58. The relationship and tension between Ezekiel's twin callings are explored in: Burden, "Esegiël, Priester en Profeet"; Odell, "You Are What You Eat"; Sweeney, "Zadokite Priest and Visionary Prophet"; Mein, "Ezekiel as a Priest"; Duguid, "Putting Priests in Their Place"; Schwartz, "A Priest Out of Place"; Patton, "Priest, Prophet, and Exile"; Betts, *Ezekiel the Priest*; Lyons, *Introduction*, 14–20. Note that Jeremiah also had the twin callings.

24:15–27). Both priest-prophets faced a rebellious (מרה) nation who refused to listen (Exod 6:9; 23:21; Ezek 2:3–8; 20:8, 13). Both urged Israel to hope in Yahweh, that God would take them from their captivity and lead them as his people into the land promised to their forefathers. The books of Exodus and Ezekiel leave the life stories of both men unfinished, and for the later prophet, one imagines a disappointing end: "Like Moses, [Ezekiel] never sets foot on the land he surveyed (in visionary form)."[59]

Perceptive readers see similarities between the call narratives of Moses and Ezekiel. In her *JSOT* article, Rebecca Idestrom mentions that, for both men, the initial encounter with God was "far from home," involved a voice speaking from a fiery spectacle, and would be "the first of many unusual divine encounters that they will have throughout their ministries."[60] D. Nathan Phinney has explored how Ezekiel's call narrative may be patterned on Moses's more closely than has hitherto been recognized, including prophetic resistance.[61] Iain Duguid helpfully summarizes a point about two commissioning texts (Exod 7:1–5 and Ezek 2:1–3:11) from J. L. Ska's research: "In both God entrusts a mission to his envoy and before it begins announces the failure of that mission."[62]

In the call narrative, might there also be some connection between the assistance Moses requires (because of mouth trouble) in order to speak on Yahweh's behalf and the mysterious hindrance of Ezekiel speaking for Yahweh? Both experienced a bridling of the tongue, either by a personal, developmental speech impediment (Exod 4:10) or through a divinely-ordered speech impediment (Ezek 3:26). Both prophets had their mouths opened (Ezek 3:27; 29:21) after a fashion so that they might fulfill their divine commission. It was true for both men that Yahweh helped them to speak and taught them what to say (Exod 4:12; Ezek 3:10, 27).[63]

In Ezek 14:1 and 20:1, the prophet meets with the זקני ישראל, the "elders of Israel," just as Moses is reported to have done (Exod 3:16 [J]; 4:29 [J]; 12:21; 17:5–6; 19:7; 24:1, 9).[64] Both men plead for the people when Yahweh seems ready to destroy them all in their idolatry (Exod 32:9–14 [J/E]; Ezek 9:8; 11:13). Greenberg has argued that Moses and Ezekiel should be associated in readers' minds

59. Milgrom, *Ezekiel's Hope*, 217.

60. Idestrom, "Echoes," 492.

61. Phinney, "Prophetic Objection." Block finds the resistance in the text more pervasive than does Phinney (*Ezekiel 1–24*, 12, 137–38, 157).

62. Duguid, *Ezekiel and the Leaders*, 105, citing Ska, "La sortie d'Égypte." In fairness, I mention that Ska discounts the idea of literary dependence.

63. For a fascinating study of the bridling of the tongue and opening of the mouth motifs, see Glazov, *Bridling of the Tongue*. A note in Kennedy, "Hebrew *piṯôn peh*," also examines the motif and makes important points: Yahweh opens the prophet's mouth that he may speak to Egypt, the land where Israel learned idolatry and the only foreign nation condemned in Ezekiel for idolatry (30:13), and the result of the prophet's oracles is that Egypt comes to acknowledge the sovereignty of Yahweh.

64. Ezekiel meets זקני יהודה ("the elders of Judah") in 8:1. Previously noted was the contrast, spiritually speaking, between the *seventy* worshiping elders of Israel in Exod 24:1 and 9 (cf. Num 11) and the *seventy* idol-worshiping elders in Ezek 8:11–12.

because of their similar role in passing down God's law. After noting that Moses was "denied any part in the formulation of the Pentateuchal laws," he writes: "The only legislator the Bible knows of is God; the only legislation is that mediated by a prophet (Moses and Ezekiel)."[65]

As already mentioned, the latter chapters of Exodus and Ezekiel reveal how the two men met with God on mountaintops, there receiving both a written law[66] and detailed plans for God's future sanctuary: the tabernacle in Moses's case (Exod 25–27 [P]), and the new temple in Ezekiel's vision (esp. Ezek 40–44). Both observed the descent of Yahweh's glory to fill the sanctuary (Exod 40:35 [P]; Ezek 43:5), precluding them "from entering into specified sacred spaces (Exod 40:35; Ezek 44:1–3)."[67] Leading scholars, in their reading of Ezek 43:18–27, are convinced that the prophet is "functioning like Moses in Exod 29:1–37 and Lev 8:15–34, consecrating the altar and executing the first offerings."[68] "The first time the altar is used, it must be Ezekiel-Moses who acts to consecrate the new altar. Ordinary priests do not suffice here. Ezekiel-Moses is only responsible for the initiation, though; the priests then are to follow in his succession."[69] Might one expect Ezekiel was conscious of these parallels?[70]

The theme of כבוד־יהוה, "the glory of Yahweh," and particularly *seeing* the glory, receives stronger emphasis in Exodus and Ezekiel than in any other books in the Hebrew Bible.[71] One discovers repetitious use of the verb כבד in Niphal in the sense of God "getting/gaining glory" (Exod 14:4, 17, 18; Ezek 28:22; 39:13). The texts in Exod 14 and Ezek 28 are remarkable for also including a closely attached RF—I find nothing comparable in the OT. The noun כבוד and the construction כבוד־יהוה appear frequently in both books,[72] and the combination of כבוד־ יהוה/כבוד with the verb ראה ("to see") marks a key pattern of usage rarely found elsewhere.[73]

65. Greenberg, "Some Postulates," 11.

66. Patton mentions this in "I Myself," 85.

67. Awabdy, "YHWH Exegetes Torah," 701.

68. Block, "In Search of," 229. See also Levenson, *Theology of the Program*, 38.

69. Fechter, "Priesthood in Exile," 35.

70. McKeating researches the many parallels between Ezek 40–48 and what he terms Mosaic traditions and calls them "uncannily close" ("Ezekiel the 'Prophet like Moses'?" 103). My study does not attempt to summarize McKeating, though his findings may be interpreted as buttressing claims advanced here (he concludes that the book of Ezekiel does indeed present the prophet as another Moses; see n. 56 above). As an aside, the name of Moses surprisingly does not appear in Ezekiel (and appears only 3× in the Major Prophets).

71. Idestrom's discussion is again valuable ("Echoes," 495–96). For up-to-date, thorough considerations of כבוד/כבד in Ezekiel, with reference back to Exodus, see: Keck, "The Glory of Yahweh"; Wu, *Honor, Shame, and Guilt*, 75–90; and de Vries, *Kābôd of YHWH*.

72. See Exod 16:7, 10: 24:16–17 (2×); 29:43; 33:18, 22; 40:34–35 (2×); Ezek 1:28; 3:12, 23 (2×); 8:4; 9:3; 10:4 (2×), 18–19 (2×); 11:22–23 (2×); 39:21; 43:2 (2×), 4 (2×); 44:4.

73. See Exod 16:7, 10; 24:17; 33:18; Ezek 1:28; 3:23; 8:4; 39:21; 44:4; cf. Isa 35:2; 60:2; 66:18.

Exodus and Ezekiel are uniquely similar among all Bible books in revealing God's explicit concern that honor be shown both to himself and his prophet. In Exodus, Yahweh intends for the covenant people to put their trust in him and also to trust in his servant (Exod 14:31 [J]; 19:9 [J]). Ezekiel's oracles state that, as the people come to recognize Yahweh, they also must recognize that Yahweh's true prophet is among them (Ezek 2:5; 33:33). The reader is especially prompted to tie this idea of twofold recognition to Exodus because Yahweh's insistence that Israel acknowledge his servant Ezekiel is expressed in the style of an RF—"When all this comes true ... then they shall know that a prophet has been among them" (33:33)—that may echo the formulas of Exodus.

In OT teaching, the wealth represented by precious metals and jewelry was a blessing from God. Israel understood that the riches gained through "plundering the Egyptians" (Exod 3:22) symbolized God's favor and provision for his people who had just been delivered from an impoverished slavery (Exod 11:2–3 [E]; 12:35–36 [E]). So, when the Israelites used the plunder to construct a golden calf at the base of Mount Sinai (Exod 32 [J/E]), it was an egregious sin against God's generosity and represented a refusal to acknowledge that it was Yahweh who had delivered them from economic oppression. Ezekiel's accusation that Israel had begun this idolatrous tradition in "the days of your youth" and that she has continued to provoke Yahweh with this same sin down to the prophet's day (16:10–17; 7:20) may be at least an indirect reference to the golden-calf episode. Was not the exodus the most memorable time when Yahweh was understood to give his people silver and gold? Ezekiel conveys the Deity's description of the materials used in Israel's idolatry (16:17): it is "my gold and my silver which I gave to you" (מזהבי ומכספי אשר נתתי לך).

In an ironic twist reminiscent of the exodus story, Ezekiel warns that Yahweh will visit upon Israel—other nations, too—some of the same judgments Egypt experienced. Israel will hand over its jewelry as plunder to foreigners (7:21; cf. Exod 12:36 [E]). Yahweh will turn the tables by leaving the women of Israel childless (5:17), even as Egypt bewailed the death of its firstborn (Exod 12:29–30 [J]). The nation will experience multiform "plagues"—afflictions generally or disease specifically (דבר). Plagues mentioned in Ezekiel like those that struck Egypt are: the flood-land (ארץ צפתך) drenched with flowing blood (32:6; cf. Exod 7:17–21 [J/P]);[74] darkness (30:18; 32:7–8; cf. Exod 10:21–23 [E]);[75] hailstones (13:11; 38:22;

---

74. John B. Taylor views 32:6 as an allusion to the earlier plague, "as if [God were] to imply that Pharaoh's final hour of judgment will follow a pattern similar to God's earlier confrontation with him through Moses" (*Ezekiel*, 209). As William A. Tooman notes, occurrences of דבר ודם in Ezekiel may be read as a hendiadys "bleeding pestilence" ("Meaning of דבר ודם"). The other option is Greenberg's "plague and bloody death" (*Ezekiel 1–20*, 101).

75. Greenberg refers to 32:7–8 as "a reminiscence of the Plague of darkness (Exod 10:21ff.)" (*Ezekiel 21–37*, 656).

cf. Exod 9:13–26 [J/E]); pestilence (דבר; bubonic?);[76] and the destruction of cattle (32:13; cf. Exod 9:1–7 [J]). Some of these plagues prophesied in Ezekiel are to strike Israel, and some will be revisited upon Egypt. The general references to "plague" may also be connected with God's judgment after the golden-calf incident (Exod 32:35 [E]).

The story in Ezek 9 of a linen-clad (לבש בדים) man with writing kit and of guards going through Jerusalem killing the idolaters without mercy may remind readers of the episode of a band of Levites sent throughout the camp to kill many idolatrous people during the golden-calf incident (Exod 32:25–29 [J/E]). (The priesthood was commanded to wear שש, "fine linen," in Exod 28.)[77] For some, Ezekiel 9 may also bear a resemblance to the Passover account when it tells of a mark being given to the righteous and their being spared in the slaughter. Those without the mark, the ungodly, are judged with death, much like those in the Passover story in Exod 12:12–13 [P], 21–30 [J/P].[78]

Turning to the final chapters of Ezekiel, one finds many parallels with Exodus, most of which are similarities.[79] In a few cases, Ezekiel proves dissimilar, but even these may point back to Exodus by way of contrast.[80] In both revelations, Yahweh insists that all the details be conveyed to the people (Exod 25:9 [P]; Ezek 40:4). Exact measurements are recorded in each book (Ezek 40–42; Exod 26–27 [P]). Directions are given in Exodus to build the main altar with undressed stones and without steps to climb (20:24–26 [E]), whereas Ezekiel specifies dressed stones for the sacrificial tables (40:42) and steps for the main altar (43:13–17). Specifications for a wooden altar or "table that is before Yahweh" in Ezek 41:22 remind one of the table's counterpart in Exod 25:23–30 [P]. There are descriptions of the courtyard surrounding the temple/tabernacle in Ezek 42:1 and Exod 27:9–19 [P].[81] Directions for sacrifices of young bulls and rams without defect are found in both Ezek 43:23 and Exod 29:1 [P]. There is a reference in Ezek 44:3 to the prince (הנשיא) of the

---

76. Ezek 5:12, 17; 6:11, 12; 7:15; 12:16; 14:19, 21; 28:23 (Sidon); 33:27; 38:22 (Gog); cf. Exod 5:3 (J); 9:3, 15 (both J); Lev 26:25 (H); Deut 28:21.

77. Levitt Kohn, *New Heart*, 57, offers details on the usage of שש in P (27×, all in Exodus) and Ezekiel (3×). Otherwise, it appears only in Gen 41:42 [E] and Prov 31:22. She also cites Hurvitz, who has argued on the basis of that usage for an early date of P in "Usage of שש and בוץ."

78. Greenberg entertains the idea of a connection with the Passover account (Exod 12:23) or the "frontlets" in Exod 28:38 (*Ezekiel 1–20*, 177), noting in passing the old talmudic interpretation that those with the mark were not spared. But does this not conflict with 9:6? The fullest treatment may be Tuell, "Meaning of the Mark."

79. Block has made a good argument that we should look beyond Exodus to compare Ezek 40–48 with Leviticus, Numbers, and Deuteronomy (*Ezekiel 25–48*, 498–501).

80. E.g., one might suggest that differences between a tabernacle, as a mobile sanctuary, and a temple should be expected (Robert I. Vasholz, private correspondence).

81. Jews of Jesus's time associated Ezekiel with Moses for this reason. "Like Moses, this man saw the pattern of the Temple, with its wall and broad outer wall" (Liv. Pro., trans. D. R. A. Hare, in *OTP*, 2:389).

people eating in the presence of Yahweh; the seventy elders of Exod 24:11 [J] "saw God, and they ate and drank." Scholars explore additional parallels that are not taken up here.[82] Though some of these listed parallels are not exact, their number, thematic range, and wide distribution suggest that Ezekiel was familiar with the whole book of Exodus (in some form). In reading Ezek 40–48, one cannot evade Zimmerli's conclusion: "The prophet himself, the charismatic addressed by God, becomes the new Moses who is permitted to inaugurate the new sacrificial cult."[83]

Numerous scholars take the view that liberation is the key theme of Exod 1–15. Lyle Eslinger, however, has published an article arguing that the knowledge of God is the primary theme of that pivotal section of Scripture.[84] If Eslinger is correct in his judgment—and it is likely that he is—one gains further encouragement to trace Ezekiel's dependence on Exodus from a theological perspective. That Ezekiel is dominated by the same motif, the knowledge of God, is rarely challenged from any quarter. The reader should expect to hear many such echoes of Exodus in the prophecy that includes some of the most extended, profound theological reflection on the exodus event found in any of the prophets.[85]

Yet another strong theological theme in Ezekiel that has attracted attention recently is the presence and absence of God.[86] Those people who had reason to believe they had been abandoned by God, the exiles in Babylonia, see the approach of the Lord (in a vision report). Also, the word of Yahweh comes to a prophet among the exiles. This is real reassurance that, though the Jews with Ezekiel have been exiled from land and temple, they are not exiled from Yahweh. All the while, those back in the land believe they themselves are the blessed ones (33:24): the Jerusalemites say the exiles "are far from Yahweh;[87] this land has been

82. See Block, *Ezekiel 25–48*, and Milgrom, *Ezekiel's Hope*, 214–20.

83. Zimmerli, *Ezekiel 2*, 436.

84. Eslinger, "Freedom or Knowledge?" Strongly in support are Ford, *God, Pharaoh and Moses*, and Middlemas, "Exodus 3." For a critique of liberationist readings of Exodus, see Levenson, *Hebrew Bible*, 127–59.

85. See especially chs. 16, 20, and 23. All of Israel's troubles, according to Ezekiel, began with the nation forgetting the covenant Yahweh made with Israel בימי נעוריך, "in the days of your youth" (16:60; cf. other references to the period using this phrase in 16:22 and 43 and 23:19). References to Israel's "youth" are common in the prophetic denunciations of the nation (see: Hos 2:17[15]; Jer 2:2; 22:21). In Ezekiel, there is also repeated mention of the אבות ("fathers"), but in those passages (2:3; 18:2; 20:4, 18, 24, 27, 30, 36, 42; 36:28; 37:25; 47:14), the prophet does not specifically have in mind the patriarchs or the exodus generation. Rather, "he refers more generally to the ancestors of the present generation" (Block, *Ezekiel 1–24*, 51).

86. See: Kutsko, *Between Heaven and Earth*; Block, "Divine Abandonment"; Strong, "God's Kābôd"; Tuell, "Divine Presence and Absence"; House, "God Who Is Present (Ezekiel)," in *Old Testament Theology*, 327–45 (ch. 13); Tooman, "Covenant and Presence"; de Vries, *Kābôd of YHWH*. For discussion of the theme in OT literature, see Balentine, *Hidden God*, and Burnett, "Question of Divine Absence."

87. The translation adopted, "they are far from Yahweh," involves a repointing of the impv. as a pf. and is widely accepted (see Zimmerli, *Ezekiel 1*, 229, and Block, *Ezekiel 1–24*, 341). Greenberg accepts

given to us as our heritage" (11:15). But according to Ezekiel's visions in chapters 8–11, God is actually abandoning Jerusalem that he may become a sanctuary for those who are scattered among many countries (11:16; cf. Jer 24:1–10; 29:1–14). It would be the exiles who would know God's blessing and inherit the land in future days (Ezek 11:17). This divine presence–absence theme is also clearly found in Exodus,[88] and the two books are profitably read together along this line. Having the divine presence is a sign of God's favor (Exod 33:13–14, 16), while divine absence is regarded as a disastrous privation (33:3–6). Exodus also teaches that the divine presence is the mark of God's people, distinguishing them from other peoples of the earth (33:16). If one reads Ezekiel in the light of Exodus, then, the visions of Yahweh's glory indicate that the future of the covenant lies with the exiles, for the glory-cloud moves with God's people in both books (even outside the land of promise).[89]

4.1.3. Ezekiel's Reshaping of Earlier "Scriptural Traditions"

No one reading Ezekiel with a knowledge of biblical literature can miss Ezekiel's frequent allusions to the language, the figures and the stories found elsewhere in that literature. While these allusions are, in the gross, sufficiently similar for establishing the connection, in particulars there is almost always a divergence large enough to raise the question, whether the prophet has purposely skewed the traditional material, or merely represents a version of it different from the extant records. From evidence that the prophet himself played variations on a given theme, the likelihood is that such divergencies arise from his own shaping of the tradition rather than from otherwise unknown varieties of it.

—Moshe Greenberg[90]

It is a mistake to dismiss Ezekiel as a "dependent mind" or to disparage him as an inveterate quoter or borrower. Though the prophet evidences his schooling "in the various types of traditional literature that are reflected in his oracles (narratives,

---

the MT's impv., but he also admits that the revocalization allows the text to "read more smoothly" (*Ezekiel 1–20*, 189).

88. Bosman, "Absence and Presence." Bosman shows that, while the divine presence–absence dialectic may be interrelated with the "fear of Yahweh" theme—the primary thrust of the article—it is broader and can be traced in many passages not containing the fear motif. According to G. H. Davies, the "Presence of the Lord" unifies Exodus: "The very heart of this presence theme is . . . 'I am Yahweh.' . . . In turn, this self-predication is the clue to the various forms of predication in Leviticus, Second Isaiah, Ezekiel, and the Fourth Gospel" (*Exodus*, 48–49). See also Carroll, "Strange Fire."

89. For discussion of the moving presence in both books, see Mark, *"Mein Angesicht geht"* (*Ex 33,14*).

90. Greenberg, "Influence of Tradition," 29.

prophecy, laments, law, ritual, temple plans),"[91] he frequently revises, reframes, and even subverts the older scriptural traditions. Along with evoking and invoking, he may revoke. Examples abound. Instead of the lion of Judah seeing the submission *of* the nations, as in Gen 49 (J), the "lions" of Judah are dragged away in submission *to* the nations (Ezek 19). The noble lion who was intended to rule God's people becomes the parody of voracious lions tearing at God's people (Ezek 22:25).[92] The sentimental figure of the vine was once used to picture Israel, and it was a figure associated with the exodus event and the conquest (Ps 80:9[8]). But that vine is now to be regarded as utterly worthless in Ezekiel's reuse of the figure (Ezek 15; 19:10–14; cf. ch. 17).[93] Further, the metaphor of marriage, with its figure of Israel as a bride in covenant with Yahweh, is employed in a pejorative manner in Ezekiel's harshest invective (chs. 16 and 23). This pattern of revision and subversion shows up in Ezekiel's use of many scriptural traditions and must also be taken into account as one reads Ezekiel's references back to the exodus story and its language (this may include the RF).

Levitt Kohn indicates that Ezekiel's severely negative reuse of traditional motifs or themes is matched by negative reuse of terminology in denouncing evil and prophesying judgment. A first representative example of such terms would be the ironic reversal in the use of נאק and נאקה. In the exodus, God's people found deliverance from hardship and "groaning" under the slave masters' cruelty (Exod 2:24; 6:5). Their mourning turned to dancing long ago (Exod 15). But Ezekiel foretells the intense groaning of Pharaoh when God judges Egypt yet again: ונאק נאקות חלל לפניו (30:24).[94] The memory of a gross injustice in history remains, and Ezekiel's oracle announces that the turning of the tables is still God's plan.

A second example of the transmogrification of terminology in Ezekiel would be the reversal in the use of "hard heart" (קשה לב). In Exodus, Yahweh announced that he would harden Pharaoh's heart (7:3 [P]), but Ezekiel says that Israel is hardhearted (3:7).[95] Such an association is both a sharply pointed condemnation of Israel and, at least by implication, a justification for the judgment Yahweh will mete out to a nation acting like the hated foe in the days of Moses, the adversary who reportedly said, לא ידעתי את־יהוה, "I do not know/acknowledge Yahweh"

---

91. Greenberg, "Influence of Tradition," 29.

92. In Ezek 22:25, we read "her chiefs" (οἱ ἀφηγούμενοι ἐν μέσῳ αὐτῆς) with the LXX, against נביאיה, "her prophets," in the MT. Even Greenberg, who is quite conservative toward the MT, agrees that the MT is corrupt at this point and that "chiefs" must be preferred (*Ezekiel 21–37*, 462).

93. Greenberg characterizes Ezekiel's language as "a grotesque distortion of the traditional use of the vine as a figure for Israel" ("Influence of Tradition," 32).

94. The root נאק is rarely found in the OT. Besides Exodus and Ezekiel, the only occurrences are in Job 24:12 (verb) and Judg 2:18 (noun). My conclusions after using the Even-Shoshan concordance were confirmed in Levitt Kohn, *New Heart*, 66–67.

95. Levitt Kohn also notes the reversal in the use of קשה לב (*New Heart*, 72).

(Exod 5:2).[96] What makes this shared terminology all the more convincing as a likely example of inner-biblical interpretation is the fact that the parallel "hard heart" texts in Exodus and Ezekiel combine חזק and קשה; see Exod 7:3, 13 (P) and Ezek 2:4.[97] The two books share the same variable vocabulary in phrasing the idea.

Ezekiel is not alone among the prophets in his strongly negative reactualization (*Vergegenwärtigung*) of ancient traditions.[98] Hosea and Jeremiah previously used the marriage metaphor and the conjoined whoredom metaphor in condemning the unfaithfulness of the covenant people,[99] though not as graphically as Ezekiel. Also, the vine figure appears in earlier prophetic denunciations of Israel.[100] What is new and noteworthy as a departure from previous prophecies is Ezekiel's more negative assessment of Israel's earliest (spiritual) history. Whereas a Hosea or an Isaiah looked back to a good and pure beginning, when Israel had loved her Savior God, Ezekiel tells the story differently.[101] Other prophets had contrasted the nation's "first love" with her later "Canaanization"[102] and her present coldness toward the divine Lover. Israel should repent and return to the Husband she once followed. Ezekiel, by contrast, writes that Israel "from the days of her youth" has proved false and faithless. Israel's idolatry had its beginning in Egypt, not Canaan (Ezek 20:7).[103] The prophet writes, ותזנינה במצרים בנעוריהן זנו, "they whored in Egypt, in their youth they whored" (23:3a). Greenberg considers this prophetic

96. This point from my 2006 dissertation is extensively developed by Nevada Levi DeLapp in a fine essay, "Ezekiel as Moses—Israel as Pharaoh," but he arrived at the insight independently. Umberto Cassuto has the stimulating thought that the initial appearance of the RF in Exod 6:7 can mean, "you shall not be like Pharaoh who said, 'I do not know YHWH'" (*Exodus*, 81).

97. Yet another parallel is לב האבן in Ezek 36:26.

98. Zimmerli makes a strong point of this, that it is characteristic for the preexilic prophets and Ezekiel to reframe older positive traditions in the proclamation of judgment ("Prophetic Proclamation and Reinterpretation," 98–99). This reframing is discussed further in ch. 6 of the present volume.

99. See, e.g., Jer 2–3, and cf. Isa 1:21.

100. Isa 5:7; Hos 10:1.

101. Zimmerli makes this same point in one of his first essays, "Gotteswort des Ezechiel," 251–53 (included also in *Gottes Offenbarung*, 134–37). However, a careful reading of Isa 48:4–8 may lead one to modify this conclusion. See Westermann, *Isaiah 40–66*, 198.

102. A term coined by Block ("Period of the Judges," 48) and later used by Dwight R. Daniels (*Hosea and Salvation History*, 53).

103. It is possible that Ezek 16:3 traces the spiritual degeneracy back further than the Egyptian sojourn. There is reference to the people's birth (מכרתיך ומלדתיך) in the land of the Canaanites. Could this hark back to the patriarchs? It is unlikely, since the reference is to Jerusalem and Samaria and Ezekiel is playing rhetorically with the pagan foundations of those cities (metonyms for the kingdoms), as is suggested in the accompanying mention of Sodom. Ezekiel's characterization was an awful affront to the Zion theology. Block offers a different perspective: "The prophet thereby announces that contrary to cherished tradition, Jerusalem's spiritual roots derive not from the pious Abraham and Sarah but from the pagan peoples whom the Israelites had been charged to drive out" (*Ezekiel 1–24*, 475).

perspective entirely unprecedented.[104] Whether it was or was not, it provides the backdrop for Ezekiel's proclamation of a new exodus in God's plan. In simple, perhaps even homiletical terms, one might posit that Ezekiel has the view that Israel was taken out of Egypt without Egypt being taken out of the people, without Egyptian idolatry being removed from Israelite hearts. A more radical, more deeply spiritual work of redemption is needed if the nation is to know their God as Yahweh. This idea will be examined further in chapter 5.

4.2. Ezekiel's Recognition Formula Borrowed from Exodus

Two distinct questions suggest themselves when one studies the issue of the origin of the RF. First, scholars have inquired as to the formula's absolute origin, its first usage in the religious speech and literature of Israel. The second question may be separated from the first and may possibly yield a different answer: what source inspired Ezekiel to use the RF? Many scholars, Zimmerli among them, have given differing answers to the two questions. This section focuses narrowly on the question of *Ezekiel's* source and inspiration for his extensive employment of the formula. Moreover, I agree with Paul Joyce's recommendation[105] that the RF be taken as a whole and not broken into two constituent parts (as Zimmerli attempts). The formula and the issue of its source are best understood by treating the RF per se, not as an amalgamation of a "statement of recognition" and a "self-introductory formula," each with a separate, prior life of its own.

4.2.1. The Formula's Usage Throughout the Old Testament

Though there is not space in this narrowly defined study to discuss thoroughly the use of the RF in other parts of the OT, those formulas must be noted (see appendix to ch. 3 and Figure 1, also in ch. 3). Zimmerli was correct in saying that the formula "is by no means an original coinage of Ezekiel himself."[106] Therefore,

---

104. Greenberg, *Ezekiel 1–20*, 365. A counterargument would be that Israel's idolatry in Exod 32:4 is a return to former religious practices (cf. Josh 24:14). Older commentaries suggest that the idolatry is "cast" as an honoring of gods who brought them out of Egypt and that the calf image derives from Egypt. Childs summarizes that viewpoint: "There is obviously a *religionsgeschichtliche* background to the choice. Among the Egyptians the bull represented Apis in the pantheon while among the Canaanites he symbolized Baal" (*Exodus*, 565). Another novelty of Ezekiel, according to Greenberg, is the "remarkable oath to exile the people, taken by God even before they entered the land," about which, Greenberg claims, "Pentateuchal traditions are silent" (*Ezekiel 1–20*, 368). Has he failed to consider Lev 26:33 and Deut 4:27? Those texts do not contain גלה or גלות, but they point to an experience of exile.

105. Joyce, *Divine Initiative*, 92.

106. Zimmerli, *I Am Yahweh*, 41.

a survey of RFs elsewhere in the Bible presents the reader of Ezekiel with various possible sources. True, there are fascinating parallels between the RF and formulas used in the secular and religious literature of surrounding nations,[107] but most scholarship has rightly concluded that we must search for an OT source rather than an extrabiblical one.

The formula is prominently used in Exodus, in both early and late sources (as classical literary criticism delineates them).[108] Thus, in older style *Literarkritik*, the connection between the exodus story and the RF is more ancient than a postexilic Priestly source, unless J is dated much later[109] or redaction criticism designates the formula a secondary accretion in the early sources of J and E.[110] Table 9 indicates where the formulas of Exodus occur in old source criticism's delineation of the sources.

Readers of Exodus may find two conclusions credible in reviewing the data on the RFs. The first is that, without recourse to late redaction proposals,[111] the likelihood of the refrain appearing in two separate, independent accounts of the exodus event seems small. Source criticism finds difficulty, perhaps even founders, in distinguishing and isolating "documents" that include the same *distinctive* theological refrain—and refrains in the same exact strict and expanded forms.[112] The second conclusion is that, if one does accept a theory approximating the traditional Documentary Hypothesis, the appearance of the formula in J portions of Exodus means it is still ancient enough to have influenced all the writing prophets, from Hosea and First Isaiah down to Ezekiel.[113]

---

107. See Harner, *Grace and Law*, ch. 2, and Bodi, *Ezekiel and the Poem of Erra*, 301–5. In ch. 6, I note yet another text showing similarities to Ezekiel's use of the RF: *The Covenant of Aššur*, "The Second Oracle of Salvation" (ca. 673 BC).

108. The RF appears in: Exod 6:7; 7:5, 17; 8:18[22]; 10:2; 14:4, 18; 16:12; 29:46; 31:13. Variations somewhat related to the strict formula are found in: Exod 8:6[10]; 9:14, 29; 11:7; 16:6; 18:11.

109. See the revisionist scholarship of Van Seters, *Abraham* and "Dating the Yahwist's History," and H. H. Schmid, *Der sogenannte Jahwist*. Source criticism has been in ferment for decades; see Dozeman and K. Schmid, *Farewell to the Yahwist?* and Gertz et al., *Formation of the Pentateuch*.

110. Long ago, this was noted as an option, though not necessarily recommended, by S. R. Driver (*Introduction*, 25).

111. E.g., Schmitt, "Tradition der Prophetenbücher."

112. Such difficulties have led a number of Pentateuch scholars to view P more as a redactor than an independent source document.

113. Hos 13:4 ("I am Yahweh your God since the land of Egypt; you know no god apart from me; besides me there is no savior") indicates that the SPF ("I am Yahweh your God") together with a highly theological use of ידע were associated with the exodus story from the earliest period of the writing prophets. Further, it has been argued that, in Hos 13:4, "the participial form 'saviour' recalls the use of the verb in the summary statement of Exod 14.30 'that day the Lord saved Israel from the power of Egypt' (NEB)" (Macintosh, *Hosea*, 527). In First Isaiah, I have in mind the restoration oracle spoken to Egypt in Isa 19:16–25, which recalls some version of the exodus story and says, "Yahweh will make himself known to the Egyptians, and in that day they shall know Yahweh" (v. 21). Note, too, the references here to "the uplifted hand" (v. 16), a new "smiting/plague" (נגף in v. 22; cf. Exod

Table 9. Classical Source Analysis and Recognition Formulas in Exodus

	Driver	**Childs**
6:7	P	P
7:5	P	P
7:17	J	J
8:18[22]	J	J
10:2	J	Addition
14:4	P	P
14:18	P	P
16:12	P	P
29:46	P	P
31:13	P (H) Driver, 297	P
8:6[10]	*J*	*J*
9:14	*J*	*Addition*
9:29	*J*	*J*
11:7	*J*	*J*
16:6	*P*	*P*
18:11	*E*	*E?*

True RFs are in Roman typeface, while texts merely related to the
formula are italicized. The reference tools used were Driver, *Introduction*, and Childs, *Exodus*.

Is Georg Fohrer correct in tracing Ezekiel's usage back to Exodus? Zimmerli
strongly asserts, contrariwise, that Ezekiel's formula derives from a certain northern Israelite prophetic tradition that comes to expression in 1 Kgs 20:13 and 28.
Other scholars such as Blank and Herbert May, writing prior to Zimmerli, point
to Second Isaiah as Ezekiel's source. Isaiah has RFs in 45:3, 49:23 and 26, and 60:16,
as well as variations easily related to the formula found in 41:20; 45:6; and 52:6.

Only two other books include the RF proper: Deut 29:5[6] and Joel 4:17[3:17].
(An additional text in the latter book, Joel 2:27, breaks into the standard structure
of the RF with the interrupting phrase, "that I am in Israel," and an additional text
in Hosea is rejected on text-critical grounds).[114] Because of its uncertain dating,

7:27; 12:13, 23, 27), and the sending (שלח) of a Moses-like "savior" (מושיע) for Egypt "when they cry
to Yahweh because of oppressors" (v. 20; cf. Exod 2:23; 3:7–10).

114. Hos 2:22[20] is not counted, though the Vulg., some Hebrew MSS, and Cyril of Alexandria
read an RF (וידעת כי אני יהוה) instead of the simple "know Yahweh" (וידעת את־יהוה). On the text-
critical issue, see: Wolff, "Erkenntnis Gottes," 428–30, and *Hosea*, 46; Andersen and Freedman, *Hosea*,
283–84; Stuart, *Hosea-Jonah*, 56, 60. Wolff suggests the readings with an RF are corruptions showing
the influence of Ezekiel and/or Second Isaiah.

Joel scarcely enters into the discussion regarding the origin of Ezekiel's formula.[115] Also to be considered is the fact that the Joel formulas are heavily loaded with added phrasing on the end and sound rather different from any RF in Ezekiel. Joel 4:17 [3:17] reads, "And you shall know that I am Yahweh your God, dwelling in Zion, my holy mountain." The Deuteronomy text also does not receive serious consideration because it is connected to a recollection of the experiences of those redeemed out of Egypt and their children who wandered in the wilderness.[116] Other passages bearing some resemblance to the RF could be cited at this point,[117] but scholars have consistently narrowed the field of Ezekiel's potential sources to Exodus, 1 Kings, and Isaiah. These will be discussed in canonical order, with particular attention paid to Exodus. Conclusions drawn in chapter 1 regarding an early (preexilic) dating of the critics' "Priestly document" will have a bearing on the discussion of Exodus as a source for Ezekiel.

4.2.2. Similarities Between the Formulas in Exodus and Ezekiel

Leaving aside completely the prophecy of Ezekiel, there are more occurrences of the RF in Exodus than in any other book of the Bible. Indeed, Exodus contains nearly twice the formulas found in Isaiah and 1 Kings *combined*. At least initially, therefore, the interpreter ought to give a decided preference to Exodus as an influence on later Scripture to use the formula. Is it not likely that the high count of RFs and their wide distribution over many chapters in Exodus (chs. 6, 7, 8, 10, 14, 16, 29, and 31) inspired an even higher count and wider distribution in Ezekiel?

Both Exodus and Ezekiel include RFs addressed to Israel *and* the nations (Egypt alone in the case of Exodus). Both Israel and the nations "shall know that I am Yahweh." Interestingly, as in Exodus, formulas in Ezekiel are addressed to Egypt and to Pharaoh himself—no other king is addressed with the RF in Ezekiel. That Egypt is selected out by Ezekiel for special attention is clear from the proportionally greater number of chapters devoted to oracles against Egypt and

---

115. Since Bernhard Duhm (1922), critical scholarship has tended to date Joel's prophecy much later than the surrounding books of Hosea and Amos. John Barton says that "a postexilic date has largely established itself as the preferred one" among commentators (*Joel and Obadiah*, 15). Also, the passage in Joel most commonly dated latest (perhaps even secondary) is 2:28–3:21, which contains the RF. As a result, some hold that Joel "incorporates . . . Ezekiel's *Erkenntnisformel*" (Strazicich, *Joel's Use of Scripture*, 208). For full-length arguments for postexilic dating, see Wolff, *Joel and Amos*, and Crenshaw, *Joel*. Recent conservative discussions of lines of evidence are Stuart, *Hosea-Jonah*, 224–35, and Longman and Dillard, *Introduction*, 411–14.

116. It would be a mistake, however, to ignore Deut 29:5[6]. The RF located there, in its theological context (29:1–5[2–6]), tends to strengthen the argument that the formula is predominantly associated with the exodus and wilderness narratives. The RF appears rooted in the storyline of Exodus.

117. See the appendix to ch. 3, including: Num 16:28, 30; Deut 4:35; Josh 3:7, 10; 4:24; 1 Sam 17:46; 1 Kgs 8:43, 60; 2 Kgs 5:8 (cf. Ezek 2:5); 2 Kgs 19:19 (= Isa 37:20); Pss 46:11[10]; 83:19[18]; 100:3; Jer 9:23[24]; 16:21; 24:7; Hos 2:22[20]; 13:4; Zech 2:13[9].

the fact that far more of the formulas (nine total) are addressed to Egypt than to any other foreign nation. (Edom follows with four spoken against her, all in Ezek 35 [but see also 25:14].) Of the total number of RFs in Exodus, 50% speak of the nations' recognition of Yahweh, as over against formulas in which Israel will recognize him, and Ezekiel is similar, with 36% pertaining to recognition by the nations rather than by Israel.[118]

Exodus and Ezekiel uniquely employ the RF in oracles of both judgment and salvation (and the proportional distinction is nearly congruent).[119] Nowhere else in the Bible is the RF attached to an oracle of judgment.[120] This is a most important similarity, while a key difference between the two books is the absence of judgment oracles spoken against Israel in Exodus. When the formula in Exodus refers to Israel knowing Yahweh, it is used in a wholly positive way, speaking of Yahweh's deliverance of Israel and his blessing on her. When it appears within Exodus to speak of judgment, pagan Egypt is always the subject, never Israel. Ezekiel, by contrast, frequently employs the RF as a conclusion to oracles of judgment against Israel. This discontinuity or disjunction is clearly important for theological interpretation and will be treated in chapter 6.

In taking a closer look at the content of the RFs in Exodus and Ezekiel, one should make ready use of Joyce's categorization of Ezekiel's formulas (see Table 1, in ch. 2). A comparison study yields the conclusion that Ezekiel largely conformed to the normal use of the refrain in Exodus, with the one exception being in Joyce's stunning category G.[121] Excepting category G, the formulas in each book primarily speak the messages that the nations "know I am Yahweh" when they are punished (Joyce's category A) and that Israel will "know I am Yahweh when I deliver her" (category H). In neither Bible book does one find a formula fitting Joyce's category B, C, or F.[122]

---

118. By comparison, 1–2 Kgs contains no RFs addressed to the nations. (Three loosely "related phrases" in Kings speak *of* the nations, but they are not addressed *to* the nations.) Isaiah has a single formula addressed to a foreigner, Cyrus (45:3), and one that speaks *of* the nations knowing Yahweh as Israel's Savior (49:26).

119. I calculate 60% of the RFs in Exodus are in a judgment context, while 72% (fifty-two out of the seventy-two) of Ezekiel's are. As argued by DeLapp ("Ezekiel as Moses," 67), the formula in Exod 10:2 is harder to assess; I place it on the judgment side ("how I dealt severely with the Egyptians"). For Ezekiel, if one excludes the oracles against the nations, RFs spoken to Israel are 57% in a judgment context (twenty-six of forty-six).

120. Some might suggest Isa 49:26 as a contradiction of this claim, but this oracle also ties the recognition of Yahweh among the nations to Israel's salvation: "Those who trouble you, I will trouble, and your children I will save" (49:25b).

121. Israel will know "I am Yahweh" when Yahweh punishes Israel.

122. Joyce's category B = The nations will know "I am Yahweh" when Yahweh delivers the nations; category C = The nations will know "I am Yahweh" when Yahweh punishes Israel; category D = Israel will know "I am Yahweh" when Yahweh delivers the nations.

Variations and expansions of the RF, along with what is termed the "strict" form, appear in both Exodus and Ezekiel. Thus, if Exodus is indeed the source, as I argue, the variations in formulas would not so much reflect Ezekiel exercising substantial liberty in composition as they would reflect a varied usage in prior Scripture. A detailed comparison of the two books reveals that the variations and expansions are remarkably similar in style and in their distribution throughout the books.[123] Some expansions are precisely the same, such as וידעתם כי אני יהוה אלהיכם, "you shall know that I am Yahweh *your God*" (Exod 6:7 [P]; Ezek 20:20), and וידעו כי אני יהוה אלהיהם, "they shall know that I am Yahweh *their God*" (Exod 29:46 [P]; Ezek 39:22, 28). The latter of these two expanded formulas is found only in Exodus and Ezekiel.

A closer look at the specific expansion just noted ("... shall know that I am Yahweh your/their God") reveals another example of how Ezekiel conformed to the normal use of the refrain in Exodus. In both books, this expansion is always addressed to Israel in oracles of salvation; not one of the occurrences of this expansion is directed to the nations.[124] Likewise, Israel is never said to "know that I am Yahweh *your/their God*" in judgment.

One expansion in Ezekiel, at 20:12, can hardly be taken any other way than as a direct quotation from Exod 31:13 (with only the minor change from third- to second-person in order to fit the context).[125]

(Exod 31:13)   לדעת כי אני יהוה מקדשכם
(Ezek 20:12)   לדעת כי אני יהוה מקדשם

Setting these two texts side by side makes for a startling comparison because the additional phrase ("who makes you holy") and the infinitive construct appear in both formulas. These are the only two places in the entire OT where an RF contains מקדש. The infinitive construct is quite rare among occurrences of the refrain: nowhere else in the Bible besides these two chapters does one find the "strict form" with the infinitive construct (but cf. Jer 9:23[24]). No RF in the OT

---

123. With one exception to the rule, all of the RFs in Exodus have an exact or nearly exact companion in Ezekiel. Exod 10:2 is the same as seventeen formulas in Ezekiel (6:7, 13; 7:4; 11:10, 12; 12:20; 13:14; 14:8; 15:7; 20:38, 42, 44; 25:5; 35:9; 36:11; 37:6, 13). There are an additional two formulas in Ezekiel that are nearly exact (13:21 and 23 have וידעתן instead of וידעתם). Exod 29:46 is the same as two formulas in Ezekiel (28:26; 39:28). Exod 6:7 and 16:12 are nearly exact companions to Ezek 20:20 (which has an inf. const. rather than a pf.). Exod 7:5 and 14:4 and 18 have a nearly exact analogue in Ezek 29:6 (the latter reads כל־ישבי מצרים instead of simple מצרים). Exod 7:17 differs from Ezek 16:62, 22:16, 25:7, and 35:4 only in that the latter have pf. verbs instead of the impf. Exod 31:13 is nearly the same as Ezek 20:12 (which reads מקדשם instead of מקדשכם) and as Ezek 20:20 (which lacks the ptc.). The one Exodus formula without a counterpart is למען תדע כי אני יהוה בקרב הארץ (8:18[22]).
    124. E.g., "they [nations] shall know that I am Yahweh your God."
    125. See also the discussion of Ezek 20:12 in 4.1.1 above, "Linguistic and Terminological Parallels."

aside from these two (plus the companion formula in Ezek 20:20) is linked theologically with Sabbath. Finally, nowhere in the OT except Exod 31:12–17 and Ezek 20:12 and 20 is the Sabbath said to be a sign (אוֹת) of Yahweh's gracious presence. It seems impossible to explain the parallel by reference to *tradition*, for here we have not only the same complex of ideas and joined motifs—Sabbath as a sign, the RF, Yahweh making his people holy, the desecration (חלל) of the Sabbath—but also the same exact, extremely rare grammatical form (ידע inf. const. with RF).

After years of reflecting on Ezek 20, I am convinced the passage makes its own simple, explicit, content-based argument for reading the RF as a recollection of the exodus and wilderness narratives. The first three RFs there (vv. 12, 20, and 26) stand alone in the prophecy as the sole references *back* to God's proclaiming, "you shall know that I am Yahweh," in salvation history. All other RFs in Ezekiel (and the rest of the Bible) have a future orientation. The retrospective plainly records Yahweh saying: "I made myself known [אוֹדַע] to [Israel] in the land of Egypt. With raised hand I declared to them, 'I am Yahweh'" (v. 5). What follows is a warning, together with another SPF: "Do not defile yourselves with the idols of Egypt. I am Yahweh your God" (v. 7). The account continues on to an RF: "I made myself known [נוֹדַעְתִּי] to them by bringing them out of the land of Egypt. So I led them out from the land of Egypt and brought them into the wilderness. I gave them my statutes and made known [הוֹדַעְתִּי] to them my decrees.... And I also gave them my Sabbaths ... so that they would know I am Yahweh who sanctifies them" (vv. 9–12). The next stage involved the second generation in the wilderness, who were told, "I am Yahweh your God. Walk in my statutes; keep and perform my decrees, and keep my Sabbaths holy ... that you may know that I am Yahweh your God who sanctifies you" (vv. 19–20). Then a third time the chapter directs the reader back to that era when God acted "that [Israel] might know that I am Yahweh" (v. 26). The prophecy is insistent that the RF belongs to the exodus/wilderness story.

A last telling similarity between Ezekiel and Exodus is the formulation and usage of what this study terms "related phrases," ידע phrases similar to the recognition formula, that replace the usual object clause כִּי אֲנִי יהוה with another, examples of which would be "they shall know *my vengeance*" (Ezek 25:14) and "the nations shall know *me* when I show myself holy through you" (Ezek 38:16). With only one exception (Exod 16:6), all the related phrases in both books are spoken in judgment.[126] The contrast is obvious when one compares the pattern observed in Ezekiel and Exodus against "related phrases" in other books. Outside Ezekiel and Exodus, all the related phrases speak a positive message (in a context of worship perhaps or an oracle of salvation), with a single exception. The loosely

---

126. A full listing of those related phrases (also available in ch. 3, section 3.1 and the appendix) is provided here: Exod 8:6[10]; 9:14, 29; 11:7; 16:6; Ezek 2:5; 14:23; 25:14; 33:33; 38:16; 39:23. The "related phrases" in Ezekiel with ראה instead of ידע are also spoken only in judgment (21:4[20:48]; 39:21).

related phrase in Jer 44:29 reads, "so that you shall know that my words of calamity against you will surely stand."

Obviously, there are numerous lines of evidence pointing toward the conclusion that Ezekiel's use of the RF is derived from, and even modeled on, the formulas of Exodus. It is best to view Ezekiel's formulas as part of, and as a continuation of, the pattern of broad dependence on Exodus argued earlier in this chapter. However, before ending the discussion of the origin of Ezekiel's formula, possible ties to 1 Kings or Isaiah should be explored. Might those two books have influenced the book of Ezekiel?

4.2.3. Comparing Ezekiel's Formulas with Those in Kings and Isaiah

While the 1 Kgs 20 narrative did encourage the employment of the RF in prophetic circles,[127] it seems unwise to trace Ezekiel's extraordinarily elaborate and extended use to a tradition represented by the two occurrences in one chapter of Kings. What other evidence can Zimmerli adduce, besides the formulas, that connects Ezekiel, his language, and his theology to 1 Kgs 20 or the prophetic tradition in the Northern Kingdom that the Kings material reflects? Some might consider it a decisive point against Zimmerli's proposal that he has largely failed to provide textual grounds for that link. Though both RFs in Kings have exact parallels in phraseology with formulas in Ezekiel,[128] the message carried by the Kings formulas is uncommon in Ezekiel. Joyce, in an examination of the RFs in 1 Kgs 20, concludes: "Of Zimmerli's examples, 1 Kgs 20.13, 28 would belong in the category 'E' and 2 Kgs 19.19 in category 'D,' both categories in which there are few cases in Ezekiel. The remaining examples cited by Zimmerli (1 Kgs 17.24; 2 Kgs 5.8, 15) would belong in category 'B,' of which there are no cases in Ezekiel."[129]

Other difficulties exist as well. Both formulas in 1 Kgs 20 have second-person verbs, not both second and third person, as in Ezekiel. Both RFs in Kings are "strict forms," with no such expansions as are frequently found in Ezekiel. In 1 Kgs 20, only Israel is said to come to a recognition of Yahweh, not Israel *and* the nations.[130]

---

127. Winfried Thiel asserts this, agreeing with Zimmerli that 1 Kgs 20 is the earliest witness to prophetic use of the RF ("Die Erkenntnisaussage," 214–15). However, with his acceptance of an early dating of J, Thiel concedes that Exod 7:17 and 8:18 stand alongside 1 Kgs 20:13, 28 as "die ältesten Belege der 'Erkenntnisformel'" (*Könige*, 379).

128. The RF in 1 Kgs 20:13 is phrased in exactly the same way as four texts in Ezekiel (16:62; 22:16; 25:7; 35:4), while 1 Kgs 20:28, like Exod 10:2, is exactly parallel to seventeen formulas in Ezekiel (6:7, 13; 7:4; 11:10, 12; 12:20; 13:14; 14:8; 15:7; 20:38, 42, 44; 25:5; 35:9; 36:11; 37:6, 13; cf. also 13:21 and 23, which have וידעתן instead of וידעתם).

129. Joyce, *Divine Initiative*, 155n27.

130. Despite the Aramean beliefs that belittle Yahweh (expressed in the speech, "their god is a god of the mountains and so they were stronger than we" [v. 23]), Yahweh does not purpose to reveal to Aram "that I am Yahweh." Yahweh intends only for warring Israel to recognize him.

Fohrer's critique of Zimmerli is cogent: "The occurrence of this formula twice in anecdotal prophetical utterances does not provide a broad enough basis for the assumption that centuries later Ezekiel made use of an early literary type [represented here]."[131]

Two more arguments seem to discount Zimmerli's proposal regarding the influence of the tradition set down in 1 Kgs 20. First, there are claims that his view "is today no longer widely accepted, since these texts are no longer assigned to such an early date."[132] Second, the Elijah narratives present that character as a second Moses in dozens of ways.[133] While 1 Kgs 20 is distinct from the surrounding stories in that the prophetic figure is anonymous, it still is lodged among them and displays similar connections to the plague/exodus narratives.[134] It is a mistake then to separate it out entirely from the Ahab-Elijah literary complex (1 Kgs 16 through 2 Kgs 2). The occurrence of the RF in the broader Elijah cycle is less than surprising if the narrator is regularly suggesting a Moses analogy throughout. In brief, the appearance of the RF in both the Elijah cycle and Ezekiel's prophecy can be explained as a facet of a second-Moses typology.

If not the prophetic tradition reflected in 1 Kings, might Isaiah's prophecy have served as Ezekiel's prototype in the use of the refrain? Critical scholars who view the vast number of RFs in Ezekiel as coming from the prophet's own hand will not be inclined to trace a literary dependence on Second Isaiah, an exilic or postexilic prophet. Zimmerli, for example, speaks of Second Isaiah as "a prophet of the generation after Ezekiel."[135] According to the critics' chronology, the idea of Ezekielian dependence on Isaiah must be put out of mind.[136] However, for conservative interpreters who attribute the whole book of Isaiah (substantially in its present form) to the eighth century prophet and who uphold the unity of the prophecy,[137] Ezekielian dependence on Isaiah may be an open question.

---

131. Fohrer, *Introduction*, 409.

132. Preuss, *Old Testament Theology*, 1:333n497 [*Theologie*, 1:235].

133. Uriel Simon thinks the narrator depicts Elijah as "like Moses in his generation" (*Reading Prophetic Narratives*, 168). See also: Carroll, "Elijah-Elisha Sagas"; Wiener, *Elijah*, 29–37; Coote, "Yahweh Recalls Elijah"; Allison, *New Moses*, 39–45; Walsh, *1 Kings*, 284–89; Reiss, "Elijah the Zealot,"; Dharamraj, *A Prophet like Moses?* (who cites the rabbinic catalog of parallels in Pesiq. Rab. 4:2).

134. Dharamraj suggests that a continuing use of ידע and of the "knowing Yahweh" motif integrates ch. 20 into the wider narrative (cf. 17:24; 18:36–37), linking the RFs (20:13, 28) to the exodus narrative (*Prophet Like Moses?* 40).

135. Zimmerli, *I Am Yahweh*, 55. H. G. M. Williamson believes Deutero-Isaiah used Ezekiel (*Book Called Isaiah*, 129). However, for Johan Lust, a Persian dating of an oracle in Ezekiel permits discussion of Isaianic influence ("Ezekiel Salutes Isaiah," 380).

136. What of the reverse? On form-critical grounds, Zimmerli rules out Isaianic dependence on Ezekiel.

137. For the traditional view (first expressed in Sir 48:22–25), see: Allis, *Unity of Isaiah*; Margalioth, *Indivisible Isaiah*; Harrison, *Introduction*, 764–95; Oswalt, *Isaiah*; Motyer, *Prophecy of Isaiah*; Smith, *Isaiah*. Today, critics who appreciate the coherence and unity of the text tend to view it as a redactional unity of later date.

Though not implausible from the standpoint of conservative chronology, Isaianic influence on Ezekiel with regard to the RF is unlikely, considering the evidence. None of Isaiah's formulas appear in judgment oracles in which the judged "know that I am Yahweh," which is the context of the majority of Ezekiel's formulas (72%). The wording of the RFs in Ezekiel seems far closer to the wording in Exodus than to that of Isaiah.[138] From a form-critical and syntactical perspective, the formulas in Isaiah lack the ringing finality of those in Ezekiel; they hardly ever serve as the conclusive target statement of an oracle (Isa 49:26 is the sole exception), which is common in Ezekiel. Also, Isaiah's RFs are invariably expanded to a great extent (there are no strict forms). From a conservative perspective, Isaiah's prophecy may merely have encouraged Ezekiel later *to* use the refrain, not provided a model of *how* to use it.

Worth noting in passing is Isa 19:21: "The Egyptians shall know Yahweh." This knowledge statement, echoing the RF, ties into an oracle that unmistakably harks back to the exodus narratives about Yahweh's self-revelation (ידע in Niphal), plagues on Egypt, oppression, a savior sent by Yahweh, and the redemptive goal of "serving" (עבד) Yahweh with sacrifices. If this text's "knowledge statement" may be interpreted as a variation on the RF and as being derived from that formula, then Isaiah provides further evidence that the RF is closely associated with the exodus story in the minds of Bible writers (cf. Deut 4:35; 7:9; 29:5[6]; Hos 2:16–25[14–23]).

4.3. Conclusion

In conclusion, Ezekiel's usage of the RF—even his entire prophecy in some measure—is grounded in Exodus. The argument for literary dependence must be a

---

138. Every RF in Isaiah is expanded, and most are expanded far more than Ezekiel's. See, e.g., Isa 49:26: "Then all mankind will know that I, Yahweh, am your Savior, your Redeemer, the Mighty One of Jacob" (cf. the exact intratext 60:16). Greenberg claims that one Ezekiel refrain, 17:24, is "a greatly expanded recognition formula," and he includes the whole verse within the formula structure: "[Ezek 17:24 is] framed by parts of a modestly expanded formula: 'All ... shall know that I, YHWH, have spoken and have done it' (= have decreed that it be and have brought it about) as in 37:14. This modestly expanded formula has been split, so that 'All ... shall know that I, YHWH' precedes the recitation of his mighty deeds, while 'I, YHWH, have spoken and have done it' concludes it triumphantly" (*Ezekiel 1–20*, 317). Greenberg may be attracted to this conclusion because Ezekiel occasionally merges the RF with the "conclusion formula for divine speech": אני יהוה דברתי. The resulting expansion, "you/they shall know that I, Yahweh, have spoken," occurs 3× (5:13; 17:21; 37:14). While possible, Greenberg's reading of 17:24 is not necessary, since there is another completed (unsplit) RF in Ezekiel that is closely followed by the commonly used "conclusion formula for divine speech"; see 36:36. This conclusion formula in 17:24 can stand on its own and be understood to function similarly to the majority of the occurrences of the formula (5:15, 17; 17:24; 21:22[17], 37[32]; 22:14; 24:14; 26:14; 30:12; 34:24; 36:36). It echoes the conclusion formula within the RF without necessarily extending the structure of the RF to the end of the verse.

cumulative one, and I have uncovered evidence, especially in the form of "multiple and sustained lexical linkages,"[139] that the prophet follows a pattern of alluding to an earlier text. In chapter 1 of this study, there was a list of qualifications to test the legitimacy of literary allusions/echoes (building upon the work of Hays and Schultz), which is re-presented here.

> The reader should look for: (1) credible chronological priority of the source text; (2) availability of a source to the author; (3) availability of the source to the original audience, if it seems that there is an expectation on the writer's part that they recognize the borrowing and find meaning in the literary relationship; and (4) "verbal and syntactical correspondence which goes beyond one key or uncommon term or even a series of commonly-occurring terms, also evaluating whether the expression is simply formulaic or idiomatic" [Schultz, "Ties that Bind"]. Additional clues for the reader would be: (5) the "volume of an echo," which Hays says "is determined primarily by the degree of explicit repetition of words or syntactical patterns," especially where "the precursor text within Scripture" is "distinctive or prominent"; (6) recurrent use of a smaller text unit that strengthens the cumulative case that the echoing is both intentional and of importance; and (7) evidence of widespread use of a particular literary corpus, such as H, which should alert the reader both to the possibility of finding additional allusions (even to the other corpora) and to the legitimacy of terming it an allusion. Such widespread use could result in a clustering of affinities. Particularly strong is (8) "interpretive re-use" of another text [Schultz, "Ties that Bind"].

Behind the present chapter's work is a conscientious effort to apply these qualifications. (1) The mountain of research and cogency of argument in the works of Avi Hurvitz, Mark Rooker, Jacob Milgrom, Michael Lyons, and others, though not fully convincing to all, establish that the chronological priority of pentateuchal materials (including P) over against Ezekiel is at least credible. (2) If one grants that Exodus (in some authoritative recension) is prior, then one is also ready to believe that the priesthood, as "the custodians of a written torah,"[140] would have access to it. (3) In Ezekiel's reproaches, which assume that the people should (but culpably do not) "remember the days of their youth" in Egypt,[141] and in the people's reported references to their history (Ezek 33:24), we discover some

---

139. Fishbane, *Biblical Interpretation*, 285.

140. Block, "In Search of," 233. See also Betts, *Ezekiel the Priest*.

141. In Ezekiel, to "remember" involves a sense of moral obligation, to reverence and obey the Lord of the covenant who had mercifully rescued the people. The reproach that Israel "did not remember" (16:22, 43) clearly is not intended to speak of ignorance resulting, say, from a failure to learn one's lessons in school. Israel had a memory of Egypt, but they "remembered" in the wrong sense (23:19–21).

evidence that the people were familiar with the narratives of Israel's founding. (4) In the present chapter, there are many examples of a "verbal and syntactical correspondence which goes beyond one key or uncommon term or even a series of commonly-occurring terms" (Schultz), and these parallels are not "simply formulaic or idiomatic." (5) There is a convincing "volume of echo" that legitimizes the claim of literary allusion. (6) Ezekiel often moves beyond a single allusion and makes recurrent use of smaller text units,[142] which observation strongly inclines one to read the linkages as intentional. (7) This chapter also has demonstrated that, along with many apparent allusions to other literary corpora such as H, Ezekiel has widespread and sustained links to the book of Exodus. There is a resultant "clustering of affinities." (8) Finally, this chapter has also found cases of "interpretive re-use," which is an especially strong piece of evidence.

Though the issue of the formula's ultimate origin or initial usage in OT literature has not been directly faced in this chapter, a massive body of evidence points to the plague/exodus narratives. Why does this language, this formula, suggest itself over and over again to biblical writers, and to such a variety of writers of different eras and backgrounds, from both northern and southern kingdoms? The RF probably finds expression again and again because it is firmly planted in earlier, identity-shaping Scriptures of Israel, texts apparently "already in the process of being preserved."[143] With this in mind, it is best to avoid all talk of a "pure form" of the refrain, at least in the sense that some wish to argue. I find no evidence of an original, strict form that was later corrupted, or from which expanded forms developed. As was pointed out in the discussion of Zimmerli's contributions, the critics' early J characteristically has expanded forms of the RF while P typically has the "strict form." It does no good to term the terse form "original" and the expanded formulas "later degenerate forms."[144] I suggest that the terse and expanded forms both came to life in the midst of Yahweh's self-revelation in the recounted events of the exodus and both were recorded for future generations in the book of Exodus in some "stabilized literary formulation."[145]

Why would Ezekiel have used Exodus? A Greenberg quote (slightly out of context) gives a partial answer to this question: "Idioms, figures and forms of expression and composition familiar to his audience must be reflected in, must indeed have determined, the formulation of a biblical author's creations."[146] Besides issues of communication style and recognizable locutions, Ezekiel and his audience shared a spiritual heritage that included authoritative Scriptures

---

142. These numerous intratextual linkages may serve as signposts for the reader to recognize cases of what Block terms "typically Ezekielian resumptive exposition" ("Gog and Magog," 89).

143. Tull [Willey], *Remember the Former Things*, 3.

144. Zimmerli, *Ezekiel 2*, 556.

145. Fishbane, *Biblical Interpretation*, 7.

146. Greenberg, *Ezekiel 1–20*, 18.

(histories, prophecies, laws, etc.).[147] Led by the Spirit of Yahweh and hearing the word of Yahweh, Ezekiel compellingly reused or echoed Scriptures with which the people were familiar. That literature, in part, had fashioned "idioms . . . and forms of expression familiar to his audience." The stories of Exodus belonged not only to the priestly class, but to all the generations of the entire nation once redeemed out of Egypt. Ezekiel's use of Scripture was not arcane, an impenetrable show of learning before an ignorant audience. It was a powerful appeal to a generation of exiles familiar with Scripture. In the next chapter, two further potential reasons for Ezekiel's use of Exodus are explored: (a) an "analogy of situation" according to which the "alien and homeless"[148] exiles could identify with the alien and homeless position of enslaved Israelites long ago; and (b) the idolatry that the prophet traces back to Israel's time in Egypt.

---

147. Recall the testimony of Hos 8:1 and 12 regarding a written law. Wolff says: "This provides us with evidence for a written tradition of ancient covenant law for the middle of the eighth century. That the law had been put into writing 'increases its authority' (G. Gloege, 'Bibel III,' *RGG*3 1, 1145), especially since it was written by God himself (Ex. 24:12; 34:1)" (*Hosea*, 144). G. I. Davies claims: "The assumption must be that already in Hosea's time laws of a reputedly divine origin had been committed to writing" (*Hosea*, 207). See also: Cassuto, "Hosea and the Books of the Pentateuch"; Daniels, *Hosea and Salvation History*, 113–15; Macintosh, *Hosea*, 293.

148. This is Greenberg's contention in "Design and Themes," 217.

CHAPTER 5

The Sociohistorical and Religious
Context of Ezekiel's Oracles

This chapter deals with narrower questions of what little can be known of Ezekiel's biography,[1] the sociohistorical and religious situation faced by the Babylonian exiles, and how the prophecies containing RFs address Ezekiel's audience in that context. One is compelled to limit the discussion to the oracles to Israel, since those delivered against foreign nations were presumably never heard by that audience (e.g., the king of Tyre). A more complete survey here of the historical background is not necessary for the pursuit of this research and its goals. In any case, that information can be obtained elsewhere.[2]

This study postulates, *pace* Volkmar Herntrich, William Brownlee, and others,[3] that the prophet was himself an exile and delivered his prophecies in Babylonia. The testimony of the book is that Ezekiel ben Buzi was numbered among the exiles of 597 who lived בְּאֶרֶץ כַּשְׂדִּים עַל־נְהַר־כְּבָר, "in the land of the Chaldeans by the Kebar river" (1:3). The prefatory statement in 1:1–3 and the references to גָלוּתֵנוּ, "our exile" (33:21; 40:1) are taken at face value.[4]

---

1. While narrative-critical research is useful (characterization, implied author, etc.), I do not regard Ezekiel as primarily a literary construct (see the position in Patton, "Priest, Prophet, and Exile"). I also avoid a hard distinction between historical prophet and literary figure (see Kratz, *Prophets of Israel*).

2. In addition to standard histories of Israel and the better commentary discussions (Zimmerli, *Ezekiel 1*, 9–21; Greenberg, *Ezekiel 1–20*, 3–17; Block, *Ezekiel 1–24*, 1–12, 26–30), one may profitably consult: Oded, "Judah and the Exile"; Smith, *Religion of the Landless*; Scott, *Exile*; Smith-Christopher, *Biblical Theology*; Lipschits and Blenkinsopp, *Judah and the Judeans*; Albertz, *Israel in Exile*; Lipschits, *Fall and Rise*; Ben Zvi and Levin, *Concept of Exile*; Faust, *Judah in the Neo-Babylonian Period*. Placing Jewish experience of exile within the course of Neo-Babylonian history are Zadok, *Jews in Babylonia*, and Vanderhooft, *Neo-Babylonian Empire*. For the general history and culture of the Neo-Babylonian Empire, see Boardman et al., *Assyrian and Babylonian Empires*, and Leick, *Babylonian World*.

3. Herntrich, *Ezechielprobleme*; Brownlee, *Ezekiel 1–19*. More recently, Karl-Friedrich Pohlmann rejects Babylonian provenance of the original oracles and contends that the portrayed diaspora setting is due especially to a major "golaorientierten Redaktion" (*Hesekiel 1–19*, 27–39.) With a hermeneutic of suspicion, Robert P. Carroll rereads Ezekiel "as a series of textual representations of Jerusalem life in terms analogous to living in the diaspora" ("Deportation and Diasporic Discourses," 81). A good defense of Babylonian provenance is Renz, *Rhetorical Function*, 27–38.

4. I am not convinced by historians who doubt the existence of a preexilic Israel/Judah (in any form similar to the biblical picture) and a historical exile as largely interrupting Jewish society in the land. To such critics the exile is little more than an ideological/theological construct; see Carroll,

The issue of Ezekiel's personality has also generated a great deal of work, especially in the twentieth century. Though he was a visionary, performed strange sign-acts, and delivered disturbing oracles, Ezekiel is understood in this study as completely sane. Older theories that he suffered from some psychopathology are largely disregarded today.[5] There are now other, sounder explanations for the bizarre behaviors he exhibited. All who have difficulty grappling with these phenomena, the rhetoric, and the emotional tensions present in the prophecy would do well to consider a point made by Gordon Matties:

> Most North American readers of Ezekiel cannot enter the agony of Ezekiel's own moment in history. The terror of losing all the foundations and structures for social identity and religious vision is scarcely comprehensible. In the context of the historical crisis of the sixth century B.C.E., Ezekiel's language reaches to the extremes in search of explanation and possibility.[6]

More to the point in this chapter is noting that Ezekiel's audience, the Jewish community in Babylon, shared the prophet's "agony" of deportation; both prophet and audience had suffered great loss and trauma. If "Ezekiel's language reaches to the extremes," then the prophet's peculiarities are better explained by studying the context in which he speaks than by speculations about his mental health.

5.1. Difficulties Faced in Studying Ezekiel's Prophecy to Understand the Sociohistorical and Religious Context

5.1.1. Little Direct Information About Life in Exile

There are at least three difficulties facing the interpreter of Ezekiel in understanding the sociohistorical context. First of all, one admits A. B. Davidson's point that

---

"Myth of the Empty Land," and Grabbe, *Leading Captivity Captive*. To follow and assess the debate, consult Day, *In Search of Pre-exilic Israel*, and van der Veen, "Sixth-Century Issues."

5. The most-cited older study is Broome, "Ezekiel's Abnormal Personality," which concluded that the prophet was psychotic and suffered from a complex of different pathologies. Also influential was Jaspers, "Der Prophet Ezechiel." The Freudian analysis of Halperin, *Seeking Ezekiel*, comes to similar conclusions, but few scholars show an inclination to follow him. I do not reject out of hand the possibility that God's prophets could suffer from psychological disorders. E.g., the lament of Jer 20:14–18 (see Lundbom, *Jeremiah 1–20*, 865) and the narrative of Elijah's flight to Horeb (1 Kgs 19) suggest depression (for further discussion on this possibility, see Kruger, "Depression in the Hebrew Bible").

6. Matties, *Ezekiel 18*, 219. Additionally, Daniel Smith-Christopher reminds us that "Ezekiel's rhetoric is the language of suffering—and the rhetoric of suffering and anger is not 'normal'" ("Ezekiel in Abu Ghraib," 149); see also Tuell, "Should Ezekiel Go to Rehab?"

the prophet's "interests were exclusively religious,"[7] and thus the picture he gives of the exiles and their circumstances is inadequate to derive definite *Sitze im Leben* for the oracles. Ezekiel does on occasion quote a saying current among the exiles, but the prophet is so focused on the divine side of the dialogue[8] that the reader is left with "little to go on." The best that can be hoped for, according to Thomas Renz, is "to present a picture that can claim more probability than any alternative proposal."[9] Davidson is inclined to turn to Jeremiah's prophecy, with its candid picture of the people's idolatry and penchant for false prophets, in order to get a better grasp of Ezekiel's situation, but clearly this is not ideal.

One also admits that Ezekiel the person is less accessible because the prophecy, which is the only source of information about him, has no biographical intent. Compared with portrayals of other prophets, the book of "Ezekiel describes a remote figure whose personality is almost completely hidden behind his prophetic message."[10] Earlier attempts at psychological analysis within an author-centered hermeneutic sought to make the shadowy prophet more comprehensible in the modern day. Ironically, this effort exacerbated interpreters' problems, given that it "tended to remove Ezekiel from the mainstream of biblical prophecy."[11] The lack of much sociohistorical information in the book of Ezekiel itself is the first handicap facing the interpreter.[12]

5.1.2. *The Credibility of the Portrayal of Jewish Religious Life*

A second difficulty is the suggestion of critics that the meager background data available from reading Ezekiel may not be historically credible. Some argue that

---

7. Davidson, *Ezekiel*, xxi.

8. Walther Zimmerli and Moshe Greenberg have emphasized this point. The latter writes: "His inner parts suffused with the scroll ... the prophet must henceforth speak 'in God's words.' This is a far-reaching limitation of the prophet's spontaneity and responsibility. Zimmerli noted, with respect to 14:1–11, that 'the individuality of Ezekiel's prophetic style is recognizable by the fact that the sin of the audience is not set forth as, say, by Amos (4:1f., cf. 5:1–3), in a reproving discourse formulated by the prophet himself, but is wholly included in the divine address [to the prophet]' (*ZAW* 66 [1954], 6). Such, indeed, is the case throughout the book: Ezekiel's denunciations are exclusively reports of what God said. The prophet's task is reduced to the conveyance of God's message; he has no further responsibility toward his audience and is answerable only to God for delivering his message and thus establishing a record that 'a prophet had been among them'" (*Ezekiel 1–20*, 77).

9. Renz, *Rhetorical Function*, 43.

10. Wilson, "Prophecy in Crisis," 117.

11. Wilson, "Prophecy in Crisis," 118–19.

12. However, as argued later in this chapter, there is more sociohistorical information to be found in Ezekiel than first appears. The relative lack of information for constructing the oracles' *Sitze im Leben* can make traditional form criticism difficult to practice in Ezekiel studies. Tying the speech forms to their original oral settings proves to be quite a challenge. For a critique of Zimmerli's modified form-critical method and its aptness as a tool for work on Ezekiel, see Davis, *Swallowing the Scroll*, 15–19.

modern readers do not have simple, direct access to "the world of Ezekiel" through his denunciations of civil and cultic sins. Michael Fishbane, for example, warns against an attempt to "read prophetic critiques as a window to popular practices."[13] This warning is necessary, they believe, because of Ezekiel's hortatory purposes. Particularly, the lengthy lists of charges against Israel in such chapters as 8–11, 18, and 22 serve a rhetorical function. Fishbane contends that the sins cataloged "are more in the nature of typical lists of behaviors deriving from a common literary pattern than 'historically accurate' indices of exactly what was or was not done in Ezekiel's day."[14] The indictment of idolatry, among others, is thrown open to question.[15]

This somewhat skeptical stance can be answered with three arguments. First, Fishbane has disputed Ezekiel's ancient witness without presenting substantial evidence upon which to base his counterclaim. The fact that recognizable literary patterns are present does not require the conclusion that the indictments were, in large part, mere inventions or were somehow falsified, as though Ezekiel had preferred charges against the people of God without solid grounds. Such a conclusion seems uncompelling and even wrong-headed, considering that his indictments are not out of accord with Jeremiah's.[16] Secondly, it requires some temerity, assuming our relative ignorance of the sociohistorical context, to contradict a prophet's more specific indictments twenty-six hundred years after they were delivered. A third argument would suggest that, if Ezekiel the preacher were slightly off-base in his denunciation, his audience would readily discount his entire message. The true prophets' stock-in-trade was scrupulous honesty and adherence to the facts of the situation. If the audience did not share the prophets' perception and evaluation of the situation, the prophets were compelled to make a case for the accusations so as to be credible. Unjustifiable exaggeration or severity could lose them their audience. Yes, there were certain literary patterns to the vice catalogs, but interpreters may create more problems than are solved by proposing that a catalog may serve as "a propaganda document whose chief concern was to justify the inevitability of the divine doom to the exiles."[17] This study accepts the general accuracy of Ezekiel's charges in the particulars they describe and their interpretation of the particulars.

---

13. Fishbane, "Sin and Judgment," 147.

14. Fishbane, "Sin and Judgment," 146.

15. Berlin, "Did the Jews Worship Idols in Babylonia?"

16. According to Jeremiah, the spiritual condition of Judah was grim. His prophecy (e.g., 44:15–19) points to a religious situation post-597, and even post-586, in which the "remaining population [in Judah] . . . interpreted the exile as punishment for Josiah's anti-syncretistic actions," and there are indications of a "resurgence of syncretistic practices" (Smith, *Religion of the Landless*, 33). Jeremiah's list of religious, moral, and social evils closely mirrors that of Ezekiel.

17. Fishbane, "Sin and Judgment," 135.

While the accuracy of Ezekiel's oracles is defended, I make two important qualifications for the sake of stricter accuracy. First, one must accept that there can be ambiguity in places regarding the target of Yahweh's indictment. Many charges are leveled specifically at Jerusalem and those who remained behind after the exile of 597, while other charges seem to apply more generally to "all the house of Israel" (3:7),[18] both the exilic community and those remaining in Judah. Second, it seems best to interpret the stinging indictments as having a transgenerational application.

When the prophet censures God's people for their actions and heart attitudes, he not infrequently mentions the ancestors as also carrying a weight of guilt. Punishment is coming upon Israel because the people "*and their fathers* have rebelled against me to this very day" (ואבותם פשעו בי עד־עצם היום הזה; 2:3). In 20:4, the prophet is to speak to the nation and "make them know [הודיעם] the abominations of their fathers." There is reason, then, to read the catalog of sins as an indictment of Ezekiel's generation and as a redemptive-historical record of the evils of previous generations. A few specific sins may have been more characteristic of earlier eras, such as the long reign of Manasseh perhaps, but it is impossible to judge for certain. We are unable to distinguish strictly between specific sins as historical or contemporary. From the theological standpoint, this inability is not necessarily a serious problem in the interpretation of the prophecy, for Ezekiel argues that there is a wretched spiritual inheritance that his generation owns (20:30–31). Even in exile, the nation's tradition of profaning God's name continues (36:16–23), and Ezekiel views the current generation as sharing fully in the wickedness of those who had gone before. There is spiritual solidarity with the ancestors.[19]

Does this reading of Ezekiel's theology conflict with the teaching of chapter 18 on the topic of individual responsibility? It does not conflict if we take into consideration that, in certain places, Ezekiel implies that guilt, perhaps in the sense of condoning evil, and deserved punishment are incurred when later generations do not mourn the sins of previous generations.[20] In order to receive the plans for a new sanctuary, the regathered people of God are required in 43:9–11 to put

18. The ambiguity appears a greater challenge when one notices that even the phrase "all the house of Israel" can refer more narrowly to the Jerusalemites (12:10) or the Jews in exile (11:15).

19. The relation of the generations, their solidarity, is a fundamental issue in Ezekiel. J. G. McConville makes the point that, within broader OT theology, this solidarity is "two-edged." On the one hand, the solidarity is the basis for claiming the covenant promises of blessing upon later generations in the community of faith. "On the other hand, it means that the people of the present have a share in the *guilt* of the past" (*Ezra, Nehemiah, and Esther*, 125 [emphasis original]).

20. Perhaps scholarship needs a fuller understanding of corporate confession of sin in the OT. In addition to psalms that include corporate confession of sin (e.g., 106:6–7, 19–47), there are numerous figures said to mourn the nation's evils, identify with sinners, and confess the sins of their "fathers" as their very own (Jer 3:25; Neh 1:6–7; 9:2, 16–18, 26, 28–29, 34; Dan 9:3, 8, 16; cf. Exod 34:9). Within the OT canonical context, how is such mourning related to the expected fulfillment of the promise of return and restoration?

away their whoring and the dead idols (וּפִגְרֵי) of kings long ago. And they are also required to feel ashamed of all they have done. If and when they mourn, the plans will be made known (הוֹדַע) to them.[21] Such mourning and feelings of shame in repentance, even for ancestors' crimes and sins, could be concomitant with, and even constitutive of, a cleansing from defilement and release from guilt. Is this the best way to interpret Ezek 9:4, where those who "mourn and groan [הַנֶּאֱנָחִים וְהַנֶּאֱנָקִים] over all the abominations" done in the city are spared death at the hands of the executioners? But defilement and profanation would remain, and even carry over to another day, in a priestly conception of things, where no cleansing (in a proper mourning of evil) had taken place. It may be suggested that those who failed to mourn would also presumably tolerate and even participate in similar sins. It is remarkable that Ezekiel's prophecy associates feelings of shame with the proclamation of salvation (16:54, 61; 36:32), rather than with judgment.[22]

5.1.3. Biblical Scholarship on the Trauma of Deportation

There is currently a third difficulty in understanding the sociohistorical and religious context of Ezekiel's prophecies. Scholarship researching the emotional, psychological, and social stresses experienced by the Jews deported to Babylonia is only beginning to mature. Though much valuable work has been done to assess the historical and cultural environment of the exilic community, there have been fewer forays into the kind of sociological and psychological analysis common in psychiatry and contemporary refugee and disaster studies. More interdisciplinary reflection is needed regarding the exiles' previous trauma (597 BC) and its possible effect on their state of being years later when Ezekiel received his call (593) and began to prophesy another trauma, the future devastation of Jerusalem.

Scholars are gradually coming to appreciate Ezekiel as "trauma literature" and the crisis of the exile as "a dislocation which was not only physical but psychological

---

21. Scholars debate two points: the meaning of וּפִגְרֵי ("dead bodies/idols") in 43:9 (cf. v. 7) and the syntax in 43:11. On the first controversy, Zimmerli takes the word to refer to memorials for kings, while Daniel Block suggests it points to "some aspect of a cult of the dead," perhaps "funerary offerings" involving "the veneration of the deified spirits of Israel's royal ancestors" (*Ezekiel 25–48*, 584, 575, 585). Regarding the second controversy, on v. 11 and what G. A. Cooke terms "the confused text" (*Ezekiel*, 465), some do not understand the divulging of the temple plans as conditional on the people being ashamed (as in MT, RSV, REB, NIV, NJB, ESV). The NJPS and NRSV render the conditional וְאִם as "when" instead. The most influential commentaries challenging the conditional in the text are Zimmerli (*Ezekiel 2*, 410) and Block (*Ezekiel 25–48*, 586–89); the latter opts for "reading *wĕhēm yikkālēmû*, with LXX and Vulg." (586). Walther Eichrodt simply deletes the entire conditional clause as an inappropriate insertion (*Ezekiel*, 553).

22. Zimmerli makes this point (*Ezekiel 2*, 418–19). Other studies touching on this are Odell, "Inversion of Shame and Forgiveness," and Wu, *Honor, Shame, and Guilt*. See also Stiebert, *Construction of Shame*.

and theological too."[23] How may that crisis setting (an experience of individual and collective trauma) have shaped Israel's exilic literature? Two book-length studies by Daniel Smith-Christopher broke new ground for biblical scholarship in the field of sociological and psychological analysis,[24] and others have followed with fruitful work.[25] For Ezekiel, we now have Ruth Poser's seven-hundred-page dissertation, published as *Das Ezechielbuch als Trauma-Literatur* (2012).[26]

Smith-Christopher approaches the literature of the exile with a view to exposing the "sociology of oppression"[27] that was a force in shaping that literature. To probe the background, rhetorical conventions, and exilic theology of the literature, he utilizes a complex sociological theory that includes a component of psychology, post-traumatic stress disorder (PTSD). He researches the coping mechanisms (survival strategies) of the dispossessed, oppressed, and vulnerable. Beyond that, Smith-Christopher urges Bible readers to see the subversive element in the text: a subtle resistance to a sociopolitical oppressor.[28] His approach, building on case studies of emotional and behavioral responses to trauma and displacement, holds real promise, especially as it moves beyond a concern with victimization to consider the renewal possibilities inherent in experiences of suffering and loss. What will be built in place of what was destroyed?

It is wise to follow Smith-Christopher's lead in asking questions about trauma among deportees, the exilic community's adjustments in leadership structures, the role of ritual in establishing and maintaining group identity, and the impulse to create an affirming "in-house" literature. There is need, however, to balance his regular focus on the book as a human response to tragedy and a human word about God with a focus on Ezekiel (a profoundly theocentric prophecy) as a divine word to human beings and as a revelation of God's purposes in and response to human suffering. I now treat this subject of properly hearing the voice of suffering in Ezekiel's prophecy (as God's word) and seek insight into the sociohistorical context in which Ezekiel delivered oracles and used the RF.

23. Joyce, "Dislocation and Adaptation," 45.

24. See Smith-Christopher, *Religion of the Landless* (1989) and *Biblical Theology of Exile* (2002). The latter develops his research in two earlier articles: "Reassessing" and "Ezekiel on Fanon's Couch." More recent is his "Trauma and Old Testament."

25. Kiefer, *Exil und Diaspora*; Middlemas, *Templeless Age*; Ahn, *Exile as Forced Migrations*; Kelle, Ames, and Wright, *Interpreting Exile*; Ahn and Middlemas, *Irrigation Canals of Babylon*; Garber, "'I Went in Bitterness'"; Garber, "Trauma Theory"; Boda et al., *Prophets Speak*.

26. Poser takes the book to be imaginative literature depicting in a fictionalized way the trauma of deportation (see *Ezechielbuch*, 110–14, 261–88); she allows that those responsible for the composition may have witnessed Jerusalem's fall.

27. Walter Brueggemann, "Editor's Foreword," in Smith-Christopher, *Biblical Theology*, viii.

28. This element is present in Ezekiel, as the Babylonians are denied bragging rights in conquering Judah: it is Yahweh who sent his people into exile.

5.2. The Value of the Prophecy as a Window on the Sociohistorical and Religious Context

Whatever the difficulties in perusing Ezekiel's prophecy as a source of information about the Jewish experience of exile, scholars have little alternative. What else is available for understanding the living situation, possible community dynamics, and value systems behind the rhetoric and theological message of Ezekiel?[29] Even newer psychosocial approaches depend on the book's content. This section draws from the prophecy in a "maximalist" fashion to assess several problems of interpretation: (1) the prophet's situation and personal difficulties in fulfilling his divine calling; (2) the exiles' traumatic experiences; (3) the theological questions that, we surmise, may have occupied the community in reflecting on their lost home and new situation; and (4) Ezekiel's portrayal of Israel's spiritual and moral state and the sins that called forth Yahweh's indictment.

5.2.1. Ezekiel's Personal Hardships in Fulfilling His Calling

As already mentioned, a commonplace in Ezekiel studies decades ago was discussion of the prophet's psychoemotional makeup. Some sought to explain the peculiarities of his sign-acts and the severity of the judgment oracles by recourse to categories of pathology.[30] Recently, however, those critics who psychoanalyze him have themselves been charged with "blaming the victim." Psychological studies have sometimes shown scant interest in understanding Ezekiel's personal hardships either as a deportee or as one carrying a heavy prophetic burden.[31] The first of these concerns, the traumas of deportation and living in exile that Ezekiel experienced together with the whole Jewish community in Babylon, will be treated following a discussion of Ezekiel's personal hardships as Yahweh's spokesperson.

Among the prophets, perhaps none but Jeremiah suffered as much travail in his spirit as Ezekiel. Though the son of Buzi may not have faced literal chains (but see הרתוק in 7:23) and did not see imprisonment in a dungeon or the extremity of a martyr's death, his suffering in ministry was great. Captured by the Babylonian army in 597, Ezekiel was a few years later a captive to Yahweh's call. He was strictly

---

29. See: Dijkstra, "Valley of Dry Bones"; Lust, "Exile and Diaspora"; Odendaal, "Exile in Ezekiel"; Smith-Christopher, "Ezekiel on Fanon's Couch."

30. E.g., catatonic or paranoid schizophrenia, misogyny stemming from abuse in childhood, etc.

31. Smith-Christopher writes: "Halperin [*Seeking Ezekiel*] mentions the exile two times in his entire book, and then only in passing. Such tendencies to read the psychological state of Ezekiel totally apart from the social and political experiences he suffered are symptoms of the same avoidance in other biblical scholarly analyses of the exile as a real event where human beings deeply suffered. Any psychological assumptions about Ezekiel derived apart from serious attention to the exile are thus tantamount to *blaming the victim*" (*Biblical Theology*, 89; emphasis added).

warned not to resist his commission when he was overwhelmed (מַשְׁמִים; 3:15)
by the initial vision of God.[32] In the first three chapters, his response to seeing
the glory of Yahweh was to fall on his face in awe (1:28) and finally sit "stunned
and withdrawn"[33] for a full week. Throughout the book, Ezekiel communicates
the irresistibility of the divine calling. When, for example, the hand of the Lord
Yahweh seizes him by the hair to carry him away to Jerusalem (8:1–3), his own
volition is of no consequence. He cannot but submit.

The warnings given to Ezekiel early in the book indicate that the Jews in Babylonia could be expected to oppose the prophet's message and possibly pose a physical danger to the messenger. This is a sensible interpretation of the exhortation
not to fear, though he may live beside "briers and thorns" or "sit upon scorpions"
(2:6); these metaphors forewarn that his compatriots will cause him pain. Ezekiel
can expect, at the very least, menacing words and looks (2:6). The hostility of the
audience and their refusal to listen (2:5, 7; 3:7, 11, 27) is a gauge of their spiritual
condition.[34] Judging from the focus of Ezekiel's judgment-speeches and the focus
of the sign-acts,[35] the people were likely to have been especially resistant to the
prophecy that Jerusalem faced certain destruction.

Warnings of strong opposition from other deportees prompt interpreters to
query whether the prophet experienced an alienation from Jewish society in Babylon. Considering the fact that Ezekiel was forced to live as an alien, one imagines
that his family was dependent on fellow exiles for social interaction and friend-
ship, business and trade, assistance and counsel in times of personal need, and
spiritual fellowship. Any social alienation would have been of great consequence
in Ezekiel's life.[36] Clearly, the prophet was never completely ostracized, for the

32. Poser interprets √שׁמם as a "Trauma-Wurzel" (*Ezechielbuch*, 334; see larger context of 311–34).
33. Allen, *Ezekiel 1–19*, 44.
34. For Ezekiel personally, there may have been a positive side to Yahweh's warning about the
exiles' stubborn refusal to hear. Renz says: "The prophet is delivered from the responsibility of having
to persuade his audience. His responsibility lies only in the delivery of the warning, not in its being
heeded" (*Rhetorical Function*, 39). Even more important is the rhetorical point Renz drives home
here: "By contrasting Ezekiel's positive, more specifically submissive, response to Yahweh's word, with
the anticipated negative response of the community at large, the first three chapters also allow for a
discontinuity between the prophet's audience and the book's audience. The audience of the book is
expected to react to the book in the same way as Ezekiel reacted to the scroll given to him, and not
to respond as the people did to the prophet."
35. All the sign-acts, except the last (37:15–17), are meant to communicate the irrevocability of
Yahweh's judgment on Jerusalem. This is true even for the sign-act of dumbness, according to Longman and Dillard: "At the very least, Ezekiel's dumbness conveyed the idea that he would not be inter-
ceding with God in the nation's behalf. God's decree that Jerusalem be destroyed was now irrevocable,
and intercession was pointless. The only words from the prophet's mouth would be announcements
of impending doom until that divine decree had come to pass" (*Introduction*, 364–65). Much the same
conclusion was earlier drawn in Wilson, "Ezekiel's Dumbness."
36. It is worth remarking at this point that the typical modern Westerner, living in a culture where
"rugged individualism" is thought a virtue and mark of personal strength, might not struggle with
social alienation to the degree an ancient Jew would.

elders repeatedly sought him out, and he seems eventually to have found some public recognition and even popularity (33:30–33). He may even have carried a leadership burden, as hyperstressed exiles "looked to intellectual experts of their community, such as Ezekiel, to decode and communicate the content and perhaps shortcomings of the institutions and ideas characteristic of Babylonian life."[37] Still, his unsparing denunciations of the Jewish nation, his notoriety for bizarre sign-acts, and his sometimes curt rejection of visitors (required by Yahweh; 14:1–3 and 20:1–4) must have brought strains in relationships.

The opening chapters provide more indications that Ezekiel's calling would be hard. They speak of the ordeal of delivering woe oracles (2:10) that gave him a bitter and burning feeling in his spirit (וָאֵלֵךְ מַר בַּחֲמַת רוּחִי; 3:14), a commission as watchman (צֹפֶה) with terrifying responsibility for souls (3:17–21), divinely appointed experiences of seclusion, being bound with cords, and dumbness (3:24–26). There are still more assignments to lie bound on his side for lengthy periods to bear Israel's and Judah's punishment (4:4–8),[38] to eat siege rations cooked over dung (4:9–17), and to perform the freakish act of cutting off his hair and beard with a sword (5:1–4).

Furthermore, Yahweh exposed the priest-prophet to horrifying idol worship in the temple (8:1–16) and the trauma of witnessing slaughter in the streets (9:1–11). The latter so distressed him that he fell on his face and cried out, "Oh Lord Yahweh! Will you destroy the whole remnant of Israel in your outpoured wrath on Jerusalem?" This is not the unfeeling, hard man many take Ezekiel to be. His distress was heightened as Yahweh ordered him to condemn those in the city who give evil counsel, including Pelatiah; while Ezekiel was prophesying he watched Pelatiah drop dead (11:1–13). Again, he could not contain his raw emotions: "Oh Lord Yahweh! Will you wipe out the whole remnant of Israel?" There was tragedy in the vivid display of the power of Yahweh's word in judgment, even if Ezekiel understood the judgment as just. He may have viewed himself as an agent of Yahweh's death-dealing word, and it stands to reason that Ezekiel is able to name the dead man, Pelatiah, because he knew him, or knew of him, as a fellow Jerusalemite.

Ezekiel's public sign-acts brought uncomfortable questions and caused consternation in his audience (12:9). One imagines he fought against discouragement as he heard fellow exiles dismiss all prophecies as "coming to nothing" (12:22), or as addressing distant days with no relevance for the present (12:26). Ezekiel saw his oracles contradicted by false prophets (ch. 13) and opposed by an audience of "people who listen to lies" (13:19). Yet another burden was the duty of fulfilling Yahweh's commission and offending the sensibilities of fellow exiles by delivering the lengthy, vulgar allegories of chapters 16 and 23. (One imagines that modern readers' disgust at them was matched by disgust among most of Ezekiel's hearers.)

37. Vanderhooft, "Ezekiel in and on Babylon," 119.
38. McKeating suggests reading this text with Exod 32:30–34, where Moses seeks atonement for the nation's sin (*Ezekiel*, 95).

Having his words dismissed as strange parables (מְשָׁלִים; 21:5[20:49]), presumably not worth the effort to try to understand, seems to have caused Ezekiel distress—and readers will note that his exclamation in responding to the disrespect,
"Ah, Lord Yahweh!" (אֲהָהּ אֲדֹנִי יהוה), appears in other texts where the prophet is
experiencing anguish (4:14; 9:8; 11:13).

Yet all the inconvenience, reproach, and distress previously mentioned cannot compare with Ezekiel's personal loss in chapter 24, where his young wife[39]
is taken away in sudden death. The delight of his eyes, the only person on earth
perhaps who was sympathetic, who understood his burdensome calling, is dead,
and Ezekiel is bereft of all human comfort. The prophet had been commanded in
the morning to prophesy her impending death (24:15–18); what faith and strength
of will must this have required! And he is not even allowed the healing experience
of mourning, as Yahweh makes the bereavement another strange sign-act. There
are to be no tears, no words of lament, no outward signs of grief "by which a
mourner ... implicitly solicited the condolences of his community."[40] A long list of
normal mourning activities are proscribed by Yahweh in the text. These events in
chapter 24 are the worst of all of Ezekiel's sufferings. It may be true that he "exhibits
none of Jeremiah's agitated suffering,"[41] but suffer he did. In conclusion, one "cannot but be impressed with the power and intensity of the prophet's experience,"[42]
and all of Ezekiel's various torments and troubles deserve consideration as one
interprets the prophet's ministry and message.

5.2.2. Assessing the Trauma of the Babylonian Exile

> Ha, banishment? Be merciful, say "death";
> For exile hath more terror in his look,
> Much more than death. Do not say "banishment"!
>   ... "Banished"?
> O friar, the damned use that word in hell;
> Howling attends it.
>
> —(Romeo) Shakespeare[43]

In the preceding reflections on Ezekiel's adversities, little has been said regarding
the twin traumas of forced deportation and surviving—hardly *living*—in exile.

---

39. In ancient Israelite marriage, "it is safe to assume the bride was considerably younger than the
groom" (King and Stager, *Life in Biblical Israel*, 54). If, as is widely thought, Ezekiel was thirty years
old when commissioned in 593, and approximately age thirty-five at the time of the events in ch. 24,
his wife may have been only in her twenties when she was taken away.

40. Greenberg, *Ezekiel 21–37*, 508.

41. Zimmerli, *Old Testament Theology*, 207.

42. Longman and Dillard, *Introduction*, 361.

43. *Romeo and Juliet*, 3.3.12–14, 3.3.46–48.

Simply put, the exile was the daily grief and hardship of Ezekiel on top of which all the troubles of ministry were piled. The Jews in Babylon who composed his audience were likewise survivors of these traumas, and we must imagine that their experiences and circumstances strongly influenced their reactions to Ezekiel's oracles. Both prophet and audience were victimized by an ancient practice of "state-sponsored terrorism"[44] calculated to destroy the will to independence. Babylon intended to humiliate, intimidate, and demoralize all political and military resistance (17:12–14), and many suffered in the process. Taking this context into account, one has a better vantage point for understanding Ezekiel's oracles and their effects, how they derive from and speak to trauma. One postmodern writer posits, "das Bedürfnis, Leiden beredt werden zu lassen, ist Bedingung aller Wahrheit."[45] Here we seek "to let suffering speak," both by listening to the sufferer and by learning from the suffering.

5.2.2.1. *Specific Traumas and Hardships Likely Experienced by the Exiles*
In many places, the book of Ezekiel evokes memories of the past sufferings of Jewish prisoners in the 597 exile by announcing a far more severe judgment that was certain to fall later upon the inhabitants of Jerusalem.[46] For example, when Ezekiel detailed the siege-works to be raised against Jerusalem and the horrors to occur inside the walls, he was speaking to those who had experienced that terror first-hand, at least in some measure (2 Kgs 24:10–16). The exiles of 597 had probably seen siege walls and ramps being built, encampments of enemy soldiers, and battering rams brought near the city walls (4:1–3). According to the portrayal of events in 2 Kgs 24, Jehoiachin capitulated and went out to Nebuchadnezzar, thus sparing the city a prolonged siege.[47] The full horror of that type of warfare was to be experienced, Ezekiel prophesies, by the Jews who remained behind in Judah. It would soon come upon friends and relatives in Jerusalem

---

44. Smith-Christopher, *Biblical Theology*, 76, quotes Stuart W. Turner and Caroline Gorst-Unsworth, who define state-sponsored terrorism as: "essentially the act of a state against an individual or group, with the aim of achieving specific psychological changes (directly) in their victims and often (indirectly) in their communities." The authors add: "The survivor of torture has not merely been the accidental victim of physical injury or threat of death such as might occur, for example in a natural disaster or accident.... He or she has received the focused attention of an adversary determined to cause the maximal psychological change.... Neither is it the individual who suffers. For every person tortured there are mothers and fathers, wives, husbands and children, friends and relatives who wait in uncertainty and fear.... Torture has effects on communities and on whole societies" ("Psychological Sequelae," 475–76).

45. Adorno, *Negative Dialektik*, 27.

46. Observe, however, that, apart from passing references to Jehoiachin's capture (17:12–14; 19:8–9), Ezekiel does not directly discuss the trauma of 597.

47. See: Hobbs, *Time for War*; Kern, *Ancient Siege Warfare*; and Eph'al, *City Besieged*. For the Babylonian account, see Wiseman, *Chronicles of Chaldean Kings*, 32–34, 73, who believes "the siege cannot have lasted more than two months" (33).

(17:17; 21:27[22]), and this prospect in all likelihood further traumatized the Jews in Babylonia.

Ezekiel's vivid oracles about Jerusalem confronted the exiles with the certainty of a judgment that staggered thought and imagination. In 4:16, Yahweh promises to "break the staff of bread" (שבר מטה־לחם) so that the inhabitants must ration food and water. The population of Jerusalem will eat less palatable foods (4:9), prepared in a shameful, sickening manner (4:12–13). They will eat "in dread" (בדאגה) and be "appalled" (שמם) as they watch their loved ones suffer deprivation and become emaciated (4:16–17). Cannibalism will break out among the starved, even within the immediate family (5:10). In addition to what the oracles term the "arrows of deadly famine" (5:16; cf. Deut 32:23–24), the Jerusalemites will experience death by wild beasts, plague, and finally bloodshed as the walls are breached and swordsmen enter the city (5:17). Though the deportees of 597 never faced the full horrors of a prolonged siege, they had faced the prospect with dread.

Another deeply imbedded memory of 597 for the prisoners of war was the humiliating capture and exile of Jehoiachin (1:2). His removal as their representative head was likely felt to be their humiliation as well. The installation of the puppet ruler Zedekiah appears to have been humiliating and unpopular with some, judging from Ezekiel's continuing acknowledgment of the deposed Jehoiachin and Yahweh's dismissive words about the "profane, wicked prince" Zedekiah (21:30[25]), who should "remove the turban and take off the crown" (21:31[26]).

In 12:11, Yahweh foretells the disaster to come in 586 when the house of Israel will "go into exile, into captivity" (בגולה בשבי; cf. 21:28[24]). One assumes that the exiles of 597 also felt themselves to be captives, especially as they recalled the day they began to be marched off to Babylon, possibly in actual chains (רתוק; 7:23; cf. 34:27). They may, too, have felt stripped and raped by their enemy.[48] It is true that most scholars believe that the Jewish exiles experienced a large measure of personal liberty in Babylon.[49] Nevertheless, the reality of their political subjugation apparently led generations of Jews to regard themselves as "slaves" and to feel "great distress" (Neh 9:36–37), even after they returned to the land and were probably living in better circumstances. The slaves needed rescue from a "yoke" (מטות) of "servitude" (עבד Qal ptc.; Ezek 34:27).

48. Fine work has been done to explain the rhetoric in chs. 16 and 23 as expressive of a trauma of violence and disgrace, a "real experience of chains, imprisonment, futility and defilement" (Patton, "'Should Our Sister Be Treated Like a Whore?'" 237). See also Smith-Christopher, "Ezekiel in Abu Ghraib," Kelle, "Wartime Rhetoric," and literature they cite. Smith-Christopher reminds readers of the semantic relationship of "to strip" and "to go into exile" in √גלה.

49. Oded writes: "One gets the impression that they had a certain internal autonomy and that they enjoyed the freedom to manage their community life (Ezek. 33.30–3).... They were allowed to live according to the customs of their fathers and were allowed to buy property (Jer. 29.5) and even slaves (Ezra 2.65)" ("Judah and the Exile," 483).

We imagine a most sorrowful journey, as the exiles of 597 trudged the long road to Babylonia. They had too much time for worrying about an uncertain future, and they must have raised unsettling practical questions. What awaited them in a foreign land? How would they overcome the language barrier?[50] Where and how would they live? Would they be treated ruthlessly and enslaved? Would they ever see home again? How would they educate their children in another culture?[51] Where would they bury their dead in Babylonia? What would happen to their extended families, their houses and fields, and their possessions back in the land of their fathers? Would they be able to retain their rights of inheritance? Alongside these practical questions, religious questions must have surfaced just as quickly.

What were the deportees' impressions of Mesopotamia? Life in Babylonia, the place of their exile, is likened to residing "in a wilderness, in a dry and parched land" (19:13). There are reasons to take this characterization as metaphorical and as speaking of a miserable experience of the soul. While it is possible that some Judahite exiles found their climate inhospitable (perhaps a settlement at drier and hotter Nippur),[52] much of the evidence points to the establishment of large Jewish settlements in close proximity to the Euphrates and the surrounding well-irrigated area of canals (Ezek 1:1; 3:15; Ps 137:1). Drought would not have been a typical problem faced by the exiles. However, they may well have felt themselves to be living in a "desert" of emptiness and despair (cf. Ps 63:2[1]).

The stresses of living as exiles in the early sixth century BC would have had many effects, including the felt need for unity and the quick establishment of community leadership. One can draw comparisons to the present day. While it is common for refugees and exiles to take opportunity to "close ranks" with their own kind in an alien society, the sense of desolation and culture shock they experience in making a new life can contribute to angry, bitter, impatient attitudes in interpersonal relationships. Hurting, needy people can find it difficult to build community without strong leadership. Even with able leadership in place, the community can sharply disagree and divide over key issues such as conformity to a host culture. Some, especially the younger members, may desire to adapt and conform in large measure (see Ezek 20:32), while others fight to conserve traditional ways. There is no reason to doubt that Jewish exiles twenty-six hundred years ago would have had struggles and needs similar to these. What leadership would emerge among the exiles to address these matters? The book of Ezekiel reveals a vital concern for unity and leadership in the exilic community.[53]

---

50. Poser discusses this aspect of culture-shock and other concerns in a most valuable section (*Ezechielbuch*, 158–248).

51. Many such acculturation challenges awaited them; see Vanderhooft, "Ezekiel in and on Babylon."

52. Judith A. Franke, "Nippur," in *ABD*, 4:1119–22.

53. See Duguid, *Ezekiel and the Leaders*.

According to the testimony of the prophecy (17:13), the community had a large pool from which to draw leaders.[54] The biblical record says Jehoiachin was young and inexperienced when he ascended the throne (2 Kgs 24:8) and was held in prison in Babylon for long years (2 Kgs 25:27),[55] which explains the lack of evidence that he played any leadership role among the deportees. In place of a Davidic ruler, the exiles seem to have been led by "elders" (זקני ישראל) in each community (8:1; 14:1; 20:1, 3).[56] Thus, there is a strong note of discontinuity between political life before and after the deportation in 597, and remarkably there is a return in Babylon to a leadership pattern said to be more characteristic of the period of the exodus (Exod 17:5; 18:12; 24:1) and wilderness wanderings (Num 11:16).

5.2.2.2. Ezekielian References to Traumatized Emotions

Already noted is the proposal of Smith-Christopher that Ezekiel and his fellow exiles, as traumatized victims of "terrorism," may have experienced what is today called PTSD.[57] The psychological disorder deserves consideration in scholarship but is less germane to the aims of this research. Also, a PTSD diagnosis today, so far removed in history, and concerning subjects (Ezekiel and the community in exile) who cannot be observed or interviewed, would be unfounded.[58] It would be unwise, however, to neglect entirely Ezekielian references to traumatized emotions.

With a variety of expressive language, the book tells of the anguish of Jerusalem's inhabitants when Yahweh pours out his wrath. One may even argue that the emotional distress of the Jerusalemites constitutes a major emphasis of the judgment oracles and is part of the punishment. Yahweh will bring "a singular evil" (7:5)[59] upon the city that will cause the residents to experience anxiety and shuddering (שממון and דאגה; 4:16; cf. 12:19), panic/dismay (מהומה; 7:7, 22:5), moaning (המות; 7:16), horror (פלצות; 7:18), anguish (קפדה; 7:25), mourning (אבל Hithpael; 7:27), quaking and trembling at mealtime (רעש and רגזה; 12:18–19), their hearts melting in fear (למוג לב; 21:20[15]), and horror (שמה; 23:33). The city's inhabitants will know such a paralyzing fear and helplessness that "all

---

54. Babylon sought to decapitate the Judahite revolt by deporting the leadership and intelligentsia, who would have had the most to lose: wealth, property, social position, political power.

55. Note the discussions in Hobbs, 2 Kings, 356–69, and Cogan and Tadmor, II Kings, 328–30.

56. Key studies of the term "elders," which was probably not stable in meaning over time, and the role of elder in the OT are: J. Conrad, "זקן," in TDOT, 4:122–31; Buchholz, Ältesten Israels; Reviv, Elders in Ancient Israel; Willis, Elders of the City. Reviv concludes the elders "maintained national identity during the Babylonian exile" (191).

57. Smith-Christopher, Biblical Theology, 75–104.

58. These obstacles do not deter some from examining figures and events in history with a view to diagnosing PTSD. See Parry-Jones and Parry-Jones, "Post-traumatic Stress Disorder," and Ben-Ezra, "Earliest Evidence of Post-traumatic Stress?"

59. For discussion of the text-critical issue at 7:5 (אחר רעה or אחת רעה) and the old Jewish understanding of the Hebrew, see Greenberg, Ezekiel 1–20, 142, 147–48.

hands are feeble/go limp and all knees run as water" (7:17), and later in the same chapter, we read, "the hands of the people of the land tremble (are palsied?) with terror" (בהל Niphal, 7:27; cf. Exod 15:15). Perhaps the most vivid description of the people's overwhelming grief comes in the allegory of chapter 23: "You will tear at your breasts" (ושדיך תנתקי; 23:34).[60] Even surrounding nations will experience horror as they witness Yahweh's judgment upon his people (5:15).

Ezekiel is called to be a sign to the people in his heartbreaking and bitter groans before them (האנח בשברון מתנים ובמרירות תאנח; 21:11[16]) and his wailing and crying (זעק והילל; 21:17[12]). God tells him, "slap your thigh" (ספק אל-ירך). A trauma so terrible is coming upon Jerusalem, and it will surely bring the strongest expressions of anguish and fear. It seems to be more the inhabitants of Jerusalem and less the exiles of 597 who are said in 21:12[7] to respond to the sword with feelings of terror and utter helplessness: "Every heart will melt, all hands will be feeble, every spirit will faint, and all knees will run as water."[61]

Ezekiel is a book of extremes, and there is a meaningful contrast between these displays of emotion and how emotions are famously suppressed in chapter 24. At the death of his precious (מחמד) wife, Ezekiel is commanded to perform a sign-act pointing to the exiles' numbed, resigned response to news of Jerusalem's fall. This could be regarded as an aspect of the exiles' prophesied response to disaster that is recognizable to psychology: emotional detachment or numbness (restricted range of emotions) within a grief cycle that can contribute to deterioration in one's personal relationships. However, there are good reasons for downplaying or even dismissing a psychological interpretation of the prophet's actions.[62]

Ezekiel's oracles, of course, have no modern psychological orientation. They do speak to the heartbreak and fears of the deportees, but these problems are discussed within a spiritual and theological frame of reference. The spiritual diagnosis

---

60. Greenberg suggests that this could also be taken as "a paroxysm of self-loathing (cf. 20:43b; 36:31b)" (*Ezekiel 21–37*, 484).

61. The last phrase, "and all knees will run as water" (וכל-ברכים תלכנה מים), is often understood in the sense of knees becoming weak as water (e.g., NIV, ESV) or turning to water (NRSV, JPS). This interpretation seems strong if "all knees run as water" is believed to be parallel to "all hands will be feeble," just as the phrases "every heart will melt" and "every spirit will faint" run parallel. Greenberg offers a rather different explanation, that it means "to urinate from fear" (*Ezekiel 21–37*, 422), with which Block agrees (*Ezekiel 1–24*, 261, 671), drawing support from the LXX and a Neo-Assyrian description.

62. Odell makes a good case that the "Ezekiel persona" is not suffering any involuntary emotional paralysis in his hour of grief (an incapacity to mourn), and she urges that less attention be paid to historical concerns than to questions of literary function. In the case of this text she brilliantly points to intertextual connections with Lev 10, especially דמם and the "acceptance of divine judgment in both contexts" ("Genre and Persona," 201). She concludes that the divine command not to mourn is decisive for our interpretation of the prophet's self-restraint and indicates not only the divine intention that Jerusalem's judgment not be mourned but also that Yahweh "has chosen the exilic community over Jerusalem" (196). The conjunction of texts that commend a mourning attitude (9:4) and prohibit mourning deserves further research.

offered by Ezekiel is not that the Jewish exiles are innocent victims of tragedy
and the cruel actions of others. Rather, they have committed wrong, especially
against Yahweh their God. The exiles undoubtedly viewed themselves as victimized, particularly when comparing their lot with those who remained in Judah.[63]
(The sentiment behind the proverb in 18:2 may have been: "Why repent and obey
God when we are already being punished for sin—the sins of our ancestors?")
Ezekiel indicts them as truly guilty people who have deserved punishment and suffering. Ezekiel denied to the deportees any victim status and insisted on a certain
explanation for the exiles' suffering. His direct, confrontational approach may be
considered imprudent and offensive by many modern interpreters. However, Ezekiel appears to have operated with the assumption that, for the Jews in Babylon,
theological truth was most necessary for processing the feelings and disturbing
thoughts issuing from both the trauma of coerced displacement and the news that
a worse disaster would (and eventually did) befall the city that was their "joy and
glory" (24:25).

5.2.2.3. An "Analogy of Situation"?

Moshe Greenberg writes that, within biblical tradition (the Jewish canon), Moses
has the central place as "the mediator of Israel's divine constitution, the Torah";
the tradition "recognizes no other legislator."[64] But then Greenberg quickly brings
forward one exception: Ezekiel. It is remarkable indeed that the priest-prophet
fills a Mosaic role in delivering a body of law to God's people, and in this respect
Ezekiel is like Moses but unlike any of the other writing prophets. To account for
this profound exception in Israel's religious history, Greenberg suggests that an
"analogy of situation" required that Ezekiel perform this duty.

As just discussed, the Jewish exiles in Babylon had suffered the loss of all their
earthly moorings: their homes and property rights; much of their social network;
their political and economic life in Judah; their personal freedom. Just as serious
was their spiritual loss, being cut off from their place of worship and the whole
religious context in which they were to have lived and died. The exilic community, Greenberg avers, needed a Moses-like leader because their situation in Babylon as the "alien and homeless" was analogous to the position of the slaves in
Egypt.[65] As in Moses's day so also in Ezekiel's, there was need not only for physical

---

63. The exiles would not have understood themselves to be "survivors," for they were worse off,
or seemed to be worse off, than their fellow Judahites who had escaped the calamity of deportation,
remaining in the land of the fathers. What is fascinating to note is that Ezekiel will disabuse them
of the notion that they are worse off. Ezekiel's oracles drive home the point that those deported in
597 are indeed the survivors, and it is with the Jewish community in Babylon that Israel's future
lies. Those Jews residing in the land post-597 will not survive the judgments Yahweh rains down on
covenant breakers.
64. Greenberg, "Design and Themes," 216–17.
65. Greenberg, "Design and Themes," 217.

redemption in an exodus accomplished by God but also for spiritual renewal in a covenant that included stipulations for holy living in God's presence.

Greenberg says Israel's flouting of the original covenant stipulations (mediated by Moses) had eventually led to disaster. There had been moral and spiritual failure: "the vehicles and guardians of God's indwelling presence—the temple, its rites, and its personnel—had proved inadequate."[66] Ezekiel witnessed how idolaters were polluting the temple and how God at last would abandon his sanctuary. But there was hope for a devastated, defiled Israel in a divine two-part plan that addressed both the breakdown of sacred institutions and human unfaithfulness. First of all, as Greenberg writes:

> The lesson of the failed experiment must be put into effect by revision of these sacred institutions. As Moses spelled out the meaning of "a holy nation" to an unformed people just liberated from Egypt, so Ezekiel specified the needful changes in the vessels and symbols of God's presence in the future commonwealth of those near redemption from the Babylonian exile.

Secondly, God announced his resolve to remove Israel's "heart of stone" and gift her with a "heart of flesh." Such a work, announced by Ezekiel, would finally deal with the problem of human unfaithfulness and ensure that the covenant stipulations would be kept.

Greenberg's conclusion is that the disaster of the exile and the deportees' experience of being "alien and homeless" were analogous to bondage in Egypt. The trauma of Israel studied in this chapter uncovered societal and personal, physical and spiritual needs that God would begin to meet through a new deliverance (exodus) and through the ministry of a new legislator, a new Moses. "Analogy of situation produced similar prophetic roles."[67] It continues to be useful to highlight the Exodus–Ezekiel link in this study.

5.2.3. The Exiles' Frame of Mind and Theological Questions as Evidenced in Ezekiel's Oracles

Οἶδ' ἐγὼ φεύγοντας ἄνδρας ἐλπίδας σιτουμένους.
—Aeschylus[68]

The trauma of exile left an impress on the Jewish nation, on the Jewish mind and faith, that endures to this day. According to the testimony of Zech 7:5–7, the exiles

66. Greenberg, "Design and Themes," 217.
67. Greenberg, "Design and Themes," 217.
68. "I know that exiles feed on hopes"; Aeschylus, *Ag.* 1668. My translation follows the suggestion of Franco Monanari, s.v. σῑτέω, in *The Brill Dictionary of Ancient Greek*, ed. Madeleine Goh and Chad Schroeder (Leiden: Brill, 2015).

fasted the fifth (Ab) and seventh (Tishri) months for seventy years in order to mourn their loss. There is also a liturgical tradition in Judaism of mourning on the 9th of Ab over Jerusalem's destruction(s). The experience of the Babylonian captivity taught the nation to grieve its loss and to hope, as exiles must, for a return home. That exile and the restoration period together became foundational for Israel and developing Judaism. Jacob Neusner asserts that the scriptural account, "that Israel died and was reborn, was punished through exile and then forgiven," has become an orienting and defining story for the people of God. He adds, "this is critical—to be Israel in a genealogical sense is to have gone into exile and returned to Zion."[69]

5.2.3.1. Devotion to Jerusalem and Yahweh's Coming Judgment

A devotion to home and a desire to return to Jerusalem were defining marks of the Jews in exile. This is recognized in the Yahweh speeches that emphasize their love for Zion, and especially for the temple, by piling up terms of endearment. Yahweh declares, "I am about to desecrate my sanctuary, the pride of your strength [גאון עזכם], the delight of your eyes [מחמד עיניכם], and the passion of your life" (24:21).[70] A few verses later (v. 25) some of these affectionate terms are repeated and others are added: "Their stronghold [מעוזם], the joy of their glory [משוש תפארתם], the delight of their eyes, and their soul's exultation [ואת־משא נפשם]." The testimony of Ezekiel regarding this devotion to home is fully in line with the lament of the deportees in Ps 137, which invokes a self-imprecation "if I do not remember you and consider Jerusalem above my greatest joy" (v. 6).

A deep longing to receive news about home probably explains the elders' continued consulting with Yahweh's prophet. In each place where Ezekiel mentions the elders in Babylon (8:1; 14:1; 20:1),[71] he reports they were "sitting before me," presumably to inquire of Yahweh about their home. In two of the oracles just mentioned, there follows an unsparing denunciation of Jerusalem's evils, especially idolatry, and a prophecy that judgment upon the city is certain (9:4–10; 11:7–12; 14:21). The elders wanted news, but not this: "I send my four harsh [רע] judgments upon Jerusalem: sword, famine, wild beasts, and plague, to kill off man and animal" (14:21). It was most unwelcome news that beloved Jerusalem (a) was an unbearable offense to Yahweh and (b) was to suffer an unprecedented (5:9), terrible desolation. But Ezekiel introduces a third idea that was even more incredible: (c) Yahweh himself would send the destroyers. Ezekiel proclaimed that Jerusalem's destruction was Yahweh's will and Yahweh's work. This must have been stunning to all those who desired to return to their ancestral home.

---

69. Neusner, *Self-Fulfilling Prophecy*, 34.
70. Block's rendering of מחמל נפשכם (*Ezekiel 1–24*, 784).
71. There are also mentions of "the elders" back in the land (8:11; 9:6), and these have a negative tone.

The deportees' longing to return to Jerusalem was to be tempered by Ezekiel's exposé of the wickedness and violence there[72] and by the announcements that utter devastation is coming upon the city. Though there was misery in the life of an exile, returning home to Jerusalem would invite worse trouble. Adapting Ezekiel's cooking pot image, one could speak of jumping from the pot into the fire. The rhetorical effect of Ezekiel's message was to cause the audience or readership to distance and distinguish themselves from the population of the land. Even more, his oracles call upon the audience to join Yahweh and him in confronting Jerusalem with her abominations (הודע את־ירושלם את־תועבתיה; 16:2) and judging the city as receiving due punishment (7:3–4, 8; 20:4; 22:2; 23:36; 33:20).[73]

5.2.3.2. Devotion to Jerusalem and Negative Reports About the Jerusalemites
Devotion to Jerusalem and a sense of kinship with the Jerusalemites are also challenged by negative divine reports about those remaining back in the land. First of all, Yahweh compares the inhabitants of Jerusalem unfavorably with the exilic community. The few who escape death in the coming destruction of Jerusalem and go into exile will prove to be a reprehensible lot, more degenerate than the deportees of 597:

> But look, any survivors left in her to be led out—sons and daughters—when they come out to you [in Babylon] and you see their manners/behavior and their deeds, you will be consoled for the disaster that I have brought upon Jerusalem, for all that I have brought upon her. They will be a consolation[74] to you when you see their manners/behavior and their deeds; then you shall know that nothing of all that I have done in her is without cause, declares the Lord Yahweh. (Ezek 14:22–23)

While Yahweh has regard for the exiles and reveals his gracious presence to them in a foreign country (ch. 1; 11:16), those living in Jerusalem and in the land of Israel are referred to as "dross" (סיג). They are waste "left in the furnace" (22:18), and Yahweh warns them—"Look! I will gather you inside Jerusalem" (v. 19)—with the intention of blasting them in his hot anger and melting them (v. 21). The revelation of the extent and brazenness of idolatry in Jerusalem (ch. 8) is meant to shock Ezekiel the exile. The evil of the city is such that Yahweh cannot find even one person of spiritual standing and integrity among all the leaders there (22:30; cf. Jer 5:1–5). The people and the leaders together are regarded as morally and spiritually bankrupt. This leads the audience or reader of the oracles to mark a

---

72. Renz makes this same point in *Rhetorical Function*, 67.

73. In this list, 20:4 ("make known" to the exilic leaders) is relevant because it is the sins of "the fathers" (both the Jerusalemites' and exiles' ancestors) being exposed.

74. "Be a consolation" seems more appropriate as a rendering of נחם (Piel) than "console," since the latter might be understood in the sense of offering words of comfort.

moral and spiritual distinction between the communities in Babylon and Judah, not an absolute distinction,[75] but a real one nonetheless.

The prophecy communicates that the Jerusalemites have been "written off" and consigned to a nearly all-consuming judgment. They may be likened to the "bad figs" of Jer 24. There is no future for that whole crowd,[76] and the handful Yahweh spares only serve as a testimony to their own corruption (6:8–10; 7:16) and as a lesson for onlookers among both the nations (12:16) and the exiles (14:22–23).[77] The exposé of Jerusalem's turpitude and the divine judgment oracles condemning the city may signal Yahweh's intention that the exiles turn away from Jerusalem's population in disgust, just as Yahweh does (23:18; cf. 24:23).

Secondly, there are divine reports that Jerusalemites hold the exiles in disregard as those who are "gone far from Yahweh" (רחקו מעל יהוה; 11:15)[78] and can no longer contest the remaining inhabitants' property claims.[79] Rather than mourn the loss of their compatriots after the exile of 597, they gleefully seize their opportunity to take possession of what formerly belonged to the privileged elite. The triumphal declaration of "to us this land is given as a possession" appears more than once (11:15; 33:24).[80] The evil in this attitude becomes apparent in the echoing text, 36:2, which quotes the surrounding enemy nations reveling in Judah's disaster: "Aha! The ancient heights have become our possession!"

The revealing of this contemptuous attitude could have had the effect of striking at the exiles' morale, as argued by Block.[81] It would have been a harsh blow to those who sought solidarity with the community back home. It is also plausible, however, that that prideful attitude in Jerusalem provoked anger (Prov 13:10) and a quarrelsome spirit in the exilic community. Perhaps there was a dual effect: discouragement and anger. Such a report would only help promote among the exiles a community identity distinct from the Jerusalemites. If the latter are distinguishing

75. Andrew Mein states: "Both before and after the fall of Jerusalem Ezekiel placed a higher value on the exiles than on those remaining in the land, but this does not mean that the exiles are absolved from responsibility, nor do they occupy the moral high ground" (*Ethics of Exile*, 235).

76. The NIV communicates the derogatory tone of Yahweh's speech against Jerusalem in 7:10–14, rendering המונה as "that crowd" or "the whole crowd." See the discussions of Ezekiel's "separatist ideology" in Rom-Shiloni, *Exclusive Inclusivity*, 139–97, and Strine, *Sworn Enemies*, 177–227.

77. Ezekiel divides Israel into two groups: those remaining in the land facing judgment and those already in exile receiving hopeful promises. See the discussion below in ch. 7 ("7.2. Rhetorical Purposes")

78. It is best to follow most scholars (since Hitzig) in repointing the impv. as a pf., despite the lack of good external evidence (Zimmerli, *Ezekiel 1*, 221; Allen, *Ezekiel 1–19*, 128; Pohlmann, *Hesekiel 1–19*, 127; Block, *Ezekiel 1–24*, 341). Retaining the MT's vocalization are Greenberg, *Ezekiel 1–20*, 189, and Brownlee, *Ezekiel 1–19*, 163–64.

79. Note that Jerusalem's attitude toward the exiles—they are far away and can take no interest in our dealings here—runs parallel to the city's attitude toward Yahweh, as one who "has forsaken the land and does not see" our dealings here (8:12; 9:9).

80. Note also the triumphalist attitude in 11:3: "This city is the pot and we are the meat."

81. Block, *Ezekiel 1–24*, 349.

themselves from the Jews in Babylonia and even disparaging them, this news would encourage a rift to develop. Perhaps that social division would somehow serve God's purpose of breaking the exiles' emotional, spiritual, and religious ties to idolatrous Jerusalem. A new identity could be forged.

Yahweh's message in 11:15, reporting the hostility of the Jerusalemites, is a response to Ezekiel firmly set in the context of his horrified complaint when Pelatiah drops dead, "Ah, Lord Yahweh! Will you finish off the remnant of Israel?" (11:13). God's word in that context appears to challenge the prophet's assumption that Pelatiah belongs to the remnant (שארית) of God's true people. The message put across might be: "Pelatiah is among those who would exclude you and the rest of the Jews in Babylon from the people of God." In Ezekiel's book, there is a theological interest in the matter of who truly belongs to Israel, those whose names are to "be enrolled in the register [כתב] of the house of Israel" (13:9; cf. Exod 32:33 [ספר]). When true Israel is included in the restoration and reenters the land (11:16–20) but observes wicked Jews being excluded (11:21; 13:9), this will be Yahweh's self-revelation: "Then you shall know that I am Lord Yahweh" (13:9).

5.2.3.3. Devotion to Jerusalem and Yahweh's Judgment in 597 BC

Among several texts that declare that Yahweh is scattering Israel among the nations (4:13; 5:10; 11:16; 12:15; 36:19), one refers back to the deportation in 597 (11:16).[82] There are additional indications, however, that the exiles understand their deportation as an act of Yahweh and are wrestling with the theological ramifications of this. They do not question or debate Yahweh's sovereignty in the tragic events that have overtaken them. Instead, prior to the destruction of Jerusalem, they assert the culpability of their ancestors (18:2) and accuse Yahweh of being "unscrupulous"[83] or unjust in punishing the undeserving (18:25, 29; cf. 33:17, 20): "The way of the Lord is not right (לא יתכן)." They believe it was wrong for Yahweh to remove them from their beloved home and bring such suffering on them.

---

82. Even without the single text, the deportees' conclusion that Yahweh has sent them into exile would have been a natural inference from the drumbeat of oracles announcing Yahweh's coming wrath on Jerusalem. The covenant God who destroys and scatters in judgment *has already* destroyed and scattered in judgment.

83. This is Block's rendering, which he prefers as more exact than other glosses such as "without principle" (lacking a standard) and "arbitrary; nonsensical" (*Ezekiel 1–24*, 584–85; 2:250–52). It is difficult to settle on an English equivalent to לא יתכן (Niphal) that works well as the people's accusation against Yahweh and also as Yahweh's counteraccusation. "Unfair," for example, does not well express the sense of Yahweh's countercharge. "Not right" (cf. Zimmerli's "nicht richtig"; *Ezechiel*, 1:392) has a wide semantic range and works well. Zimmerli posits that the point of attack in the people's accusation is "Jahwes Handeln … in seiner Ordnung" (*Ezechiel*, 1:413), which is similar to Block's view. *HALOT* suggests "to measure up, be in order, be correct." Allen translates לא + the verb as "inconsistent" (*Ezekiel 1–19*, 264), following Greenberg's proposal that the verb be read "as tolerative nif'al" in the sense of "determinable" (*Ezekiel 1–20*, 333); Greenberg has "does not conform to rule" (but see n. 85 below).

Evidence that the exiles continue to wrestle with the theological issues of guilt and their relationship to Yahweh is found in 33:10. Perhaps this reported saying shows some openness on the part of the exiles to accepting Ezekiel's accusations:[84] "Our transgressions and sins weigh upon us, and because of them we waste away. How then can we live?" Adding to the struggle to comprehend their own disaster of 597 are Ezekiel's judgment oracles about the nearing devastation of Jerusalem and the slaughter of "your sons and daughters" (24:21, 25). And Ezekiel insists that all the destruction and horror is Yahweh's will and work! What kind of God draws the sword against his own people?

Though Ezekiel does not provide much of a record of how the exiles of 597 voice their agonizing theological questions and search for explanations,[85] one must understand their traumatic experience as having provoked a soul searching. Martin Buber gave voice to the agony of the Jewish querist in times of suffering, whether forcibly marched off to Babylon in 597 BC or deported by cattle car to the *Vernichtungslager* at Auschwitz-Birkenau in 1943:

> How is a life with God still possible in a time in which there is an Oświęcim? The estrangement has become too cruel, the hiddenness too deep. One can still "believe" in the God who allowed those things to happen, but can one still speak to Him? Can one still hear His word? Can one still, as an individual and as a people, enter into a dialogic relationship with Him? Can one still call to Him? Dare we recommend to the survivors of Oświęcim, the Job of the gas chambers: "Call to Him, for He is kind, for His mercy endurest [*sic*] forever"?[86]

The thought that Yahweh has exiled his own people carries most troubling implications for the emotionally traumatized. "How can I trust such a God?" An exile's whole world, whole conception of the world and its order, is thrown over. But that thought—"Yahweh has done this!"—which develops from an awareness of God's sovereign power, also carries a seed of hope. "If God has uprooted

---

84. Those inclined toward psychological analysis might at this point bring forward the notion of a "grief cycle." After an initial denial (it was the fathers, not we, who sinned) and possible withdrawal, there is a succession of anger, bargaining, depression ("how can we live?"), acceptance, and hope.

85. Could Ezek 33:17, translated slightly differently, hint at the exiles' frustrated search for an understanding of God's ways? In his second volume, Greenberg questions his earlier rendering of לֹא יִתָּכֵן: "But it is hard to see why the demoralized audience of vs. 10 (or any other) should cavil at the hope-inspiring way of judgment or consider it 'not conforming to rule'" (*Ezekiel 21–37*, 674). Greenberg here then cites Adrian Graffy's proposed translation, "the way of the Lord cannot be fathomed" (*Prophet Confronts His People*, 76–77), to which Greenberg responds positively: "This is an expression of surprise and difficulty in understanding how they can avoid wasting away in their sin, and hints at reluctance to change their ways. God throws it back in their face, declaring that their way—knowing the way to life (= repentance) and not following it—is incomprehensible."

86. Buber, *At the Turning*, 61.

us, then surely he can plant us again." The hope of return to their beloved home, which daily sustained the spirits of the exiles, had to center on Yahweh. It was not love for Jerusalem that Ezekiel would have opposed, but the futile hope that Jerusalem would remain unmolested by Babylon and that a return to an unjudged, still defiled Jerusalem was yet possible for the exiles. Return was promised for a purified people, return to a purified city, after Yahweh had shown himself to be holy among his people in the sight of the nations (20:41). "Then you shall know that I am Yahweh, when I bring you into the land of Israel, the land I promised on oath to give your fathers" (20:42).

The exile from beloved Jerusalem provoked the Jewish community to wrestle with profound theological questions, and the struggle proved to be the remaking of them. Their day of torment was also a day of opportunity for Israel to understand Yahweh and his ways, the nature of the covenant, and their calling to live in holiness for the sake of the Name. Again, Buber puts it well:

> From the moment when a national disaster appears inevitable, and especially after it has become a reality, it can, like every great torment, become a productive force from the religious point of view: it begins to suggest new questions and to stress old ones. Dogmatized conceptions are pondered afresh in the light of the events, and the faith relationship that has to stand the test of an utterly changed situation is renewed in a modified form. But the new acting force is nothing less than the force of extreme despair, a despair so elemental that it can have but one of two results: the sapping of the last will of life, or the renewal of the soul.[87]

5.2.4. Israel's Spiritual and Moral State According to Yahweh's Indictment

If the reader focuses on Ezekiel's references to the nation and her sins, a picture of corrupted popular religion and morality emerges and one better understands the prophetic assessment of Israel's spiritual condition. Even those who dispute the accuracy of Ezekiel's portrayal of popular Jewish religion and morality[88] must

---

87. Buber, *Prophetic Faith*, 183.

88. This has been done in two ways. First of all, as mentioned earlier (see n. 13), some doubt the historical accuracy of Ezekiel's charges. Secondly, some scholars repudiate the biblical writers' condemnation of "pagan and syncretistic abuses" (Fohrer, *Introduction*, 237) as propaganda in a rhetorical battle to define the religion. E.g., Susan Ackerman contends that *authentic* Yahwism was pluriform and could include such allegedly "foreign" features as child-sacrifice, burning incense at the במות, honoring the Queen of Heaven, mourning Tammuz, and bowing down to the sun and that, further, the doctrine of the prophets and Deuteronomists that such activities were an abhorrent corruption, even a falling away from Yahwism, is narrow and false, promoting the views and interests of but one faction within Yahwism and repressing others' views; thus their partisan treatises should be subjected to ideological criticism (*Under Every Green Tree*, 213–17). In such a reconstruction of Israel's religion, Ezekiel's prophecy will not be heard *as Scripture*.

seek to understand his particular perspective on these subjects, for the theological outlook and message of the prophecy will be partially hidden if one fails to weigh the prophet's words about Israel's sins.

From the beginning of the book, the Israelites are described as a nation in rebellion, not only against Nebuchadnezzar, to whom they were politically subject, but against their God. Five times in the short second chapter, Israel is called "rebellious,"[89] and the revolt against Yahweh has been of long duration (2:3). Later on (20:7–8, 13, 21; cf. 23:3, 8, 19), Ezekiel traces this rebelliousness back to the days of the exodus. Perhaps the theme of the nation's rebellion is a key for understanding what Matties termed the "extremes" in Ezekiel's language, including the repetition of the RF. Note that the term "rebellious" is found in close proximity to the RF and related phrases (2:5; 20:21, 38).

The prominence of the rebellion theme in Ezekiel can be demonstrated in the frequency of vocabulary. The בית מרי ("rebellious house") characterization appears a total of fourteen times.[90] The verbs מרד and מרה (both for "to rebel") occur six times in the prophecy to describe Israel's hostile attitude toward Yahweh (2:3; 5:6; 20:8, 13, 21, 38 [ptc.]), and the adjective מרי ("rebellious") occurs fifteen times.[91] Among the specific actions of Israel that accord with the "rebel" indictment is the refusal to listen (3:7; cf. 20:8, 39).[92] In some texts, the particle לא negates the verb שמע, while elsewhere the verb חדל is used in conjunction with שמע (2:5, 7; 3:11, 27).

"Refusal to listen" deserves more reflection. At the beginning of the book, Yahweh issues a solemn charge to Ezekiel: "Hear what I say to you!" (2:8; 3:10). The submissive Ezekiel is a foil to his compatriots whom Yahweh rebukes: "The house of Israel is not willing to hear you because they are not willing to hear me" (3:7). The insistent, repetitive character of the prophecy cannot be explained without reference to this hard-headed and hard-hearted resistance to God's word. Ezekiel (יחזקאל) was personally fitted in his disposition (3:8–9) for his appointment to proclaim Yahweh's word to a people who were of a hard countenance (חזקי־מצח) and a stubborn heart (וקשי־לב). It is also true that the prophet's *message* was

---

89. In just ten short verses, the term מרי appears 5× (2:5, 6, 7, 8 [2×]). Additionally, the verb מרד or its participle are used 2× in v. 3 to describe the nation of Israel. Finally, note the appearance in 2:3 of the verb פשע, a synonym of מרד, and in 2:4, the adjectives קשי and חזק (cf. 3:7–9).

90. See: 2:5, 6, 8; 3:9, 26, 27; 12:2 (2×), 3, 9, 25; 17:12; 24:3; 44:6; cf. the similar 20:13.

91. Almost always in the phrase "rebellious house." The exception is in 2:7.

92. Ezek 20:39 presents translation difficulties. A few understand the phrase ואחר אם־אינכם שמעים אלי as a strongly worded affirmative, "and hereafter you shall certainly listen to me" (e.g., NIV, JB, but changed in NJB), but the vast majority of interpreters render the Hebrew conditional in a directly literal way: "and afterwards, if you will not listen to me . . . ," with a missing apodosis (NJPS, NRSV, ESV, Greenberg, Allen, Block). Zimmerli regards the "fragmentary clause" as possibly "corrupted at the beginning" and best expunged (*Ezekiel 1*, 403), but few today follow Zimmerli on this point. Eichrodt tried to resolve the difficulty by deleting ואחר as "a relic of an alternative reading" (*Ezekiel*, 262).

fitted for such a resistant people. Perhaps the message needed constant repetition because the word was not being heard much of the time, as Yahweh indicated would be the case (2:7; 3:7). Here one recalls with Greenberg that Moses had been forewarned that Pharaoh would not listen to him and Yahweh's word (Exod 3:19; 7:22).[93] Is this another instance where Israel has become like her old nemesis in the land of slavery, the tyrant who declared, "I do not know Yahweh" (Exod 5:2), and refused to listen?[94] Just as Pharaoh in Moses's time was hardened against Yahweh and his servant Israel,[95] the nation of Israel in Ezekiel's day is shown to be hardened (חזק) against Yahweh and his servant.

The prophet accuses his rebellious nation of a wide variety of cultic and civil sins, and the religious sins are counted more grave than the civil. Far less attention is given to civil sins, and they are treated in a more general way. For example, Ezek 7:23 speaks of the land as "full of bloodshed" and Jerusalem as "full of violence." Those especially responsible for this are political leaders, the princes (22:6, 27), but religious leaders are not innocent (22:25). Other civil sins cited are breaking covenant with Yahweh by forging alliances with a series of ungodly nations (16:26–29;[96] ch. 23) and violating the suzerainty treaty, or "covenant" (ברית; 17:18), established with victorious Babylon. Ezekiel 18 lists various sins as examples of crimes against the moral law that merit divine judgment, including sexual immorality, oppression of the poor, usury, robbery, and the breaking of pledges. Chapter 22 also gives a catalog of civil sins: showing contempt for parents, mistreating the alien and the widow, incest and other sexual perversion, political conspiracy, and robbery.[97]

As noted, however, more attention is given to cultic sins. As a priest concerned for purity and holiness, Ezekiel details the religious offenses that pollute the people and their worship. They have rejected Yahweh's laws and decrees (5:6–7; 11:12), presumably a reference to Sinai, or generally the laws of Moses. Instead of following in the ways of Yahweh, the people "have behaved according to the standards

---

93. Greenberg, *Ezekiel 1–20*, 75.

94. Pharaoh's refusal to hear (שמע + לא) Moses is emphasized in Exod 7:4, 13, 22; 8:15, 19; 9:12; 11:9. Notably, Israel also fails earlier to listen to Moses (Exod 6:9, 12; 16:20). As mentioned earlier (ch. 4, n. 96), this point in my dissertation is more fully developed in DeLapp, "Ezekiel as Moses."

95. Exodus has an abundance of texts referring to Pharaoh's hardness of heart employing חזק (Piel: 4:21; 10:20, 27; 11:10; 14:4, 8, 17; Qal: 7:13, 22; 8:15; 9:12; 9:35) and כבד (Hiphil: 8:15, 32; 9:7, 34; 10:1).

96. Block aptly says: "Jerusalem flirted with the world powers. The order in which these nations are named reflects the history of Israel's contacts with them" (*Ezekiel 1–24*, 495).

97. Other passages in Ezekiel detailing civil sins are: 8:17; 9:9; 11:6; 12:19; 22:3; 24:6, 9. Could Exodus in some recension, especially the book of the covenant, have served as a legal source for the prophet's indictment of particular sins? Ezekiel's vice catalogs include: contempt for parents (Exod 20:12; 21:15, 17); oppressing the alien (Exod 22:21; 23:9) and the widow (Exod 22:22–24); sexual sins (Exod 20:14; 22:16–17, 19); robbery (Exod 20:15; 22:1–4); and usury (Exod 22:25–27). Eichrodt suggests (*Ezekiel*, 270) Ezekielian dependence on the book of the covenant to explain כל־פטר רחם in Ezek 20:25–26 (cf. Exod 34:19–20).

of the nations [כמשפטי הגוים] around [them]" (5:7; 11:12). This breaking of the covenant brings Yahweh's judgments (משפטים), which will be performed in the sight of the nations (לעיני הגוים). Israel is censured repeatedly for dishonoring Yahweh by breaking the Sabbath (20:13, 16, 21, 24; 22:8, 26; 23:38). "Your abominations" (תועבתיך; practices or idols) are cause for unprecedented divine judgment (5:8–10), which will involve cannibalism during siege. There will be no pity "because you have defiled my sanctuary with all your detestable things/idols and your abominations" (5:11).

The worst of the cultic sins is idolatry, which Ezekiel condemns eighty-two times.[98] In chapter 6, Yahweh pledges to destroy the high places, pagan altars, incense altars, and idols, together with the people who set them up. This must be done to teach the nation how Yahweh "[has] been broken by their whoring heart, which has turned away from [him], and by their eyes, which go whoring after their idols" (6:9). The wealth, especially the jewelry with which their covenant God had blessed them, they used to make "detestable idols and vile images" (7:20; cf. 16:10–19; Exod 32).

In a profound passage, 11:16–21,[99] the reader learns of Israel's true plight. They continue to practice idolatry with each passing generation because their "heart goes after [הלך] their detestable things/idols and abominations" (11:21; cf. 14:3). The conversion of the nation is necessary. A new deliverance is needed "to recapture the hearts of the house of Israel, which are estranged from me because of their idols" (14:5; cf. 1 Kgs 18:37). After Israel's heart renewal, the nation will keep Yahweh's ordinances (ואת־משפטי ישמרו; 11:20).[100]

A deep-seated cynicism added to the religious problems of the exiles and those remaining back in Judah (see Jer 5:13). The proverb in 12:22 records the popular disdain for prophets and their visions: "The days pass, and every vision comes to nothing." The confusion of voices, as Yahweh's true prophets and the false prophets gave out conflicting oracles, fed the cynicism of the people. God denounces those who lead the people astray: "They have seen false visions and divined a lie. They say, 'Yahweh declares,' when Yahweh has not sent them, and yet they expect the word to be fulfilled. . . . Because you have spoken worthless lies and seen delusions, I am against you, declares the Lord Yahweh" (13:6, 8). The problem was twofold: false prophets had multiplied, and the people liked to listen to lies (13:19; cf. Jer 5:30–31). The people chose to practice a sort of syncretism, consulting idols

98. See Milgrom, "Nature and Extent of Idolatry," 1, and Ganzel, "Transformation of Pentateuchal Descriptions," 35.
99. I say "profound" because prominent themes of Ezekiel are gathered together: the return from exile as a type of "new exodus," the bestowal of a new spirit and a responsive heart to the restored people of God, and individual responsibility.
100. Note Ezekiel's use of משפטים to refer variously to the "practices" of the nations, Yahweh's punishing "judgments," and his holy "ordinances," which God will enable Israel to keep.

and then inquiring of Yahweh (14:7; 20:3). The end result of this habit was a curiosity about the oracles of Yahweh (from any prophet, false or true), but without any intention to heed the oracles or take action (33:30–33; cf. Jer 23:14–40). As Jeremiah also had complained, "no one turns from his wickedness," (לבלתי־שׁבו אישׁ מרעתו; Jer 23:14).

Ezekiel 16 refers to the practice of child sacrifice, which characterized Baal worship (cf. Jer 19:5) and the cult of Molech. Child sacrifice was one of several historic sins of Judah, according to this chapter. So depraved did Jerusalem become that Ezekiel compares the city unfavorably with Samaria and Sodom (16:46–47)! "Samaria did not commit half the sins you did" (16:51; NIV). Ezekiel declares that the apostasy derives from a failure of memory: "You did not remember the days of your youth" (16:22, 43). What is meant by the reference to "the days of your youth" (ימי נעוריך)? The end of chapter 16 (vv. 59–62) mentions "covenant" five times, the holy covenant Israel had forgotten but Yahweh would remember.

> I shall deal with you according to what you have done, you who have despised the oath in breaking the covenant. Yet I will remember the covenant I made with you in the days of your youth, and I will establish for you an everlasting covenant. . . . And so I will establish my covenant with you, and you shall know that I am Yahweh. (16:59–62)

Here it is most likely that "the days of your youth" is a reference to Israel's stay in and deliverance from Egypt. As readers move on to chapter 23, this interpretation is confirmed. There is no doubt that, in Ezekiel's idiom, "the days of your youth" *can* refer to the nation's time in Egypt. See the dual references in 23:19–21 and the chiastic parallelism in 23:3a:[101]

ותזנינה במצרים

בנעוריהן זנו

The reference of 16:60 to the covenant made "in the days of your youth" would appear to point to Sinai, indicating that, in Ezekiel's own historical and theological understanding, the covenant is ancient indeed. For comparison's sake, one may add that the early prophet Hosea equated "the days of her youth" with "the day she came up out of Egypt" (Hos 2:17[15]; cf. also Jer 2:2).[102]

---

101. Conclusions drawn from chs. 16 and 23, with their "unsurpassing harshness" in recounting Israel's history, should be given full weight: the chapters "are impossible to deny to Ezekiel" (Zimmerli, *Ezekiel 2*, xv).

102. There is abundant material for studying an intertextual relationship between Hosea and Ezekiel. One can begin with the trope of a "new exodus" common to both. Hosea 2 is of special interest because of (a) the description of Israel as an adulterous wife, (b) the divine Lover's threat to

Ezekiel intends to mark a sharp contrast between Israel, whom he indicts with the words "you did not remember the days of your youth" (16:43), and Yahweh, who says, "I shall remember my covenant with you in the days of your youth" (16:60). It seems a good and necessary inference that Israel is being charged with forgetting the covenant, though one does not read that exact language ("you did not remember the covenant I made with you in the days of your youth"). The covenant violation is described in strong terms: "despised the oath in breaking covenant" (אֲשֶׁר־בָּזִית אָלָה לְהָפֵר בְּרִית; 16:59). The term אָלָה, often translated as "oath,"[103] also carries the idea of a curse, and indeed KBL and *HALOT* recommend the rendering "curse" for 16:59. There is reason to translate the noun as "curse-oath."[104] Marten Woudstra makes good sense of the text when he writes: "Indeed it may well be that the evil which the prophet is here denouncing is first of all a light-heartedness with respect to the sanctions of the covenant, its oath and its curse. Inevitably this leads to a breaking of the covenant. It is as it were designed to do this."[105]

When comparing chapters 20 and 16, interpreters become more certain of the prophet's intent in harking back to Israel's foundations. Ezekiel 20 forms the core of his argument for an unbroken history of idolatry. The covenant people "have shown themselves from the very beginning to be a generation infected with heathenism at their very roots."[106] In Egypt, God made himself known (וָאִוָּדַע לָהֶם בְּאֶרֶץ מִצְרַיִם) to Abraham's descendants using the statement "I am Yahweh" (20:5).[107] Even before Yahweh brought the nation out of Egypt, with redemption still only a promise, Yahweh commanded them to get rid of their images and not defile themselves with the idols of Egypt (20:6–7). Because Israel did not forsake

---

strip (פשט Hiphil) the adulteress and expose her shame, (c) the promise of a new covenant, (d) the references to the exodus event, (e) the development of the covenant formula in 2:25[23], and (f) the ידע statements which echo the RF: וִידַעַתְּ אֶת־יהוה (2:10[8]) and וְהִיא לֹא יָדְעָה כִּי אָנֹכִי נָתַתִּי לָהּ הַדָּגָן (2:22[20]).

103. Zimmerli's "Eid" (*Ezechiel*, 1:333) follows the strong German tradition since Luther. Cf. NIV, NRSV, and ESV, as well as BDB. NJPS reads "spurned the pact."

104. Greenberg, *Ezekiel 1–20*, 291. Marten Woudstra says: "The two meanings of the Hebrew אָלָה are not very far apart. An oath is a conditional form of self-malediction. He who showed no respect for the oath would by implication be also wanting in his respect for the curse which the oath entailed. But since oaths were an essential part of covenant-making, so much so that Mendenhall can rightly say that 'a covenant is essentially a promissory oath' ('Ancient Oriental and Biblical Law,' *BA* 17 [1954]: 28), it follows that the despising of the oath is tantamount to the 'breaking of the covenant'" ("Everlasting Covenant," 27).

105. Woudstra, "Everlasting Covenant," 28.

106. Eichrodt, *Ezekiel*, 28.

107. As noted by Lyle Eslinger, out of the Bible's twenty-six instances of ידע in Niphal, only six have Yahweh as the subject, all of which are distinctive in describing Yahweh's "self-manifestation through historical intervention" ("Ezekiel 20 and the Metaphor," 103). The distribution follows a pattern Ezekiel scholars recognize as predictable:1× in Exod 6:3; 1× in Isa 19:21; and 4× in Ezekiel (2× in ch. 20). The motif of divine self-revelation is securely tied to the exodus narrative.

the idols of Egypt, God considered pouring out his wrath on them *in Egypt itself* (20:8). But mercy prevailed, and for the sake of his holy name, Yahweh did bring them out of bondage.

Continuing his rehearsal of Israel's appalling history, Ezekiel tells the story of their rebellion in the desert. There they rejected God's laws, "for their heart was devoted to their idols"—the idols of Egypt (20:16). Next, Yahweh commanded the second generation,

> Do not walk in the statutes of your fathers or follow their rules or defile yourselves with their idols. I am Yahweh your God; walk in my statutes and be careful to follow my laws. And hallow my Sabbaths, that they may be a sign between us. Then you shall know that I am Yahweh your God. (20:18–20)

This second generation also rebelled against Yahweh, according to Ezek 20:21. Because of this, Yahweh swore an oath (cf. Lev 26:27–45) that Israel would be dispersed among the nations "because they had not kept my laws but had rejected my statutes and desecrated my Sabbaths, and their eyes were set on their fathers' idols" (20:24).

Turning to Israel's history in the land, Ezekiel contends that idolatry became a way of life there too. The prophet recounts how the nation provoked Yahweh with its high places, sacrifices to idols, offerings, and incense (20:28). Perhaps one could say that, spiritually, the nation of Israel had never finally left Egypt. She refused to give up the "whoring she began in Egypt" (23:8, 27). Gustav Oehler's *Theology of the Old Testament* makes the point that "during the stay in Egypt the foundation was laid of the religious syncretism which came up in different forms in the following centuries and which was in general characteristic of Israel, which was never independently productive in polytheistic forms of worship."[108]

Ezekiel implies that the former slaves never left Egypt behind (23:3, 8, 19, 21, 27). Even in exile, Israel's tendency is to continue to "defile yourselves the way your fathers did and go whoring after their detestable things" (20:30–31; cf. 20:1). But Yahweh will not allow the continued idolatry (20:32). Ezekiel promised that the exodus history would be repeated as Yahweh purified the nation by bringing her "into the desert of the nations," judging her there (20:34–38), and finally bringing her back into the land of Israel (20:40–42).[109] In the end, Ezekiel's oracle strikes the note of grace: "You shall know that I am Yahweh, when I deal with you for my

---

108. Oehler, *Theology of the Old Testament*, 1:99. John Calvin makes a similar point commenting on 20:8 and the ease with which Israel adopted the idolatry of Egypt (*Commentaries... Ezekiel*, 2:292).

109. Scholarship is divided as to whether Ezekiel likens the exiles to the first generation to leave Egypt (Rom-Shiloni, Levitt Kohn) or the second (Strine). See: Rom-Shiloni, "Ezekiel as the Voice"; Levitt Kohn, "'As Though You Yourself'"; Strine, "Role of Repentance."

name's sake, not according to your evil ways and your corrupt doings" (20:44). The judgment meted out will be corrective and restorative in design.

Chapter 23 refers to the idolatry originally begun Egypt as "prostitution" (זנה or זנות), "lewdness" (זמה), or an "adultery" (נאף).[110] The association of this idolatry with Israel's stay in Egypt is strong: explicit references to מצרים appear six times in chapter 23 (vv. 3, 8, 19, 21, 27 [2×]). Yahweh intends to put a stop to "her prostitution since [her days in] Egypt" (תזנותיה ממצרים; 23:8; cf. 23:19). When God deals with his people, "they shall not remember Egypt anymore" (v. 27). Instead of forgetting Yahweh (23:35; cf. 22:16) and remembering the idols of Egypt, the chastened people will remember Yahweh (6:9) and forget Egypt.

To understand the historical and religious context, it is useful to trace how Ezekiel often identifies the exiles with the entire nation. With this key, one can turn to such sections as the Spirit-given vision of Jerusalem (chs. 8–11) and gain significant insight into the religious life of the exiles. The apostasy back in the homeland was appalling to Ezekiel, as he envisioned the idol of jealousy in the inner court of Solomon's Temple (8:3–5). He also saw Israel's elders burning incense before pictures of unclean animals and idols (8:10–12), women sitting mourning for Tammuz (8:14), and twenty-five men in the inner court bowing to the rising sun (8:16). Gross idolatry characterized the lives of "old men, young men and maidens, children and women" (9:6). These visions concerned life in Judah prior to the fall of Jerusalem, while the practices of those remaining in the land *after* Jerusalem's fall are described in 33:22–29.

Ezekiel 20:32 indicates that the exiles[111] were indeed like the Jews back in Jerusalem. The deportees reportedly say: "Let us be like the nations, like the tribes of [other] lands, who worship wood and stone." Idolatry was a strong temptation for them, surrounded as they were by pagan neighbors. This one verse is an excellent key for understanding the background to the regular RF. God had always opposed himself to idol worship with the resounding claim, "I am Yahweh, your God" (see Exod 20:2–3; cf. Lev 19:4 and Ps 81:9–10). According to the perspective in Ezekiel, this pattern is traceable all the way back to the time of the exodus. We read in 20:5–7:

> And I made myself known to them in Egypt. On that day I swore to them that I
> would bring them out of the land of Egypt.... And I said to them, "Each of you
> must cast away the detestable things [before] his eyes, and do not defile yourselves
> with the idols of Egypt. *I am Yahweh your God.*"

110. "Prostitution": 23:3 (2×), 5, 7, 8, 11 (2×), 14, 18, 19, 27, 29 (2×), 30, 35, 43 (2×). "Lewdness": 23:21, 27, 29, 35, 44, 48, 49. "Adultery": 23:37 (2×), 43, 45.

111. Because 20:31 contains Yahweh's rebuke as he refuses any attempt of the wicked to "inquire of me," and the elders of the exilic community are seeking to make an inquiry in 20:1, it is best to read v. 32 as addressed to an exilic audience "scattered among the nations" (20:34).

To serve idols was to profane Yahweh's holy name (Ezek 20:39), and contrariwise, to worship God truly on his holy mountain was to know him by name as Yahweh (vv. 40–44).[112]

Another instructive passage is Elijah's challenge to the prophets of Baal on Mount Carmel.[113] After his opponents had exhausted themselves in asking their god for fire, Elijah intercedes for the covenant people with this magnificent prayer: "O Yahweh, God of Abraham, Isaac and Israel, let it be *known* today that you are God in Israel. . . . Answer me, O Yahweh, answer me, so these people will *know* that you, O Yahweh, are God and that you have turned their hearts back again" (1 Kgs 18:36–37). Nearly three hundred years later, according to the biblical chronology, Ezekiel too knew that the conversion of the heart was necessary. The prophet's oracles imply that this same people would come to confess with their ancestors, "Yahweh—he is God! Yahweh—he is God!"

112. Comparing Ezekiel's and Jeremiah's theology at this point is instructive. The "weeping prophet" condemns false prophets as those "who think that by the dreams they recount they can make my people forget my name, even as their fathers forgot my name for Baal [worship]" (Jer 23:27). Idolatry, then, is to be equated with forgetting the name Yahweh. It is fascinating to compare literature from the wider ANE. Unfaithfulness to political treaties (refusal to pay tribute) can be equated with "forgetting" the suzerain's gods. E.g., the annals of Ashurbanipal speak of "Tirhakah, king of Egypt and Cush," who "forgot the might of the god Ashur, the god Ishtar and the great gods, my lords, and trusted in his own strength" (Cogan, *Raging Torrent*, 150 ["Campaigns to Egypt—Edition A / Rassam Cylinder" Col. i, 53–58; cf. *ANET*, 294].

113. Zimmerli calls this account "particularly valuable" for discussing the recognition event (*I Am Yahweh*, 67). This is so because the account includes (1) the request for Yahweh to act in order that "these people will know," (2) the report of the divine act, and (3) a full and graphic depiction of the event's effect, recognition of Yahweh by his prostrate people.

CHAPTER 6

Intertextuality and Theological
Interpretation of the Formula

In many ways, Ezekiel is the grandfather of intertextual composition, con-
sciously attempting to echo the language of earlier prophetic tradition, deuteronomic themes, priestly concerns, and the cosmic imagery of the temple
liturgy. But the book is also very deliberately composed with a narrower
"intra-textual" design, in which foreshadowings of later salvational themes
in chs. 33–39 are regularly included in earlier judgment warnings (cf. chs. 11,
16, and 20).

—Lawrence Boadt[1]

This chapter interprets Ezekiel's recognition formula alongside the book of Exodus as an intertext. The argument of this study as a whole is that the two books
have such a density of linguistic and theological links, the RF chief among them,
that an intertextual reading is not only justified, but necessary. Ezekiel may well
be regarded, according to Boadt's suggestion, as "the grandfather of intertextual
composition," and the keynote formula may be understood as an echo of the language of Exodus (in some authoritative recension).

Acknowledging the literary, intertextual relationship between Ezekiel and Exodus, while crucial, does not necessarily simplify the task of interpreting the prophet's RF. Research in this chapter shows that, while the formula's usage in Exodus
probably guided Ezekiel's usage in some particulars, he refashions and reinterprets
the RF for his own time. There is not only strong continuity but also jarring discontinuity in his use of the formula. As mentioned previously, the prophet can
both evoke and revoke. The interpreter, then, ought not to regard Ezekiel's RF as
a mere transposition from a different time and place (or literary context) with the
exact same meaning attached. The demonstrable literary borrowing from Exodus
compels the interpreter to study both similarities and dissimilarities in the usage
and interpretation of the formula as employed by Exodus and Ezekiel. That study
yields the conclusion that, with regard to theological themes and emphases contained in or accompanying the refrain, continuity is stronger than discontinuity.

---

1. Lawrence Boadt, review of Block, *Ezekiel 1–24*, 136.

From a purely synchronic intertextual perspective, one would phrase things somewhat differently. There is a dialogue between texts read, and in the case of Exodus and Ezekiel, which have so much in common, the reader hears an involved and extended dialogue with both perceived "disjunctions" and "conjunctions," the latter being more pronounced in this reader's perception. In this chapter, which seeks to interpret the RF theologically, the reader may wisely move "from text via text to meaning."[2] The main focus will be on a synchronic reading of Ezekiel and Exodus together, but diachronic questions will not be entirely avoided.

6.1. Theological Disjunction
Between the Formulas in Ezekiel and Exodus

As already emphasized, Ezekiel's RFs have tremendous emotive power because they echo a prominent feature of the story of Israel's redemption with which, the reader may surmise, Ezekiel's audience was familiar. Whether one posits an "intertextuality of text production" or an "intertextuality of text reception,"[3] it is fascinating to "read between" Exodus and Ezekiel with special focus on the RF. As we listen to Exodus and Ezekiel in concert, what do we hear? How do the refrains in Ezekiel echo those in Exodus? Is a clear, strong echo heard in which the accents, the tones, and the articulation of a message in the original voice are recognizable? (Here I am of a diachronic mind with the idea of an originating voice or source.) The RF usage in Ezekiel, it might be expected, could have much in common with the usage and meaning it has in Exodus. And it does, but there is also a disjunction that proved not just counterintuitive, but scandalous to the audience. What caused Ezekiel's formula to be so gripping and awful was the prophecy's "radical inversion of its former usage."[4] As one listens to Ezekiel's RFs in concert with the formulas elsewhere in the Bible, there is discord or dissonance. Nowhere else in all the Bible does the RF appear in an oracle of judgment against Israel. The formula previously sounded a triumphant, encouraging note: the enemies of God's people would be destroyed, and through that divine intervention, Israel would be saved and "know that I am Yahweh." Now, however, it is Israel who will be given into the hands of her enemies, and it is she who will know the severe punishment Yahweh brings upon his enemies.

Walther Zimmerli does not make this exact point, that the prophet Ezekiel has departed from the consistently positive use of the RF with relation to Israel elsewhere in the OT, but he does discuss how dreadful the judgment oracles sound

2. Van Wolde, "From Text via Text," 160.
3. Van Wolde, "Texts in Dialogue with Texts," 4.
4. Carley, *Ezekiel*, 39.

for Israel, who likely found it inconceivable that Yahweh could be other than an
ally. Zimmerli says that, in the tradition represented in 1 Kgs 20, Yahweh "reveals
himself in his actions as the Lord who intervenes on behalf of his people and
historically proves his loyalty to Israel."

> However, this picture is severely disturbed and unexpectedly illuminated by the
> plethora of judgment statements against Israel (Judah) in the first half of this book.
> Even the prophetic stories from the time of Elijah and Elisha spoke about the judg-
> ment of transgressors among the people and even the sinful king. The intensification
> in Ezekiel is so terrifying because, on the one hand, it has been expanded to include
> the entire people and its entire political existence; on the other, the recurring direct
> association of this judgment of Israel with the strict statement of recognition virtually
> identifies it as the locus at which Yahweh reveals himself in his most personal essence.
> Yahweh's revelatory self-introduction is to be recognized in his judgment over Israel.[5]

Zimmerli follows Gerhard von Rad in placing the RFs of 1 Kgs 20 in a holy-
war tradition. Regardless of one's opinion regarding such a distinct tradition,[6] it is
clear that, in Ezekiel, we have a "radical inversion" of the idea that Yahweh joins
battle on the side of his people to grant them victory. At the time of the exodus,
Moses rallied the Israelites with a prophecy of divine intervention: "Do not fear.
Stand firm and you will see the salvation of Yahweh which he will accomplish for
you today. The Egyptians whom you see this day you will not see again, not ever.
Yahweh will fight [לחם] for you; you will keep still" (Exod 14:13–14).

That prophecy was fulfilled in the destruction of the charioteers who cried,
"Let us flee from before the Israelites, for Yahweh fights for them against Egypt"
(14:25). Israel was then awe-struck and could not contain her joy: "Who among
the gods is like you, Yahweh? Who like you is glorious in holiness, dreadful in
praiseworthy deeds, a worker of wonders? *You stretched out your right arm* [נטית
ימינך] and the earth swallowed them" (Exod 15:11–12). This was the fulfillment
of Yahweh's earlier promise in Exod 6:6 which has an attached RF: "I shall bring
you out (והוצאתי אתכם) ... and I shall redeem you with outstretched arm (בזרוע
נטויה) and with great judgments."

However, in Ezekiel's oracles (20:33–35), Yahweh promises a new exodus with
Yahweh's arm outstretched in wrath and judgment against Israel:

> As I live, declares the Lord Yahweh, surely with a mighty hand and an outstretched
> arm (בזרוע נטויה) and with outpoured wrath I shall rule over you. I shall bring you

5. Zimmerli, *I Am Yahweh*, 92–93.
6. The idea of Yahweh as warrior and as entering battle for Israel is strong in Exodus (14:14, 25 [both alleged to be J/E]; 15:3 [J]; 17:16 [E]).

out (והוצאתי אתכם) from the peoples and gather you out of the lands among whom you were scattered with a mighty hand and outstretched arm (בזרוע נטויה) and with outpoured wrath. And I shall bring you into the wilderness of the peoples and I shall judge you there face to face.

The "radical inversion" of exodus language is stunning, and in examining the oracles more closely, the reader finds further examples of this inversion.

The same type of revisionary reuse with even harsher language occurs where Ezekiel speaks of Yahweh's *hand* (also in 20:33–34 above). Exodus has numerous texts declaring that Yahweh will extend his hand against Egypt.[7] Indeed, Exodus says that the willful Pharaoh, who does not know Yahweh (5:2), will not let the children of Israel go unless compelled by Yahweh's hand (3:19). The hand of Yahweh is against Pharaoh but not against Israel's leaders in Exod 24:11 (ואל־אצילי בני ישראל לא שלח ידו), who are spared judgment when they have a covenant meal with a holy God. Ezekiel, however, inverts this language in oracles against Israel: "I shall stretch out my hand against them [ונטיתי את־ידי עליהם] and make the land a desolation and waste. . . . Then they shall know that I am Yahweh" (6:14).[8] He envisages a war of Yahweh against his people. Instead of Egyptian dead lying on the seashore (Exod 14:30), the dead bodies of Israelites will lie in front of their idols (Ezek 6:5). The prophet says, "The slain shall fall among you, and you shall know that I am Yahweh" (6:7).

Jeremiah also contains this stunning reversal of the Divine Warrior motif, though without the RF. When the king's messengers inquire about the outcome of the war with Nebuchadnezzar, they receive this answer (21:4–6):

Thus says Yahweh, the God of Israel: See, I shall turn back against you the weapons of war that are in your hands, [weapons] with which you are fighting against the king of Babylon and the Babylonians who are besieging you outside the wall. And I will bring them inside this city. *I myself will fight against you* with an outstretched

---

7. See Exod 3:20; 7:4, 5; 9:3, 15; 13:3, 9, 14, 16; cf. 32:11.

8. Since the phrases "stretch out the hand" and "stretch out the arm" are a common idiom, one need not *necessarily* view Ezekiel's use of the phrase as being closely tied to Exodus. Exodus repeatedly uses נטה in these phrases to describe divine action (Exod 6:6; 7:5; 15:12) and Moses's and Aaron's action (Exod 7:19; 8:1[5]; 9:22; 10:12, 21; 14:16, 26; and elsewhere). In two places, Exodus uses שלח with the same meaning (3:20; 9:15). What is significant in Ezekiel is the radical inversion of this language, together with the RF, using it to describe divine action in oracles of judgment *against Israel* (see Ezek 6:14; 14:9, 13; 16:27; 25:7, 13; 35:3), in addition to oracles against the nations (e.g., Ezek 25:16). As noted before, Moshe Greenberg writes: "Ezekiel characteristically utilizes a traditional phrase with a shocking twist: in the new Exodus the ferocity that tradition asserted was unleashed upon Egypt in the old one will be turned against rebellious Israel in order to force it finally to accept what it never had before—God's kingship over it in the land he chose for it" (*Ezekiel 1–20*, 372). Worth mentioning is Isaiah's use of this same phrase in judgment oracles (9:11, 16, 20; 10:4).

hand and a strong arm (ביד נטויה ובזרוע חזקה) in anger, fury, and great wrath. *I will strike down* the inhabitants of this city, both man and beast, and they shall die of a great plague.[9]

The inversion of Exodus's wholly positive use of the RF in a majority of Ezekiel's formulas addressed to Israel is highly significant as another facet of this overall pattern of "skewing" previously positive language.[10] In this one matter—a negative context versus a positive one for the use of the RF—Isaiah's formulas are more similar to Exodus's than are Ezekiel's. The distinction in usage of the formula is a prime reason to reject the idea of Ezekiel's formulas deriving from so-called Second Isaiah (*pace* Sheldon Blank and Herbert May), whose use of the refrain is wholly positive, whether it is addressed to Israel or the nations.

Because the fulfillment of his call necessitated faithful interpretation of Scripture, one may question how Ezekiel understood the tension between Exodus and his own oracles. Might there have been any unease over the appropriateness of the radical inversion? This study answers that question in the negative for several reasons. First, Ezekiel presents the judgment oracles as coming from God, with complete faith that his oracles carried absolute divine authority. The reader sees this in his repeated use of the introductory phrases: "the word of Yahweh came to me," "thus says Yahweh," and "hear the word of Yahweh."[11] In addition to the introductory phrases, there is also the constant use of certain concluding phrases that highlight the divine origin of the oracles ("the utterance of Yahweh" and "I, Yahweh, have spoken").[12] Thus, in Ezekiel's theocentric orientation, the radical inversion is authored by Yahweh, not the prophet.

Secondly, while the book of Exodus contains no RFs set in judgment oracles *against Israel*, Yahweh reportedly did judge his people in terrible ways at the time of the exodus. Ezekiel argues in 20:36 that his theme of judgment against Israel did have its precedent in Exodus: "As I judged your fathers in the wilderness of the land of Egypt, so I shall judge you, declares the Lord Yahweh." The scriptural testimony is that Israel *had* experienced certain plagues in Egypt (Exod 7:14–8:19)

9. This Jeremiah text (v. 5 in particular) is cited by Greenberg: "Jeremiah partly anticipated Ezekiel in this skewed usage" (*Ezekiel 1–20*, 372).

10. Of the forty-six RFs addressed to Israel, thirty are found in oracles of judgment.

11. The "word-event/prophetic word formula," ויהי דבר־יהוה אלי לאמר, occurs over 50× and is said by Zimmerli to demarcate separate oracles. The "messenger formula," כה אמר (אדני) יהוה, is also extensively used (about 125×). The phrase Ronald Hals terms the "call to attention formula" (*Ezekiel*, 359), שמעו דבר־אדני יהוה, can appear alongside the messenger formula (e.g., 6:3); Ezekiel has some ten occurrences.

12. The "prophetic utterance formula" (Hals, *Ezekiel*, 361) or "signatory formula" (Block, *Ezekiel 1–24*, 33), נאם אדני יהוה, appears about 85× in Ezekiel and is discussed in detail in Baumgärtel, "Die Formel." The "conclusion formula for divine speech" (mentioned in ch. 3), אני יהוה דברתי, is found approximately 15×, occasionally in conjunction with the RF.

and other judgments in the wilderness (Exod 32:25–29, 35; Lev 10; Num 11:33). Their wickedness[13] during the period Ezekiel described as "the days of your youth" was such that Yahweh had threatened to consume (כלה) the nation in his anger (Exod 32:10, 12; 33:3, 5; cf. Ezek 20:13).[14]

Note a third reason. Immediately after the deliverance from Egypt, as Moses exhorts the redeemed people to follow in God's ways, there seems to be both a promise of mercy and a latent threat in Moses's speech in Exod 15:26: "If you truly listen to the voice of Yahweh your God, and do what is right in his eyes, and heed his commandments, and keep all his requirements, then all the diseases I brought upon the Egyptians I will not bring upon you, for I am Yahweh your healer." But what if the nation in future years does *not* "truly listen to the voice of Yahweh . . . and heed his commandments"? Is there the implication that "all the diseases I brought upon the Egyptians" might, at a later time, be visited upon Israel in God's judgment? Such a threat lines up with pentateuchal theology elsewhere (e.g., Num 33:56).

The fourth reason depends on a well-known Exodus text that explicates the name *Yahweh*. Exodus 34:5 records that Yahweh came down to Moses on Sinai and "called out the name Yahweh."[15] Then, in the following verses, there is an additional double declaration of the name with what seems to be a divine exposition of the name.[16]

(6) And Yahweh passed before him and called out, "Yahweh, Yahweh, a God compassionate and gracious, slow to anger, abounding in covenant-love[17] and faithfulness, (7) maintaining covenant-love for thousands, and forgiving guilt and rebellion and sin. Yet he does not leave them unpunished, visiting the sin of the fathers upon the children and grandchildren, to three and four generations.

Verse 7b disperses illusions that Yahweh will never judge his people. On the positive side, this covenant text (v. 10) establishes that Yahweh intends to pour out an

13. Exodus refers to the nation as: "stiff-necked" (32:9; 33:3, 5; 34:9); having corrupted themselves (32:7); being "prone to evil" (32:22); testing and grumbling against Yahweh (16:8; 17:7); breaking the Sabbath command (16:28); and needing an atonement for their sin (32:30; 34:9). Thus, Exodus presents no idyllic picture of Israel's spiritual and moral state in the beginning.

14. Exodus contains multiple threats. Israel was warned to keep God's command not to approach Mount Sinai, otherwise "Yahweh will break out against them" (Exod 19:22, 24). Exodus 32:34 reads: "But in the day of my visitation I shall visit vengeance upon them for their sin." There was also Yahweh's warning that he would withdraw his presence from the people (33:3–5).

15. In Exod 34:5, I read ויתיצב and ויקרא with Yahweh as subject. See: Cassuto, *Exodus*, 439; Childs, *Exodus*, 603, 611–12; Durham, *Exodus*, 453; Houtman, *Exodus*, 3:707. William Propp disagrees (*Exodus 19–40*, 609).

16. Durham agrees: "Yahweh's confession of his nature is a powerful exegesis of the meaning of 'Yahweh! Yahweh!,' one brilliantly matched to (or by) the narrative of which it is a part and one that summarizes dramatically that Yahweh will not accommodate his nature to the vagaries of his people's commitment" (*Exodus*, 454).

17. Following Glueck, *Ḥesed in the Bible*.

abundance of love upon his chosen people. They can also expect to see Yahweh work unparalleled wonders in the future, convincing surrounding nations of his awesome power on behalf of Israel. But, on the negative side, the covenant renewal in chapter 34, made necessary by the covenant violation with the golden calf, also offers stern warnings. Yahweh's name is "Jealous" (v. 14), and he will certainly not clear the guilty. The sin especially in view is any covenant with the peoples in the land God gives them (vv. 12–16), for such will lead Israel to worship other gods, a worship characterized as spiritual "prostitution" (זנה; vv. 15–16).

In an intertextuality of text reception, one might read backward in the canon, from Ezekiel to Exodus, and discover in Exodus (through Ezekiel) a certain potential latent in the RF for a negative use.[18] Coming to know Yahweh, Lord of the covenant, can occur in judgment as well as in salvation, and Israel may "know that I am Yahweh" in a broader situational context than deliverance from her enemies. If Yahweh may make himself known to Egypt through acts of judgment, might he not reveal himself to Israel in judgment when the nation has for generations violated the covenant? Is it unthinkable for him to display to rebels what one of my students termed "the other side of his power"[19] that they may "know that I am Yahweh"?

It may be suggested that Ezekiel's radical inversion of the RF was more shocking to his audience than to him and that it follows Ezekiel's pattern, noted earlier,[20] of what Zimmerli might have termed a negative reactualization of tradition. Zimmerli prompted scholarship to consider the relation of Ezekiel's message to the older theological *traditum* (as he calls it) and what transformation occurs in the reuse of the *traditum*:

> For all of this, is it appropriate to speak of "interpretation" of historical traditions? To be sure, old traditions emerge throughout. Yet in terms of the actual function which "tradition" should serve, namely, the function of wholesome assurance for the present in "memory" and in "actualization" of past events, the *traditum* crumbles to pieces wherever the great pre-exilic prophets take hold of it. In their preaching it becomes the accuser of the present. And even at the price sometimes (especially in Ezekiel) of radical recasting with all beneficial aid eliminated, the *traditum* is made to serve entirely the prophets' immediate proclamation of judgment, the sole locus of emphasis. The God who comes in judgment emerges from the entire pious tradition. He is to be known in his impending judgment, and no longer in tradition about previous deeds (*Erweiswort*). Alongside this, the old traditions have nothing of their own to emphasize. "Tradition," in the salutary sense of the word, shatters

18. If the interpreter rejects the idea of such a negative curse/judgment *potential*, one might at least understand the language of Exod 15:26, and similar texts such as 23:22, as threatening the withdrawal of positive benefits (e.g., protection).

19. Harold Kazekula, Theological College of Central Africa, 2000.

20. See chapter 4, section 4.1.3.

and becomes an empty shell of mere historical recollection, over which a completely different word of God is proclaimed.[21]

Zimmerli certainly has an important point to make here, but perhaps he over-states his case. If Ezekiel himself reuses the RFs not only in oracles of judgment but also, still, in oracles of salvation, have the traditions completely crumbled or shattered? (E.g., Ezekiel prophesies that Yahweh will graciously lead Israel in a new exodus back to the land of their "fathers" [20:41–42] after he has led them by a new exodus to know his judgment [20:34–38].) There is need to see the conjunctions (or continuities), alongside the "shattering" disjunctions (or discontinuities).

6.2. Theological Conjunctions Between the Formulas in Ezekiel and Exodus

Chapter 4 demonstrated that Exodus and Ezekiel have numerous points of contact. Evidence was adduced that Ezekiel drew the RF from Exodus as well. Therefore, it may be supposed that the interpretations of the formula in the two books will also have points of contact, and this supposition is correct. Fuller meaning in the RF and several conjunctions are discovered through an intertextual reading of Ezekiel and Exodus.

6.2.1. No Positive Use of the Formula When Spoken to the Nations

As is true even in Isaianic studies,[22] there is a lack of consensus regarding the prophet's conception of the relationship of the nations to Yahweh. Some believe Ezekiel envisaged the nations' full salvation alongside Israel, but others contest this idea.[23] Debate has centered on the interpretation of the RF. Are chapters 25–32 in fact oracles *against* the nations, to be read in a wholly negative way? Because

21. Zimmerli, "Prophetic Proclamation," 98–99.
22. Van Winkle, "Relationship of the Nations."
23. For arguments in favor, see: Zimmerli, "Knowledge of God" (29–98 in *I Am Yahweh*), esp. 88–90; Reventlow, "Die Völker"; Reventlow, *Wächter über Israel*, 134–57 (esp. 138); von Rad, *Old Testament Theology*, 2:237; Ackroyd, *Exile and Restoration*, 115–17; Eichrodt, *Ezekiel*, 44–45, 586; Vogels, "Restauration de l'Égypt," 473–94; Martens, "Ezekiel's Contribution"; Wright, *Message of Ezekiel*, 37–38, 255–72 (Wright cites his student, D. A. Williams, "'Then They Will Know that I Am the Lord': The Missiological Significance of Ezekiel's Concern for the Nations as Evident in the Use of the Recognition Formula" [MA thesis, All Nations Christian College, 1998]). For arguments against, see: Keil, *Prophecies of Ezekiel*, 1:358; Cooke, *Ezekiel*, xxxi; Kaufmann, *Religion of Israel*, 446; Zimmerli, *Ezekiel 1*, 66; Darr, "Wall Around Paradise"; Joyce, *Divine Initiative*, 90, 94–97; Strong, "Ezekiel's Use"; Block, *Ezekiel 1–24*, 53; Block, "Ezekiel: Theology of," in *NIDOTTE*, 4:618–19. Baruch J. Schwartz thinks the oracles take such a "dim view" of even Israel's future with Yahweh that they can hardly be said to promise salvation or grace to the covenant people ("Ezekiel's Dim View").

the formulas are addressed to the nations as well as to Israel, questions arise as to whether the former will "know that I am Yahweh" in the same sense as Israel does. Currently, the strong trend among specialists is to view the prophecy as more exclusivistic than inclusivistic in theology and missional focus. The direction of scholarship, then, would be to interpret the RFs addressed to the nations as *not* having conversion and saving knowledge in view.

Zimmerli's position in the controversy is hard to discern.[24] In places, his writings seem to encourage the view that Ezekiel's RF anticipates the conversion of the nations. As explained in chapter 2, Zimmerli's form-critical approach understands the formula as consisting of two parts: the "assertion/statement of recognition" (*Erkenntnisaussage*)[25] and the "formula of self-introduction" (*Selbstvorstellungsformel*). The latter (אני יהוה) is supposed to have had an original cultic setting and to have served as the "personal self-introduction of the attendant God" in worship.[26] The logical next step for Zimmerli is to interpret the RF as anticipating a worshipful response to the "word-event." In his 1954 essay, he writes of "the knowledge of God coming about in the worshiping confession, Yahweh is God (1 Kings 18)," and "the adoration that kneels because of divinely inspired recognition, an orientation toward the one who himself says 'I am Yahweh.'" Zimmerli then asserts that "this same recognition is expected from the rest of the world's nations. In this Ezekiel is similar to Deutero-Isaiah."[27]

But Zimmerli's introduction to his commentary (1969) contradicts that theological conclusion. He distances his own position from Henning Graf Reventlow's and distinguishes between Ezekiel's and Deutero-Isaiah's outlook on the nations' future. Zimmerli mentions "the future age of *Israel's* salvation which is announced," and then he writes:

> The message of the prophet Ezekiel *lacks a completely universal interest.* "The nations" can sometimes (mostly in sayings from the school) be mentioned in the Recognition Formula as witnesses (36:23; 37:28; 38:16; 39:7, 21, 23). *Unlike Deutero-Isaiah,* the prophet of the late exilic age, Ezekiel lacks a fully-developed message about the world of the nations.[28]

24. Martens claims Zimmerli for his view—long associated with Reventlow—that ידע in the RF includes an "adoration" of Yahweh ("Ezekiel's Contribution," 76), while Darr believes Zimmerli "departs from this view" ("Wall Around Paradise," 272).

25. Zimmerli can use "statement of recognition" in a rather broad sense (even as a synonym for "recognition formula"). I note here that he terms כי ידע (the first element in the RF) "die Erkenntnisaussage im engeren Sinne" (*Gottes Offenbarung*, 90).

26. Zimmerli, *I Am Yahweh*, 26.

27. Zimmerli, *I Am Yahweh*, 88. The end of this particular essay expands on this, mentioning "confession, worship, and obedience" (98).

28. Zimmerli, *Ezekiel 1*, 66 (emphasis added). The word "completely" in the English translation is unnecessary and even misleading (modifying "universal"). The original reads simply, "Das universale Interesse fehlt der Verkündigung des Propheten Ezechiel" (*Ezechiel*, 1:101*–102*).

Zimmerli wrote the introduction at the conclusion of his work on the commentary, more than a decade after his essays of the 1950s, and so it represents his mature views, which do not agree with Reventlow. At the same time, I doubt he would have asserted his disagreement in strong terms, as is common today among Ezekiel specialists.

Among those who lean toward an inclusive interpretation of Ezekiel's theology, there is a tendency to understand all RFs in Ezekiel as having essentially the same content and meaning, whether spoken to Israel or to the nations, whether in prophecies of judgment or salvation. What Israel comes to "know" the nations will also "know." What it means *to know* remains fairly constant and uniform. One finds this interpretation in both critical and conservative scholarship. Among several on the critical side, Klaus Koch may be quoted:

> Knowing that Yahweh *is* means recognizing him as the One who, in any event, will ultimately prevail. The act of human knowledge does not merely imply theoretical insight. It involves modified behaviour as well; for the Hebrew word for knowing, *yada'*, does not mean objective and detached observation. It means arriving at an understanding of something through use and association. In Ezekiel, this knowledge does not become the common property of eschatological Israel alone. It is given to the other nations as well (36.36 . . .).[29]

Koch is a careful scholar and expresses his conclusion in a nuanced way that is agreeable in most respects. One may raise questions, however, when he writes of a knowledge of Yahweh involving something like repentance ("modified behavior") on the part of the nations as well as Israel. Does Ezek 25:7 lead us to expect that Ammon will behave differently in coming to know a wrathful Yahweh? The oracle reads: "I shall cut you off from the peoples, and I shall exterminate [אבד Hiphil] you from the countries. I shall destroy [שמד Hiphil] you, and you shall know that I am Yahweh."

The conservative work of my former professor, Gerard Van Groningen, on Messianism also reflects this tendency to interpret all content of knowledge (or result of knowing) as much the same regardless of whether the RF addresses Israel or the nations, whether in oracles of judgment or salvation:

> The covenant people would come to a realization that when Yahweh spoke, "I am Yahweh" and "You shall know that I am Yahweh," he meant exactly that! Not only were his dealings with Israel and Judah in exile to realize that truth, *but Yahweh's dealings with other nations were to have them come to know and acknowledge that Yahweh is the only God.* . . . Thus the particular *and universal* dimensions of Yahweh's covenantal relationships were at the very heart of the exile."[30]

29. Koch, *Prophets*, 2:105.
30. Van Groningen, *Messianic Revelation*, 733 (emphasis added).

Such scholars are applying a sound hermeneutical principle: *authors commonly use terms and phrases in much the same fashion when repeated within a single document*. We tend to believe key terms or phrases occurring repeatedly in a larger text will be fairly consistent in meaning, and we wish to read them together and take cues from the larger context in interpreting the parallels. For example, we might expect the meaning of the "Day of Yahweh" in Joel 4:14[3:14] to be in line with that of the earlier occurrences (1:15; 2:1, 11; 3:4[2:31]). By use of this principle, one might deduce that, in Ezekiel's RFs, Israel and the nations will know in the same way. If the recognition of Yahweh by Israel is God's grace and means salvation (e.g., at 36:38), then the recognition of Yahweh by the nations may mean salvation too. Because of the strong covenantal overtones in the RF, it is thought by some that the formulas spoken to the nations indicate God's covenantal interest in the nations.

There is another hermeneutical principle, however, to be taken into account. Professor C. F. D. Moule instructed students that "statements may vary strikingly in emphasis as a result of the very different circumstances to which they were severally addressed."[31] One needs, then, to balance a concept- or lexeme-oriented approach with a field-oriented approach that seeks to understand how "the situational and semantic context modulates the sense of included lexical units."[32] When situational, rhetorical, and literary contexts are examined, it becomes clear that occurrences of νόμος in Paul or ידע in Ezekiel can have different senses, and one is bound to give close scrutiny to the context. I turn to apply this hermeneutical principle in studying Ezekiel's RF.

Does ידע "vary strikingly" in meaning depending on the context, or does it have a fairly consistent, generalized meaning in Ezekiel's RFs, both in those addressed to Israel and in those addressed to the nations? Before examining relevant texts in Ezekiel, I propose a thesis to be tested: reading Exodus as an intertext, taking into account the context of its RFs as to whether they address Israel or a foreign nation, may illuminate the study of Ezekiel's formula on this point. Do we hear echoes of Exodus usage?

A careful reading of Exodus leads to the conclusion that there are two distinct kinds of knowing implied by the RFs there. The knowledge of Yahweh attained by Egypt in judgment is of a completely different order than that attained by Israel in their experience of a gracious redemption. It seems impossible to interpret the formulas spoken to Israel in 6:5–7 and to Egypt in 7:3–5 as having the same kind of knowledge in view.[33] Israel is to see Yahweh's plan fulfilled in her redemption from

31. Dunn, review of Carson, O'Brien, and Seifrid, *Justification and Variegated Nomism*, vol. 1, 113.
32. Cotterell and Turner, *Linguistics and Biblical Interpretation*, 147.
33. Some try to interpret these Exodus RFs the same way. Victor P. Hamilton writes: "The divine purpose is that the Pharaoh and his people—to say nothing of the Israelites—will indeed acquire knowledge of the true God.... It will be a knowledge based on observation and confrontation, not

slavery and in Yahweh's presence coming to dwell with the covenant people. They come to "fear" Yahweh and "put their trust" (אָמַן Hiphil) in him and his prophet (14:31). However, the story is different with an Egypt that *knows*.

Rather than revealing a disposition to be known by a humbled Egypt in his grace, Yahweh declares he will harden the hearts of the Egyptians (14:17) that they might resist him to the point of being utterly broken. It is in Egypt's final destruction that Yahweh will be known, when Pharaoh's charioteers cry out, moments before being engulfed, "Let us flee from before the Israelites for Yahweh fights for them against Egypt" (14:25). The narrative reveals God's intention to destroy human lives as a judgment (14:17), and therefore, according to the divine perspective and purpose, one is mistaken to say, "Egypt has learned *too late* the lesson of the Plagues, that 'I am Yahweh.'"[34] In the plan of God as described in the narrative, the timing is right. Yahweh's glory is revealed not in Egypt's willing submission to the God of Israel, but in Yahweh hardening Pharaoh's heart that the king might pursue his scheme to reenslave Israel (14:4) and find destruction. "Then the Egyptians shall *know* that I am Yahweh" in a very different sense than Israel *knows*.[35] For the former, G. Johannes Botterweck says, it is "a painful and helpless surprise [*leidvolle und ohnmächtige Betroffenheit*]."[36] This negative perspective on the nations as awed but unconverted observers of Yahweh's mighty acts for Israel carries over into Exod 15. Among hostile nations in 15:9 (many of the same nations mentioned in Ezekiel), Israel sings in Exod 15:11–17:

> Who among the gods is like you, Yahweh?
> > Who like you is glorious [אדר Niphal] in holiness,
> > > dreadful in praiseworthy deeds [תהלות], a worker of wonders?
> You extended your right arm,
> > and the earth swallowed them.
> In your covenant mercy [חסד] you lead
> > the people you have redeemed.

---

on hearsay. To know the Lord as Lord means to recognize and then submit to his authority. This is the choice the Pharaoh needs to make and is invited to make" (*Handbook*, 159). Exodus makes clear that Pharaoh did not submit to Yahweh's authority, even after the plague on the firstborn. Instead, Pharaoh and his advisers chose to chase after Israel to enslave them again (Exod 14:1–9). There is inconsistency in Hamilton's quote above. He first states that Yahweh's purpose is that Pharaoh "will *indeed* acquire knowledge of the true God" and "submit" (repent?). He then backs away and makes it a "choice Pharaoh . . . is invited to make."

34. Propp, *Exodus*, 1:500.

35. Exodus texts containing RFs spoken against Egypt, besides 7:3–5 above, have a similarly severe tone and contain harsh judgment against Israel's oppressors. Those texts are Exod 7:17 (the plague of blood) and 8:18[22] (Yahweh spares Israel while he plagues Egypt again). Cf. the phrases related to the formula in 8:10; 9:14, 29; and 11:7.

36. G. Johannes Botterweck, "ידע *yādaʿ*," in *TDOT*, 5:473.

In your might you lead them
   to your holy dwelling place.
The nations hear; they shudder;
   dread seizes the inhabitants of Philistia.
Then Edom's chiefs are terrified;
   [as for] the rams [strong men] of Moab, trembling seizes them;
   all the inhabitants of Canaan melt away [מוג].
Fear and terror fall upon them.
  By the greatness of your arm
  they are still as a stone,
until your people pass by, Yahweh,
   until the people you have acquired [קנה][37] pass by.
You bring them and plant them
  on the mountain of your inheritance,
the place you make into your dwelling, Yahweh,
   the sanctuary, Lord, your hands establish [כון Polel].

Israel's consolation amid the surrounding nations was to be in Yahweh's promise, "I shall be an enemy to your enemies" (Exod 23:22). The expectation, then, is that Egypt, Edom, Moab, and the rest would know Yahweh in his hostility to all Israel's foes.

As with the RFs in Exodus, it seems wise to differentiate between Ezekiel's formulas and not assume ידע should be construed the same way whether the formula addresses Israel in "salvation-oracles" or the nations in "judgment-oracles." I propose that what *should* be construed in much the same way is the knowledge connoted in Ezekiel's RFs that occur in oracles of *judgment against Israel* and the knowledge that occurs in oracles of *judgment against the nations*. The kinds of knowledge connoted by the RF do not differ according to addressee (Israel knows in one sense, the nations in another), but according to oracle type (the judged know in one sense, but the redeemed in another). I will proceed by examining, first of all, where the knowledge connoted by Ezekiel's RFs differs and, secondly, where the knowledge connoted by Ezekiel's formulas is similar.

6.2.1.1. Construing the Knowledge Connoted by the Formula Differently
As noted in chapter 3, approximately 75% of Ezekiel's RFs appear in prophecies of judgment and the remaining formulas occur in prophecies of mercy and restoration addressed to Israel. Yahweh promises, "I shall establish my covenant with you,

---

37. Some wish to translate קנה as "create" instead of "purchase" or "acquire." See Durham, *Exodus*, 200, 202, and KBL, 843. *HALOT* suggests "acquire" (1112).

and you shall know that I am Yahweh" (16:62; cf. 34:25; 37:26). God also purposes to be known in his mercy as he returns his people to their own land: "You shall know that I am Yahweh when I bring you into the land of Israel, the country which I swore [lit.: raised my hand] to give to your fathers" (20:42).[38] The restoration will be like a national resurrection (37:1–14): "I shall put breath in you, and you shall live, and you shall know that I am Yahweh" (37:6). The blessings of restoration will include:

1. atonement for Israel's sin (16:63)
2. cleansing from defilement and idolatry (36:25, 29, 33)
3. inward spiritual renewal (36:26)
4. rescue from slavery (34:27)
5. protection from selfish rulers (34:10), enemies (34:28; 38:8; 39:26), and wild animals (34:25, 28)
6. Yahweh's fierce judgment upon foreign attackers (38:21–23)
7. abundant harvests (34:27; 36:8, 29–30, 34–36)
8. multiplication of Israel's population and livestock (ורבו ופרו; 36:10–11, 37–38)
9. rebuilt cities (36:34–36)
10. removal of neighbors' scorn (36:15, 30)

There will be a new David to rule (34:23; 37:24–25), true justice under Yahweh's shepherding care (34:11–16), and the reestablishment of Yahweh's dwelling among his people (34:30; 37:26–28), which a Christian interpreter may link to the bestowal upon Israel of God's Spirit (36:27; 37:14; 39:29). The fullness of God's blessing may be summed up in the covenant formula: "You will be my people, and I will be your God" (36:28; 37:23, 27).[39] Israel will know and trust Yahweh as her saving God.

Ezekiel's oracles against the nations contain no promises of salvation or blessing similar to those above. Only doom and woe (with awe in observing Yahweh's blessing upon Israel) are prophesied to them. Yahweh's word to the nations is: "See, I am against you" (הנני אליך; 26:3; 28:22; 29:3, 10; 35:3; 38:3; 39:1).[40] There is nothing in Ezekiel similar to Isaiah's oracle that the Egyptians will "swear allegiance to Yahweh Sebaoth" (19:18), "build an altar to worship Yahweh in the midst of Egypt"

38. Cf. Ezek 36:8, 24; 37:12, 14, 21, 25; 38:8; 39:25–28.

39. For discussion, see Rendtorff, *Covenant Formula*, and Sedlmeier, "'Sie werden mir zum Volk.'"

40. These texts are matched by a number that address the wicked of Israel (Ezek 13:8; 21:8; 34:10). The contrast would be a text speaking blessing such as 36:9—כי הנני אליכם ופניתי אליכם—which Block says "recalls Yahweh's covenant promise in Lev. 26:9, 'I will turn to you (*ûpāniti ʾălêkem*) and make you fruitful and multiply you, and I will confirm my covenant with you'" (*Ezekiel 25–48*, 333).

(v. 19), "turn to Yahweh" (v. 22), and hear "Yahweh Sebaoth saying, 'Blessed be my people Egypt'" (v. 25). With no oracles of salvation addressed to the nations, one might guess that there will be no RFs addressed to the nations that speak of them knowing Yahweh in deliverance and blessing. This supposition is confirmed as true by a careful reading of Ezekiel and by the best scholarship—see Paul Joyce's catalog (Table 1 in ch. 2). Not a single RF is spoken positively to the nations in all of the prophecy. Even those who believe that Ezekiel anticipates some future blessing on the nations admit this fact. In his fine expositional commentary, Christopher Wright says:

> It has to be said, however, that all the texts which apply the recognition formula to the nations (as distinct from Israel) do so either in relation to anticipated punishment of the nations in the oracles directed against them, or in relation to the predicted restoration of Israel in their midst. There is no clear text that expresses the expectation that the nations would know Yahweh as a result of his delivering or saving *them* in any way that parallels the deliverance of Israel.[41]

A distinction can and should be made between the knowledge connoted by RFs (with their variations) addressed to the nations and the knowledge connoted by RFs in salvation oracles spoken to Israel. Those judged "know" Yahweh in a different sense than do those who are saved,[42] and the formulas included in oracles of restoration spoken to Israel have less bearing on the interpretation of formulas spoken to the nations. It is a misreading to interpret in a salvific sense those formulas that say the nations "shall know that I am Yahweh." The theology in Ezekiel differs from that in Isa 19:21: "Yahweh shall make himself known to the Egyptians, and the Egyptians shall know Yahweh [וידעו מצרים את־יהוה] in that day and worship with sacrifice and offering. They shall make vows to Yahweh and perform them." Contrary to the position of Reventlow and others, Ezekiel's RFs do not lead readers to expect the nations either to trust in Yahweh and repent or to experience covenantal blessing.

6.2.1.2. *Construing the Knowledge Connoted by the Formula Similarly*
Though salvation oracles (Israel) and judgment oracles (nations) are not so comparable, with regard to the kind of knowledge connoted by Ezekiel's RF, the judgment oracles against Israel and the nations are. This research concludes that the RFs found in judgment oracles against the nations are best interpreted alongside

---

41. Wright, *Message of Ezekiel*, 37.
42. As argued above, knowing Yahweh in deliverance/restoration takes place only among those whose hearts are transformed. Florian Markter demonstrates in *Transformationen* that Ezekiel envisages only the Jewish exiles experiencing this.

and in basic accord with those spoken in judgment against Israel, and vice versa. Ezekiel's various judgment oracles often read in a similar way, and here, to give a set of examples,[43] one might compare 6:14 and 33:29 (Israel) with 29:9 (Egypt) and 35:3–4 (Mount Seir):

> 6:14 — And I shall stretch out my hand against them and make the land desolate [שממה] and a waste [ומשמה] from the wilderness to Diblah throughout all their settlements. And then they shall know that I am Yahweh.

> 33:29 — And they shall know that I am Yahweh, when I have made the land a desolation (שממה) and a waste [ומשמה] because of all their abominations which they have done.

> 29:9 — And the land of Egypt shall be a desolation [שממה] and a waste [וחרבה]. And then they shall know that I am Yahweh.

> 35:3–4 — Behold, I am against you, Mount Seir, and I shall stretch out my hand against you, and I shall make you a desolation [שממה] and a waste [ומשמה]. Your cities I shall lay waste [חרבה], and you shall be a desolation [שממה]. And then you shall know that I am Yahweh.

"Reading between" such texts sensitizes the reader to intratextual relationships that Boadt says abound in Ezekiel. Surely these oracles are to be heard/read together, and recognizing such intratextuality proves heuristically useful. There is no hopeful tone, no expectation of mercy from Yahweh, no hint of a saving knowledge in judgment oracles that contain the RF. Those in Israel who defiantly break covenant with Yahweh are destroyed in a manner similar to the nations who attack the covenant people and awaken Yahweh's vengeance. Both experience Yahweh's outpoured wrath: Israel (7:3, 8; 36:18; etc.) and the nations (25:14; 38:18; etc.). Just as there seems to be no hope whatsoever that the Israelites destroyed in Yahweh's wrath will ever "know that I am Yahweh" in salvation and blessing, the reader cannot expect the nations judged in wrath to know him in a saving sense. We again may compare texts in Ezekiel spoken to Israel and to the nations in oracles of judgment.

> 6:3b, 5–7 — Behold I, even I, shall bring a sword upon you, and I shall destroy your high places. . . . And I shall lay the corpses of the sons of Israel before their altars, and I shall scatter your bones all around your altars. In all of your settlements the cities shall be laid waste and the high places ruined. . . . The slain shall fall in your midst and you shall know that I am Yahweh.

---

43. Other good comparisons are: Ezek 22:15–16 with 30:26; 5:13 with 25:17.

28:23—And I shall send plague upon her [Sidon] and blood into her streets, and in her midst the slain shall fall by the sword that is against her on every side. And they shall know that I am Yahweh.

32:11b–15—The sword of the king of Babylon shall come upon you. By the swords of mighty men I shall cause your multitude to fall, by the most terrible of all the nations. They shall bring to nothing the pride of Egypt, and all its multitude shall perish. I shall destroy all her beasts from beside her great waters, which shall not be disturbed anymore by human feet or beasts' hooves. . . . When I make the land of Egypt a desolation, and when the land is stripped of all that fills it, and when I strike down all who live in her, then they shall know that I am Yahweh.

One faces a tall challenge in interpreting ידע as used in Ezekiel's RFs spoken in judgment. In the texts above, what does it mean to "know that I am Yahweh" as the sword cuts the subject down? What is the content of the "knowledge"? The book of Ezekiel teaches that the nations will know Yahweh's vengeance and wrath. They will learn who is punishing them, the identity of Yahweh as Israel's covenant God, who may by turns punish Israel with exile (39:23) or defend Israel from other nations. The nations will not only experience the truth that Yahweh is wrathful toward them; they will also be confronted by Yahweh himself, who announces in his prophesied actions "I am Yahweh." It is not merely truths *about* Israel's God that the nations come to know. Yahweh announces to Gog: "I shall bring you against my land that *the nations may know me* when before their eyes I show my holiness through you" (38:16), and "I will show my greatness and my holiness and *make myself known* in the eyes of many nations, and they shall know that I am Yahweh" (38:23).[44]

6.2.1.3. *Three Texts that May Raise Questions*
Ezekiel 36:36, one of two texts to which some appeal may be made in support of the idea that the RF comports with a promise of blessing upon the nations, does not truly contradict the conclusion in this section. The nations in 36:36 do not receive any blessing, covenantal or otherwise; they are mere onlookers, observing that the destroyed nation of Israel has been rebuilt: "And/then the nations which remain around you shall know that I am Yahweh, I have rebuilt the ruined places and replanted what was desolate. I, Yahweh, have spoken, and I shall do it."

---

44. Another verse may make the same point: Ezek 35:11 records Yahweh's declaration to Edom: "I shall make myself known among you when I judge you." The MT reads "make myself known among them [ונודעתי בם]," but many scholars follow the LXX reading (σοι = בך) as "more to the point" (Greenberg, *Ezekiel 21–37*, 716). Greenberg follows Zimmerli's lead (*Ezekiel 2*, 226) in suggesting the "MT may have arisen by inadvertent assimilation to the preceding *bm*." Those who favor the MT, perhaps as the *lectio difficilior*, include Allen (*Ezekiel 20–48*, 168) and Block (*Ezekiel 25–48*, 313).

The nations are clearly outside the covenant community looking on with amazement at the restoration of agriculture to such a verdant state—"like the Garden of Eden" (36:35).

Some scholars' mistaken notion that the nations share in the spiritual and material blessings Yahweh rains down upon his own people may result from a confounding of Isaiah and Ezekiel. Studies in Isaiah, the better-known prophecy, can color one's perspective on Ezekiel. Isaiah's use of the creation–creator motif easily moves toward the portrayal of Yahweh's universal concern.[45] In Isaiah, nations are gathered to the land of Israel. Ezekiel's theological focus is more on the exodus event, and so he emphasizes Israel's "new exodus"[46] *out of the nations* and into a renewed covenant relation to Yahweh (36:24–30).

The second text to be referenced as possibly calling into question my conclusion is Ezek 29:16. Preceding verses promise that Yahweh "will gather the Egyptians from the peoples among whom they were scattered and restore the fortunes of Egypt and return them to the land of Pathros" (vv. 13–14a). However, the pericope's overall tone is quite negative: "They shall be a lowly kingdom, the most lowly of kingdoms it shall be, and will never again exalt herself above other nations. I shall make them so small that they shall never again dominate the nations" (14b–15). Joyce has good reason to assert that "the restoration of Egypt which is envisaged in Ezek. 29.13–16 in fact amounts to a humiliation."[47] Ezekiel 29 certainly speaks of no covenant blessing for Egypt. Instead, God's dealings with that land will ensure that the Israelites never again rely on their southern neighbor for political and military assistance, thus "recalling their iniquity in turning to them" (v. 16). The prophesied "restoration" amounts to such a humiliation that it would be folly to depend on Egypt rather than Yahweh (cf. Ps 40:5[4]).[48]

Daniel Block sheds light on why Egypt, in this single text,[49] might have been viewed differently from other nations and been addressed in "a modified restoration oracle," rather than with a prophecy of utter destruction. In an intertextual approach (without using that terminology), he points to the close correspondence between 29:16 and an earlier text, 28:24, articulating Yahweh's purpose in destroying the nations surrounding Israel. His comparison is reproduced below (but adding the RF).[50]

45. See: Isa 42:1–6, 10–12; 45:3–22; 49:6; 52:10; 55:5; 56:3–7; 60:1–9; 61:11; 66:18.

46. Motif analysis of Isaiah shows that he also prophesies a "new exodus," but that motif functions differently (Isa 41:9; 43:5–6, 16–19; 49:17–18; 51:10–11; 52:12; 56:8; 58:8). Isaiah's numerous allusions to Exodus are mostly passing allusions, poetic in nature. See also Zimmerli, "Le nouvel 'exode.'"

47. Joyce, *Divine Initiative*, 154. In his later work, he indicates his uncertainty as to whether the RF in 29:16 has Egypt or Israel as the subject (*Ezekiel*, 182).

48. Greenberg quotes the Psalm text in his commentary (*Ezekiel 21–37*, 607).

49. This text stands out among Ezekiel's oracles against Egypt already quoted in this chapter, which generally read as harshly as any oracles against other nations.

50. Block, *Ezekiel 25–48*, 144.

28:24	29:16

28:24

ולא־יהיה עוד לבית ישראל
סלון ממאיר וקוץ מכאב
מכל סביבתם השאטים אותם
וידעו כי אני אדני יהוה:

29:16

ולא יהיה־עוד לבית ישראל
למבטח
מזכיר עון בפנותם אחריהם
וידעו כי אני אדני יהוה:

And there will be no more
for the house of Israel
a prickling briar or painful thorn
from any of their neighbors
who treated them with contempt.
And they shall know
that I am Lord Yahweh.

And there will be no more
for the house of Israel
an object of trust—
a reminder of iniquity
because they turned to them [Egypt].
And they shall know
that I am Lord Yahweh.

Block says that, in juxtaposition, these two texts show "the differences in the charges Ezekiel had leveled against the six neighbor states on the one hand and against Egypt on the other." While the former are to be condemned and removed from the scene for hostility toward the covenant people, their *Schadenfreude* when Judah collapsed, and their intent to appropriate Judah's territory for themselves (see 35:12), Egypt may be treated with moderation because that nation "had tried to prevent the collapse of Judah." Yahweh can accomplish his purpose of removing Egypt as an "object of trust" for his people "by merely reducing Egypt to vassal status and neutralizing its imperialistic ambitions."[51] This hardly spells covenant blessing and salvation for Egypt. The RFs that conclude these texts are identical and unique in Ezekiel: there are no other examples of the formula in the third person with the double designation for God, אדני יהוה. This strengthens Block's case that these texts echo each other and should be read together: they begin and end the exact same way. In summary, the two texts commonly brought forward (29:16 and 36:36) do not support the contention that RFs anticipate the nations experiencing deliverance or covenantal blessing.

The third text contains no RF addressed to the nations and, therefore, does not call into question the main conclusion of this section (no positive use of the formula when spoken to the nations). However, it may raise doubts about the ancillary conclusion that there is no hopeful message or salvation oracle directed toward the nations in Ezekiel. Chapter 16, which contains plenty of difficulties as an allegory, has an enigmatic conclusion that speaks of Jerusalem's two "sisters," Samaria being an older sibling and Sodom a younger. There is certainly

51. Block, *Ezekiel 25–48*, 145. As Ralph W. Klein suggests, it is best to downplay the notion that Egypt's judgment is moderated because she tried to help Judah (*Ezekiel*, 137). Rather, she posed a more minor threat as a wrong "object of trust."

"restoration" language in 16:53, where Yahweh gives promises and exhortations in the larger text including adjacent verses:

> They are more in the right than you, and so you, too, be ashamed and bear your disgrace, for you have made your sisters look righteous. I shall restore their fortunes (וְשַׁבְתִּי אֶת־שְׁבִיתְהֶן), the fortunes of Sodom and her daughters and the fortunes of Samaria and of her daughters, and I shall restore your fortunes in the midst of them, so that you may bear your disgrace and be ashamed of all that you have done, becoming a consolation to them.

In Ezekiel's rhetoric, the more-righteous Samaria and Sodom must be restored somehow if Jerusalem is to be restored by God.

But what kind of restoration awaits Samaria and Sodom? Should interpreters follow Moshe Greenberg in saying, "a decision of God to *forgive* and restore her [Jerusalem] must in all fairness entail the same for her sisters"?[52] How similar are the restorations of Jerusalem and Samaria/Sodom? The idea of forgiveness does not seem to be required by the text, which speaks instead of the sisters' "return [שׁוּב] to their former state/situation [לְקַדְמָתָן]." Chapter 16 is careful, it seems, to distinguish Jerusalem's restoration from those of other nations, and a comparison of an instance of clear *similitude* (v. 55) with one of clear *distinction* (vv. 60–63) reveals the precise element in which they differ: forgiveness. Verse 55 exemplifies similitude in the application of key terms ("return" and "former state") to both: "And of your sisters, Sodom with her daughters shall return to their former state, and Samaria with her daughters shall return to their former state, and you and your daughters shall return to your former state." But only for Israel does verse 63 add "forgiving" (כָּפַר Piel inf. constr.) to the restoration. The distinction is also emphasized when verses 60–62 employ the language of covenant in conjunction with an RF addressed to Israel:

> But I myself will remember the covenant with you in the days of your youth, and I shall establish [קוּם Hiphil] an everlasting covenant. And you shall remember your ways and be ashamed in taking your sisters, both your elder and your younger; and I shall give them to you as daughters but not on account of the covenant with you [וְלֹא מִבְּרִיתֵךְ]. I myself shall establish my covenant with you, and you shall know that I am Yahweh.

The last phrase of verse 61 is definitely "difficult to interpret,"[53] with its preposition, and one cannot be certain of the best rendering. But good sense can be made of

---

52. Greenberg, *Ezekiel 1–20*, 289 (emphasis added).
53. Zimmerli, *Ezekiel 1*, 353.

the Hebrew in context by taking it to mean "though not as participants in your covenant" (Zimmerli) or "not on the basis of my covenant with you" (NIV).[54]

6.2.1.4. Conclusion

Within Ezekiel's prophecy and during the time of national calamity, attention has reverted almost exclusively to the covenant community. There appears to be little concern for or issue made of the nations, apart from the major section of chapters 25 through 32. (The speeches against Gog in chs. 38–39 are lodged in the section of salvation oracles spoken to Israel.) And what attention is paid to them, when the focus shifts briefly to Yahweh's relationship to the nations, seems subordinate to other interests. The note struck in such passages is always and only one of vindication of Yahweh's name (cf. Exod 9:16) or the defense of the covenant community (through retribution upon her enemies). The note of grace is missing, as is the idea of evangelization, though the public vindication of Yahweh's honor might be viewed as a necessary step toward a future work of grace among the nations.[55] This theme of vindication is a key to understanding the majority of the RFs in Ezekiel (those attached to judgment oracles). The more exclusive focus on Israel, on her correction and restoration, makes sense from any angle. Israel is primary in Yahweh's plan of intervention unfolded in Ezekiel because (though Ezekiel does not make this plain) Israel's restoration is preliminary to her serving fruitfully as a witness to Yahweh among the nations. Ezekiel leaves unsaid the truth so prominent in Isaiah: gracious divine action toward the covenant community is directed toward the goal of blessing the nations. One must study elsewhere in the OT to learn that the nations will be blessed only through a revitalized covenant people, through Abraham's *true* seed.

One properly draws the conclusion that the idea of the nations' salvation as a part of Yahweh's plan is neither propounded nor contradicted; it is simply absent in Ezekiel. The RFs spoken to the nations lend no support to those who wish to interpret Ezekiel as prophesying the conversion of the nations to trust and worship of Yahweh as their own God. Paul Hanson argues for a more inclusive vision: "His judgment and his salvation were both parts of a universal plan of bringing the knowledge of Yahweh to all the world, and bringing šālôm to a people living in obedience, righteousness, and purity in a city named 'Yahweh is there.'"[56] It is true that "all the world," the nations, will come to "know that I am Yahweh," but, as in

54. Zimmerli, Ezekiel 1, 333. Cf. NJPS ("though they are not of your covenant") and ESV. Greenberg prefers to read the preposition causatively with the sense of "not because you [Jerusalem] have kept the covenant" (Ezekiel 1–20, 292). Block explains well the interpretive options and renders the phrase "even though they are not your covenant partners" (Ezekiel 1–24, 512).

55. Concern for the vindication of Yahweh's name before the nations in his dealings with his people is also evident in Exodus (see 32:12–14).

56. Hanson, People Called, 222.

Exodus so in Ezekiel, the interpreter should mark a difference between "knowing Yahweh" and "knowing Yahweh's salvation." In terms of the loci in systematic theology, one can distinguish between revelation and salvation. In Ezekiel, the recipients of the former outnumber the recipients of the latter.

6.2.2. *The Formula Connected to Yahweh's Acting in History*

When Jehoiakim burns the scroll of Jeremiah's prophecies (Jer 35), he exemplifies what the Bible presents as a common sin of Israel over the centuries: stubborn refusal to heed the word of Yahweh through his messengers. When Moses is sent to speak Yahweh's comforting promises of salvation to the elders, they listen at first (Exod 4:31) but later "did not listen to Moses because of their despondency [קֹצֶר רוּחַ] and cruel servitude" (6:9). Even Moses himself struggles with unbelief and impatience: "And rescued? You have not rescued your people" (5:23). Because the people faithlessly ignore his word, God chooses to reveal himself in another way, one that would prove irrefutable (cf. Exod 14:31). He would directly intervene in the history of the nation. In Ezekiel we see a similar pattern where the people refuse to believe the word. Yahweh tells the prophet, "the house of Israel is unwilling to listen to you for they are unwilling to listen to me" (3:7). There is the strong implication in the judgment oracles that follow that Yahweh has decided to add to his words powerful actions that the nation will be unable to gainsay.

In Exodus, the RF is always connected with Yahweh's self-revelation in the area of historical experience, with a direct act of Yahweh, or with his giving the sign of the Sabbath.[57] Key phrasing often combined with the RF is: "I shall do *x*; then you shall know" and "when I make/have made *x*, you shall know." The same connection to experience of Yahweh's acts or to the institution of the Sabbath in history is characteristic of Ezekiel's RFs. Hardly any formula in Ezekiel falls outside this pattern. That connection to historical event is crucial. It seems misleading to say, "history is only ancillary to Yahweh's self-demonstration, for the 'I am Yahweh' addressed to the listener is the real focus."[58] In Ezekiel's theology, Yahweh's words are being disregarded by the people, and the time has come for Yahweh to act so as to prove "I did not threaten in vain to bring this evil upon them" (6:10). God says, "I, Yahweh, have spoken and I shall do it" (22:14), and "all my words which

---

57. See the extensive arguments of Austin Surls that, in Exodus, the name "Yahweh" cannot be understood according to etymology: the name has meaning and is recognized (the RF) in its use within the story of God's saving acts, and this literary context determines how Israel and Egypt "could now ascribe terrifying power, sovereignty, faithfulness to promises, and salvific concern for his covenant people in the name 'YHWH'" (*Making Sense*, 115). Cf. Eslinger's research discussed above in ch. 2, n. 202.

58. Zimmerli, "'Offenbarung' im Alten Testament," 30. Cited in Botterweck, "יָדַע *yada'*," in *TDOT*, 5:471.

I speak, each will be performed" (12:28). The strongest assertion comes in 24:14: "I, Yahweh, have spoken. It shall come to pass and I shall do it. I shall not go back, and I shall not spare, and I shall not repent" (cf. Num 14:35: אני יהוה דברתי אם־לא זאת אעשה לכל־העדה הרעה הזאת).

All of the strict formulas and expansions cannot point to anything other than direct divine intervention in the realm of history and personal experience. The following selection of RFs from Exodus and Ezekiel may be taken as representative:

1. You shall know that I am Yahweh your God, who brought you out from under the burdens of the Egyptians.
2. The Egyptians shall know . . . when I stretch out my hand against Egypt and bring the children of Israel out from them.
3. I will distinguish the land of Goshen on that day . . . no swarm of flies will be there, so that you shall know that I, Yahweh, am in this land.
4. You may tell your children . . . how I toyed [עלל Hithpael] with the Egyptians and set my signs among them, that you may know . . . [59]
5. The Egyptians shall know . . . when I get glory through Pharaoh, his chariots . . .
6. You shall fall by the sword, and at the border of Israel I shall judge you. Then you shall know . . .
7. They shall know . . . when I scatter them among the nations.
8. You shall know . . . when I bring you into the land of Israel.
9. To the people of the East . . . I shall give it [Moab] as a possession . . . I shall execute judgments upon Moab and then they shall know . . . [60])

In short, Israel and the nations will know that Yahweh himself "strikes the blow" when judgment comes. And, in salvation oracles, they will have a revelation of God when Yahweh himself has accomplished the restoration of the people to their land and to a proper covenant relationship. They can come to that realization because a clarifying, interpreting word has been spoken by Yahweh along with his acting in the realm of history. Word and action in tandem bring recognition and knowledge of Yahweh.

One possible exception to the rule requires attention. Greenberg says the "recognition-clause" in 11:12 "is unique in its reference to Israel's sin rather than to God's action, which will bring about recognition of his authority." Beginning with the end of 11:11, the text reads: אשפט אתכם: וידעתם כי־אני יהוה אשר בחקי לא הלכתם. Further, Greenberg remarks on how "this singular turn-about, emphasizing the ground of

59. "Toyed" is the rendering suggested by Brevard Childs (*Exodus*, 126). Durham has an expansive translation: "amused myself aggravating" (*Exodus*, 131).
60. The references for these nine passages are: Exod 6:7; 7:5; 8:18[22]; 10:2; 14:18; Ezek 11:10; 12:15; 20:42; 25:10–11.

the punishment rather than the punishment itself, inverts the order of the elements of 5:7–10 (where ground [vs. 7] precedes consequence) and thus calls attention to its echoing character."[61] Greenberg chooses to read אֲשֶׁר as a conjunction introducing a causal clause: "for" or "because." Others agreeing with this rendering are Block, Ronald Hals,[62] and the translators of the NIV and ESV. Another option widely accepted is to translate אֲשֶׁר as a relative particle—"according to whose statutes you have not walked"—a rendering favored by Zimmerli, Leslie Allen, and the translators of NJPS and NRSV.[63] If one confronts grammatical ambiguity in connecting 11:12a and 12b, and if the RF follows immediately after the word about Yahweh's punishment of Jerusalem's leadership ("at the border of Israel I shall judge you"), can one say with conviction that the recognition is not attributable to God's action? No, one cannot, especially in light of the parallel in 11:10. This section's claim that the RF (and the recognition of which it speaks) is connected to Yahweh's acting in history still appears to stand. Even where a few of the *expansions* of the formula "point to God's qualities, not to the events in which these features become known,"[64] the linkage with God's action remains strong within the oracle that contains the RF (e.g., 38:16; 39:7). In no case is Yahweh known apart from his actions.

Related to this topic is the question of why the RF does not appear in chapters 40–48. A partial answer may be that that formula has a strongly prophetic element, while the last nine chapters mainly describe a golden age as though it has come, an age when prophecies of restoration seem already to be fulfilled.[65] There hardly seems any place for declarations that Israel "shall know that I am Yahweh," for the people dwell safely in the land in fellowship with Yahweh (וְשֵׁם־הָעִיר מִיּוֹם יְהוָה שָׁמָּה; 48:35). That is, in the perfect restoration of Israel with their permanent temple, kingdom, land inheritance, covenant relationship, and so on, the prophecy latent in the formula is fulfilled.[66] But some might require a fuller answer to the question of why the RF fails to appear in chapters 40–48. Two observations are helpful: the prophecy rarely employs the formula in the vision-report genre,[67] and

61. Greenberg, *Ezekiel 1–20*, 188.
62. Block, *Ezekiel 1–24*, 328, 337–38; Hals, *Ezekiel*, 65.
63. Zimmerli, *Ezekiel 1*, 229; Allen, *Ezekiel 1–19*, 128.
64. Odell, "Are You He?" 128. In examining the formulas, the expansions, and their immediate contexts, Odell draws "the conclusion that the recognition formula retains its connection to the idea that God will be made manifest in history" (129).
65. "The fact that God has already constructed the Temple" in the concluding vision raises questions for interpreters like Jon Levenson (*Theology of the Program*, 45). Does this "mean that man has no role in its construction"? Levenson firmly says no; he avers that Ezekiel sees a mere model and that Israel must follow that pattern in her construction. But there is little evidence for this.
66. The restoration may accompany the knowledge "that I am Yahweh," or it may be premised on that knowledge.
67. As already noted, there are no RFs in Ezek 1–3, 8–11 (except for the oracle of judgment against Jerusalem's leadership in 11:5–12, which interrupts the vision report), or 40–48. The only RFs occurring in a vision report are found in ch. 37.

40–48 contain no oracles prophesying Yahweh's intervention in history, which is the context for all RFs.

Because of this extraordinary stress on recognizing Yahweh in his actions, quite a few interpreters of both Exodus and Ezekiel translate the formula so as to reflect this link. Martin Luther used *erfahren sollen* almost exclusively in translating the RF in Exodus and Ezekiel, rather than *merken, erkennen,* or another verb. *Erfahren* tends to carry the connotation of "coming to know by experience," at least more so than its synonyms. Luther's choice continues to be reflected in German Bibles to this day.[68] W. Schottroff speaks of translating ידע with *erfahren* because the Hebrew verb so often denotes perception of objects and circumstances in the world through either experience or the reports of others.[69] (Recall how ראה replaces ידע in the formula at Ezek 21:4[20:48].)[70] In his Exodus commentary, John Durham translates, "you will know by experience that I am Yahweh."[71] Though such a translation might be termed more of a paraphrase because it fails to capture the terseness that usually characterizes the formula, it does communicate in a general way the means whereby the knowledge of Yahweh is apprehended. "Knowing by experience" can be overstressed, however, and should not be taken as the definition of ידע in all occurrences in Ezekiel, even where used near the RF (see 39:23).

The prophet is clear in saying that Yahweh is known by interpreted historical events. G. A. Cooke says that "one of the chief truths emphasized throughout the Book is that God reveals Himself in history, especially in the history of his people."[72] The relationship between revelation and history has in the past been of great interest to contemporary theologians and is worth exploring at a depth not feasible here. I merely note that there was a protracted debate, especially following the publication of Pannenberg (ed.), *Offenbarung als Geschichte,* in 1961,[73] and that several positions have been adopted by scholars.

How is the revelation or knowledge of God mediated to us? Some give strong emphasis to historical events as the locus of revelation (G. Ernest Wright),[74] while

---

68. One exception would be the old Kautzsch study Bible, which consistently uses *erkennen sollen* to translate the RF in both Exodus and Ezekiel. See Kautzsch, *Mose bis Ezechiel.*

69. W. Schottroff, "ידע *jdᶜ* erkennen," in *THAT,* 1:686.

70. The lexemes ידע and ראה are often used in tandem. See especially Exod 16:6–7 and Ezek 21:4[20:48] and 39:21–22, which are related to the RF. But one may also note: Exod 2:25; Num 24:16–17; Deut 11:2; Isa 29:15; 41:20; 44:9, 18; 58:3; 61:9; Jer 2:23; 5:1; 12:3.

71. Durham, *Exodus,* 72. He later expands on his translation by saying the exodus "will be a rescue that will teach Israel by experience the truth of the claim made in the name 'Yahweh' and in the statement 'I am Yahweh'" (78).

72. Cooke, *Ezekiel,* 423.

73. Examining the controversy over "revelation as history" and "revelation as word" within OT studies specifically are Knierim, "Offenbarung im Alten Testament," and Preuss, *Theologie des Alten Testaments,* 1:228–58.

74. G. E. Wright writes that "history is the chief medium of revelation" (*God Who Acts,* 13).

others stress the divine word (Th. C. Vriezen).[75] While the more refined positions of Zimmerli and Rendtorff give an important place to both historical event and the divine word, they prioritize them differently. Rendtorff follows von Rad more closely in giving priority to historical events (as tradition) in revelation. Von Rad famously said that "the Old Testament is a history-book (*Geschichtsbuch*)," and that "from first to last Israel manifestly takes as her starting-point the absolute priority in theology of event over '*logos*.'"[76] Zimmerli gave priority to the word instead of event, and this generated a conflict with Rendtorff. Setting quotes representing their positions alongside each other is illuminating. When Rendtorff argued that history "is *not* something penultimate which has only a subservient function in relation to the self-manifestation of Jahweh," Zimmerli said, "history is only ancillary to Yahweh's self-demonstration, for the 'I am Yahweh' addressed to the listener is the real focus."[77] The present study draws the conclusion that event and word need be neither set at variance with each other nor separated. Event without the word is uninterpreted and possibly meaningless for the observer, while word without event is not the demonstration Ezekiel's oracles claim it is.[78] This linkage comes to the fore especially in Ezek 29:21, where Yahweh promises to "make a horn spring forth for the house of Israel" *and* to open Ezekiel's mouth among them (to interpret?); "then they shall know that I am Yahweh."

In Ezekiel's theology, and in the prophets more generally, there is frequently a merging of event and word. This occurs where the prophet's proclamation (word) of God's mighty acts (history) in the past is also the occasion for declaring (word) both what God intends to accomplish among his people (event) and how those future events should be interpreted (word).[79] Reventlow finds a similar insight in von Rad:

> However, history and word are related to each other, for the way in which these
> historical actions are open to constantly new interpretations by later generations

75. See Vriezen, *Outline of Old Testament Theology*, 133: "In other words, Israel owes this knowledge to the special revelation granted to the prophets, from the earliest times (Abraham or Moses); and it was preserved to the end by the Prophets alone, who spoke the explanatory Word of God all through Israel's history." Vriezen does not completely overlook the historical (see 136–38).

76. Von Rad, *Old Testament Theology*, 2:357, 1:116.

77. Rendtorff, "The Concept of Revelation," 46; Zimmerli, "'Offenbarung' im Alten Testament," 30.

78. Here, the intention is to be true (in a descriptive sense) to Ezekiel's prophecy and its categories. While many today speak of "the collapse of history" within OT Theology, historical reference and meaningfulness are of monumental importance in the proclamation of the prophets and cannot be dispensed with or disparaged. Ezekiel (not sharing any post-Enlightenment problems or strategies) could never have granted Gotthold Lessing's premise that there is, in the events prophesied, something "accidental." On the "collapse," see Perdue, *Collapse of History* and *Reconstructing Old Testament Theology*.

79. In one place, Zimmerli mentions another linkage between event and word: "Ezekiel . . . sets in motion mighty events through his word" (*Ezekiel 1*, 259).

"in a direct ratio to their understanding of their own position in the light of their fathers' history with God" (II, 375 = ET 361) provides an ongoing context of interpretation: "History becomes word and word becomes history" (II, 371 = ET 358). Here the future, too, is always interpreted in the light of experiences of the past.[80]

6.2.3. Yahweh Acts to Reveal His Holy Name and to Guard Its Honor

From a literary and rhetorical standpoint, the RF in Ezekiel usually forms the conclusion (*letzten Bestandteil*) or "target statement of a larger discursive sequence" (*Ziel- und Schlußaussage eines Wortgefüges*).[81] Theologically, it states both the purpose and goal of God's self-revelation in historical events. He acts and, just as importantly, tells the interpretation of his acts in history, so people should recognize and acknowledge the Actor's claim, "I am Yahweh," the God who maintains the honor of his holy name by keeping covenant. In both Exodus and Ezekiel, God is re-revealing himself by his name, Yahweh, to a nation that has forgotten him.[82] But there is something more. Great dishonor has been brought to the name Yahweh by an insolent Pharaoh who sneers: "Who is Yahweh, that I should listen to his voice and let Israel go? I do not know Yahweh and I will not let Israel go" (Exod 5:2). Therefore, Yahweh will strike Egypt with plague after plague in order to vindicate his name. Through his spokesman, God declares to Pharaoh, "by this you will know that I am Yahweh" (Exod 7:17). In Ezekiel's time, dishonor is being brought upon the name of Yahweh by the detestable practices (תועבת; 43×[83]) of his people to whom he is bound by covenant, and also by the punishment of exile that Israel has endured (36:20–21).

In Exodus and in Ezekiel, covenant promises, sealed by the attached name *Yahweh*, have been made and must be kept. In light of God's explanation of his own acts in Ezek 36, one might assert that the true context of the divine oracles is not so much the condition of the people as it is the injury done to Yahweh's name and honor and his commitment to act to vindicate his name. "It is not for your sake, O house of Israel, that I am about to act, *but for the sake of my holy name*, which you have profaned among the nations to which you have gone. I will vindicate the holiness of my great name" (36:22–23). This commitment brings him to act against his own people, and also for them, but this is no contradiction. C. Hassell Bullock points out:

<hr/>

80. Reventlow, *Problems of Old Testament Theology*, 74.
81. Zimmerli, *I Am Yahweh*, 33 (*Gottes Offenbarung*, 46).
82. In Ezekiel's historical retrospective, the nation had already corrupted themselves with the idols of Egypt during their slavery (Ezek 20:7–8; 23:27); this turning away from the God of their ancestors was a *forgetting*. The prophet then makes his case that the Israel of his day is in spiritual solidarity with the earlier idolatrous generations (20:30) and has forgotten Yahweh (שׁכח; 22:12 and 23:35).
83. Humbert, "Le substantif *to'ēbā*," 217.

When [Yahweh's] covenant people and the nations around them came to acknowledge who he was, then he would be truly vindicated. To say, however, that he was intent upon protecting his own reputation is not in the least to suggest that he had no concern with Israel's. Rather it is to suggest that the Lord was most true to his people when he was most true to himself. When he was true to himself, he could not be false to Israel.[84]

Ezekiel so stresses Yahweh's side of the argument with Israel because, if the exiles were to understand Yahweh himself, they needed to understand Yahweh's grievances and his impulsion to act on behalf of his name. Yahweh was compelled to act not only because his covenant people had refused to guard the honor of his holy name (sin of omission), but because Israel herself had actively profaned the name (sin of commission).

In Exodus, one senses that the revelation of the divine name is nearly identical to the revelation of Yahweh himself. It has been argued that, in OT times, to know a person's name was much the same as knowing the person.[85] Though this idea has been challenged and caution is in order,[86] there is some validity to it. Scholars today still make the claim that:

> In the ancient Sem. world a person's name often carried more significance than an identification mark; it was considered to be a description of character or conditions. Having or giving a name was related to, if not determinative of, one's existence (Gervitz, "Of Patriarchs and Puns," *HUCA* 46, 1975, 33).... It is because the name of a person, place, or thing was considered deeply bound up with the character and perhaps the destiny that naming played an important part in the narratives.[87]

Especially through its link to accounts of God's mighty acts (see n. 57 above), the name *Yahweh* does communicate something of the power and nature of the God of the OT, carrying with it the authority and the holiness of Yahweh himself. For this reason, that name must be hallowed, not misused (the third commandment). Ignorance of that name can be tragic and dangerous. This seems an accurate

---

84. Bullock, *Introduction*, 251.

85. Walther Eichrodt has written: "If the saying *nomina sunt realia* is valid in any context, it is surely that of the divine name in the ancient world" (*Theology of the Old Testament*, 1:178).

86. Issuing a challenge and urging caution are: Barr, "Symbolism of Names"; A. S. van der Woude, "שֵׁם *šēm* Name," in *THAT*, 2:935–63; and F. V. Reiterer with H.-J. Fabry, "שֵׁם *šēm*," in *ThWAT*, 8:122–76. The most current discussions, offering valuable correctives, are Hess, "Names," and Surls, *Making Sense*.

87. Allen P. Ross, "שֵׁם," in *NIDOTTE*, 4:147. Ross steers clear of earlier excessive claims, e.g., "a name is regarded as possessing an inherent power which exercises a constraint upon its bearer; he must conform to his essential nature as expressed in his name" (quoted from R. Abba, "Name," in *IDB*, 3:501).

assessment when one recalls Moses's plea to God to reveal his name before he took God's message to Israel. He said, "they might ask, 'what is his name?'" (Exod 3:13). Were Moses not to have an answer, he would be disqualified as Yahweh's spokesperson. God granted Moses to know his name and told him, "Yahweh is my name forever, by this [name] I am to be remembered from generation to generation" (3:15). Thereafter, with the name committed to him, Moses could go confidently to Pharaoh to speak in the name of Yahweh (5:23).

The plagues upon Egypt became a declaration of Yahweh's name, both to the judged and to the redeemed, with the accompanying RFs. God sent Moses to Pharaoh with a terrifying message: "I have raised you up for this very purpose, that I might show you my power and *that my name might be proclaimed* in all the earth" (Exod 9:16; NIV). Beyond the plague narratives, Yahweh intends the deliverance at the Red Sea to be the occasion when his name is declared. "I shall get glory for myself over Pharaoh and all his forces, and the Egyptians shall know that I am Yahweh" (14:4, cf. vv. 17–18). In fulfillment of this prophecy, all Israel sings praise to Yahweh. Viewing the bodies of their pursuers washing up on the shore (14:30), they sing, "Yahweh is a warrior; Yahweh is his name!" (15:3). The nation ought, then, to have understood the importance of jealously guarding the name (Exod 20:7).

According to the Exodus narratives and Ezekiel's recounting of Israel's history, the generation who experienced the exodus—God's own people—did not guard the honor of the name, but rather ruined or defiled themselves with idolatry when they were in the wilderness (Exod 32:7–8; cf. Ezek 20:13–20). On what basis does Moses plead with Yahweh to spare the rebel nation? Moses appeals to Yahweh that he should relent from his anger against the people he has so famously delivered because, if Yahweh does destroy Israel, then Egypt can then slander him for having an "evil purpose in bringing them out" (32:12). Concern for God's reputation is an all-important issue in Exod 32 and in Ezekiel's reflections on Yahweh's purposes in the wilderness to act "for the sake of my name."[88]

Gaining perspective with a look back over the course of redemptive history, Ezekiel realizes the importance of guarding the honor of the name, and he also realizes, perhaps with a sense of horror, the guilt attached to the sin of profaning it. His response to this truth is first to explain to the exiles how Yahweh vindicated his holiness at the time of the exodus, and he provides this account in chapter 20. Ezekiel records Yahweh as saying, "But I acted for the sake of my name, to keep it from being profaned" (vv. 9, 14, 22). The second aspect of his response is to explain how Yahweh is vindicating his holy name in their own day. Four times over, Ezekiel

---

88. This explanation contrasts with certain ideological criticism, positing that Yahweh's jealousy for his name reflects an egomaniac threatening ecojustice. See the labeling of the RF as the "divine ego formula" in Habel, "Silence of the Lands," 135–36, and Kelle, "Dealing with the Trauma," 477–78.

denounces the people for polluting (טמא Piel) and profaning (חלל Piel) Yahweh's "holy name" (20:39; 36:20–23; 39:7; 43:8). In Ezekiel's day, because Yahweh's people do not honor and protect his name, Yahweh himself is compelled to pity (חמל; 36:21), consecrate (קדש Piel; 36:23), make known (ידע Hiphil; 39:7), and jealously guard (קנא Piel; 39:25) his name. Certain judgment for Israel is bound up with their abuse of the name, and the mere declaration of "Yahweh" in the RF serves to emphasize the connection between judgment and the name. Every utterance of the name in judgment oracles reinforces in hearers' minds that profanation of the name has roused Yahweh to guard his honor. How profound that Yahweh's response to a profaning of his holy name is the fresh declaration of it in the RF!

Beyond judgment, Yahweh will also act to restore his people "for his name's sake." The grace of this holy God is seen in his promise to deal with his people "for my name's sake and not according to your evil ways nor according to your corrupt practices" (20:44). The restoration and blessing of the nation announced with the RF also vindicate and glorify the name. This is the significance of the final vision (chs. 40–48). Ezekiel is given a detailed look at the perfect restoration that awaits God's people. The glory of Yahweh enters the future temple, and there at the foot of the throne, Ezekiel hears: "[This is] where I will live among the children of Israel forever. And the house of Israel will not defile my holy name any longer—neither they nor their kings—by their whoring and by the lifeless idols [בפגרי; dead bodies?] of their kings at their high places" (43:7). Israel will give evidence that they finally know the name and revere it when they have put away all idolatry. The God who had to depart his temple because the people defiled his name will never need depart it again.

6.2.4. The Irresistibility of Yahweh's Self-Revelation

Considering how Ezekiel "is concerned above all else to defend the honor of Yahweh's name," Zimmerli joins others inclined to regard him as "the Calvin of the prophets."[89] Yet there is another "Calvinistic" emphasis in Ezekiel's theology besides God-centeredness and the focus on God's majesty: the stress on absolute divine sovereignty. God may be resisted up to a point, either by his prophet or by his people,[90] but his ultimate purposes cannot be thwarted. This is another similarity between the prophecy and Exodus, for much is made of divine initiative in both. Theologians have long been drawn to the two books in discussions of the

---

89. Zimmerli, *Old Testament Theology*, 207. Marten Woudstra calls Ezekiel "the John Calvin of the Old Testament" ("Edom and Israel," 26).

90. In Exodus, Moses's resistance to Yahweh's call is plain to see. Was Ezekiel also reluctant and resistant? Block and others point to suggestions in the text that Ezekiel was reluctant, at least in some measure (*Ezekiel 1–24*, 11–12). Phinney, "The Prophetic Objection," suggests that 4:12–15 may have been added to the call narrative of chs. 1–3 so as to conform to the Mosaic paradigm of a resisted call.

Table 10. Divine Promises to Act in Exodus 6:6–8

I am Yahweh (אני יהוה)
   ↳ I will bring you forth (והוצאתי אתכם)
   ↳ I will free you (והצלתי אתכם)
   ↳ I will redeem you (וגאלתי אתכם)
   ↳ I will take you as my people (ולקחתי אתכם לי לעם)
   ↳ I will be God to you (והייתי לכם לאלהים)
    Recognition Formula (וידעתם כי אני יהוה אלהיכם)
   ↳ I will bring you into the land (והבאתי אתכם אל־הארץ)
   ↳ and I will give it to you (ונתתי אתה לכם)
I am Yahweh (אני יהוה)

---

relationship between the sovereignty of God and human responsibility.[91] What do we make of the narratives in Exodus in which Pharaoh hardens his own heart, and Yahweh also hardens Pharaoh's heart?[92] How do we understand the prophecy of Ezekiel in which Israel, on the one hand, is exhorted to "get a new heart and new spirit" (18:31) but, on the other, also hears assurances that Yahweh will give a "new heart and new spirit" (36:26; cf. 11:19)?

For the RFs in Exodus and Ezekiel, is "knowing" contingent on a favorable human response, perhaps even conversion? In Exod 6:6–8, there is deep significance in the seven verbal clauses ("I will" statements) being, first, syntactically subordinate to the SPF, and, second, connected with the first RF in the book (Table 10). Only in the context of Yahweh's sure promise to act and his fulfillment of his promises will the nation know him and the glory of his covenant name. But, when he acts, it seems there is no hazard that those acts will fail to result in human recognition or acceptance of Yahweh's self-assertion. In Ezekiel, in the face of Israel's rebellion—מרי and related forms occur twenty-two times—Yahweh purposes to act incontrovertibly to assert himself and the honor of his name. No matter whether Pharaoh and Israel are hard-hearted (קשה; e.g., Exod 7:3 and Ezek 3:7) toward God's word, Yahweh will have his way.

There seems little basis for Zimmerli's attempt to find some human freedom of decision to respond when confronted with God's intervention. Though Zimmerli acknowledges "the fact that the statement of recognition in the divine view must always resonate something of a concluding finality,"[93] he wishes to join the "purely indicative translation" ("they *shall* know that I am Yahweh") to another

---

91. Or, alternatively, divine initiative and human response. For extended discussion, see especially Joyce, *Divine Initiative*.

92. Pharaoh is said to harden (כבד) his own heart in Exod 8:15 and 32 and 9:34, and Yahweh hardens (חזק) Pharaoh's heart in Exod 4:21; 7:3 (קשה); 9:12; 10:1 (כבד), 20, 27; 11:10; 14:4, 8, 17. In other texts there is ambiguity about who hardens (7:13, 14, 22; 8:19; 9:7, 35).

93. Zimmerli, *I Am Yahweh*, 37.

less forceful one: "They *should* recognize that I am Yahweh." Positing that both elements are always contained in prophetic pronouncements, Zimmerli says that accepting the second sense alongside the first "allows the imperative that confronts human beings to resonate in their freedom of decision and calls them to obedience." He adds that it is difficult "to determine which of the two accents emerge [*sic*] more strongly in any given instance."[94] I disagree. Given that "the statement of recognition here in the *perfectum consecutivum* seems quite unobtrusively to follow the foregoing *perfecta consecutiva* that depict Yahweh's acts,"[95] it is best to interpret the prophesied acts and prophesied recognition as of equal certainty. Perhaps one may go further and suggest that both the prophesied acts and the human recognition of God result from a divine work,[96] the recognition in accord with the gift of a new heart and spirit where saving knowledge is concerned.

The RF in Exodus and Ezekiel hardly carries any intonation of appeal. It intones a certainty,[97] not an invitation to reflect on and accept the truths and divine Person revealed. Pharaoh *shall*, not should, "know that I am Yahweh" when God acts in judgment (Exod 7:17; Ezek 29:3–6). The RF not only "expresses the *intended effect* of the event predicted in the oracle";[98] it expresses what Yahweh will inevitably accomplish. Any shouted opposition to his self-assertion is drowned out by the reassertion "I am Yahweh!" backed by divine action. God will brook no reply. Any contrary response is answered by God's action.

This pattern characterizes the cycle of plagues upon Egypt in Exodus and judgments upon Israel throughout her history as recorded in Ezekiel. Human resistance to God's plan, far from frustrating the divine purpose, ironically seems a part of God's plan.[99] There is a grand and also terrible aspect of divine sovereignty here, where both Pharaoh's and, later, Israel's stubbornness and rebellion are prophesied (Exod 3:19; 7:3, 13, 22; 8:15, 19; 9:12, 35; 11:9; Ezek 2:3–5; 3:7; 14:21–23). In all human resistance, Yahweh is working out his purpose to show his power and have his name proclaimed in all the earth (Exod 9:16; 10:1–2; 11:9; 14:4, 17–18; Ezek 38:16, 17–23; 39:1–7).

94. Zimmerli, *I Am Yahweh*, 37.

95. Zimmerli, *I Am Yahweh*, 37.

96. In keeping with much Protestant theology since the Reformation, Karl Barth writes, "Knowledge of God is a knowledge completely effected and determined from the side of its object, from the side of God" (*Dogmatics in Outline*, 24).

97. Cf. Zimmerli's view that the RF "demands acknowledgment of this God who comes in history and is near in his revelation" (*I Am Yahweh*, 97) with Lapsley's criticism of a latent imperative, "should" (*Can These Bones Live?* 123).

98. Greenberg, *Ezekiel 1–20*, 133 (emphasis added).

99. In Exodus, each decision of Pharaoh is prophesied: his refusal to allow Israel to leave throughout the first nine plagues, his decision to expel Israel after the tenth, his decision to chase after Israel when the former slaves appeared to be hemmed in by the sea, and finally the decision to follow Israel into the sea. Time after time, Pharaoh and his officials act "just as Yahweh had said" (כאשר דבר יהוה; 7:13, 22; 8:15, 19; 9:12, 35).

Perhaps Zimmerli has not fully considered the link between the RFs of Exodus and Ezekiel at this point: most formulas—as an absolute declaration (perfect *waw*-conjunctive),[100] "they *shall* know"—are directed to those who have no
inclination or will to acknowledge Yahweh. The assertions are emptied of power
and meaning if they must forever wait for a willing response. It is false to say that
Yahweh is not known on account of his actions and self-revelation *until* human
beings accept the validity of the actions with their accompanying claim. To say
that God is known not so much in his actions and word as in human response to
a divine encounter is some distance removed from the theology of Ezekiel, with
its "radical theocentricity" (Joyce). There is no escaping the cumulative force of
the repeated refrain. The truth of Yahweh and about Yahweh will be hammered
home. Yes, the repetitions of the RF, which seem to irk Zimmerli and others, must
say something about the receptivity of the prophet's audience. (Driving a nail into
an oak plank requires many more hammer blows than driving it into pine.) One
must be careful, however, not to miss the additional point made by the repetitions:
Yahweh's determination that he be known. Whether people "listen or refuse to
listen" matters not for the inevitable outcome; "they shall know" (2:5).

Though there is theological conjunction between Exodus and Ezekiel on this
point that Yahweh's self-revelation is ultimately irresistible, the reader notes a difference as well. The narratives of Exodus reveal the fulfillment of the prophecy in
the RF: Egypt and Israel do come to know Yahweh. Ezekiel, however, offers no
similar narrative of human response to the oracles; there is no real testimony to
recognition. The divine prophecy, "you shall know that I am Yahweh," is truly the
last word. In Exodus, Israel's doubts that God will fulfill his word are overcome
(6:9; 14:10–12) and the nation evinces they recognize Yahweh (12:27; 14:31). In the
case of Pharaoh, who initially denies Yahweh (5:2), he gradually, grudgingly comes
to recognize Yahweh's power.[101] The prophecy of the RF in Exodus is finally fulfilled in two stages. Pharaoh initially submits and sends Israel out, but Yahweh
intends a final Egyptian recognition, not in submission but in the destruction of
the hard-hearted. The Egyptians die "knowing Yahweh" as their enemy (14:25).

Yahweh's holy name is to be vindicated when Israel and the nations *know* him.
As already stated, that acknowledgment will differ widely in its practical effect,
depending on whether it is effected by unstoppable destruction (upon Israel or
the nations) or by fulfilled promises of blessing and restoration (for Israel alone).
Ezekiel does not appear to entertain for a moment the notion that Yahweh could

100. See n. 62 in ch. 3.

101. At first, Pharaoh is defiant (Exod 5:2, 6–9; 7:22–23), but the severity of the plagues begins to
show an impact in 8:8 and 18, where Pharaoh asks Moses to intercede for him with Yahweh. In 9:27–28,
the proud ruler confesses: "I have done wrong [חָטָאתִי] this time; Yahweh is the righteous one; I and
my people are the guilty. Pray to Yahweh!" Other texts to note in the progressive recognition of
Yahweh are 10:7 and 16–17 and 12:31–32.

be frustrated in vindicating himself because of people's failure to cooperate. In Ezekiel's theology, as in Exodus, God is surely able to accomplish his will, and his stated will is that his mighty acts in concert with his word will elicit from his creatures the acknowledgment of Yahweh. God's acts do not occur for their own sake, but rather are purposefully directed at Israel and the other nations who "shall know."

6.2.5. The Nature of the Knowledge of God Implied by the Formula

John Calvin is surely right that different kinds of knowledge are denoted in the different contexts of the RFs in Ezekiel.[102] On the one hand, those the Reformer terms "the reprobate" will know Yahweh as their judge through historical "proofs of His anger," while on the other, some will come to a knowledge that "brings a sweet taste of paternal love."[103] He indicates that there is no simple, consistent answer to the question about the nature of the knowledge of God implied by the RF.[104] It is necessary here to interpret more broadly the theological content of the formula.

It was once the custom in biblical theology to distinguish between ancient Greek and Hebrew modes of thought. James Barr subjected this approach to a thorough critique in *The Semantics of Biblical Language*, showing that faulty exegesis usually results if and when that sharp distinction between the dynamic, concrete, and totality type of Hebrew thought and the static, abstract, division-producing Greek thought is said to tie in to distinctions of language.[105] Mode of thought ought to be more carefully differentiated from expression.

Barr's criticisms do apply to the following quote from Geerhardus Vos, in which the old Princeton theologian contrasts a Western (essentially Greek) concept of knowledge with the oriental:

> According to the former, "to know" means to mirror the reality of a thing in one's consciousness. The Shemitic and Biblical idea is to have the reality of something practically interwoven with the inner experience of life. Hence "to know" can stand in the Biblical idiom for "to love," "to single out in love." Because God desires to be known after this fashion, He has caused his revelation to take place in the milieu of the historical life of the people.[106]

102. Calvin, *Commentaries . . . Ezekiel*, 2:341.
103. Calvin, *Commentaries . . . Ezekiel*, 2:341.
104. As mentioned earlier, Exodus and Ezekiel together reveal two distinct experiences of *knowing*. For the judged, it is a helpless, despairing *realization* that God is powerfully acting against them and announcing, "I am Yahweh." For those delivered, it is a willing, full *recognition* of Yahweh as their covenant-keeping God.
105. Barr, *Semantics*, esp. ch. 2.
106. Vos, *Biblical Theology*, 8.

While today's reader may discount some of Vos's explanation or phrase things differently, it is true that ידע often carries the connotation of practical, even intimate, knowledge gained through experience.[107] In his classic *TDOT* article, Botterweck says, "'To know Yahweh' refers to a practical, religio-ethical relationship," and other scholars agree.[108] Indeed, a close study of the RFs in Exodus and Ezekiel suggests that ידע in those texts has far more to do with one's experience *of* God than with any comprehension of doctrinal points *about* God.

The formulas of Exodus and Ezekiel imply a knowledge of God not to be associated with schooling and mere intellectual capacity. This knowledge is to be construed differently from the wisdom-literature theme of "seeking knowledge," which is closely related to wisdom (חכמה); this *knowledge* does not come to human beings as their own attainment, through any quest, study, or test (see Prov 2:4–5).[109] Rather, it is a personal knowledge gained as God's acts and self-revelation grip the whole person and, in the case of God's gracious deliverance, lead to conversion and begin to inform all of life. One of Ezekiel's variations on the formula definitely points in this direction, toward a personal knowledge of God. Yahweh declares, "I will bring you against my land, so that the nations *may know me*, when I show my holiness through you before their eyes, O Gog" (38:16).[110] This observation helps explain the tight linkage between God's action in people's lives and their knowledge of him. An experience of Yahweh's hand on them for judgment (cf. Ps 32:4) was taken as a sign of his self-revelation, and there was no denying the "knowledge" they gained.

Though the RF indicates a coming to know God, there is need for careful reflection on the phrasing of the formula with the embedded SPF, "I am Yahweh." (As mentioned earlier, one does not read in Ezekiel a straightforward "you shall know Yahweh.") In his interpretation, Zimmerli highlights the "extremely important" SPF:

> [It] expresses an event or process that is of central significance for Israel's faith. It is
> the formula that stands at the inception of the fundamental revelatory encounter

107. For a fuller accounting of the verb's semantic range, see *DCH*, 4:99–110. Botterweck writes, "The great semantic range of *yādaʿ* from purely apperceptive knowledge to 'be careful of, pay attention to' is clear from its use in parallel with *śim*, 'take to heart'" ("ידע *yādaʿ*," in *TDOT*, 5:462). Here I am concerned to understand ידע with "Yahweh" (or כי אני יהוה) as the object.

108. Botterweck, "ידע *yādaʿ*," in *TDOT*, 5:469; cf. Terence Fretheim, "ידע," in *NIDOTTE*, 2:413.

109. If there is a similarity between ידע in the Ezekiel/Exodus RF and דעת in the wisdom literature, it may be a certain loose connection to learning by observation/experience and to the theology of the "fear of Yahweh" (with resultant submission to God, pursuit of holiness, discipline, etc.) that is said to be the "beginning of knowledge" in Prov 1:7; 9:10; cf. 2:5. See Schöpflin, *Theologie als Biographie*, 113 and 116, for a stronger stress on a wisdom connection in what she names the *Erkenntnisansage*.

110. Above (n. 44), I noted other texts making this point: Ezek 38:23; 35:11. One may add Yahweh's assertion that those in Israel who escape the nation's judgment "will remember *me*" (6:9). Cf. the Jeremiah versions of the RF (9:23[24]; 24:7), which speak of "knowing *me*, that I am Yahweh." Jeremiah also indicts Israel for not knowing Yahweh: 2:8; 4:22; 8:7; 9:2[3], 5[6].

(Exod. 3:6) between Yahweh and Moses, who is the divine tool of Israel's liberation from Egypt. It is also the formula governing the most important legal exposition ... in the context of the making of the covenant (Exod. 20).[111]

Ezekiel is strict about preserving that "I am Yahweh" element within the RF. But how exactly does the SPF function there? It can be a discrete formula, certainly, to be interpreted on its own in both Exodus (6:2, 6, 8, 29; 20:2) and Ezekiel (20:5, 7, 19). Because of the collocation of the distinct SPF and the RF, as well as the inner-biblical interpretation of Exod 6 in Ezek 20 detailed above in chapter 4, I draw the conclusion that the RF in both books is including the SPF *as the SPF*.[112] In other words, the RF appears to offer a citation of the often independent SPF—"you shall know *I am Yahweh* when I . . ."—and there are grounds for giving prominence to the SPF element as a key to the meaning of the RF (see Table 10). Just as Rendtorff has understood the covenant formula and RF to amplify each other when they resound in the same oracle,[113] I contend that the SPF and RF can amplify each other.

Several nuances of the SPF guide my theological interpretation. (1) As previously argued, "I am Yahweh" has clear associations with the exodus event in Exodus, Ezekiel, and elsewhere in the OT.[114] (2) The SPF reinforces God's promises as trustworthy and the prohibitions of the law as binding, the formula serving almost as a divine signature. (3) It also is equated with God's swearing an oath to act in both Exodus and Ezekiel. In line with these points, I suggest the RF of the two books implies that God is reasserting the "I am Yahweh" signature-phrase when he fulfills his age-long promises to save or judge (enacting the sanctions of the law).[115] Bible readers may paraphrase the RF to mean: "When I bring judgment or deliverance according to my threats and promises, you shall know me as the one who declared 'I am Yahweh' in connection with those promises."[116]

Of all the expansions of the strict RF in Exodus and Ezekiel combined, relatively few call the reader's attention to doctrinal points (propositions) in the area of theology proper. An example of such a point that is so referenced would be the holiness of God that leads him to sanctify his people (Exod 31:13; Ezek 20:12). The infrequent addition of the title אדני to the name יהוה in the formula structure

111. Zimmerli, *I Am Yahweh*, 83. For further discussion see ch. 2, nn. 51–54, in the present volume.

112. In Zimmerli's view, it is a "combined formula" (*Ezekiel 1*, 38).

113. Rendtorff, *Covenant Formula*, 91–92. Cf. Jer 24:7: "And I shall give to them a heart to know me, that I am Yahweh, and they shall be my people and I shall be their God."

114. See n. 83 in ch. 3 and n. 113 in ch. 4 of the present volume, and Diesel, "Ich bin Jahwe," 377–80.

115. Exodus (2:24; 32:13) and Ezekiel both assert that Yahweh is acting on old covenant commitments.

116. Schöpflin has a similar view: "Die konsequent und damit stereotyp eingesetzte Erkenntnisansage im Ezechielbuch zielt auf Zweierlei ab: Die Erkenntnissubjekte erkennen die (All)Macht YHWHs anhand seiner in Aussicht gestellten Taten, und zugleich zeigt sich ihnen die Zuverlässigkeit des Gotteswortes, das ihnen Zukünftiges im Voraus mitteilt" (*Theologie als Biographie*, 119).

might indicate that Yahweh is Lord over all and that his sovereign power commands attention. Such truths about God are subordinate to the less specific, experiential knowledge of Yahweh. The formula is not intended to direct our attention
to various attributes of God. This is not to deny that there is regularly a connection
between a content of knowledge about God and the experiential knowledge of
God, but that is not the main thrust in Exodus or Ezekiel.[117]

It may be asked what the RF suggests negatively as it is spoken to Israel and
the nations. Does it mean that they *do not know* him?[118] Does it indicate that they
do not know him *as Yahweh*? One of the charges leveled at the nation in Ezek 23
may point to a partial answer to the question regarding Israel. Yahweh declares,
"Because *you have forgotten me* and thrust me behind your back, bear (נשׂא Qal
impv.) the consequences of your lewdness and whoring!" (23:35). When one combines accusations referring to the nation's failure of memory (לא זכר in 16:22, 43;
שׁכח in 22:12) with assertions that Israel will "remember" as the result of Yahweh's
actions (6:9; 16:61, 63; 20:43; 36:31), the interpreter notices a pattern and theme.[119]
To "know Yahweh" is to remember his saving acts and his acts of judgment and to
respond appropriately. Failure to know or recognize Yahweh results from a failure
to remember his mighty acts. Israel would not *know* until her historical memory
was jogged, and Ezekiel delivers oracles to accomplish that very purpose.

Ezekiel's RF is one example among many of the prophetic *Rückblick* to what
Ezekiel presents as Israel's covenantal foundations, especially Yahweh's salvation
and claiming a people for himself in the exodus. The formula not only accompanies the necessary history lesson in an interpretive role (20:12, 20, 26); it may be
regarded as part of the history lesson as an echo of Exodus.[120] And the formula

117. Zimmerli agrees on form-critical grounds, i.e., his *Erweiswort* (see *I Am Yahweh*, 79).
Fretheim, makes this point: "Knowing God leads naturally into, and cannot be separated from, a more
specific content of the knowledge of God" ("ידע," in *NIDOTTE*, 2:413).

118. Ezekiel does not include this specific indictment (contrast Hos 2:10[8]; 4:1, 6; 5:4; Isa 1:3;
27:11; 52:5–6; 56:10; Jer 2:8; 4:22; 5:4; 8:7; 9:2[3], 5[6]).

119. The "remember" motif in Ezekiel is complex. Not only does Israel fail to remember what
she ought; she calls to mind what she ought not. What she has remembered is the sin of her youth,
not her salvation. Yahweh censures Israel for remembering Egypt with all its idols (23:19), and he
pledges that that memory with its baneful, evil influence would be expunged (23:27). (Cf. the assertion in 16:61–63 that Jerusalem will recall her former sins only with shame.) Also, Ezekiel refers to
Yahweh's remembering Israel (16:60), and this is covenant language. On the use and meaning of זכר,
see: Childs, *Memory and Tradition*; Schottroff, *'Gedenken' im Alten Orient*; H. Eisling, "זכר *zākhar*,"
in *TDOT*, 4:64–82; and L. Allen, "זכר," in *NIDOTTE*, 1:1100–06. Regarding cultural memory, see
Pioske, "Retracing a Remembered Past."

120. The literary theory of "echo" was developed by English scholar John Hollander and has come
to be used in biblical intertextual studies too (Richard B. Hays can be mentioned). Timothy K. Beal
writes: "The figure of echo concerns both the means by which texts relate and a more general theory
of textuality. Texts echo other texts, and as such can be understood as 'echo chambers.' In an echo
chamber—that is, in a literary context for echoing—any text being echoed will *sound* differently than
it has elsewhere. One value of the theory is that it expresses the intertextual character of all writing

points to Yahweh's single-minded, consistent purpose throughout Israel's history. The nation would "know that I am Yahweh" in recalling both deliverance and judgment at the time of the exodus and in recognizing Yahweh's hand in her present judgment and future deliverance. With regard to other nations in Exodus and Ezekiel, their knowing is an awareness and identification of Yahweh specifically as the God of Israel. Yahweh is the God of Israel, by turns fighting for his people (Exod 14:25; Ezek 38:23), showing himself holy in Israel (Ezek 37:28; 38:16; 39:7), or punishing them for unfaithfulness (Ezek 39:23).

The connection between "know" and "remember" just explored indicates to me that Zimmerli may be overstating his case when he denies that ידע as used in the RF relates to any human psychological process. Yes, he is correct that "an inquiry into Ezekiel concerning the psychological processes involved in recognition of Yahweh does not seem very promising."[121] The prophecy has little interest in such processes (the oracles concentrate on him who is known), and one questions how there could be some process in coming to realize "I am Yahweh" when the subject is suddenly cut down by the sword. This may be Zimmerli's point where he writes:

> In the book of Ezekiel, the organization of the statements of recognition shows that the knowledge of Yahweh is not the emergence of an image that has first become clear in the human interior; neither is it a process of speculative combination [nicht als der Vorgang eines spekulativen Kombinierens] nor the result of an analysis of one's creaturely condition. Knowledge or recognition of Yahweh is rather an event occurring in the face of Yahweh's acts, acts to which the prophet as proclaimer draws one's attention.[122]

In many of the judgment scenarios, Zimmerli's claim holds true. But what of the oracles of salvation that promise an experience of delightful restoration—"and they shall know that I am Yahweh their God; I am with them" (34:30)? One could assume a mental process here, a developing knowledge as Israel reflects on undeserved blessings. What of an RF promising an enduring knowledge: "from that day onward the house of Israel will know…" (39:22)? What of a knowledge gained while receiving the sign of Sabbath (20:12, 20) or while remembering one's sins of the past (20:41–44)?

Michael Carasik rightly critiques Zimmerli for an overreach;[123] the latter goes beyond the evidence in claiming that "the event of recognition is not an inward,

---

while maintaining, in the metaphor at least, a sense of closure (walls) around the text's structure. There can be no echo in a wide open 'field.'" ("Glossary," 21.)

121. Zimmerli, *I Am Yahweh*, 88.

122. Zimmerli, *I Am Yahweh*, 35–36 (*Gottes Offenbarung*, 49).

123. Carasik, *Theologies of the Mind*, 22–23.

reflective, or spiritual occurrence."[124] For a few Ezekiel passages, interpreters should not rule out some (undescribed) "psychological process" of reflection being involved in the knowing. There is a danger of oversimplification and a flattening of the knowledge of Yahweh as he acts to reveal himself. On a text-by-text basis, one must allow for variety in how the subjects in the RF come to know. Like the Egyptian charioteers in Exod 14, subjects may be suddenly overtaken by disaster and realize in their dying moment that Yahweh has acted (cf. Ezek 13:14). Others may progressively realize the truth of "I am Yahweh" when God rescues and begins to shepherd them (Ezek 34). In summary, there may or may not be a "psychological process" in knowing. At the same time, Zimmerli is correct that the prophecy gives such a process hardly any attention. Block and Jacqueline Lapsley offer an astute conclusion on human involvement in "knowing": both Exodus and Ezekiel use the RF to send the message that Israel and the nations are "spectators in their acquisition of the knowledge of God," that "their participation is . . . passive."[125]

6.2.6. The Recognition Formula's Link to Covenant

6.2.6.1. The Biblical Evidence

Leslie Allen makes reference to "the covenant goal of recognition of Yahweh"[126] in the book of Ezekiel. To what extent is recognition of Yahweh linked to the covenant? Is it even covenantal in nature? Many factors lead scholars to view the RF against the backdrop of covenant,[127] and these are worth enumerating. (1) The formula makes its first appearance in the canon of Scripture set within a series of promises following Yahweh's statements of "I also made a covenant with them" and "I have remembered my covenant" (Exod 6:4, 5–8).[128] (2) That same initial occurrence of the RF at Exod 6:7 has "framing introductory formulas" (*rahmenden*

---

124. Zimmerli, *I Am Yahweh*, 67. Is his interpretation of the "event of recognition" influenced by a neo-orthodox "theology of crisis," with its rejection of an old liberal interior religion (Schleiermacher's *Gefühl*)? Is Zimmerli presenting the event as a crisis of decision thrust upon a person who encounters the transcendant God and the awful antithesis of God and the world, Creator and creation?

125. Lapsley, *Can These Bones Live?* 124; cf. Block, *Ezekiel 1–24*, 39. Decades prior, Botterweck made a similar point (*"Gott erkennen,"* 98).

126. Allen, *Ezekiel 20–48*, 12.

127. Beyond the formula's covenantal significance, prominent scholars have argued that covenant is the underlying concern of the entire book of Ezekiel; see Boadt, "Function of the Salvation Oracles," and Fishbane, "Sin and Judgment."

128. Deuteronomy's single true RF (29:5[6]) is also firmly in a covenant context, whether or not one interprets 28:69[29:1] and its reference to ברית as attaching to the preceding chapters or introducing chap. 29. On this question, see van Rooy, "Deuteronomy 28,69," McConville, *Deuteronomy*, , 401–2, and the literature they cite.

Einleitungsformeln)[129] on either side (6:6, 8; cf. v. 2): אני יהוה. That formula serves as the key theological component of the RF, but where it appears independently in Exodus, Ezekiel, and elsewhere in the OT, it also commonly names the God speaking as he who brought Israel out of Egypt and bound them to himself in covenant at Sinai.[130] (3) Also, that initial RF in Exod 6 immediately follows a version of the covenant formula, "you shall be my people and I shall be your God," and the two formulas frequently appear together in Scripture as the result of "highly conscious reflection."[131] (4) Throughout Ezekiel, nearly every place one finds reference to covenant, one finds the RF close at hand.[132] (5) Many argue that, in some contexts, ידע has clear covenantal significance,[133] and that it finds use in ANE suzerainty treaties. (6) It is commonplace to refer to the name יהוה as God's covenant name, especially because of its revelation/reiteration in Exod 3 and 6;[134] therefore the phraseology, "know that I am *Yahweh*," would seem to imply a covenantal recognition of some sort. (7) Covenant is also tied into the RF by the not infrequent expansion that adds אלהיכם or אלהיהם ("your God," or "their God") to the end (Exod 6:7; 16:12; 29:46; Ezek 20:20; 28:26; 34:30; 39:22, 28).[135] The sense of this expansion—which is thought to echo the covenant formula—seems to be that Yahweh has sole claim on Israel's loyalty because he and they are bound together in covenant. Faithfulness to Yahweh and the avoidance of all idolatry is of the essence of the covenant (2 Kgs 17:35–39).

There is no full understanding of the RF and its varied usage apart from the idea of covenant. However, on the face of things, the connection between the formula

129. Zimmerli, *I Am Yahweh*, 13 (*Gottes Offenbarung*, 23).

130. Again, see n. 83 in ch. 3 and n. 113 in ch. 4 of this volume.

131. Rendtorff, *Covenant Formula*, 91.

132. Using the delineation of oracles in Table 8, eleven of twelve references to God's *covenant* stand within oracles that also contain the RF (the exception being 44:7). E.g., see the connection in 16:62 ("I will establish my covenant with you, and you shall know that I am Yahweh").

133. See: Huffmon, "Treaty Background"; Huffmon and Parker, "Further Note"; W. Schottroff, "ידע *jdʿ* erkennen," in *THAT*, 1:691–93; Stuart, *Hosea–Jonah*, 53, 60. Also supporting this interpretation of the lexeme's usage are Garr, "Grammar and Interpretation," 406–8, and Hugenberger, *Marriage as Covenant*, 267–73. The latter evaluates the contradicting arguments of Botterweck ("ידע *yādaʿ*," in *TDOT*, 5:478) and Nicholson (*God and his People*, 80). I do not think ידע in Ezekiel's RFs consistently indicates "mutual legal recognition on the part of suzerain and vassal" (Huffmon, "Treaty Background," 34). It would be contrary to the evidence presented earlier to suggest Yahweh is "recognized" by the nations as their covenant Lord. They might, however, recognize him as Israel's divine suzerain, who can act in vengeance to protect his covenant people (Exod 14:25).

134. See David Noel Freedman and M. P. O'Connor, "יהוה YHWH," in *TDOT*, 5:518, and Garr, "Grammar and Interpretation," 401–8. Henry O. Thompson summarizes a large body of scholarship: "But most important to the biblical tradition, Yahweh is the god [*sic*] of the covenant" ("Yahweh," in *ABD*, 6:1012).

135. Odell argues that the formulation "they shall know that I am Yahweh, *their God*" reflects a "covenantal confession" ("Are You He?" 128): "[That] covenantal language provides the frame of reference for interpreting not only the Gog event but also the final modification of expectations embedded in the recognition formula" (146–47).

and covenant is not always so apparent. For example, what was the covenantal content of formulas spoken to Pharaoh and Egypt in the exodus narratives? One might make the same query regarding the RFs addressed to Egypt and the other nations in Ezekiel. There might also be some difficulty in a covenantal interpretation of the judgment oracles against Israel. How were the exiles to comprehend the punishment of Jerusalem in terms of covenant?

This chapter has already discussed the "radical inversion" of the formulas addressed to Israel, but a few additional comments are in order before explaining the covenant orientation of RFs spoken against the nations. If Israel had any real "expectation of God's punitive intervention" (which is questionable), she looked for "individual divine acts of judgment"[136] as retribution for individual sins. Israel possibly figured on national reversals, but she did not expect national destruction. The covenant and the temple were insurance against such a disaster. In the popular mind, the covenant could not have indicated or explained the catastrophic events of the several exiles to Babylon. It was unthinkable that Israel could be considered Yahweh's enemy and be punished along with the nations, or even worse, be punished by the nations (cf. Hab 1). That they did in fact suffer such a catastrophe at the hand of Yahweh dealt a blow to the presumption in their belief system (cf. Jer 7:4) from which the exiles would not recover. Ezekiel's calling was not to come up with a "new theology" incorporating this startling reality into an existing belief system, but to summon errant Israel back to its foundations, back to a truer understanding of what Yahweh's covenant meant and included for them, and most importantly back to the covenant God whose name is Yahweh.[137] Israel will "remember" the God they have forgotten (6:9; 22:12; 23:35).

Though the Jewish nation in his day failed to appreciate the doctrine, Ezekiel insisted that the unheard-of severity of Yahweh's judgment was in line with the ancestral covenant. It was not being violated or abrogated from Yahweh's side, but was being upheld in the horrors of siege and exile.[138] Deuteronomy stipulates that, among the many curses (כל־הקללות) to fall upon those who break the covenant,

---

136. Eichrodt, *Theology of the Old Testament*, 1:458.
137. The earlier prophecy of Hosea, taking into account its theological similarities with Ezekiel, is a touchstone on these points. Hosea has a prophetic *Rückblick* over the nation's history, reaching back to the time of David (3:5), the exodus (2:15; 9:10; 11:1; 12:9, 13; 13:4), and even the patriarchs (12:3–5, 12). He indicts Israel for forgetting Yahweh (2:13; 8:14; 13:6) and his Torah (4:6; cf. 8:1, 12). Despite false claims to know Yahweh (8:2), Israel has rejected "knowledge" (4:6); "they do not know Yahweh" (5:4; cf. 2:8; 4:1, 6), as demonstrated by their "prostitution." A proper punishment would be for Yahweh to return the nation to Egypt (8:13; 9:3; 11:5). The experience of salvation and covenant renewal includes "knowing Yahweh" (2:20; 6:3; cf. 6:6).
138. The case for this is convincingly made in Wong, *Idea of Retribution*. This is opposite the view of A. B. Ehrlich as cited by Greenberg: "If Israel behaves in such a way as to break the covenant with YHWH, YHWH will do similarly and behave toward them contrary to his covenant obligations" (*Ezekiel 1–20*, 291).

there will be reminders of the miseries in Egypt (28:27, 60), plagues (28:21–22), siege (28:52), and even exile (28:36–37), where sons and daughters will go "into captivity" (בשבי; 28:41), being "scattered among all the nations" (28:64). Also, the covenant curses found in the Pentateuch include a prediction that, when hard-pressed by the enemy, Israel would experience such famine that parents would eat their children (Lev 26:29; Deut 28:53–57).[139] Ezekiel reiterates this judgment (5:10), and there is testimony it did happen (Lam 2:20). These passages shed light on Yahweh's asseveration in Ezek 6:10 that "they shall know that I am Yahweh; I did not threaten in vain to bring this evil upon them." As I argued in chapter 5, the punishments meted out to Israel are regarded by Ezekiel as a divine response to the nation's covenant-breaking. They may be interpreted as covenant enforcement.

Turning to the RFs addressed to the nations in oracles of judgment, the interpreter seeks some covenantal significance, and there is indeed a tie to covenant for each formula spoken against the nations. Did not Yahweh's covenant with Israel include reprisals upon all who mistreat his chosen people? Though the term ברית is not found in the promises of Gen 12:2–3, a covenant orientation is apparent in the multiple "I will" declarations.[140] Yahweh promises: "I will bless those who bless you, and whoever curses (קלל) you I will curse (ארר)" (12:3). Each of Ezekiel's RFs spoken against the nations is accompanied by accusations of wrongs committed against Israel.[141] Other prophetic books contain similar arguments: for example, Joel 4:17–21[3:17–21] uses the formula and then quickly defines the heaven-sent covenant blessing as protection from and punishment of neighboring nations:

> Then you shall know that I am Yahweh your God,
> who dwells in Zion, my holy mountain.
> And Jerusalem shall be holy,
> *and strangers shall never invade her again.*
> In that day the mountains shall drip with pressed grapes
> and the hills shall flow with milk,
> and all the stream-channels shall flow with water.
> A fountain shall spring forth from the house of Yahweh,[142]
> and shall water the Valley of Shittim.

139. Moshe Weinfeld is inclined to read such treaty curses more as rhetoric, contra the view that they are later interpolations that reflect subsequent historical developments: "Maledictions of this type do not necessarily reflect a real situation but belong rather to the typology of the political documents current in the eighth and seventh centuries BC" (*Deuteronomy and the Deuteronomic School*, 127).

140. For the promissory aspect of the divine covenant, see: Gen 12:2–3, with five promises (first-person); 17:3–8, with five; 28:13–15, with four; and Exod 6:6–8, with seven.

141. Ammon (25:3, 6); Moab (25:8); Mount Seir/Edom (25:12; 35:5, 10–15); Philistia (25:15); Tyre (26:2); Egypt (29:6–7); Gog (38:18).

142. Cf. Ezek 47.

Egypt [however] shall become a desolation,
and Edom shall be a desolate wilderness,
because of violence against the people of Judah
and because they shed innocent blood in their land.

The same argument applies in Exodus where RFs are spoken against Israel's slave-masters: Yahweh will be recognized by both Egyptians and Israelites in the punishment he metes out to the oppressors of the covenant people (Exod 8:22–23; 10:2; 14:4, 18).

Over fifty years ago, F. Charles Fensham took up the "problem" in the prophets "that maledictions against foreign nations are clothed in the same language as those against a disobedient Israel."[143] His research indicated a close connection between the two sets of curses connected with the covenant and that the similarity in calamities pronounced against Israel and the other powers meant "the Lord will punish his disobedient people in the same way as his enemies." In diachronic analysis, Fensham concluded: "The important trend of thought was that maledictions against a disobedient people shall overtake them, because they have breached the covenant. Calamities predicted against foreign nations must have developed out of these maledictions."[144] No matter what the vector of influence with similar maledictions, the tie to covenant helps to explain the similarity.

Ezekiel's RFs included in Yahweh's promises to restore his people have the most obvious covenant content, since they most exactly echo the formulas of Exodus (when context is taken into consideration). Standing out in the midst of a chapter filled with condemnation, one formula reads: "I shall establish [וַהֲקִימוֹתִי] my covenant with you, and you shall know that I am Yahweh" (16:62). Another formula draws in the themes of covenant and emancipation: "I shall make [וְכָרַתִּי] a covenant of peace with them. . . . They shall know that I am Yahweh, when I break the bars of their yoke and deliver them from the hand of those who enslaved them" (34:25, 27b). Leading into the concluding chapters' vision of Israel's glorious future, an oracle declares that that covenant of peace will be everlasting:

And I shall make [וְכָרַתִּי] a covenant of peace with them; it shall be an everlasting covenant with them. I shall establish[145] them and multiply them, and I shall set my sanctuary among them forever. My dwelling place will be with them, and I will be their God, and they will be my people. Then the nations shall know that I, Yahweh, make Israel holy, when my sanctuary is among them forever. (37:26–28)

---

143. Fensham, "Common Trends," 172.
144. Fensham, "Common Trends," 173.
145. Following *DCH*, s.v. "נתן," 5:802.

Here the effect of the covenant-making for Israel is threefold: the nation will be multiplied in population; they will have Yahweh's glorious presence among them in a restored sanctuary; and they will experience a renewed covenant relationship (expressed in the covenant formula). For the nations, the effect of the covenant-making is the recognition of Yahweh as Israel's God, who sanctifies his people with his own presence.

What stands out in Ezekiel's salvation oracles is the unconditional nature of the promises to which the formula attaches. I previously noted that 43:11 (without an RF) may perhaps be interpreted as a conditional blessing: if the people of Israel are ashamed of their wicked past, then the prophet will make known to them the design of the new temple. However, the strong impression left by the restoration promises is their unconditionality. Fulfillment of these promises does not await the repentance, obedience, and covenant faithfulness of the people. Rather, the repentance and new obedience are presented as a divine gift, as the "heart-work" of Yahweh, who thereby reveals himself to be the sanctifier of Israel (11:19–20; 36:25–27). The blessings of the restoration come as a gracious initiative of Yahweh, apparently not as a divine response to any human action. (Again, Ezekiel's theology is seen to be theocentric.) Yahweh's salvation comes to those who deserve nothing of it; all the mercies shown are based on the character of God and are for the sake of his name.

Thomas Raitt argues that the unconditional nature of the restoration promises in Jeremiah and Ezekiel represents a shift away from earlier covenant theology and its consistent emphasis on human obligation (Mosaic covenant) and stipulations that the people can find forgiveness only through repentance.[146] The two exilic prophets' doctrine of restoration as a wholly gracious gift based on the faithful character of God is said to be without precedent. In his dissertation on Exod 32–34, R. W. L. Moberly replies that Raitt's thesis cannot be sustained. He says, "in fact Ex. 32–34 contains precisely such a theology of the Mosaic covenant, and Jeremiah and Ezekiel may have been explicitly taking their stand within the ancient tradition." He writes further here:

> Ex. 32–34 is the tradition, *par excellence,* which deals with the question of what happens after Israel is unfaithful to her covenant obligations. It presents a theology of the Mosaic covenant in which the covenant is renewed precisely because it depends upon the character of Yahweh as gracious and merciful and not on the people who continue to be stiff-necked and unrepentant. According to our present text, the Mosaic covenant, as the Davidic, rests ultimately upon the faithfulness of Yahweh and as such can hardly be less enduring.[147]

146. Raitt, *Theology of Exile,* 106–8.
147. Moberly, *At the Mountain,* 189, 188.

One should posit a tight conjunction between the covenant theology of Exodus and Ezekiel. Yahweh is known in both books as Israel's God of the covenant who will strictly enforce the covenant sanctions, judging the guilty, and will also intervene in the nation's history to uphold his gracious promises.

6.2.6.2. *The Extrabiblical Evidence*

Ezekiel scholars find some extrabiblical confirmation of the RF's covenant orientation in an Assyrian prophecy brought to light in the nineteenth century. It may have been Manfred Weippert, in 1972, who first drew attention to the connection between the *Covenant of Aššur* and the biblical *Erkenntnisaussage*.[148] The Assyrian oracles were delivered by the prophet "La-dagil-ili" to King Esarhaddon, son of Sennacherib, circa 673 BC.[149] In a desperate conflict with other nations (Cimmerians and land of Ellipi), the king entreats his god for help, and Aššur replies that he has heard his servant's complaint and announces how he has dealt with the threat. Weippert quotes the covenant's "Second Oracle of Salvation" only in part (K.2401 ii:22–25) and his translation reads,

> Deine Feinde bringe ich als Schlachtopfer dar.
> Mit ihrem Blut fülle ich den Fluß.
> Man möge erkennen (und) mich (dafür) preisen,[150]
> *daß* ich Aššur bin, der Herr der Götter!

The "Second Oracle" in full provides the larger literary context, mentioning "covenant," and is worth quoting in the translation published by the Neo-Assyrian Text Corpus Project of the University of Helsinki (Table 11).[151]

In what some regard as a bygone era, there was strong interest in the "treaty analogy" and scholars explored formal and thematic parallels between ANE covenants (international suzerainty treaties) and Yahweh's covenant with Israel.

---

148. Weippert, "'Heiliger Krieg,'" esp. 481–82. As Weippert mentions the *Erkenntnisaussage* in this connection, he has the full RF in view (in an Akkadian variation).

149. The portion of text within the *Covenant of Aššur* of greatest relevance to this study, "The Second Oracle of Salvation," is well established and without need for reconstruction. All the other sections have entire lines missing.

150. This is Weippert's 2001 revised translation of line 24 ("Ich bin Jahwe," 43). His 1972 rendering was "Man möge (es) sehen und mich preisen."

151. Parpola, *Assyrian Prophecies* (SAA 9), §3.3. Parpola draws attention to parallels between this Assyrian oracle and Ezekiel. Others emphasizing the similarities between Assyrian oracles—commonly this one—and OT prophecy in its covenant orientation are: Weippert, "Heiliger Krieg," 482; Huffmon, "Prophecy in the Ancient Near East," in *IDBSup*, 697–700; Fensham, "Malediction and Benediction"; Fensham, "Common Trends"; McCarthy, *Treaty and Covenant*; Millard, "La prophétie et l'écriture"; Weippert, "Aspekte israelitischer Prophetie"; Huffmon, "Prophecy, Ancient Near Eastern Prophecy," in *ABD*, 5:477–82; Nissinen, "Die Relevanz"; Weippert, "Ich bin Jahwe"; and Diesel, *"Ich bin Jahwe,"* 177–82.

Table 11 *The Covenant of Aššur* (K.2401 / *ABRT*, 1:22f / SAA 9, §3),
"The Second Oracle of Salvation" (ca. 673 BC; SAA 9, §3.3)

10 *an-nu-rig* LÚ.*sar-sar-a-ni¹ an¹-nu-⌈ti¹⌉*	¹⁰Now then, these traitors provoked
11 *us-sa-ad-bi-bu-ka us-se-ṣu-nik¹-ka*	you, had you banished, and surrounded
12 *il-ti-bu-ka at-ta pi-i-ka*	you; but you opened your mouth (and
13 *tap-ti-ti-a ma-a a-ni-na* ᵈ*aš-šur¹*	cried): "Hear me, O Aššur!"
14 *a-na-ku kil-la-ka as-se-me*	¹⁴I heard your cry. I issued forth as a
15 TA* ŠÀ-*bi* KÁ.GAL AN-*e*	fiery glow from the gate of heaven, to hurl
16 *at-ta-qa-al-la-al-la*	down fire and have it devour them.
17 *la¹-ak-ru-ur i-šá-tu lu-šá-kil-šú-nu*	
18 *at-ta ina bir-tu-šú-nu ta-za-az*	¹⁸You were standing in their midst, so I
19 TA* *pa¹-ni-ka at-ti-ši*	removed them from your presence. I drove
20 *a-na* KUR-*e us-se-li-šú-nu*	them up the mountain and rained (hail)
21 NA₄.MEŠ *aq-qul-lu ina* UGU-*hi-šú-nu a-zu-nu-un*	stones and fire from heaven upon them.
22 LÚ.KÚR.MEŠ-*ka uh-ta-ti-ip*	²²I slaughtered your enemies and
23 *da-me-šú-nu* ÍD *um-tal-li*	filled the river with their blood. Let them
24 *le-mu-ru lu-na-i¹-⌈du¹-ni*	see (it) and praise me, (knowing) that I
25 *a-ki* ᵈ*aš-šur* EN DINGIR.MEŠ *an-na-ku-ni*	am Aššur, lord of the gods.
26 *an-nu-u šul-mu šá ina* IGI *ṣa-al-me*	²⁶This is the well-being (placed) before the Image.
27 *ṭup-pi a-de-e an-ni¹-u šá* ᵈ*aš-šur*	²⁷This covenant tablet of Aššur enters
28 *ina* UGU *ha-ʾu-u-ti ina* IGI LUGAL *e-rab*	the king's presence on a *cushion.* Fragrant
29 Ì—DÙG.GA *i-za-ar-ri-qu*	oil is sprinkled, sacrifices are made, incense
30 UDU.SISKUR.MEŠ *ep-pu-šú*	is burnt, and they read it out in the king's
31 ŠEM.HI.A *il-lu-ku*	presence.
32 *ina* IGI LUGAL *i-sa-as-si-u*	

Interest has waned, and Dennis McCarthy is right to explain this development as, first of all, a response to "the too-sweeping claims made for the treaty analogy" and, secondly, "an over-reaction of criticism."[152] It would be an unfortunate mistake, however, if the *Covenant of Aššur* were ignored in study of Ezekiel's RF.

There are numerous affinities between Ezekiel's prophecies and this Neo-Assyrian text. (1) According to the accepted dating schemes, the two are only a century apart: 673 for the *Covenant of Aššur* and 571 for the latest oracle of Ezekiel (29:17–21). (2) They share the genre of prophetic oracle and are completely dominated by reported direct divine speech. (3) Both record the deity's announcement of his dramatic intervention in the nation's affairs, and (4) the actions are related to a divine–human covenant relationship.[153] Finally, (5) the deity makes a

152. McCarthy, "Preface to the Second Edition," in *Treaty and Covenant*, ix.

153. Some might protest that the Neo-Assyrian covenant is royal, between Aššur and the king, and that the idea of a national covenant is unique to Israel. However, scholars have discovered that a covenant between deity and nation is not so uniquely Israelite; see Gordon, "'Comparativism,'" 49–51.

declaration, in the style of an RF, of his expectation that his sovereignty be widely acknowledged.[154] Thus, this is no far-fetched analogy, say, between an international treaty in the second millennium and a divine–human biblical covenant of a much later era.

Simo Parpola, editor of the Helsinki volume containing the *Covenant of Aššur* (SAA 9), has suggested that, among the texts in biblical prophecy, Ezekiel's oracle against Gog is most similar to the language in the "Second Oracle of Salvation" within the *Covenant of Aššur* (hereafter, CA ii).[155] In Ezek 38:22–23 we read,

> I shall execute judgment on him with pestilence and bloodshed and flooding rains and hailstones. Fire and brimstone I shall rain down upon him and his hordes, and the many nations that are with him. So I shall show my greatness and my holiness, making myself known in the eyes of many nations. Then they shall know that I am Yahweh.

In a closer reading of the Neo-Assyrian text and Ezek 38, one uncovers still more affinities. There are said to be overwhelming odds militarily in favor of the attacking enemy (CA ii:10–13, 18; Ezek 38:11–12, 15–16). In his intervention, the deity makes use of cosmic weapons, (hail)stones and fire from heaven, to overcome the enemy of his servant/people (CA ii:14–17, 20–21; Ezek 38:22).[156] All the apocalyptic-type imagery and language lead to a kind of RF spoken by the deity; the Akkadian at CA ii:24–25, is well translated as: "Let them recognize and praise me, that I am Aššur, lord of the gods." The declaration, "I am Yahweh" or "I am Aššur," functions as the rhetorical conclusion of the oracle section, identifying the deity and indicating the deity's expectation that the nations acknowledge and praise him[157] and his activity in the preceding cataclysm. Later on, in the same *Covenant of Aššur*, there is yet another divine declaration in the style of an RF, but

---

154. Weippert writes: "Die Erweisformel wird in der assyrischen Prophetie, wenn man die beiden Belege verallgemeinern darf, mit dem Verbum *amāru* 'sehen, gewahr werden, erkennen' und Objektsatz gebildet, nicht mit *edû*, dem akkadischen Äquivalent des im Hebräischen gebrauchten ידע" ("Ich bin Jahwe," 44). See *CAD*, A/II:13 (s.v. *amāru*, A.2d) for numerous examples of √*amāru* meaning "to come to know, realize, recognize, see" in a demonstration or proof context.

155. Parpola, *Assyrian Prophecies*, 24.

156. For discussion of this feature of ANE and OT prophecy, see Stökl, "'I Have Rained Stones.'"

157. Worth noting is how the Akkadian oracle expresses Aššur's expectation of praise from the nations. In biblical scholarship, some choose to read the formula אני יהוה as self-praise. K. Günther writes: "Die Selbstvorstellungsformel ... ist im alten Orient weit bereitet.... Durch Verweis der Gottheit auf eigene Taten und Eigenschaften gewinnt die Selbstvorstellungsformel den Charakter des Selbstlobes (im AT bei Dtjes: Jes 44,24; 45,7; auch in Gerichts- und Disputationsreden; vgl. Westermann, ATD 19, 124–132; H.-M. Dion, Le genre littéraire sumérien de l'«hymne à soi-même» et quelques passages du Deutéro-Isaïe, *RB* 74, 1957, 215–234)" ("אני *'ani* ich," in *THAT*, 1:219). Jan L. Koole reads the RFs in Isaiah in similar fashion, speaking of "God's self-praise 'I am Yahweh'" (*Isaiah 49–55*, 70).

in the mouth of Aššur's companion goddess in the Assyrian pantheon, Ištar.[158] (Why has the deity acted on behalf of her people? She says, "From this you shall see/recognize [√*amāru*] that I am Ištar of Arbela.") Both the "Second Oracle of Salvation" and Ezek 38:22–23 are a part of a larger prophecy that speaks repeatedly of a covenant relation between the deity and his people (CA ii:27, 36; CA iii:11, 14; Ezek 16:60–63; 34:25; 37:26). There appear to be good grounds, both biblical and extrabiblical, for a covenantal interpretation of the RF.

After this chapter's consideration of the prime theological disjunction and the several conjunctions between the formulas in Ezekiel and Exodus, what remains is to conclude the study with a summary of the overall argument, a discussion of the rhetorical purposes in Ezekiel's use of the RF, and an effort to define the theological meaning of the formula in Ezekiel.

---

158. In column iv, a continuation of "Word of Ištar of Arbela" (begins at iii:16), we read the following oracle in Parpola's translation (*Assyrian Prophecies*, 27). (There are minor breaks, indicated by brackets, which required restoration by comparing with other texts; only in iv:19 is the restoration said to be conjectural.)

> 14 [No]w rejoice, Esarhaddon! [I have
>   be]nt [the four doorjamb]s of Assyria and
>   given them to you; I have vanquished yo[ur
>   enemy. The *mood* of the *people*] who stand
>   with you has been turned upside down.
> 20 [From thi]s you shall see [that] I am
>   [Ištar of] Arbela.

The relationship between Aššur and Ištar in Assyrian theology is treated in Parpola, *Assyrian Prophecies*, XXI–XXXI. For similar divine "I-statements" addressed to King Esarhaddon, see K.4310 in Parpola, *Assyrian Prophecies*, 4–11 (= *ANET*, 449–50: "Akkadian Oracles and Prophecies" [trans. Robert H. Pfeiffer]), "Oracles Concerning Esarhaddon," i.14–24, 30; iii.15).

CHAPTER 7

Conclusion: Defining the Rhetoric and
Theological Meaning of Ezekiel's Formula

This study illuminates the literary and theological function of what S. R. Driver calls Ezekiel's "keynote formula" by undertaking a fresh examination of its use, and especially by identifying and interpreting the RF as one aspect of an intertextual relationship between Ezekiel and the book of Exodus. The research presented here has moved beyond a consideration of Ezekiel's relationship to an Exodus "tradition." That such a relationship exists is widely agreed, and the Bible's RF has often been interpreted with reference to that Exodus tradition. For example, K. Günther discusses the formula in *THAT* and writes, "Erkenntnis Jahwes geschieht im Zusammenhang mit seinem geschichtlichen Selbsterweis (vgl. Exodus-tradition)."[1] My research, however, has led me beyond talk of *tradition* to explore a *textual* dimension in which Ezekiel's prophecy shows "many signs of being influenced by a study of Israel's sacred writings" (Brevard Childs).

7.1. Summary of the Argument

My work argued specifically that the seventy-two RFs in Ezekiel mark a theological nexus between the prophecy and the book of Exodus and that those formulas are best interpreted alongside the numerous RFs in Exodus. With the proposal that Ezekiel signals a dependence on earlier "Scriptures"—especially Exodus in some authoritative recension—this study ran into critical debate over the compositional history of the Pentateuch and the dating of alleged "documents" or of the literary deposit of pentateuchal traditions. In building the argument at this controversial point, I showed that: (1) OT scholarship is presently in such ferment over source analysis, dating pentateuchal materials, and questions of redaction, that the conclusions of the older *Literarkritik* (e.g., P is postexilic) are no longer privileged in the debate; (2) a body of exegetical evidence and sophisticated linguistic analysis by the likes of Avi Hurvitz, Michael Fishbane, Mark Rooker, Jacob Milgrom, and Risa Levitt Kohn supports the contention that Ezekiel drew from P in some stabilized and authoritative literary deposit; and (3) the presence of several RFs in the

1. K. Günther, "אני *'anî* ich," in *THAT*, 1:220.

242

allegedly older J/E strata of Exodus would convince many who perhaps reject the
revisionist scholarship cited in 2 above that those formulas are ancient enough to
have influenced all the writing prophets. Strictly speaking, a preexilic dating of P is
not necessary for recognizing the influence of the Exodus narratives upon Ezekiel.

Chapter 2, with its review of scholarship, laid a foundation, not only by establishing how others previously have built up research on the formula but also by
indicating the problems of controversy and confusion in past scholarship. I noted
at least three important points, the first being a confusion over the exact number
of occurrences of the RF, and the second a controversy over the biblical source[2]
influencing Ezekiel's usage of that formula. The third point was the area of theological interpretation. Among other disagreements, scholars dispute whether the
RFs addressed to the nations speak of a saving knowledge of Yahweh. The contro-
versies and confusion reveal both the need for further research and opportunities
to move beyond existing scholarship.

Chapter 3 presented the results of basic exegetical spadework focused on details
of the formula's usage in Ezekiel: defining the formula;[3] cataloging the surprising
variety of RFs; confirming the correct tally of formulas; examining genre, syntax,
and literary context; searching for "clusters" of formulas; and discussing text-critical
and redaction-critical issues. Because this monograph meant to engage in close
comparative work examining Ezekiel's RFs alongside those in other biblical books,
chapter 3 also provided a lengthy appendix with a "List of Recognition Formulas
and Related Phrases Outside Ezekiel." This appendix proved useful later in the
study when pursuing questions of inner-biblical interpretation and intertextuality.

Chapter 4 was central to the book's argument. Following chapter 1 and the criteria set down there for recognizing the phenomena of allusion and inner-biblical
interpretation, this chapter presented abundant evidence that Ezekiel alludes to
the book of Exodus (J/E and P materials). The linguistic and terminological
parallels (4.1.1.) showed a clear pattern of reference from Ezekiel back not only
to the exodus story in the prophet's historical retrospectives, and not only to a
theological exodus tradition, but also to Exodus texts. There is what might be
termed a "demonstrable relationship between texts" (van Wolde) with "multiple
and sustained lexical linkages" (Fishbane).[4] This conclusion, arrived at inductively
through research of specific examples, served as a deductive "warrant" to read the
many similarities of theme, event, and theology in Exodus and Ezekiel as further

2. The study also noted some of the proposals of a nonbiblical source for Ezekiel's RF, but these
were not explored in depth. Scholarship has been more intent on studying the formula in its canonical
context, looking for a biblical source.

3. The "true" RF was defined as divine speech consisting of the verb ידע and the attached clause,
כי אני יהוה, which may be variously expanded. The only exception to this rule was Ezek 20:26, where
אשר replaces כי.

4. Fishbane, Biblical Interpretation, 285.

support for the claim that Ezekiel's prophecy alludes to Exodus (4.1.2). Additional evidence of a broad Ezekielian dependence on Exodus was brought forward in the section treating "Ezekiel's Reshaping of Earlier 'Scriptural Traditions'" (4.1.3), and radical revision or "skewing" (Greenberg) of traditional materials was understood as compelling evidence for allusion. I built on this cumulative case when averring (section 4.2) that Ezekiel's RFs are one of the "multiple and sustained linkages," are most similar to the formulas in Exodus, and are best understood as another echo of Exodus texts. Many points of similarity were mentioned, including the striking correspondence between Exod 31:13 and Ezek 20:12. Ezekiel's RFs were also compared and contrasted with formulas in other books (esp. 1 Kings and Isaiah). I judged that a much stronger case can be made for the influence of Exodus on Ezekiel than for the influence of some northern Israelite prophetic tradition reflected in 1 Kgs 20 (Walther Zimmerli's contention).

Because Ezekiel scholarship should give greater attention to the trauma of the Jewish exiles, and because certain rhetorical features of Ezekiel's prophecy can be at least partially explained by researching the sociohistorical situation, chapter 5 examined "the sociohistorical and religious context of Ezekiel's oracles." There is "the need to let suffering speak" (Theodor Adorno). Perhaps Ezekiel's multiplication of RFs indicates something about the receptivity of a traumatized and embittered community in exile? When one turns to consider Yahweh's indictment of Israel in her spiritual and moral state (5.2.4), Ezekiel's allusions to Exodus (as text and event) take on new meaning. Ezekiel traced the rebellion of Israel and her pollution with idolatry all the way back to the nation's sojourn in Egypt. The covenant people had never put away the idols of Egypt, and Ezekiel declared that, in response, Yahweh will act as the God of exodus. The spiritual and moral state of Israel was so grave that a new exodus done in judgment must precede a new exodus to usher the saved into the land promised to the ancestors (20:34–38, 41–44). Though Yahweh had made himself known to Israel in Egypt, declaring to them "I am Yahweh" and promising their deliverance, Ezekiel says the people did not forsake their idols. Generation after generation were devoted to their idols, and Israel would not give up the "prostitution she began in Egypt" (23:8, 27). The RFs spoken to Israel in Egypt had continuing relevance for the nation in Ezekiel's day, for Yahweh would reveal himself yet again as he put an end to what Ezekiel could have characterized as Israel's old Egyptian habits.

In chapter 6, the argument of this book proceeded on the premise that Ezekiel as a text generates more meaning in its fuller canonical context, as it is read with other texts. Exodus and Ezekiel have such a density of linguistic and theological links—the RF chief among them—that an intertextual reading is not only justified, but necessary. Focusing more on a synchronic intertextuality of reception than on an intertextuality of production,[5] chapter 6 offered a theological

5. Again, this differentiation is borrowed from van Wolde, "Texts in Dialogue," 4.

interpretation of Ezekiel's formulas alongside those in Exodus. I discovered both jarring disjunctions and strong conjunctions between Ezekiel and Exodus in the interpretive work. Exploring both the disjunctions and the conjunctions took me deeper into the theology of the two books and prepared me to drive at answers to the primary questions about the topic of study. How does the formula function rhetorically in the prophecy? What does Ezekiel's RF mean? What does it mean to "know that I am Yahweh"? What is the formula saying where it appears as a theological conclusion to oracles of judgment or deliverance? Such questions now lead into two brief sections of conclusions.

7.2. Rhetorical Purposes in Ezekiel's Use of the Formula

A whole book could be written exploring the rhetoric of Ezekiel's RF; this is but a brief, suggestive treatment of the prophecy's persuasive strategy in the use of the formula. I begin with the basics. (1) The RF is the book's heartbeat,[6] signaling the prophecy's overriding concern that Yahweh be known. Interpreters are mistaken to take the formula as "Ezechiels theologisches *ceterum censeo*,"[7] tacked on the end of oracles. (2) Being so widespread, it serves to unify Ezekiel as a whole; more specifically, it integrates oracles of judgment with those of restoration, indicating the way in which all Yahweh's actions are directed toward a single goal. (3) Daniel Block correctly observes that the formula "transforms . . . oracles from mere announcements of coming events into announcements of Yahweh's self-manifestation."[8] (4) The RF seems purposed both to illustrate and to reinforce the theocentricity of the book,[9] especially through the cumulative impact of all the repetition. (5) Accompanying the retelling of Israel's *un*holy-history and prophecies of coming divine intervention, the formula contributes to the argument that Yahweh is purposefully and powerfully engaged with the nation—past, present, and future.[10] More than just a claim to power and authority over world events, the RF is Yahweh's claiming in his speeches all those events as his own doing. (6) The prophecy sharply focuses on divine acts[11] and sets forth in the RF God's

---

6. As noted previously (ch. 6, n. 82), it functions literarily and rhetorically as the regular conclusion or target statement of individual oracles.

7. Lang, *Ezechiel*, 96. Contra Lang, it is precisely where Ezekiel is most repetitive in style that his rhetorical intentions are best read.

8. Block, *Ezekiel 1–24*, 39.

9. See ch. 2, n. 135.

10. Thus answering the obloquy that Yahweh will not act (12:22–28).

11. Thomas Renz illustrates this point by remarking, when discussing Ezek 4, that the prophecy pays little attention to either the audience or Ezekiel's carrying out God's directives: "Strictly speaking, it is not the sign acts that are reported, but Yahweh's commands to the prophet to perform the sign acts. This is one of the techniques used to establish the book's theocentricity" (*Rhetorical Function*, 66).

dual purpose in taking action: to reveal himself in the glory and holiness of his name and to gain acknowledgment and honor as Israel's covenant Lord (note the abundant appearances of אדני).

The RF, however, is more than a rhetorical technique for asserting that God is acting in judgment and deliverance so as to remove the profanation of his name. It is more than explanatory. The "I am Yahweh" in the RF is itself a resounding redeclaration of the name in honor. For Ezekiel, the most grievous consequence of Israel's sordid behavior (טמא; 20:30–31, 43; 22:3–4; 23:13) is the defilement of the divine name (טמא Piel; 43:7–8). The prophecy's use of the RF may be understood rhetorically as a protest and reassertion of the name in honor and holiness. Further, the RF should be read as God's own testimony: "My holy name I shall make known among my people Israel, and I shall not let my holy name be profaned [חלל] anymore. And the nations shall know that I am Yahweh, the Holy One in Israel" (39:7; cf. 20:5, 9).

Relating the RF to the phrase "for the sake of my (holy) name" (20:9, 14, 22; 36:22–23),[12] one may profitably explore how Ezekiel's theme of the honor/sanctity of God's name (declared in the RF) radically reorients Israel's hope of deliverance. Previously, the nation had trusted in Jerusalem's inviolability[13] while claiming God's electing love and promises of peace (13:10, 16). Ezekiel's tone and portrayal of Yahweh subvert that conventional theology, as W. Dommershausen explains. "It is striking that Ezekiel here [36:20–23] stresses the honor and holiness of Yahweh rather than his mercy and love toward the exiles. It is obviously the prophet's purpose to provide the exiles, who had gone astray with their talk of God's mercy, with a new basis for their hope of deliverance."[14] In light of Israel's awakened sense of sin and shame (see 33:10), perhaps it is even a merciful relief for the exiles to hear that God will act to rescue "*not* for your sake" (36:22). (Why would he turn to save the likes of us!) Instead, there is a more believable reason: he acts in his zeal (קנא; 39:25) for his name, known in the asseveration "I am Yahweh."

Scrutiny of the RF can reveal the intended audience and thrust of an oracle where other clues are lacking. Consider, for example, how Ezekiel divides Israel into two groups: those remaining in the land facing judgment and those already in exile receiving hopeful promises. The exiles are implicitly threatened if they identify with those who are breaking the covenant back in the land and fail to turn from the nation's historical idolatry. Those in Babylon "shall know that I am Yahweh" in acts of judgment if they do not take warning. This is understood more clearly by examining the seeming grammatical inconsistency where second-person RFs appear in

---

12. The RF and the phrase are joined in 20:44.

13. For a fresh examination of the topic, see Tooman, "Ezekiel's Radical Challenge."

14. W. Dommershausen, "חלל *ḥll* I," in *TDOT*, 4:411. Intriguingly, there are similarities here to Moses's argument for divine forebearance and forgiveness after the golden-calf incident in Exod 32. His plea is grounded in concern for God's reputation among the nations (32:11–12; cf. 9:16; Josh 7:9).

prophecies speaking of those judged in the third person: *you* shall know ... when *they* fall slain (e.g., 6:13; 13:9). Sometimes there is a subsequent shift to addressing the judgment oracle and attached RF to the offenders in the second person (13:14). Those who experience judgment and those who are observers are both led to "know," but from the rhetorical angle it is the exiles who are the primary audience.

I agree with Thomas Renz on Ezekiel's rhetoric: "[The aim] is to shape Israel's present self-understanding as a community in exile. While the book ostensibly looks at the past (pre-destruction) and the future (restoration) much more than at the present situation (exile), it deals with the past and future to make a point for the present."[15] With regard to the RF, the prophecy states there *was* a knowing in times past and there *will be* a knowing in the future. In the present, the exiles receive from Ezekiel ben-Buzi vision reports of the glory of Yahweh, who draws near to them, abandoning his Jerusalem sanctuary. God also deigns to speak oracles to the community and correct their proverbial sayings. There is no question but that the formula communicates the expectation that Israel is *presently* to acknowledge Yahweh as their God. Chapter 20 has Yahweh confronting any of his people who are determined to be like tribes of other lands and serve wood and stone (v. 32). God's reply is fierce (vv. 32–38): I will not allow it to happen; I will rule over you (exiles). I will also bring you into the desert of the nations to execute judgment upon you—a judgment that had its precedent *in Egypt* at the time of the exodus (v. 36). You will be barred from the land. Then you shall know I am Yahweh.

One can detect a polemical function in Ezekiel's use of the RF. He avoids an explicit indictment that Israel *does not know* God in reverence and covenant-keeping,[16] but that implication is drummed home in the repetitious formula. That is to say, the RF may be interpreted from a privative angle: "In your spiritual condition, you fail to 'know' and regard Yahweh!" Perhaps the message that Israel's wickedness and pollution amount to godlessness (refusing to know the one declaring "I am Yahweh") strikes home with greater force when left unsaid. A lack of recognition of Yahweh on the part of Israel and the nations is plausibly taken to be the chief human problem addressed by the oracles.[17] The secondary

---

15. Renz, *Rhetorical Function*, 57. Pushing beyond Renz and quoting Fishbane, I stress how "the exodus tradition was used [in Ezekiel], from first to last, as a paradigmatic teaching for present and future generations" (*Text and Texture*, 121). Ezekiel shapes the community's self-understanding in a variety of ways, but particularly with the message of the exilic community's solidarity with preceding generations: its idolatrous tendencies (20:30–31), exodus into a desert, being spared destruction in the desert, awareness of onlooking nations, and a need to look "to the first exodus as the archetypal expression of its own future hope" (121). The RF belongs to this narrative and bolsters the argument. See also Sweeney, "Ezekiel's Conceptualization," who underlines allusions to Exodus.

16. See ch. 6, n. 118, and the surrounding discussion.

17. As argued above (n. 96 in ch. 4 and nn. 94 and 95 in ch. 5), Ezekiel polemically sets up an analogy with the ancient nemesis Pharaoh when charging Israel with hardheartedness and suggesting she refuses to "know" Yahweh.

and consequent problem is Israel's failure to recognize her own "abominations," a fault to be put right by the prophet's accusing disclosure (יד"ע Hiphil impv., 16:2; 20:4; 22:2; cf. 23:36).

The polemics continue as the prophecy argues that the refusal to know is a disgusting, age-old problem. Ezekiel presses on Israel Yahweh's historical covenant claim, which she has faithlessly rejected by playing the harlot, even as long ago as Egypt (20:8; 23:3, 8, 19, 21, 27). The profuse RF and its related SPF, echoing the narratives in Exodus, form a part of that claim: "I said to them [then], 'throw away, each of you, the detestable images before your eyes, and do not defile yourselves with the idols of Egypt. I am Yahweh your God!'" (20:7).[18] Beyond that, the repeated RF is rhetoric of a continuing claim on Israel, from the wilderness period (20:20, 26), to a wilderness experience of exile (20:38), and into the future (20:42–44).[19] The formula highlights the divine intention ultimately to redo an exodus-like redemption of Israel and renew the covenant with an outcome never before enduringly realized: Israel and the nations "shall know that I am Yahweh."

7.3. Defining the Theological Meaning of the Formula in Ezekiel

Drawing from all the research presented, I propose that the RF in Ezekiel indicates that the subjects of the verb יד"ע will assuredly "know" Yahweh in the sense of recognizing his powerful presence as God in his acts and his word (which cohere) according to the covenant made with Israel. The keynote formula speaks not so much of knowing something about Yahweh,[20] but of knowing him in his personal presence (cf. "may know me" in 38:16). In the past, the God of Israel had revealed himself (יד"ע Niphal)[21] and spoken his name to his people as a sure guarantee that

18. The RF not only accompanies the prophet's "history lesson" in an interpretive role (20:12, 20, 26); it may be regarded as *part* of the history lesson as an echo of Exodus's narratives themselves.

19. C. A. Strine makes a related point about the usefulness of the exodus tradition: "Ezekiel employs the exodus tradition to offer hope to those who would resist assimilation into the surrounding culture. To wit, just as YHWH guided the people out from under Pharaoh and the Egyptian deities, YHWH could and would guide the exiles out from under the king of Babylon and his patron deity Marduk. When Ezek 17, 20, and 34 maintain that it was YHWH who scattered the Judahites into Babylon in the first place, they do so to make a case that YHWH can also gather them back to Judah. Coinciding with this interpretation, Ezekiel produces a boundary marker by which the community can demonstrate its allegiance to this interpretation of history: the rejection of image-based worship" (*Sworn Enemies*, 282).

20. Though not the core message, there are truths *about* Yahweh not to be missed, such as his sovereignty over the nations and Israel's history—"I shall rule over you!" (20:33).

21. According to *DCH*, the Niphal of יד"ע rarely has Yahweh as the subject in the Hebrew Bible ("יהוה," 4:128). Texts cited are: Exod 6:3 [allegedly P]; Isa 19:21; Ezek 20:5, 7; Ps 9:17[16]. (Hab 3:2 is noted as another possible text, but that requires emendation of the Hiphil.) Fascinatingly, with the exception of Ps 9:17, all these texts relate theologically to the exodus narratives.

he would fulfill his covenant promises. "I made myself known to them in the land of Egypt and I swore [lit.: raised my hand] to them, saying, 'I am Yahweh your God'" (Ezek 20:5). As then, so now, Yahweh's acts and word are authoritatively declared with a kind of signature seal, "I am Yahweh," within the RF.[22] And he will be known in those acts and words that, for the prophet Ezekiel, hark back to previous mighty acts and a previous word of God in the exodus story.[23]

Yahweh's acts and words together—past, present, and future—direct people to know him in both salvation and judgment. He is profoundly the God of both. Yahweh is the God of deliverance (Exod 14:1–31; 17:8–16) and gracious provision (plunder, guidance, water, manna, quail) from the time of "the fathers." However, the same Yahweh is to be feared by his enemies (Exod 9:30) and his own people (Exod 20:20) as a God of holiness, jealousy, judgment, and wrath against all godlessness. The proclamation of Ezekiel the preacher is that there is life and refuge *in* Yahweh for those who turn from evil (18:23) to keep faith with him, but there is no life and no refuge *from* him, if one is wicked and unfaithful.

If Yahweh is the covenant name of the God of the Bible, then his actions performed with the attendant RF can be interpreted as covenant enforcement. What should "Yahweh" mean to the nations? That is the name of the deity in covenant with Israel who fulfills his covenant word in defending his people with terrible judgments upon their foes.[24] The nations who trouble Israel will know the outpoured wrath of Yahweh, perhaps in answer to the prayers of Israel post-586: "Pour out your wrath on the nations that do not know you!" (Ps 79:6; Jer 10:25).[25] And to Israel, Yahweh will be known as the God of the covenant who cannot allow his people to repudiate the "bond of life and love"[26] so as to engage in idolatry like other nations (20:33). Yahweh is insistent: "I shall make you pass under the rod and bring you into the bond of the covenant" (20:37). He will enforce the

---

22. The *Selbstvorstellungsformel*, אני יהוה, appears only 3× on its own in Ezekiel. In the first text, 20:5, it not only coincides with Yahweh's action in taking an oath (the uplifted hand) to his covenant people in Egypt, but seems to *be* the oath. God is swearing by God that he will fulfill his promise. In the second and third texts, 20:7 and 19, the phrase אני יהוה asserts God's authority to claim Israel's allegiance and proscribe idolatry. But the phrase is predominantly (73×) found embedded in the RF, plus one related statement with the verb ראה.

23. As noted in ch. 4, the prophet not only takes his hearers/readers back in time to recall the exodus story (Ezek 20); he reuses in a startling way the language of that watershed passage in Exod 6, where the RF first appears and indicates God's covenant goal. "I am Yahweh. . . . I have remembered my covenant. . . . You shall know that I am Yahweh your God, *who brought you out of forced labor in Egypt*."

24. The nations are never said to "know that I am Yahweh" when Yahweh punishes his people.

25. "It seems to us indisputable that the event [calling forth the psalm's pathos] was the destruction of the Temple and Jerusalem," say Frank-Lothar Hossfeld and Erich Zenger (*Psalms* 2, 304). They believe this "psalm is in an intertextual conversation with the book of Jeremiah" (305), but there are connections with Ezekiel as well.

26. Gerard Van Groningen's characterization of the OT ברית.

covenant sanctions, purging out the rebels and making certain that his holy name is no longer profaned. In all the judgments, "you shall know that I am Yahweh" (20:38–39). "Whether they listen or refuse to listen, . . . they shall know" (2:5),[27] and ultimately they shall recognize that a prophet was among them and that God has given a compelling self-revelation in word ("I am Yahweh") and in deed.

Yet, after Yahweh's severity, there will be another chapter opened in which both the nations and Israel will recognize Yahweh in the restoration of the covenant people. The arm that reached out to gather the covenant people from the nations for judgment (20:34–38) will reach out again—another "new exodus"—to bring a repentant and purified people into "the land I swore to give to your fathers" (20:41–44). Yahweh will show himself holy in the sight of many nations (39:27) and be known through a "covenant of peace" as he protects his people and sends "showers of blessing."

> And they shall know that I am Yahweh when I break the bars of their yoke and deliver them from the hand of those who had enslaved them. They shall no longer be prey to the nations, and the beasts of the land shall not devour them; they shall dwell securely and none shall frighten them. And I shall provide famously productive farms for them, so they shall not be consumed with hunger and not suffer any longer the taunts of the nations. They shall know that I, Yahweh, their God am with them and that they, the house of Israel, are my people. The declaration of Yahweh. (34:27b–30)

To sum up, Ezekiel's recognition formula points to a redemptive covenant in the past and a covenant yet to be (16:60, 62), the conclusion of which will be the eternal dwelling of Yahweh with his people. The formula reflects a historical perspective on God's saving acts, asserts that Yahweh acts to reveal himself as covenant Lord in the nation's current situation, and expresses Israel's only hope for the future: that Yahweh will continue to act in history to reveal himself and to redeem and sanctify his people. According to Ezekiel's theology, Yahweh was, and is, and shall be, the God of exodus.[28]

---

27. The crucial point here is that "knowing" is not dependent on the subject's repentance—cf. the experience of Egypt and Pharaoh in Exodus. However, it is certainly the case that repentance ("repent and live!"; 18:32) has a bearing on whether Yahweh will be known in judgment or restoration. In "The Role Of Repentance," Strine seems to equate the demand for repentance with the call to know Yahweh (485n70).

28. A similar point regarding Isaiah is made in Zenger, "The God of Exodus," 22–33. Compare also Mic 7:15.

Abba, Raymond. "Name." *IDB* 1:500–508.

———. "Priests and Levites in Ezekiel." *VT* 28 (1978): 1–9.

Ackerman, Susan. *Under Every Green Tree: Popular Religion in Sixth Century Judah.* HSM 46. Atlanta: Scholars Press, 1992.

Ackroyd, Peter R. *Exile and Restoration.* OTL. Philadelphia: Westminster, 1968.

Adorno, Theodor W. *Negative Dialektik.* Frankfurt: Suhrkamp, 1966.

Ahn, John J. *Exile as Forced Migrations: A Sociological, Literary, and Theological Approach on the Displacement and Resettlement of the Southern Kingdom of Judah.* BZAW 417. Berlin: de Gruyter, 2011.

Ahn, John J., and Jill Middlemas, eds. *By the Irrigation Canals of Babylon: Approaches to the Study of the Exile.* LHBOTS 526. London: T&T Clark, 2012.

Aichele, George. *The Control of Biblical Meaning: Canon as Semiotic Mechanism.* Harrisburg: Trinity Press International, 2001.

Aichele, George, and Gary A. Phillips, eds. *Intertextuality and the Bible. Semeia* 69/70 (1995).

Alberti, Leon Battista. *On Painting.* Translated by John R. Spencer. New Haven: Yale University Press, 1970.

Albertz, Rainer. *Israel in Exile: The History and Literature of the Sixth Century B.C.E.* StBibLit 3. Atlanta: Society of Biblical Literature, 2003.

Allen, Graham. *Intertextuality.* 2nd ed. London: Routledge, 2011.

Allen, Leslie C. *The Books of Joel, Obadiah, Jonah and Micah.* NICOT. Grand Rapids: Eerdmans, 1976.

———. *Ezekiel 1–19.* WBC 28. Waco, TX: Word, 1994.

———. *Ezekiel 20–48.* WBC 29. Waco, TX: Word, 1990.

———. "Structure, Tradition and Redaction in Ezekiel's Death Valley Vision." Pages 127–42 in *Among the Prophets: Language, Image and Structure in the Prophetic Writings.* Edited by Philip R. Davies and David J. A. Clines. JSOTSup 144. Sheffield: JSOT Press, 1993.

———. "The Structuring of Ezekiel's Revisionist History Lesson (Ezekiel 20:3–31)." *CBQ* 54 (1992): 448–62.

Allis, O. T. *The Unity of Isaiah.* London: Tyndale, 1951.

Allison, Dale C. Jr. *The New Moses: A Matthean Typology.* Edinburgh: T&T Clark, 1993.

Alonso Schökel, Luis. "Jeremías como anti-Moisés." Pages 245–54 in *De la Tôrah au Messie: Études d'exégèse et d'herméneutique bibliques offertes à Henri Cazelles pour ses 25 années d'enseignement à l'Institut catholique de Paris, octobre 1979.* Edited by Maurice Carrez et al. Paris: Desclée, 1981.

Alt, Albrecht. *Die Ursprünge des Israelitischen Rechts.* Leipzig: Hirzel, 1934.

Andersen, Francis I. *The Hebrew Verbless Clause in the Pentateuch.* JBLMS 14. Nashville: Abingdon, 1970.

Andersen, Francis I., and David Noel Freedman. *Hosea.* AB 24. Garden City, NY: Doubleday, 1980.

Anderson, George W. "Hebrew Religion." Pages 283–310 in *The Old Testament and Modern Study.* Edited by H. H. Rowley. Oxford: Clarendon, 1951.

Auvray, Paul. *Ézéchiel.* 2nd ed. Paris: Cerf, 1957.

Awabdy, Mark A. "YHWH Exegetes Torah: How Ezekiel 44:7–9 Bars Foreigners from the Sanctuary." *JBL* 131 (2012): 685–703.

Bailey, Randall C. "'And They Shall Know that I Am YHWH!': The P Recasting of the Plague Narratives in Exodus 7–11." *JITC* 22 (1994): 1–17.

Bakhtin, Mikhail M. *The Dialogic Imagination.* Translated by Caryl Emerson and Michael Holquist. Austin: University of Texas Press, 1981.

Balentine, Samuel E. *The Hidden God: The Hiding of the Face of God in the Old Testament.* Oxford: Oxford University Press, 1983.

Ball, David Mark. *"I Am" in John's Gospel: Literary Function, Background and Theological Implications.* JSNTSup 124. Sheffield: Sheffield Academic, 1996.

Baltzer, Klaus. *Das Bundesformular.* WMANT 4. 2nd. ed. Neukirchen-Vluyn: Neukirchener Verlag, 1964.

Barr, James. *The Semantics of Biblical Language.* Glasgow: Oxford University Press, 1961.

———. "The Symbolism of Names in the Old Testament." *BJRL* 52 (1969): 11–29.

Barstad, Hans M. "No Prophets? Recent Developments in Biblical Prophetic Research and Ancient Near Eastern Prophecy." *JSOT* 57 (1993): 39–60.

Barth, Karl. *Dogmatics in Outline.* Translated by G. T. Thomson. London: SCM, 1949.

Barthes, Roland. "The Death of the Author." Pages 142–48 in *Image-Music-Text.* Translated by Stephen Heath. New York: Hill & Wang, 1977. Translation of "La mort de l'auteur." *Mantéia* 5 (1968): 12–17.

Barton, John. "*Déjà lu*: Intertextuality, Method or Theory?" Pages 1–16 in *Reading Job Intertextually.* Edited by Katharine Dell and Will Kynes. LHBOTS 574. New York: Bloomsbury T&T Clark, 2013.

———. *Joel and Obadiah: A Commentary.* OTL. Louisville: Westminster John Knox, 2001.

Baumann, Eberhard. "'Wissen um Gott' bei Hosea als Urform von Theologie?" *EvT* 15 (1955): 416–25.

Baumgärtel, Friedrich. "Die Formel *neʾum Jahwe.*" *ZAW* 73 (1961): 277–90.

Baumgartner, Walter, and Ludwig Koehler. *Hebrew and Aramaic Lexicon of the Old Testament.* Revised by Walter Baumgartner and Johann Jakob Stamm. Translated and edited under M. E. J. Richardson. 5 vols. Leiden: Brill, 1994.

Beal, Timothy K. "Glossary." Pages 21–24 in *Reading between Texts: Intertextuality and the Hebrew Bible.* Edited by Danna Nolan Fewell. Louisville: Westminster John Knox, 1992.

Becker, Joachim. "Erwägungen zur ezechielischen Frage." Pages 137–49 in *Künder des Wortes: Beiträge zur Theologie der Propheten (Josef Schreiner zum 60. Geburtstag).* Edited by Lothar Ruppert et al. Würzburg: Echter, 1982.

———. "Ez 8–11 als einheitliche Komposition in einem pseudepigraphischen Ezechielbuch." Pages 136–50 in Lust, *Ezekiel and His Book.*

———. "Zur 'Ich bin'-Formel im Alten Testament." *BN* 98 (1999): 45–54.

Beetham, Christopher A. *Echoes of Scripture in the Letter of Paul to the Colossians.* BibInt. Leiden: Brill, 2008.

Ben-Ezra, Menachem. "Earliest Evidence of Post-traumatic Stress?" *British Journal of Psychiatry* 179 (2001): 467.

Ben Zvi, Ehud, and Christoph Levin, eds. *The Concept of Exile in Ancient Israel and Its Historical Contexts.* BZAW 404. Berlin: de Gruyter, 2010.

Bergman, Jan. *Ich bin Isis: Studien zum memphitischen Hintergrund der griechischen Isisaretalogien.* Historia Religionum 3. Uppsala: Uppsala Universitet; Stockholm: Almqvist & Wiksell, 1968.

Berlin, Adele. "Did the Jews Worship Idols in Babylonia?" Pages 323–33 in *Homeland and Exile: Biblical and Ancient Near Eastern Studies in Honour of Bustenay Oded.* Edited by Gershon Galil et al. VTSup 130. Leiden: Brill, 2009.

Betts, T. J. *Ezekiel the Priest: A Custodian of Tôrâ.* StBibLit 74. New York: Lang, 2005.

Beuken, Willem A. M. *Isaiah II/2, Isaiah Chapters 28–39.* HCOT. Leuven: Peeters, 2000.

———. "Jesaja 33 als Spiegeltext im Jesajabuch." *ETL* 67 (1991): 5–55.

———. "Servant and Herald of Good Tidings: Isaiah 61 as an Interpretation of Isaiah 40–55." Pages 411–42 in *The Book of Isaiah—Le livre d'Isaïa: Les oracles et leurs relectures: Unité et complexité de l'ouvrage.* Edited by J. Vermeylen. BETL 81. Leuven: Leuven University Press, 1989.

Blank, Sheldon H. *Prophetic Faith in Isaiah.* Detroit: Wayne State University Press, 1967.

———. "Studies in Deutero-Isaiah." *HUCA* 15 (1940): 1–46.

Blenkinsopp, Joseph. "An Assessment of the Alleged Pre-Exilic Date of the Priestly Material in the Pentateuch." *ZAW* 108 (1996): 495–518.

———. *Ezekiel.* Interpretation. Louisville: John Knox, 1990.

———. *Isaiah 1–39.* AB 19. New York: Doubleday, 2000.

———. "Prophecy and the Prophetic Books." Pages 323–47 in *Text and Context.* Edited by A. D. H. Mayes. Oxford: Oxford University Press, 2000.

Bloch, Renée. "Ezéchiel XVI: Exemple Parfait du Procédé Midrashique dans la Bible." *Cahiers Sioniens* 9 (1955): 193–223.

———. "Midrash." Pages 1263–81 in *Supplément au Dictionnaire de la Bible,* vol. 5. Paris: Letouzey et Ané, 1957.

Block, Daniel I. *Beyond the River Chebar: Studies in Kingship and Eschatology in the Book of Ezekiel.* Cambridge: James Clarke, 2013.

———. *The Book of Ezekiel, Chapters 1–24.* NICOT. Grand Rapids: Eerdmans, 1997.

———. *The Book of Ezekiel, Chapters 25–48.* NICOT. Grand Rapids: Eerdmans, 1998.

———. *By the River Chebar: Historical, Literary, and Theological Studies in the Book of Ezekiel.* Eugene, OR: Cascade, 2013.

———. "Divine Abandonment: Ezekiel's Adaptation of an Ancient Near Eastern Motif." Pages 15–42 in Odell and Strong, *The Book of Ezekiel.*

———. "Ezekiel's Boiling Cauldron: A Form-critical Solution to Ezekiel XXIV 1–14," *VT* 41 (1991): 12–37.

———. "The God Ezekiel Wants Us to Meet: Theological Perspectives on the Book of Ezekiel." Pages 162–92 in Joyce and Rom-Shiloni, *The God Ezekiel Creates.*

———. "Gog and Magog in Ezekiel's Eschatological Vision." Pages 85–116 in *The Reader Must Understand.* Edited by K. E. Brower and M. W. Elliott. Leicester: Apollos, 1997.

———. "In Search of Theological Meaning." Pages 227–39 in Cook and Patton, *Ezekiel's Hierarchical World.*

———. "The Period of the Judges: Religious Disintegration Under Tribal Rule." Pages 39–57 in *Israel's Apostasy and Restoration: Essays in Honor of Roland K. Harrison.* Edited by Avraham Gileadi. Grand Rapids: Baker, 1988.

Bloom, Harold. *The Anxiety of Influence.* New York: Oxford University Press, 1973.

Boadt, Lawrence. "Ezekiel, Book of." *ABD,* 2:711–22.

———. *Ezekiel's Oracles against Egypt: A Literary and Philological Study of Ezekiel 29–32.* BibOr 37. Rome: Pontifical Biblical Institute, 1980.

———. "The Function of the Salvation Oracles in Ezekiel 33 to 37." *HAR* 12 (1990): 1–21.

———. "Mythological Themes and the Unity of Ezekiel." Pages 211–31 in *Literary Structure and Rhetorical Strategies in the Hebrew Bible.* Edited by L. J. de Regt, J. de Waard, and J. P. Fokkelman. Assen: Van Gorcum, 1996.

———. Review of *The Book of Ezekiel, Chapters 1–24,* by Daniel I. Block. *Biblica* 80 (1999): 134–37.

Boardman, John, I. E. S. Edwards, N. G. L. Hammond, and E. Sollberger, eds. *The Assyrian and Babylonian Empires and Other States of the Near East, from the Eighth to the Sixth Centuries B.C.* Vol. 3/2 of *The Cambridge Ancient History.* 2nd ed. Cambridge: Cambridge University Press, 1991.

Boda, Mark J. *The Book of Zechariah.* NICOT. Grand Rapids: Eerdmans, 2016.

Boda, Mark J., Frank Ritchel Ames, John Ahn, and Mark Leuchter, eds. *The Prophets Speak on Forced Migration.* Atlanta: SBL Press, 2015.

Boda, Mark J., Michael H. Floyd, and Colin Toffelmire, eds. *The Book of the Twelve and the New Form Criticism.* ANEM 10. Atlanta: SBL Press, 2015.

Boda, Mark J., and J. Gordon McConville, eds. *Dictionary of the Old Testament: Prophets* [*DOTPr*]. Downers Grove, IL: IVP Academic, 2012.

Bodi, Daniel. *The Book of Ezekiel and the Poem of Erra.* OBO 104. Fribourg: Universitätsverlag; Göttingen: Vandenhoeck & Ruprecht, 1991.

Bogaert, Pierre-Maurice. "Le deux rédactions conservées (LXX et TM) d'Ézéchiel 7." Pages 21–47 in Lust, *Ezekiel and His Book.*

Bosman, Hendrik. "The Absence and Presence of God in the Book of Exodus as Theological Synthesis." *Scriptura* 85 (2004): 1–13.

Botterweck, G. Johannes. *"Gott erkennen" im Sprachgebrauch des Alten Testamentes.* BBB 2. Bonn: Hanstein, 1951.

Botterweck, G. Johannes, Helmer Ringgren, and Heinz-Josef Fabry, eds. *Theological Dictionary of the Old Testament.* 15 vols. Translated by John T. Willis, Geoffrey W. Bromiley, David E. Green, Douglas W. Stott. Grand Rapids: Eerdmans, 1974–2006.

Botterweck, G. Johannes, Helmer Ringgren, and Heinz-Josef Fabry, eds. *Theologisches Wörterbuch zum Alten Testament.* 10 vols. Stuttgart: Kohlhammer, 1973–2000.

Boyarin, Daniel. *Intertextuality and the Reading of Midrash.* Bloomington: Indiana University Press, 1990.

Boyd, J. Oscar. "Ezekiel and the Modern Dating of the Pentateuch." *Princeton Theological Review* 6 (1908): 29–51.

Bridges, Robert. "Prometheus the Firegiver" (1883). *Poetical Works of Robert Bridges, Excluding the Eight Dramas.* 2nd ed. London: Oxford University Press, 1936.

Briggs, Richard S. *Words in Action: Speech Act Theory and Biblical Interpretation.* New York: Continuum T&T Clark, 2001.

Bright, John. *A History of Israel.* 4th ed. Philadelphia: Westminster John Knox, 2000.

Broome, Edwin C. Jr. "Ezekiel's Abnormal Personality." *JBL* 65 (1946): 277–92.

Brown, F., Samuel R. Driver, and C. A. Briggs, eds. *A Hebrew and English Lexicon of the Old Testament.* Oxford: Clarendon, 1907.

Brownlee, William H. *Ezekiel 1–19.* WBC 28. Waco, TX: Word, 1986.

Bruce, Don. "Bibliographie annotée: Écrits sur l'intertextualité." *Texte* 2 (1983): 217–58.

Brueggemann, Walter. *An Introduction to the Old Testament: The Canon and Christian Imagination.* Louisville: Westminster John Knox, 2003.

———. *Theology of the Old Testament: Testimony, Dispute, Advocacy*. Minneapolis: Fortress, 1997.

Buber, Martin. *At the Turning: Three Addresses on Judaism*. New York: Farrar, Straus and Young, 1952.

———. *The Prophetic Faith*. Translated by Carlyle Witton-Davies. New York: Macmillan, 1949.

Buchholz, Joachim. *Die Ältesten Israels im Deuteronomium*. Göttinger Theologischer Arbeiten 36. Göttingen: Vandenhoeck & Ruprecht, 1988.

Bullock, C. Hassell. *An Introduction to the Old Testament Prophetic Books*. Chicago: Moody, 1986.

Bultmann, Rudolf. "The Significance of the Old Testament for Christian Faith." Pages 8–35 in *The Old Testament and the Christian Faith*. Edited by Bernhard W. Anderson. New York: Harper & Row, 1963.

Burden, J. J. "Esegiël, Priester en Profeet." *Theologica Evangelica* 18 (1985): 14–21.

Burnett, Joel S. "The Question of Divine Absence in Israelite and West Semitic Religion." *CBQ* 67 (2005): 215–35.

Burrows, Millar. *The Literary Relations of Ezekiel*. Philadelphia: Jewish Publication Society, 1925.

Buss, Martin. *The Changing Shape of Form Criticism: A Relational Approach*. HBM 18. Sheffield: Sheffield Phoenix, 2010.

Buttrick, George Arthur, ed. *The Interpreter's Dictionary of the Bible*. 4 vols. New York: Abingdon, 1962.

Callender, Dexter, Jr. "The Recognition Formula and Ezekiel's Conception of God." Pages 71–86 in Joyce and Rom-Shiloni, *The God Ezekiel Creates*.

Calvin, John. *Commentaries on the First Twenty Chapters of the Book of the Prophet Ezekiel*. Translated by T. Myers. Grand Rapids: Baker, 1981 (reprint).

———. *Commentary on the Book of the Prophet Isaiah*. Translated by William Pringle. Vol. 1. Grand Rapids: Baker, 1981 (reprint).

Campbell, Athony. "Form Criticism's Future." Pages 15–31 in Sweeney and Ben Zvi, *The Changing Face of Form Criticism*.

Carasik, Michael. *Theologies of the Mind in Biblical Israel*. StBibLit 85. New York: Lang, 2006.

Carew, M. Douglas. "To Know or Not to Know: Hosea's Use of *ydʿ/dʿt*." Pages 73–85 in *The Old Testament in the Life of God's People: Essays in Honor of Elmer A. Martens*. Edited by Jon Isaak. Winona Lake, IN: Eisenbrauns, 2009.

Carley, Keith W. *Ezekiel among the Prophets*. Naperville, IL: Allenson, 1974.

Carr, David M. "Data to Inform Ongoing Debates about the Formation of the Pentateuch—From Documented Cases of Transmission History to a Survey of Rabbinic Study." Pages 87–106 in Gertz, Levinson, and Rom-Shiloni, *The Formation of the Pentateuch*.

———. "Method in Determination of Direction of Dependence: An Empirical Test of Criteria Applied to Exodus 34,11–26 and its Parallels." Pages 107–40 in *Gottes Volk am Sinai: Untersuchungen zu Ex 32–34 und Dtn 9–10*. Edited by Matthias Köckert and Erhard Blum. Gütersloh: Kaiser-Gütersloher, 2001.

Carroll, Robert P. "Deportation and Diasporic Discourses in the Prophetic Literature." Pages 63–85 in Scott, *Exile*.

———. "The Elijah-Elisha Sagas: Some Remarks on Prophetic Succession in Ancient Israel." *VT* 19 (1969): 400–15.

————. "Intertextuality and the Book of Jeremiah: Animadversions on Text and Theory." Pages 55–78 in Exum and Clines, *The New Literary Criticism and the Hebrew Bible.*

————. "The Myth of the Empty Land." *Semeia* 59 (1992): 79–93.

————. "Strange Fire: Abstract of Presence Absent in the Text, Meditations on Exodus 3." *JSOT* 61 (1994): 39–58.

Cassuto, Umberto. *A Commentary on the Book of Exodus.* Translated by Israel Abrahams. Jerusalem: Magnes, 1967.

————. "The Prophet Hosea and the Books of the Pentateuch." Pages 79–100 in *Biblical and Oriental Studies I.* Translated by Israel Abrahams. Jerusalem: Magnes, 1973.

Chapman, Stephen B. *The Law and the Prophets: A Study in Old Testament Canon Formation.* FAT 27. Tübingen: Mohr Siebeck, 2000.

Charles, R. H. *A Critical and Exegetical Commentary on the Revelation of St. John.* Vol. 1. ICC. Edinburgh: T&T Clark, 1920.

Childs, Brevard S. *The Book of Exodus: A Critical, Theological Commentary.* OTL. Philadelphia: Westminster, 1974.

————. "The Canon in Recent Biblical Studies." *ProEccl* 14 (2005): 26–45.

————. "The Canonical Shape of the Prophetic Literature." *Int* 32 (1978): 46–55.

————. *Introduction to the Old Testament as Scripture.* Philadelphia: Fortress, 1979.

————. *Memory and Tradition in Israel.* SBT 37. Naperville, IL: Allenson, 1962.

————. "Midrash and the Old Testament." Pages 45–59 in *Understanding the Sacred Text: Essays in Honor of Morton S. Enslin.* Edited by J. Reumann. Valley Forge, PA: Judson Press, 1972.

————. "Speech-Act Theory and Biblical Interpretation." *SJT* 58 (2005): 375–92.

Clayton, Jay, and Eric Rothstein, eds. *Influence and Intertextuality in Literary History.* Madison: University of Wisconsin Press, 1991.

Clements, Ronald E. "Beyond Tradition-History: Deutero-Isaianic Development of First Isaiah's Themes." Pages 78–92 (ch. 5) in *Old Testament Prophecy: From Oracles to Canon.* Louisville: Westminster John Knox, 1996.

Clines, David J. A. "Beyond Synchronic/Diachronic." Pages 52–71 in *Synchronic or Diachronic? A Debate on Method in Old Testament Exegesis.* Edited by Johannes C. de Moor. OtSt 34. Leiden: Brill, 1995.

————, ed. *The Dictionary of Classical Hebrew.* 8 vols. Sheffield: Sheffield Academic, 1993–2011.

Cogan, Mordechai. *The Raging Torrent: Historical Inscriptions from Assyria and Babylonia Relating to Ancient Israel.* Jerusalem: Carta, 2008.

Cogan, Mordechai, and Hayim Tadmor. *II Kings.* AB 11. Garden City, NY: Doubleday, 1988.

Cohen, Menachem, ed. *Book of Jeremiah.* Vol. 11 of *Mikra'ot Gedolot "Haketer."* Ramat-Gan, Israel: Bar-Ilan University Press, 2012. [Hebrew]

Collins, John J. *Introduction to the Hebrew Bible.* Minneapolis: Fortress, 2004.

Cook, Stephen L. "Innerbiblical Interpretation in Ezekiel 44 and the History of Israel's Priesthood." *JBL* 114 (1995): 193–208.

Cook, Stephen L., and Corrine L. Patton, eds. *Ezekiel's Hierarchical World: Wrestling with a Tiered Reality.* SBLSymS 31. Atlanta: Society of Biblical Literature, 2004.

Cooke, G. A. *A Critical and Exegetical Commentary on the Book of Ezekiel.* ICC. Edinburgh: T&T Clark, 1936.

Coote, Robert B. "Yahweh Recalls Elijah." Pages 115–20 in *Traditions in Transformation: Turning Points in Biblical Faith.* Edited by Bruce Halpern and Jon Levenson. Winona Lake, IN: Eisenbrauns, 1981.

Cotterell, Peter, and Max Turner. *Linguistics and Biblical Interpretation*. London: SPCK, 1989.

Crane, Ashley S. *Israel's Restoration: A Textual-Comparative Exploration of Ezekiel 36–39*. VTSup 122. Leiden: Brill, 2008.

Crenshaw, James L. *Joel*. AB 24C. New York: Doubleday, 1995.

———. *Prophetic Conflict: Its Effect upon Israelite Religion*. BZAW 124. Berlin: de Gruyter, 1971.

Crim, Keith, ed. *The Interpreter's Dictionary of the Bible, Supplementary Volume*. Nashville: Abingdon, 1976.

Cross, Frank Moore. *Canaanite Myth and Hebrew Epic: Essays in the History of the Religion of Israel*. Cambridge, MA: Harvard University Press, 1973.

Culler, Jonathan. *The Pursuit of Signs*. Ithaca: Cornell University Press, 1981.

Daniels, Dwight R. *Hosea and Salvation History: The Early Traditions of Israel in the Prophecy of Hosea*. BZAW 191. Berlin: de Gruyter, 1990.

Darr, Katheryn Pfisterer. "The Book of Ezekiel." Pages 1073–607 of vol. 6 of *The New Interpreter's Bible*. Nashville: Abingdon, 2001.

———. "Ezekiel among the Critics." *CurBS* 2 (1994): 9–24.

———. "Literary Perspectives on Prophetic Literature." Pages 127–43 in *Old Testament Interpretation: Past, Present, and Future: Essays in Honor of Gene M. Tucker*. Edited by James Luther Mays et al. Nashville: Abingdon, 1995.

———. "The Wall Around Paradise: Ezekielian Ideas About the Future." *VT* 37 (1987): 271–79.

Davidson, A. B. *The Book of the Prophet Ezekiel*. CBSC. Cambridge: Cambridge University Press, 1892.

Davies, G. Henton. *Exodus: Introduction and Commentary*. TBC. London: SCM, 1967.

Davies, G. I. *Hosea*. NCBC. Grand Rapids: Eerdmans, 1992.

———. Review of *A Linguistic Study of the Relationship Between the Priestly Source and the Book of Ezekiel*, by Avi Hurvitz. *VT* 37 (1987): 117–18.

Davis, Ellen F. "Swallowing Hard: Reflections on Ezekiel's Dumbness." Pages 217–37 in *Signs and Wonders: Biblical Texts in Literary Focus*. Edited by J. Cheryl Exum. SemeiaSt. Atlanta: Scholars Press, 1989.

———. *Swallowing the Scroll: Textuality and the Dynamics of Discourse in Ezekiel's Prophecy*. JSOTSup 78. Sheffield: Almond, 1989.

Day, John, ed. *In Search of Pre-exilic Israel: Proceedings of the Oxford Old Testament Seminar*. JSOTSup 406. London: T&T Clark, 2004.

Deijl, Aarnoud van der. *Protest or Propaganda: War in the Old Testament Book of Kings and in Contemporaneous Ancient Near Eastern Texts*. SSN 51. Leiden: Brill, 2008.

Deist, Ferdinand E. "On 'Synchronic' and 'Diachronic': Wie es eigentlich gewesen." *JNSL* 21 (1995): 37–48.

DeLapp, Nevada Levi. "Ezekiel as Moses—Israel as Pharaoh: Reverberations of the Exodus Narrative in Ezekiel." Pages 51–73 in *Reverberations of the Exodus in Scripture*. Edited by R. Michael Fox. Eugene, OR: Pickwick, 2015.

Dentan, Robert C. *The Knowledge of God in Ancient Israel*. New York: Seabury, 1968.

Dharamraj, Havilah. *A Prophet Like Moses? A Narrative-Theological Reading of the Elijah Stories*. Milton Keynes, UK: Paternoster, 2011.

Di Pede, Elena. "'C'est par un prophète qu'Adonaï a fait monter Israël d'Égypte': Moïse 'prophète' dans le livre de l'Exode." Pages 55–71 in *A Pillar of Cloud to Guide: Text-Critical, Redactional, and Linguistic Perspectives on the Old Testament in Honour of Marc Vervenne*. Edited by Hans Ausloos et al. BETL 269. Leuven: Peeters, 2014.

Diesel, Anja Angela. *"Ich bin Jahwe": Der Aufstieg der Ich-bin-Jahwe-Aussage zum Schlüsselwort des alttestamentlichen Monotheismus*. WMANT 110. Neukirchen-Vluyn: Neukirchener Verlag, 2006.

Dijkstra, Meindert. *Gods Voorstelling: Predikatieve expressie van zelfopenbaring in oudoosterse teksten en Deutero-Jesaja*. DNST 2. Kampen: Kok, 1980.

———. "The Valley of Dry Bones: Coping with the Reality of Exile in the Book of Ezekiel." Pages 127–32 in *The Crisis of Israelite Religion: Transformation of Religious Tradition in Exilic and Post-Exilic Times*. Edited by Bob Becking and M. C. A. Korpel. OtSt 42. Leiden: Brill, 1999.

Dimant, Devorah. *Qumran Cave 4.XXI: Parabiblical Texts, Part 4: Pseudo-Prophetic Texts*. DJD 30. Oxford: Clarendon, 2001.

Dion, H.-M. "Le genre littéraire sumérien de l' «hymne à soi-même» et quelques passages du Deutéro-Isaïa." *RB* 74 (1967): 215–34.

Dodd, C. H. *The Interpretation of the Fourth Gospel*. Cambridge: Cambridge University Press, 1954.

Dozeman, Thomas B. "Inner-biblical Interpretation of Yahweh's Gracious and Compassionate Character." *JBL* 108 (1989): 207–23.

Dozeman, Thomas B., and Konrad Schmid, eds. *A Farewell to the Yahwist? The Composition of the Pentateuch in Recent European Interpretation*. SBLSymS 34. Atlanta: Society of Biblical Literature, 2006.

Dozeman, Thomas B., Konrad Schmid, and Baruch J. Schwartz, eds. *The Pentateuch: International Perspectives on Current Research*. FAT 2.78. Tübingen: Mohr Siebeck, 2011.

Draisma, Sipke, ed. *Intertextuality in Biblical Writings: Essays in Honour of Bas van Iersel*. Kampen: Kok, 1989.

Driver, S. R. *An Introduction to the Literature of the Old Testament*. 9th ed. Edinburgh: T&T Clark, 1913.

Dubbink, Joep. "A Story of Three Prophets: Synchronic and Diachronic Analysis of Jeremiah 26." Pages 13–30 in *Tradition and Innovation in Biblical Interpretation: Studies Presented to Professor Eep Talstra on the Occasion of his Sixty-Fifth Birthday*. Edited by W. Th. van Peursen et al. SSN 57. Leiden: Brill, 2011.

Duguid, Iain M. *Ezekiel and the Leaders of Israel*. VTSup 56. Leiden: Brill, 1994.

———. "Ezekiel: History of Interpretation." *DOTPr*, 229–35.

———. "Putting Priests in Their Place: Ezekiel's Contribution to the History of the Old Testament Priesthood." Pages 43–59 in Cook and Patton, *Ezekiel's Hierarchical World*.

Dunn, James D. G. Review of *Justification and Variegated Nomism*, vol. 1, *The Complexities of Second Temple Judaism*, edited by D. A. Carson, Peter T. O'Brien, and Mark A. Seifrid. *TJ* 25 (2004): 111–13.

Durham, John I. *Exodus*. WBC 3. Waco, TX: Word, 1987.

Eichrodt, Walther. *Ezekiel*. Translated by Cosslett Quin. OTL. London: SCM, 1970. Translation of *Der Prophet Hesekiel*. ATD 22. Göttingen: Vandenhoeck & Ruprecht, 1966.

———. "Der Sabbat bei Hesekiel: Ein Beitrag zur Nachgeschichte des Prophetentextes." Pages 65–74 in *Lex tua Veritas, Festschrift H. Junker*. Edited by H. Gross et al. Trier: Paulinus, 1961.

———. *Theology of the Old Testament*. Translated by J. A. Baker. 2 vols. OTL. Philadelphia: Westminster, 1961–1967.

Eissfeldt, Otto. *The Old Testament: An Introduction*. Translated by Peter Ackroyd. Oxford: Blackwell, 1965.

————. "The Prophetic Literature." Pages 115–61 in *The Old Testament and Modern Study.* Edited by H. H. Rowley. Oxford: Clarendon, 1951.

Eliot, T. S. *Selected Essays.* New ed. New York: Harcourt, Brace & World, 1950.

Elliger, Karl. *Deuterojesaja [1. Teilband: Jesaja 40,1–45,7].* BKAT 11/1. Neukirchen-Vluyn: Neukirchener Verlag, 1978.

————. "Das Gesetz Leviticus 18." *ZAW* 67 (1955): 1–25.

————. "Ich bin der Herr—euer Gott." Pages 9–34 in *Theologie als Glaubenswagnis: Festschrift für Karl Heim zum 80. Geburtstag.* Edited by Tübingen Theological Faculty. Hamburg: Furche-Verlag, 1954.

Engnell, Ivan. *Critical Essays on the Old Testament.* Translated and edited by John T. Willis. London: SPCK, 1970.

————. "Methodological Aspects of Old Testament Study." Pages 13–30 in *Congress Volume, Oxford 1959.* Edited by G. W. Anderson. VTSup 7. Leiden: Brill, 1960.

Eph'al, Israel. *The City Besieged: Siege and Its Manifestations in the Ancient Near East.* CHANE 36. Leiden: Brill, 2009.

Eslinger, Lyle M. "Ezekiel 20 and the Metaphor of Historical Teleology: Concepts of Biblical History." *JSOT* 81 (1998): 93–125.

————. "Freedom or Knowledge? Perspective and Purpose in the Exodus Narrative (Exodus 1–15)." *JSOT* 52 (1991): 43–60.

————. "Inner-biblical Exegesis and Inner-biblical Allusion: The Question of Category." *VT* 42 (1992): 47–58.

————. "Knowing Yahweh: Exodus 6:3 in the Context of Genesis 1—Exodus 15." Pages 188–98 in *Literary Structure and Rhetorical Strategies in the Hebrew Bible.* Edited by L. J. de Regt, J. de Waard, and J. P. Fokkelman. Assen: Van Gorcum; Winona Lake, IN: Eisenbrauns, 1996.

Evans, John F. "Death-Dealing Witchcraft in the Bible? Notes on the Condemnation of the 'Daughters' in Ezekiel 13:17–23." *TynBul* 65 (2014): 57–84.

————. "An Inner-Biblical Interpretation and Intertextual Reading of Ezekiel's Recognition Formulae with the Book of Exodus." DTh diss., Stellenbosch University, 2006.

————. Review of *A New Heart and a New Soul,* by Risa Levitt Kohn. *OTE* 16 (2003): 538–40.

Even-Shoshan, Abraham, ed. *A New Concordance to the Old Testament.* Introduction by John H. Sailhammer. Grand Rapids: Baker, 1984.

Ewald, Georg Heinrich August von. *Commentary on the Prophets of the Old Testament.* Translated by J. Frederick Smith. 5 vols. London: Williams & Norgate, 1880.

Exum, J. Cheryl, and David J. A. Clines, eds. *The New Literary Criticism and the Hebrew Bible.* Valley Forge, PA: Trinity, 1993.

Faust, Avraham. *Judah in the Neo-Babylonian Period: The Archaeology of Desolation.* Atlanta: Society of Biblical Literature, 2012.

Fechter, Friedrich. "Priesthood in Exile According to the Book of Ezekiel." Pages 27–41 in Cook and Patton, *Ezekiel's Hierarchical World.*

Feist, Udo. *Ezechiel: Das literarische Problem des Buches forschungsgeschichtlich betrachtet.* BWANT 138. Stuttgart: Kohlhammer, 1995.

Fensham, F. Charles. "Common Trends in Curses of the Near Eastern Treaties and *Kudurru*-Inscriptions Compared with Maledictions of Amos and Isaiah." *ZAW* 75 (1963): 155–75.

————. "Malediction and Benediction in Ancient Near Eastern Vassal-Treaties and the Old Testament." *ZAW* 74 (1962): 1–9.

Feuillet, André. "Les *Ego Eimi* christologiques du quatrième Évangile." *RSR* 54 (1966): 5–22, 213–40.

Fewell, Danna Nolan, ed. *Reading Between Texts: Intertextuality and the Hebrew Bible.* Louisville: Westminster John Knox, 1992.

Filson, Floyd V. "The Omission of Ezek. 12:26–28 and 36:22b–38 in Codex 967." *JBL* 62 (1943): 27–32.

Fischer, Georg. "Zurück nach Ägypten: Exodusmotivik im Jeremiabuch." Pages 73–92 in *A Pillar of Cloud to Guide: Text-critical, Redactional, and Linguistic Perspectives on the Old Testament in Honour of Marc Vervenne.* Edited by Hans Ausloos et al. BETL 269. Leuven: Peeters, 2014.

Fishbane, Michael. *Biblical Interpretation in Ancient Israel.* Oxford: Clarendon, 1985.

———. *The Exegetical Imagination: On Jewish Thought and Theology.* Cambridge, MA: Harvard University Press, 1998.

———. *The Garments of Torah: Essays in Biblical Hermeneutics.* Bloomington: Indiana University Press, 1989.

———. *Haftarot: The Traditional Hebrew Text with the New JPS Translation.* JPS Bible Commentary. Philadelphia: Jewish Publication Society, 2002.

———. "Inner-Biblical Exegesis." Pages 33–48 in vol. 1/1 of *Hebrew Bible/Old Testament: The History of Its Interpretation.* Edited by Magne Sæbø. Göttingen: Vandenhoeck & Ruprecht, 1996.

———. "Revelation and Tradition: Aspects of Inner-Biblical Exegesis." *JBL* 99 (1980): 343–61.

———. "Sin and Judgment in the Prophecies of Ezekiel." *Int* 38 (1984): 131–50.

———. *Text and Texture: Close Readings of Selected Biblical Texts.* New York: Schocken, 1979.

———. "Torah and Tradition." Pages 275–300 in Knight, *Tradition and Theology in the Old Testament.*

———. "Types of Biblical Intertextuality." Pages 38–44 in Lemaire and M. Sæbø, *Congress Volume, Oslo 1998.*

Floss, Johannes Peter. *Jahwe Dienen—Göttern Dienen: Terminologische, literarische und semantische Untersuchung einer theologischen Aussage zum Gottesverhältnis im Alten Testament.* BBB 45. Cologne: Hanstein, 1975.

Fohrer, Georg. "Die Glossen im Buche Ezechiel." Pages 204–21 in *Studien zur alttestamentlichen Prophetie (1949–1965).* BZAW 99. Berlin: Töpelmann, 1967.

———. *Die Hauptprobleme des Buches Ezechiel.* BZAW 72. Berlin: Töpelmann, 1952.

———. *Introduction to the Old Testament.* Translated by David E. Green. Nashville: Abingdon, 1968.

———. "Remarks on Modern Interpretation of the Prophets." *JBL* 80 (1961): 309–19.

———. Review of *Studien zum Ezechielbuch,* by Jörg Garscha. *ZAW* 87 (1975): 396.

Fohrer, Georg, and Kurt Galling. *Ezechiel.* 2nd ed. HAT. Tübingen: Mohr Siebeck, 1955.

Ford, William A. *God, Pharaoh and Moses: Explaining the Lord's Actions in the Exodus Plague Narratives.* Milton Keynes, UK: Paternoster, 2006.

Fox, Michael V. "The Identification of Quotations in Biblical Literature." *ZAW* 92 (1980): 416–31.

Freedman, David Noel, ed. *The Anchor Bible Dictionary.* 6 vols. New York: Doubleday, 1992.

Frye, Northrop. *The Great Code: The Bible and Literature.* New York: Harcourt Brace Jovanovich, 1982.

Fuhs, Hans Ferdinand. *Ezechiel 1–24*. Würzburg: Echter, 1986.

Gaboriau, F. "La connaissance de Dieu dans l'Ancien Testament." *Angelicum* 45 (1968): 145–83.

Galambush, J. G. "Ezekiel." Pages 231–37 in *Hebrew Bible: History of Interpretation*. Edited by John H. Hayes. Nashville: Abingdon, 2004.

———. "Necessary Enemies: Nebuchadnezzar, Yhwh, and Gog in Ezekiel 38–39." Pages 254–67 in *Israel's Prophets and Israel's Past: Essays on the Relationship of Prophetic Texts and Israelite History in Honor of John H. Hayes*. Edited by Brad E. Kelle et al. LHBOTS 446. New York: T&T Clark, 2006.

Ganzel, Tova. "Transformation of Pentateuchal Descriptions of Idolatry." Pages 33–49 in *Transforming Visions: Transformations of Text, Tradition, and Theology in Ezekiel*. Edited by William A. Tooman and Michael A. Lyons. PTMS. Eugene, OR: Pickwick, 2010.

Garber, David G. "'I Went in Bitterness': Theological Implications of a Trauma Theory Reading of Ezekiel." *RevExp* 111 (2014): 346–57.

———. "Trauma Theory and Biblical Studies." *CurBS* 14 (2015): 24–44.

Garfinkel, S. P. "Studies in Akkadian Influences in the Book of Ezekiel." PhD diss., Columbia University, 1983.

Garr, W. Randall. "The Grammar and Interpretation of Exodus 6:3." *JBL* 111 (1992): 385–408.

Garscha, Jörg. *Studien zum Ezechielbuch: eine redaktionskritische Untersuchung von 1–39*. Europäische Hochschulschriften 23. Bern: Herbert Lang; Frankfort: Peter Lang, 1974.

Gertz, Jan C., Bernard M. Levinson, Dalit Rom-Shiloni, and Konrad Schmid, eds. *The Formation of the Pentateuch: Bridging the Academic Cultures of Europe, Israel, and North America*. FAT 2.111. Tübingen: Mohr Siebeck, 2016.

Gile, Jason. "Deuteronomy and Ezekiel's Theology of Exile." Pages 287–306 in *For Our Good Always: Studies on the Message and Influence of Deuteronomy in Honor of Daniel I. Block*. Edited by Jason S. DeRouchie et al. Winona Lake, IN: Eisenbrauns, 2013.

Glazov, Gregory Yuri. *The Bridling of the Tongue and the Opening of the Mouth in Biblical Prophecy*. JSOTSup 311. Sheffield: Sheffield Academic, 2001.

Glueck, Nelson. *Ḥesed in the Bible*. Translated by Alfred Gottschalk. New York: KTAV, 1975.

Gordis, Robert. "The Book of Ezekiel in Contemporary Criticism." *The Jewish Review* 4 (1946): 57–77.

———. "Midrash and the Prophets." *JBL* 49 (1930): 417–22.

Gordon, Robert P. "'Comparativism' and the God of Israel." Pages 45–67 in *The Old Testament in Its World*. Edited by R. P. Gordon and J. C. de Moor. OtSt 52. Leiden: Brill, 2005.

Goshen-Gottstein, Moshe H., Shemaryahu Talmon, and Galen Marquis, eds. *Sefer Yehezkel/The Book of Ezekiel*. HUB. Jerusalem: Hebrew University Magnes, 2004.

Grabbe, Lester L., ed. *Leading Captivity Captive: The Exile as History and Ideology*. JSOTSup 278. Sheffield: Sheffield Academic, 1998.

Graffy, Adrian. *A Prophet Confronts His People*. AnBib 104. Rome: Biblical Institute Press, 1984.

Greenberg, Moshe. "The Design and Themes of Ezekiel's Program of Restoration." Pages 215–36 in *Interpreting the Prophets*. Edited by James Luther Mays and Paul J. Achtemeier. Philadelphia: Fortress, 1987.

———. *Ezekiel 1–20*. AB 22. Garden City, NY: Doubleday, 1983.

———. *Ezekiel 21–37*. AB 22A. New York: Doubleday, 1997.

———. "Notes on the Influence of Tradition on Ezekiel." *JANES* 22 (1993): 29–37.

———. "Prolegomenon." Pages xi–xxxv in Torrey, *Pseudo-Ezekiel*.

———. "Some Postulates of Biblical Criminal Law." Pages 5–28 in *Yehezkel Kaufmann Jubilee Volume: Studies in Bible and Jewish Religion Devoted to Yehezkel Kaufmann on the Occasion of His Seventieth Birthday*. Edited by Menaḥem Haran. Jerusalem: Magnes, 1960.

———. "The Use of Ancient Versions for Interpreting the Hebrew Text: A Sampling from Ezekiel ii 1—iii 11." Pages 131–48 in *Congress Volume, Göttingen 1977*. Edited by J. A. Emerton. VTSup 29. Leiden: Brill, 1978.

———. "What Are Valid Criteria for Determining Inauthentic Matter in Ezekiel?" Pages 123–35 in Lust, *Ezekiel and His Book*.

Gruenthaner, Michael J. "Recent Theories about Ezechiel." *CBQ* 7 (1945): 438–46.

Gunneweg, A. H. J. *Understanding the Old Testament*. Translated by John Bowden. OTL. Philadelphia: Westminster, 1978.

Haag, Herbert. *Was lehrt die literarische Untersuchung des Ezechiel-Textes?* Freiburg: Universitätsbuchhandlung, 1943.

Habel, Norman. "The Silence of the Lands: The Ecojustice Implications of Ezekiel's Judgment Oracles." Pages 127–40 in Cook and Patton, *Ezekiel's Hierarchical World*.

Hahn, Scott Walker, and John Sietze Bergsma. "What Laws Were 'Not Good'? A Canonical Approach to the Theological Problem of Ezekiel 20:25–26." *JBL* 123 (2004): 201–18.

Halperin, David J. *Seeking Ezekiel: Text and Psychology*. University Park: Pennsylvania State University Press, 1993.

Hals, Ronald M. *Ezekiel*. FOTL. Grand Rapids: Eerdmans, 1989.

Hamilton, P. C. "Theological Implications of the Divine Title Adonai Yehovah in Ezekiel." PhD diss., Southwestern Baptist Theological Seminary, 1990.

Hamilton, Victor P. *Handbook on the Pentateuch*. 2nd ed. Grand Rapids: Baker Academic, 2005.

Hänel, Johannes. *Das Erkennen Gottes bei den Schrift-Propheten*. BWANT 2.4. Stuttgart: Kohlhammer, 1923.

Hanhart, Robert. *Sacharja 1–8*. BKAT 14/7.1. Neukirchen-Vluyn: Neukirchener Verlag, 1998.

Hanson, Paul D. *The People Called: The Growth of Community in the Bible*. San Francisco: Harper & Row, 1986.

Haran, Menachem. "Behind the Scenes of History: Determining the Date of the Priestly Source." *JBL* 100 (1981): 321–33.

———. "The Character of the Priestly Source: Utopian and Exclusive Features." Pages 131–38 in World Union of Jewish Studies, *Eighth World Congress*.

———. "Ezekiel, P, and the Priestly School." *VT* 58 (2008): 211–18.

———. "The Law-Code of Ezekiel xl–xlviii and Its Relation to the Priestly School." *HUCA* 50 (1979): 45–71.

———. *Temples and Temple Service in Ancient Israel*. Oxford: Clarendon, 1978.

Harnack, Adolf von. *Marcion. Das Evangelium vom fremden Gott. Eine Monographie zur Geschichte der Grundlegung der katholischen Kirche*. Leipzig: Hinrichs, 1921.

Harner, Philip B. *Grace and Law in Second Isaiah: "I Am the Lord."* ANETS 2. Lewistown, NY: Edwin Mellen, 1988.

Harrison, R. K. *Introduction to the Old Testament*. Grand Rapids: Eerdmans, 1969.

Hartman, G. H., and S. Budick, eds. *Midrash and Literature*. New Haven: Yale University Press, 1986.

Hays, Christopher B. "Echoes of the Ancient Near East? Intertextuality and the Comparative Study of the Old Testament." Pages 20–43 in *The Word Leaps the Gap: Essays on Scripture and Theology in Honor of Richard B. Hays*. Edited by J. Ross Wagner et al. Grand Rapids: Eerdmans, 2008.

Hays, Richard B. *The Conversion of the Imagination: Paul as Interpreter of Israel's Scripture*. Grand Rapids: Eerdmans, 2005.

———. *Echoes of Scripture in the Letters of Paul*. New Haven: Yale University Press, 1989.

Hegel, Georg Wilhelm Friedrich. *The Philosophy of Right/The Philosophy of History*. Translated with notes by T. M. Knox. Great Books of the World 46. Chicago: Encyclopædia Britannica, 1952.

Herntrich, Volkmar. *Ezechielprobleme*. BZAW 61. Giessen: Töpelmann, 1932.

Herrmann, Johannes. *Ezechiel*. KAT. Leipzig: Deichert, 1924.

———. *Ezechielstudien*. Leipzig: Hinrichs, 1908.

Herrmann, Siegfried. *Die prophetischen Heilserwartungen im Alten Testament*. BWANT 85. Stuttgart: Kohlhammer, 1965.

Heschel, Abraham. *Heavenly Torah*. Edited and translated by Gordon Tucker with Leonard Levin. New York: Continuum, 2005.

Hess, Richard S. *Israelite Religions: An Archaeological and Biblical Survey*. Grand Rapids: Baker Academic, 2007.

———. "Names." *DDL* 3:429–58.

———. *The Old Testament: A Historical, Theological, and Critical Introduction*. Grand Rapids: Baker Academic, 2016.

Hobbs, T. R. *2 Kings*. WBC 13. Waco, TX: Word, 1985.

———. *A Time for War: A Study of Warfare in the Old Testament*. Wilmington, DE: Glazier, 1989.

Hoftijzer, J. "Review: The Nominal Clause Reconsidered." *VT* 23 (1973): 446–510.

Holladay, William L. "The Background of Jeremiah's Self-Understanding: Moses, Samuel, and Psalm 22." *JBL* 83 (1964): 153–64.

———. *Jeremiah 1: A Commentary on the Book of the Prophet Jeremiah Chapters 1–25*. Hermeneia. Philadelphia: Fortress, 1986.

———. *Jeremiah 2: A Commentary on the Book of the Prophet Jeremiah Chapters 26–52*. Hermeneia. Philadelphia: Fortress, 1989.

———. "Jeremiah and Moses: Further Observations," *JBL* 85 (1966): 17–27.

Hollander, John. *The Figure of Echo: A Mode of Allusion in Milton and After*. Berkeley: University of California Press, 1981.

Holman, C. Hugh, and William Harmon, eds. *A Handbook to Literature*. 6th ed. New York: Macmillan, 1992.

Hölscher, Gustav. *Hesekiel, der Dichter und das Buch*. Giessen: Töpelmann, 1924.

———. *Die Profeten: Untersuchung zur Religionsgeschichte Israels*. Leipzig: Hinrichs, 1914.

Horst, Friedrich. *Leviticus xvii–xxvi und Hezekiel: Eine Beitrag zur Pentateuchkritik*. Colmar: Barth, 1881.

Hossfeld, Frank Lothar. *Untersuchungen zu Komposition und Theologie des Ezechielbuches*. FB 20. Würzburg: Echter, 1977.

Hossfeld, Frank-Lothar, and Erich Zenger. *Psalms 2: A Commentary on Psalms 51–100*. Translated by Linda M. Maloney. Hermeneia. Minneapolis: Fortress, 2005.

House, Paul R. *Old Testament Theology*. Downers Grove, IL: InterVarsity Press, 1998.

Houston, Walter. "What Did the Prophets Think They Were Doing? Speech Acts and Prophetic Discourse in the Old Testament." Pages 133–53 in *The Place Is Too Small for Us: The Israelite Prophets in Recent Research*. Edited by Robert P. Gordon. Winona Lake, IN: Eisenbrauns, 1995.

Houtman, Cornelis. *Exodus*. Vol. 3. *Exodus 20–40*. Translated by Sierd Woudstra. HCOT. Leuven: Peeters, 2000.

———. *Der Pentateuch: Die Geschichte seiner Erforschung neben einer Auswertung*. Biblical Exegesis and Theology 9. Kampen: Kok Pharos, 1994.

Howie, C. G. *The Date and Composition of Ezekiel*. JBLMS 4. Philadelphia: Society of Biblical Literature, 1950.

Hubbard, David A. *Joel and Amos*. TOTC. Downers Grove, IL: InterVarsity Press, 1989.

Huffmon, H. B. "The Treaty Background of Hebrew *yāda*." *BASOR* 181 (1966): 31–37.

Huffmon, H. B., and S. B. Parker. "A Further Note on the Treaty Background of Hebrew *yāda*." *BASOR* 184 (1966): 36–38.

Hugenberger, Gordon. *Marriage as Covenant*. VTSup 52. Leiden: Brill, 1994.

Humbert, Paul. "Le substantif *to'ēbā* et le verbe *t'b* dans l'Ancien Testament." *ZAW* 72 (1960): 217–37.

Hummel, Horace D. *Ezekiel*. 2 vols. St. Louis: Concordia, 2005–2007.

Hurvitz, Avi. "Can Biblical Texts Be Dated Linguistically? Chronological Perspectives in the Historical Study of Biblical Hebrew." Pages 143–60 in Lemaire and Sæbø, *Congress Volume, Oslo 1998*.

———. "Dating the Priestly Source in Light of the Historical Study of Biblical Hebrew a Century after Wellhausen." *ZAW* 100 Supplement (1988): 88–100.

———. "The Evidence of Language in Dating the Priestly Code—A Linguistic Study in Technical Idioms and Terminology." *RB* 81 (1974): 24–56.

———. "The Language of the Priestly Source and Its Historical Setting—The Case for an Early Date." Pages 83–94 in World Union of Jewish Studies, *Eighth World Congress*.

———. *A Linguistic Study of the Relationship between the Priestly Source and the Book of Ezekiel*. CahRB 20. Paris: Gabalda, 1982.

———. "Once Again: The Linguistic Profile of the Priestly Material in the Pentateuch and its Historical Age, a Response to J. Blenkinsopp." *ZAW* 112 (2000): 180–91.

———. "The Recent Debate on Late Biblical Hebrew: Solid Data, Experts' Opinions, and Inconclusive Arguments." *Hebrew Studies* 47 (2006): 191–210.

———. "The Usage of שש and בוץ in the Bible and Its Implications for the Date of P." *HTR* 60 (1967): 117–21.

Idestrom, Rebecca G. S. "Echoes of the Book of Exodus in Ezekiel." *JSOT* 33 (2009): 489–510.

Irwin, William A. "Ezekiel Research Since 1943." *VT* 3 (1953): 54–66.

———. *The Problem of Ezekiel*. Chicago: University of Chicago Press, 1943.

Jahn, Gustav. *Das Buch Ezechiel auf Grund der Septuaginta hergestellt*. Leipzig: Pfeiffer, 1905.

Jaspers, Karl. "Der Prophet Ezechiel: Eine pathographische Studie." Pages 13–21 in *Aneignung und Polemik: Gesammelte Reden und Aufsätze zur Geschichte der Philosophie*. Edited by H. Saner. Munich: Piper, 1968.

Jenni, Ernst, and Claus Westermann, eds. *Theologisches Handwörterbuch zum Alten Testament*. 2 vols. Munich: Kaiser; Zürich: Theologischer Verlag, 1971–1976.

Jenny, Laurent. "The Strategy of Form." Pages 34–63 in *French Literary Theory Today*. Edited by Tzvetan Todorov. Translated by R. Carter. Cambridge: Cambridge University Press, 1982.

Jepsen, Alfred. *Untersuchung zum Bundesbuch*. BWANT 3.5. Stuttgart: Kohlhammer, 1927.

Joosten, Jan. "Diachronic Linguistics and the Date of the Pentateuch." Pages 327–44 in Gertz, Levinson, and Rom-Shiloni, *Formation of the Pentateuch*.

Joüon, P., and T. Muraoka. *A Grammar of Biblical Hebrew*. 2nd ed. (with corrections). SubBi 27. Rome: Gregorian and Biblical Press, 2011.

Joyce, Paul M. "Dislocation and Adaptation in the Exilic Age and After." Pages 45–58 in *After the Exile: Essays in Honour of Rex Mason*. Edited by John Barton and David J. Reimer. Macon, GA: Mercer University Press, 1996.

———. *Divine Initiative and Human Response in Ezekiel*. JSOTSup 51. Sheffield: JSOT Press, 1989.

———. *Ezekiel: A Commentary*. LHBOTS 482. New York: T&T Clark, 2009.

———. "Synchronic and Diachronic Perspectives on Ezekiel." Pages 115–28 in *Synchronic or Diachronic? A Debate on Method in Old Testament Exegesis*. Edited by Johannes C. de Moor. Leiden: Brill, 1995.

Joyce, Paul M., and Dalit Rom-Shiloni, eds. *The God Ezekiel Creates*. LHBOTS 607. London: Bloomsbury T&T Clark, 2015.

Kaiser, Otto. *Einleitung in das Alte Testament*. 5th ed. Gütersloh: Gütersloher, 1984.

———. *Introduction to the Old Testament*. Translated by John Sturdy. Minneapolis: Augsburg, 1975

Kaufmann, Yehezkel. *History of the Religion of Israel*. Vol. 4. Translated by C. W. Efroymson. New York: KTAV; Jerusalem: Hebrew University; Dallas: Institute for Jewish Studies, 1977.

———. *The Religion of Israel*. Translated by Moshe Greenberg. New York: Schocken, 1960.

Kautzsch, E., ed. *Gesenius' Hebrew Grammar*. Translated by A. E. Cowley. 2nd ed. Oxford: Clarendon, 1983 (reprint).

———. *Die Heilige Schrift des Alten Testaments*. 4th ed. Edited by A. Bertholet. Vol. 1, *Mose bis Ezechiel*. Tübingen: Mohr Siebeck, 1922.

Keck, Elizabeth. "The Glory of Yahweh in Ezekiel and the Pre-Tabernacle Wilderness." *JSOT* 37 (2012): 201–18.

Keil, Karl/Carl Friedrich. *Manual of Historico-Critical Introduction to the Canonical Scriptures of the Old Testament*. Translated by George C. M. Douglas. 2 vols. Edinburgh: T&T Clark, 1869.

———. *The Prophecies of Ezekiel*. Translated by James Martin. 2 vols. Grand Rapids: Eerdmans, 1986 (reprint).

Kelle, Brad E. "Dealing with the Trauma of Defeat: The Rhetoric of the Devastation and Rejuvenation of Nature in Ezekiel," *JBL* 128 (2009): 469–90.

———. "Wartime Rhetoric: Prophetic Metaphorization of Cities as Female." Pages 95–111 in *Writing and Reading War: Rhetoric, Gender, and Ethics in Biblical and Modern Contexts*. Edited by Brad E. Kelle and Frank Ritchel Ames. SBLSymS 42. Atlanta: Society of Biblical Literature, 2008.

Kelle, Brad E., Frank Ritchel Ames, and Jacob L. Wright, eds. *Interpreting Exile: Displacement and Deportations in Biblical and Modern Contexts*. Atlanta: Society of Biblical Literature, 2011.

Kennedy, James M. "Hebrew *pitḫôn peh* in the Book of Ezekiel." *VT* 41 (1991): 233–35.

Kern, Paul Bentley. *Ancient Siege Warfare*. Bloomington: Indiana University Press, 1999.

Kiefer, Jörn. *Exil und Diaspora: Begrifflichkeit und Deutungen im antiken Judentum und in der Hebräischen Bible*. Leipzig: Evangelische Verlagsanstalt, 2005.

Kim, Dong-Hyuk. *Early Biblical Hebrew, Late Biblical Hebrew, and Linguistic Variability*. VTSup 156. Leiden: Brill, 2013.

King, Philip J., and Lawrence E. Stager. *Life in Biblical Israel*. Louisville: Westminster John Knox, 2001.

Klein, Anja. *Schriftauslegung im Ezechielbuch: Redaktionsgeschichtliche Untersuchungen zu Ez 34–39*. BZAW 391. Berlin: de Gruyter, 2008.

Klein, Ralph W. *Ezekiel: The Prophet and His Message*. Columbia: University of South Carolina Press, 1988.

Klostermann, August. "Ezechiel und das Heiligkeitsgesetz." Pages 368–418 (ch. 7) in *Der Pentateuch: Beiträge zu seinem Verständnis und seiner Enstehungsgeschichte*. Leipzig: Deichert, 1893.

Knierim, Rolf P. "Offenbarung im Alten Testament." Pages 206–35 in *Probleme biblischer Theologie: Gerhard von Rad zum 70. Geburtstag*. Edited by Hans Walter Wolff. Munich: Kaiser, 1971.

Knight, Douglas A. *Rediscovering the Traditions of Israel*. Revised ed. SBLDS 9. Missoula, MT: Scholars Press, 1975.

———, ed. *Tradition and Theology in the Old Testament*. Philadelphia: Fortress, 1977.

Knight, Douglas A., and Gene M. Tucker, eds. *The Hebrew Bible and Its Modern Interpreters*. Philadelphia: Fortress; Decatur, GA: Scholars Press, 1985.

Knohl, Israel. *The Sanctuary of Silence: The Priestly Torah and the Holiness School*. Minneapolis: Fortress, 1995.

Koch, Klaus. *The Prophets*. Vol. 2. Translated by Margaret Kohl. Philadelphia: Fortress, 1982.

Koehler, Ludwig, and Walter Baumgartner. *Lexicon in Veteris Testamenti libros*. 2nd ed. Leiden: Brill, 1958.

Koole, Jan L. *Isaiah*. Vol. 3/2, *Isaiah 49–55*. Translated by Anthony P. Runia. HCOT. Leuven: Peeters, 1998.

Kowalski, Beate. *Die Rezeption des Propheten Ezechiel in der Offenbarung des Johannes*. SBB 52. Stuttgart: Katholisches Bibelwerk, 2004.

Krapf, Thomas M. *Die Priesterschrift und die vorexilische Zeit: Yehezkel Kaufmanns vernachlässigter Beitrag zur Geschichte der biblischen Religion*. OBO 119. Freiburg: Universitätsverlag; Göttingen: Vandenhoeck & Ruprecht, 1992.

Kratz, Reinhard. *The Prophets of Israel*. Winona Lake, IN: Eisenbrauns, 2015.

Kraus, Hans-Joachim. *Geschichte der historisch-kritischen Erforschung des Alten Testaments*. 3rd ed. Neukirchen-Vluyn: Neukirchener Verlag, 1982.

———. *Die prophetische Verkündigung des Rechts in Israel*. Theologische Studien 51. Zollikon-Zürich: Evangelischer Verlag, 1957.

Kristeva, Julia. *The Kristeva Reader*. Edited by Toril Moi. Translated by Seán Hand and Léon S. Roudiez. Oxford: Blackwell, 1986.

Kruger, Paul A. "Depression in the Hebrew Bible: An Update." *JNES* 64 (2005): 187–92.

Kugel, James L. Review of *Biblical Interpretation in Ancient Israel*, by Michael Fishbane. *Prooftexts* 7 (1987): 269–83.

Kuhl, Curt. "Neuere Hesekiel-Literatur." *TRu* 20 (1952): 1–26.

———. "Zum Stand der Hezekiel-Forschung." *TRu* 24 (1957): 1–53.

———. "Zur Geschichte der Hesekiel-Forschung." *TRu* 5 (1933): 92–118.

Kuhn, Reinhard. *Corruption in Paradise.* Hanover, NH: University Press of New England, 1982.

Kutscher, E. Y. *The Language and Linguistic Background of the Isaiah Scroll (1QIsaᵃ).* Leiden: Brill, 1974.

Kutsko, John F. *Between Heaven and Earth: Divine Presence and Absence in the Book of Ezekiel.* Biblical and Judaic Studies 7. Winona Lake, IN: Eisenbrauns, 2000.

Lang, Bernhard. *Ezechiel: Der Prophet und das Buch.* EdF 153. Darmstadt: Wissenschaftliche Buchgesellschaft, 1981.

Lange, Armin. "Ancient Hebrew Texts." Pages 570–72 (§8.2) in Lange and Tov, *The Hebrew Bible.*

Lange, Armin, and Emanuel Tov, eds. *The Hebrew Bible: Pentateuch, Former and Latter Prophets.* Vol. 1B of *Textual History of the Bible.* Edited by Armin Lange. Leiden: Brill, 2017.

Lapsley, Jacqueline E. *Can These Bones Live? The Problem of the Moral Self in the Book of Ezekiel.* BZAW 301. Berlin: de Gruyter, 2000.

LaSor, William Sanford, David Allan Hubbard, and Frederic Wm. Bush. *Old Testament Survey.* 2nd ed. Grand Rapids: Eerdmans, 1996.

Leick, Gwendolyn, ed. *The Babylonian World.* New York: Routledge, 2007.

Lemaire, A., and M. Sæbø, eds. *Congress Volume, Oslo 1998.* VTSup 80. Leiden: Brill, 2000.

Levenson, Jon D. "Ezekiel in the Perspective of Two Commentators." *Int* 38 (1984): 210–17.

———. *The Hebrew Bible, the Old Testament, and Historical Criticism: Jews and Christians in Biblical Studies.* Louisville: Westminster John Knox, 1993.

———. *Theology of the Program of Restoration of Ezekiel 40–48.* HSM. Missoula, MT: Scholars Press, 1976.

Levine, Baruch A. "Late Language in the Priestly Source: Some Literary and Historical Observations." Pages 69–82 in World Union of Jewish Studies, *Eighth World Congress.*

———. *Numbers.* 2 vols. AB 4 and 4a. New York: Doubleday, 1993–2000.

———. "Research in the Priestly Source: The Linguistic Factor." *Eretz-Israel* 16 (1982): 124–31 [Hebrew].

Levitt Kohn, Risa. "'As Though You Yourself Came Out of Egypt': The Ethos of Exile in Ezekiel." *HeBAI* 3 (2014): 185–203.

———. "Ezekiel at the Turn of the Century." *CurBR* 2 (2003): 9–31.

———. *A New Heart and a New Soul: Ezekiel, the Exile and the Torah.* JSOTSup 358. London: Continuum Sheffield Academic, 2002.

———. "A Prophet like Moses? Rethinking Ezekiel's Relationship to the Torah." *ZAW* 114 (2002): 236–54.

———. "'With a Mighty Hand and an Outstretched Arm': The Prophet and the Torah in Ezekiel 20." Pages 159–68 in Cook and Patton, *Ezekiel's Hierarchical World.*

Lilly, Ingrid E. *Two Books of Ezekiel: Papyrus 967 and the Masoretic Text as Variant Literary Editions.* VTSup 150. Leiden: Brill, 2012.

Lind, Millard A. "A Political Alternative: An Examination of Ezekiel's Recognition Statements." Pages 260–74 (ch. 24) in *Monotheism, Power, Justice: Collected Old Testament Essays.* Elkhart, IN: Institute of Mennonite Studies, 1990.

Lindblom, J. *Prophecy in Ancient Israel.* Philadelphia: Fortress, 1962.

Lipschits, Oded. *The Fall and Rise of Jerusalem: Jerusalem Under Babylonian Rule.* Winona Lake, IN: Eisenbrauns, 2005.

Lipschits, Oded, and Joseph Blenkinsopp, eds. *Judah and the Judeans in the Neo-Babylonian Period*. Winona Lake, IN: Eisenbrauns, 2003.

Longman, Tremper III, and Raymond B. Dillard. *An Introduction to the Old Testament*. 2nd ed. Grand Rapids: Zondervan, 2006.

Lundbom, Jack R. *Jeremiah 1–20*. AB 21A. New York: Doubleday, 1999.

———. *Jeremiah 21–36*. AB21B. New York: Doubleday, 2004.

———. *Jeremiah 37–52*. AB21C. New York: Doubleday, 2004.

Lust, Johan. "אדני יהוה in Ezekiel and Its Counterpart in the Old Greek." *ETL* 72 (1996): 138–45.

———."The Divine Titles האדון and אדני in Proto-Isaiah and Ezekiel." Pages 131–49 in *Isaiah in Context: Studies in Honour of Arie van der Kooij on the Occasion of His Sixty-Fifth Birthday*. Edited by Michaël N. van der Meer et al. VTSup 138. Leiden: Brill, 2010.

———. "Exile and Diaspora: Gathering from Dispersion in Ezekiel." Pages 99–122 in *Lectures et Relectures de la Bible (Festschrift P.-A. Bogaert)*. Edited by J.-M. Auwers et al. Leuven: Peeters, 1999.

———. "Ez., XX, 4–26 une parodie de l'histoire religieuse d'Israel." *ETL* 43 (1967): 488–527.

———. "Ezéchiel dans la Septante." Pages 337–58 in *Les recueils prophétiques de la Bible: Origine, milieux et contexte proche-oriental*. Edited by Jean-Daniel Macchi, Christophe Nihan, Thomas Römer, and Jan Rückl. Le Monde de la Bible. Geneva: Labor et Fides, 2012.

———, ed. "Ezekiel." Fascicle 12 in *Biblia Hebraica quinta editione cum apparatu critic novis curis elaborato*. Edited by Robert Althann and Adrian Schenker. Stuttgart: Deutsche Bibelgesellschaft, forthcoming.

———. "Ezekiel 36–40 in the Oldest Greek Manuscript." *CBQ* 43 (1981): 517–33.

———, ed. *Ezekiel and His Book: Textual and Literary Criticism and their Interrelation*. BETL 74. Leuven: Leuven University Press; Peeters, 1986.

———. "Ezekiel Manuscripts in Qumran: Preliminary Edition of 4Q EZa and b." Pages 90–100 in Lust, *Ezekiel and His Book*.

———. "Ezekiel Salutes Isaiah: Ezekiel 20.32–44." Pages 367–82 in *Studies in the Book of Isaiah: Festschrift Willem A. M. Beuken*. Edited by J. van Ruiten et al. BETL 132. Leuven: Leuven University Press; Peeters, 1997.

———. "The Ezekiel Text." Pages 153–68 in *Sôfer Mahîr: Essays in Honour of Adrian Schenker Offered by the Editors of "Biblia Hebraica Quinta."* Edited by Yohanan A. P. Goldman et al. VTSup 110. Leiden: Brill, 2006.

———. "Major Divergences between LXX and MT in Ezekiel." Pages 83–92 in *The Earliest Text of the Hebrew Bible: The Relationship between the Masoretic Text and the Hebrew Base of the Septuagint Reconsidered*. Edited by Adrian Schenker. SCS 52. Atlanta: Society of Biblical Literature, 2003.

———. "Multiple Translators in LXX-Ezekiel?" Pages 654–69 in *Die Septuaginta—Texte, Kontexte, Lebenswelten: Internationale Fachtagung veranstaltet von Seputaginta Deutsch (LXX.D), Wuppertal 20–23 Juli, 2006*. Edited by M. Karrer et al. WUNT 219. Tübingen: Mohr Siebeck, 2008.

Lyons, Michael A. *From Law to Prophecy: Ezekiel's Use of the Holiness Code*. LHBOTS 507. New York: T&T Clark, 2009.

———. *An Introduction to the Study of Ezekiel*. London: Bloomsbury T&T Clark, 2015.

Macintosh, A. A. *A Critical and Exegetical Commentary on Hosea*. ICC. Edinburgh: T&T Clark, 1997.

Mackie, Timothy P. *Expanding Ezekiel: The Hermeneutics of Scribal Addition in the Ancient Text Witnesses of the Book of Ezekiel*. FRLANT 257. Göttingen: Vandenhoeck & Ruprecht, 2015.

Margalioth, R. *The Indivisible Isaiah*. New York: Yeshiva University Press, 1964.

Mark, Martin. *"Mein Angesicht geht" (Ex 33,14): Gottes Zusage personaler Führung*. HBS 66. Freiburg: Herder, 2011.

Markter, Florian. *Transformationen: Zur Anthropologie des Propheten Ezechiel unter besonderer Berücksichtigung des Motivs "Herz."* FB 127. Würzburg: Echter, 2013.

Martens, Elmer. "Ezekiel's Contribution to a Biblical Theology of Mission." *Direction* 28 (1999): 75–87. http://www.directionjournal.org/article/?1003.

Matties, Gordon H. *Ezekiel 18 and the Rhetoric of Moral Discourse*. SBLDS 126. Atlanta: Scholars Press, 1990.

May, Herbert G. "The Book of Ezekiel (Introduction and Exegesis)." Pages 41–338 in vol. 6 of *The Interpreter's Bible*. Nashville: Abingdon, 1956.

———. "Theological Universalism in the Old Testament." *JBR* 16 (1948): 100–107.

Mayfield, Tyler D. *Literary Structure and Setting in Ezekiel*. FAT 2.43. Tübingen: Mohr Siebeck, 2010.

———. "A Re-Examination of Ezekiel's Prophetic Word Formulas." *HS* 57 (2016): 139–55.

McCarthy, Dennis J. *Treaty and Covenant*. 2nd ed. AnBib 21A. Rome: Pontifical Biblical Institute, 1978.

McConville, J. Gordon. *Deuteronomy*. ApOTC. Leicester: Apollos, 2002.

———. *Ezra, Nehemiah, and Esther*. Daily Study Bible. Philadelphia: Westminster, 1985.

———. "Priests and Levites in Ezekiel: A Crux in the Interpretation of Israel's History." *TynBul* 34 (1983): 3–31.

McGregor, Leslie John. *The Greek Text of Ezekiel: An Examination of Its Homogeneity*. SCS 18. Atlanta: Scholars Press, 1985.

McKeating, Henry. *Ezekiel*. OTG. Sheffield: JSOT Press, 1993.

———. "Ezekiel as a Priest in Exile." Pages 199–213 in *The Elusive Prophet: The Prophet as a Historical Person, Literary Character and Anonymous Artist*. Edited by Johannes C. de Moor. OtSt 45. Leiden: Brill, 2001.

———. "Ezekiel the 'Prophet Like Moses'?" *JSOT* 61 (1994): 97–109.

———. "Ezekiel: Structure, Themes, and Contested Issues." Pages 190–206 in *The Oxford Handbook of the Prophets*. Edited by Carolyn J. Sharp. Oxford: Oxford University Press, 2016.

Mein, Andrew. *Ezekiel and the Ethics of Exile*. OTM. Oxford: Oxford University Press, 2001.

Mein, Andrew, and Paul M. Joyce, eds. *After Ezekiel: Essays on the Reception of a Difficult Prophet*. LHBOTS 535. New York: T&T Clark, 2011.

Meinhold, Johannes. *Einführung in das Alte Testament*. Giessen: Töpelmann, 1919.

Michel, Diethelm. "Nur ich bin Jahwe: Erwägungen zur sogenannten Selbstvorstellungsformel." Pages 1–12 in *Studien zur Überlieferungsgeschichte alttestamentlicher Texte*. TB 93. Gütersloh: Kaiser/Gütersloher, 1997.

Middlemas, Jill. "Exodus 3 and the Call of Moses: Re-reading the Signs." Pages 131–44 in *The Centre and the Periphery: A European Tribute to Walter Brueggemann*. Edited by Jill Middlemas et al. Sheffield: Sheffield Phoenix, 2010.

———. *The Templeless Age: An Introduction to the History, Literature, and Theology of the "Exile."* Louisville: Westminster John Knox, 2007.

Milgrom, Jacob. "The Case for the Pre-Exilic and Exilic Provenance of the Books of Exodus, Leviticus and Numbers." Pages 48–56 in *Reading the Law: Studies in Honour of Gordon J. Wenham.* Edited by J. G. McConville et al. LHBOTS 461. New York: T&T Clark, 2007.

———. *Ezekiel's Hope: A Commentary on Ezekiel 38–48.* With Daniel I. Block. Eugene, OR: Cascade, 2012.

———. *Leviticus.* 3 vols. AB 3–3b. Garden City, NY: Doubleday, 1991–2001.

———. "Leviticus 26 and Ezekiel." Pages 57–62 in *The Quest for Context and Meaning: Studies in Biblical Intertextuality in Honor of James A. Sanders.* Edited by Craig A. Evans et al. Leiden: Brill, 1997.

———. "The Nature and Extent of Idolatry in Eighth-Seventh Century Judah." *HUCA* 69 (1998): 1–13.

———. "Priestly ('P') Source." *ABD*, 5:546–61.

———. "Response to Rolf Rendtorff." *JSOT* 60 (1993): 83–85.

———. *Studies in Cultic Theology and Terminology.* SJLA 36. Leiden: Brill, 1983.

Millard, Alan. "La prophétie et l'écriture: Israël, Aram, Assyrie." *RHR* 202 (1985): 125–44.

Miller, Cynthia L., ed. *The Verbless Clause in Biblical Hebrew: Linguistic Approaches.* LSAWS 1. Winona Lake, IN: Eisenbrauns, 1999.

Miller, Geoffrey D. "Intertextuality in Old Testament Research." *CurBR* 9 (2010): 283–309.

Miller-Naudé, Cynthia L., and Ziony Zevit, eds. *Diachrony in Biblical Hebrew.* LSAWS 8. Winona Lake, IN: Eisenbrauns, 2012.

Miller, Patrick D. Review of *Biblical Interpretation in Ancient Israel*, by Michael Fishbane. *ThTo* 44 (1987): 377–80.

Miner, Earl. "Allusion." *The New Princeton Encyclopedia of Poetry and Poetics.* Edited by Alex Preminger and T. V. F. Brogan. Princeton: Princeton University Press, 1993.

Miranda, José Porfirio. *Marx and the Bible: A Critique of the Philosophy of Oppression.* Translated by John Eagleson. Maryknoll, NY: Orbis, 1974.

Miscall, Peter D. "Isaiah: New Heavens, New Earth, New Book." Pages 41–56 in Fewell, *Reading Between Texts.*

Moberly, R. W. L. *At the Mountain of God: Story and Theology in Exodus 32–34.* JSOTSup 22. Sheffield: JSOT Press, 1983.

———. *The Old Testament of the Old Testament: Patriarchal Narratives and Mosaic Yahwism.* OBT. Minneapolis: Fortress, 1992.

Moran, W. L. "Gen 49,10 and Its Use in Ez 21,32." *Bib* 39 (1958): 405–25.

Morgan, Thaïs E. "Is There an Intertext in This Text? Literary and Interdisciplinary Approaches to Intertextuality." *American Journal of Semiotics* 3 (1985): 1–40.

———. "The Space of Intertextuality." Pages 239–79 in O'Donnell and Davis, *Intertextuality and Contemporary American Fiction.*

Mosis, Rudolf. "Ez 14,1–11—ein Ruf zur Umkehr." *BZ* 19 (1975): 161–94.

Motyer, J. Alec. *The Prophecy of Isaiah: An Introduction and Commentary.* Downers Grove, IL: InterVarsity Press, 1993.

Mowinckel, Sigmund. *Die Erkenntnis Gottes bei den alttestamentlichen Profeten.* TNTT. Oslo: Grøndahl, 1941.

Müller, Reinhard. "A Prophetic View of the Exile in the Holiness Code: Literary Growth and Tradition History in Leviticus 26." Pages 207–28 in Ben Zvi and Levin, *The Concept of Exile.*

Naudé, J. A. "The Language of the Book of Ezekiel: Biblical Hebrew in Transition?" *OTE* 13 (2000): 46–71.

Neusner, Jacob. *Canon and Connection: Intertextuality in Judaism.* Lanham, MD: University Press of America, 1987.

———. *Self-Fulfilling Prophecy: Exile and Return in the History of Judaism.* Atlanta: Scholars Press, 1990.

———, ed. *The Talmud of Babylonia: An Academic Commentary.* 22 vols. SFACS. Atlanta: Scholars Press, 1994.

Newsom, Carol. "Bakhtin, the Bible, and Dialogic Truth." *JR* 76 (1996): 290–306.

Newsome, James D. Jr. *The Hebrew Prophets.* Atlanta: John Knox, 1984.

Niccacci, Alviero. "Types and Functions of the Nominal Sentence." Pages 215–48 in Miller, *Verbless Clause.*

Nicholson, Ernest W. *God and His People: Covenant and Theology in the Old Testament.* Oxford: Clarendon, 1986.

———. *The Pentateuch in the Twentieth Century: The Legacy of Julius Wellhausen.* Oxford: Clarendon, 1998.

Niditch, Susan. *War in the Hebrew Bible.* New York: Oxford University Press, 1993.

Nielsen, Eduard. *Oral Tradition: A Modern Problem in Old Testament Interpretation.* SBT. London: SCM, 1954.

Nielsen, Kirsten. "Intertextuality and Hebrew Bible." Pages 17–31 in Lemaire and Sæbø, *Congress Volume, Oslo 1998.*

Nissinen, Martti. "Die Relevanz der neuassyrischen Prophetie für die alttestamentliche Forschung." Pages 217–58 in *Mesopotamica—Ugaritica—Biblica.* Edited by M. Dietrich and O. Lorentz. AOAT 232. Neukirchen-Vluyn: Neukirchener Verlag; Kevelaer: Butzon & Bercker, 1993.

O'Day, G. R. "Intertextuality." Pages 155–57 in *Methods of Biblical Interpretation.* Edited by John H. Hayes. Nashville: Abingdon, 2004.

Oded, Bustenay. "Judah and the Exile." Pages 435–88 in *Israelite and Judaean History.* Edited by J. Maxwell Miller and John H. Hayes. OTL. Philadelphia: Westminster, 1977.

Odell, Margaret S. "'Are You He of Whom I Spoke by My Servants the Prophets?' Ezekiel 38–39 and the Problem of History in the Neobabylonian Context." PhD diss., University of Pittsburgh, 1988.

———. *Ezekiel.* SHBC. Macon, GA: Smyth & Helwys, 2005.

———. "Ezekiel Saw What He Saw." Pages 162–76 in Sweeney and Ben Zvi, *The Changing Face of Form Criticism.*

———. "Genre and Persona in Ezekiel 24:15–24." Pages 195–219 in Odell and Strong, *The Book of Ezekiel.*

———. "The Inversion of Shame and Forgiveness in Ezekiel 16.59–63." *JSOT* 56 (1992): 101–12.

———. "You Are What You Eat: Ezekiel and the Scroll." *JBL* 117 (1998): 229–48.

Odell, Margaret S., and John T. Strong, eds. *The Book of Ezekiel, Theological and Anthropological Perspectives.* SBLSymS 9. Atlanta: Society of Biblical Literature, 2000.

Odendaal, Marietjie. "Exile in Ezekiel: Evaluating a Sociological Model." *NGTT* 40 (1999): 133–39.

O'Donnell, Patrick, and Robert Con Davis, eds. *Intertextuality and Contemporary American Fiction.* Baltimore: Johns Hopkins University Press, 1989.

Oehler, Gustav F. *Theology of the Old Testament.* Translated by Ellen D. Smith. Vol. 1. Edinburgh: T&T Clark, 1874.

O'Kane, Martin. "Isaiah: A Prophet in the Footsteps of Moses." *JSOT* 69 (1996): 29–51.

Olley, John W. "Divine Name and Paragraphing in Ezekiel: Highlighting Divine Speech in an Expanding Tradition." *BIOSCS* 37 (2004): 87–105.

———. *Ezekiel: A Commentary based on Iezekiēl in Codex Vaticanus.* SComS. Leiden: Brill, 2009.

———. "Trajectories of Ezekiel." *CurBR* 9 (2011): 137–70; 10 (2011): 53–80.

Orlinsky, Harry M. "Nationalism-Universalism and Internationalism in Ancient Israel." Pages 206–36 in *Translating and Understanding the Old Testament: Essays in Honor of Herbert Gordon May.* Edited by Harry Thomas Frank et al. Nashville: Abingdon, 1970.

Oswalt, John N. *The Book of Isaiah.* 2 vols. NICOT. Grand Rapids: Eerdmans, 1986–1998.

Park, Joon Surh. "Theological Traditions of Israel in the Prophetic Judgment of Ezekiel." PhD diss., Princeton Theological Seminary, 1978.

Parpola, Simo. *Assyrian Prophecies.* SAA 9. Illustrations edited by Julian Reade and Simo Parpola. Helsinki: Helsinki University Press; Neo-Assyrian Text Corpus Project, 1997.

Parry-Jones, B., and W. L. L. Parry-Jones. "Post-traumatic Stress Disorder: Supportive Evidence from an Eighteenth Century Natural Disaster." *Psychological Medicine* 24 (1994): 15–27.

Patmore, Hector M. "The Shorter and Longer Texts of Ezekiel: The Implications of the Manuscript Finds from Masada and Qumran." *JSOT* 32 (2007): 231–42.

Paton, Lewis Bayles. "The Holiness-Code and Ezekiel." *PRR* 7 (1896): 98–115.

Patrick, Dale. *The Rhetoric of Revelation in the Hebrew Bible.* OBT. Minneapolis: Fortress, 1999.

Patton, Corrine. "I Myself Gave them Laws that Were Not Good: Ezekiel 20 and the Exodus Traditions." *JSOT* 69 (1996): 73–90.

———. "Priest, Prophet, and Exile: Ezekiel as a Literary Construct." Pages 73–89 in Cook and Patton, *Ezekiel's Hierarchical World.*

———. "'Should Our Sister Be Treated Like a Whore?' A Response to Feminist Critiques of Ezekiel 23." Pages 221–38 in Odell and Strong, *The Book of Ezekiel.*

Pease, Donald E. "Author." Pages 105–17 in *Critical Terms for Literary Study.* 2nd ed. Edited by Frank Lentricchia and Thomas McLaughlin. Chicago: University of Chicago Press, 1995.

Peckham, Brian. *History and Prophecy.* ABRL. Garden City, NY: Doubleday, 1993.

Perdue, Leo G. *The Collapse of History: Reconstructing Old Testament Theology.* OBT. Minneapolis: Fortress, 1994.

———. *Reconstructing Old Testament Theology: After the Collapse of History.* OBT. Minneapolis: Fortress, 2005.

Perlitt, Lothar. *Bundestheologie im Alten Testament.* WMANT 36. Neukirchen-Vluyn: Neukirchener Verlag, 1969.

Petter, Donna Lee. *The Book of Ezekiel and Mesopotamian City Laments.* OBO 246. Fribourg: Academic Press; Göttingen: Vandenhoeck & Ruprecht, 2011.

Pfister, Manfred. "Konzepte der Intertextualität." Pages 1–30 in *Intertextualität, Formen, Funktionen, anglistische Fallstudien.* Edited by Ulrich Broich and Manfred Pfister. Konzepte der Sprach- und Literaturwissenschaft 35. Tübingen: Niemeyer, 1985.

Phillips, Gary A. "Drawing the Other: The Postmodern and Reading the Bible Imaginatively." Pages 403–31 in *In Good Company: Essays in Honor of Robert Detweiler.* Edited by David Jasper et al. Atlanta: Scholars Press, 1994.

Phinney, D. Nathan. "The Prophetic Objection in Ezekiel IV 14 and Its Relation to Eze-kiel's Call." *VT* 55 (2005): 75–88.

Pioske, Daniel. "Retracing a Remembered Past: Methodological Remarks on Memory, History, and the Hebrew Bible." *BibInt* 23 (2015): 291–315.

Pippin, Tina. *Apocalyptic Bodies: The Biblical End of the World in Text and Image*. London: Routledge, 1999.

Platter, Charles. Review of *Intratextuality: Greek and Roman Textual Relations*, edited by Alison Sharrock and Helen Morales. *RelSRev* 28 (2002): 260.

Plottel, Jeanine Parisier, and Hanna Charney, eds. *Intertextuality: New Perspectives in Criticism*. New York: New York Literary Forum, 1978.

Poebel, Arno. *Das appositionell bestimmte Pronomen der 1. Pers. Sing. in den westsemitischen Inschriften und im Alten Testament*. OIAS 3. Chicago: University of Chicago Press, 1932.

Pohlmann, Karl-Friedrich. *Das Buch des Propheten Hesekiel (Ezechiel)*. 2 vols. ATD 22. Göttingen: Vandenhoeck & Ruprecht, 1996–2001.

———. *Ezechiel: Der Stand der theologischen Diskussion*. Darmstadt: Wissenschaftliche Buchgesellschaft, 2008.

———. "Forschung am Ezechielbuch 1969–2004." *TRu* 71 (2006): 60–90, 164–91, 265–309.

———. "Synchrone und diachrone Texterschließung im Ezechielbuch." *HeBAI* 1 (2012): 246–70.

Porter, Stanley E. "The Use of the Old Testament in the New Testament: A Brief Com-ment on Method and Terminology." Pages 79–96 in *Early Christian Interpretation of the Scriptures of Israel*. Edited by Craig A. Evans and James A. Sanders. JSNTSup 148. Sheffield: Sheffield Academic, 1997.

Poser, Ruth. *Das Ezechielbuch als Trauma-Literatur*. VTSup 154. Leiden: Brill, 2012.

Preuss, Horst Dietrich. *Old Testament Theology*. Translated by Leo G. Perdue. OTL. Lou-isville: Westminster John Knox, 1995–1996. Translation of *Theologie des Alten Testa-ments*. 2 vols. Stuttgart: Kohlhammer, 1991–1992.

Pritchard, James B., ed. *Ancient Near Eastern Texts Relating to the Old Testament*. 3rd ed. with supplement. Princeton: Princeton University Press, 1969.

Propp, William H. C. *Exodus*. 2 vols. AB 2 and 2a. New York: Doubleday, 1999–2006.

———. "The Priestly Source Recovered Intact?" *VT* 46 (1996): 458–78.

Provan, Iain, V. Philips Long, and Tremper Longman III. *A Biblical History of Israel*. 2nd ed. Louisville: Westminster John Knox, 2015.

Pury, Albert de, ed. *Le Pentateuque en Question: Les origines et la composition des cinq pre-miers livres de la Bible à la lumière des recherches récentes*. Geneva: Labor et Fides, 1989.

Rad, Gerhard von. "The Form-critical Problem of the Hexateuch." Pages 1–78 in *The Problem of the Hexateuch and Other Essays*. Translated by E. W. Trueman Dicken. New York: McGraw-Hill, 1966.

———. *Holy War in Ancient Israel*. Translated by Marva J. Dawn. Grand Rapids: Eerd-mans, 1991. Translation of *Der heilige Krieg im alten Israel*. Fifth ed. Göttingen: Van-denhoeck & Ruprecht, 1969.

———. *Old Testament Theology*. Translated by D. M. G. Stalker. 2 Vols. New York: Harper & Row, 1962–1965.

Raitt, Thomas M. *A Theology of Exile: Judgment/Deliverance in Jeremiah and Ezekiel*. Philadelphia: Fortress, 1977.

Regt, Lénart J. de. "Macrosyntactic Functions of Nominal Clauses Referring to Participants." Pages 273–96 in Miller, *Verbless Clause.*

Reiss, Moshe. "Elijah the Zealot: A Foil to Moses." *JBQ* 32, no. 3 (2004): 174–80.

Rendsburg, Gary. "Late Biblical Hebrew and the Date of P." *JANES* 12 (1980): 65–80.

Rendtorff, Rolf. "Between Historical Criticism and Holistic Interpretation: New Trends
in Old Testament Exegesis." Pages 298–303 in *Congress Volume, Jerusalem 1986.* Edited
by J. A. Emerton. Leiden: Brill, 1988.

———. *Canon and Theology: Overtures to an Old Testament Theology.* Translated and
edited by Margaret Kohl. OBT. Minneapolis: Fortress, 1993.

———. "The Concept of Revelation in Ancient Israel." Pages 25–53 in *Revelation as
History.* Edited by Wolfhart Pannenberg. New York: Macmillan, 1968. Translation
of "Die Offenbarungsvorstellungen im alten Israel." Pages 21–41 in *Offenbarung als
Geschichte.* Edited by Wolfhart Pannenberg. Göttingen: Vandenhoeck & Ruprecht,
1961.

———. *The Covenant Formula: An Exegetical and Theological Investigation.* Translated by
Margaret Kohl. OTS. Edinburgh: T&T Clark, 1998.

———. "Geschichte und Wort im Alten Testament." *EvT* 22 (1962): 621–49.

———. "The Paradigm Is Changing: Hopes—and Fears." *BibInt* 1 (1993): 34–53.

———. *The Problem of the Process of Transmission in the Pentateuch.* Translated by John J.
Scullion. JSOTSup 89. Sheffield: JSOT Press, 1990.

Renz, Thomas. *The Rhetorical Function of the Book of Ezekiel.* VTSup 76. Leiden: Brill, 1999.

Reventlow, Henning Graf. *Problems of Old Testament Theology in the Twentieth Century.*
Translated by John Bowden. Philadelphia: Fortress, 1985.

———. "Die Völker als Jahwes Zeugen bei Ezechiel." *ZAW* 71 (1959): 33–43.

———. *Wächter über Israel: Ezechiel und seine Tradition.* BZAW 82. Berlin: Töpelmann,
1962.

Reviv, Hanoch. *The Elders in Ancient Israel: A Study of a Biblical Institution.* Translated by
Lucy Plitmann. Jerusalem: Magnes, 1989.

Riffaterre, M. "Intertextual Representation: On Mimesis as Interpretive Discourse."
Critical Inquiry 11 (1984): 141–62.

Ringgren, Helmer. "Oral and Written Transmission in the O.T." *ST* 3 (1949): 34–59.

Robbins, Vernon K. *Exploring the Texture of Texts: A Guide to Socio-Rhetorical Interpretation.* Valley Forge, PA: Trinity Press International, 1996.

Roberts, J. J. M. *First Isaiah.* Hermeneia. Minneapolis: Fortress, 2015.

Robson, James. *Word and Spirit in Ezekiel.* LHBOTS 447. London: T&T Clark, 2006.

Rogerson, John. *Old Testament Criticism in the Nineteenth Century: England and Germany.* Philadelphia: Fortress, 1985.

Rom-Shiloni, Dalit. *Exclusive Inclusivity: Identity Conflicts Between the Exiles and the
People who Remained (6th–5th Centuries BCE).* LHBOTS 543. New York: Bloomsbury T&T Clark, 2013.

———. "Ezekiel and Jeremiah: What Might Stand Behind the Silence?" *HeBAI* 1 (2012):
203–30.

———. "Ezekiel as the Voice of the Exiles and Constructor of Exilic Ideology." *HUCA*
76 (2005): 1–45.

Rom-Shiloni, Dalit, and Corrine Carvalho, eds. *Ezekiel in its Babylonian Context.* WO 45,
no. 1 (2015).

Rooker, Mark F. *Biblical Hebrew in Transition: The Language of the Book of Ezekiel.*
JSOTSup 90. Sheffield: JSOT Press, 1990.

———. "Ezekiel and the Typology of Biblical Hebrew." *HAR* 12 (1990): 133–55.

Rooy, H. F. van. "Deuteronomy 28,69—Superscript or Subscript?" *JNSL* 14 (1988): 215–22.

Rowley, H. H. "The Book of Ezekiel in Modern Study." *BJRL* 36, no. 1 (1953–1954): 146–90.

———. *The Changing Pattern of Old Testament Studies*. London: Epworth, 1959.

Ruiten, J. T. A. G. M van. "The Intertextual Relationship between Isa 11,6–9 and Isa 65,25." Pages 31–42 in *The Scriptures and the Scrolls: Studies in Honour of A. S. van der Woude on the Occasion of His 65th Birthday*. Edited by F. García Martínez et al. VTSup 49. Leiden: Brill, 1992.

Ryken, Leland. *Words of Delight: A Literary Introduction to the Bible*. Grand Rapids: Baker, 1987.

Sanders, James A. Review of *The Garments of Torah*, by Michael Fishbane. *ThTo* 47 (1991): 433.

———. *Torah and Canon*. Philadelphia: Fortress, 1972.

Sandmel, Samuel. "The Haggada Within Scripture." *JBL* 80 (1961): 105–22.

———. *The Hebrew Scriptures: An Introduction to Their Literature and Religious Ideas*. New York: Oxford University Press, 1978.

Sarna, Nahum M. *Exodus = Šemōt*. JPS Torah Commentary. Philadelphia: Jewish Publication Society, 1991.

———. "Psalm 89: A Study in Inner-Biblical Exegesis." Pages 29–46 in *Biblical and Other Studies*. Edited by A. Altmann. Brandeis Texts and Studies. Cambridge, MA: Harvard University Press, 1963.

Satake, Akira. *Die Offenbarung des Johannes*. Edited by Thomas Witulksi. KEK 16. Göttingen: Vandenhoeck & Ruprecht, 2008.

Saussure, Ferdinand de. *Course in General Linguistics*. Translated by Roy Harris. Edited by C. Bally and A. Sechehaye. Chicago: Open Court, 1986.

Savran, George W. *Telling and Retelling: Quotation in Biblical Literature*. Indiana Studies in Biblical Literature. Bloomington: Indiana University Press, 1988.

Sawyer, John F. A. "A Change of Emphasis in the Study of the Prophets." Pages 233–49 in *Israel's Prophetic Tradition: Essays in Honour of Peter R. Ackroyd*. Edited by Richard Coggins et al. Cambridge: Cambridge University Press, 1982.

———. *Sacred Languages and Sacred Texts*. London; New York: Routledge, 1999.

Schleiermacher, Friedrich. *The Christian Faith*. Translated by H. R. Mackintosh and J. S. Stewart. Edinburgh: T&T Clark, 1928.

Schmid, H. H. *Der sogenannte Jahwist*. Zurich: Theologischer Verlag, 1976.

Schmidt, Werner H. *Old Testament Introduction*. Translated by Matthew J. O'Connell. 2nd ed. New York: de Gruyter; Louisville: Westminster John Knox, 1999.

Schmitt, Hans-Christoph. "Tradition der Prophetenbücher in den Schichten der Plagenerzählung Ex 7,1–11,10." Pages 196–216 in *Prophet und Prophetenbuch: Festschrift für Otto Kaiser zum 65. Geburtstag*. Edited by Volkmar Fritz, Karl-Friedrich Pohlmann, et al. Berlin: de Gruyter, 1989.

Schoors, Antoon. *I Am God Your Saviour: A Form-Critical Study of the Main Genres in Is. XL-LV*. VTSup 24. Leiden: Brill, 1973.

Schöpflin, Karin. *Theologie als Biographie im Ezechielbuch: Ein Beitrag zur Konzeption alttestamentlicher Prophetie*. FAT 2.36. Tübingen: Mohr Siebeck, 2002.

Schottroff, W. *"Gedenken" im Alten Orient und im Alten Testament*. 2nd ed. WMANT 15. Neukirchen-Vluyn: Neukirchener Verlag, 1967.

Schultz, Richard L. "Intertextuality, Canon, and 'Undecidability': Understanding Isaiah's 'New Heavens and New Earth' (Isaiah 65:17–25)." *BBR* 20 (2010): 19–38.

————. *The Search for Quotation: Verbal Parallels in the Prophets.* JSOTSup 180. Sheffield: Sheffield Academic, 1999.

————. "The Ties that Bind: Intertextuality, the Identification of Verbal Parallels, and Reading Strategies in the Book of the Twelve." Pages 39–57 in *SBL 2001 Seminar Papers.* Atlanta: Society of Biblical Literature, 2001.

Schulz, Hermann. *Das Todesrecht im Alten Testament: Studien zur Rechtsform der Mot–Jumat–Sätze.* BZAW 114. Berlin: Töpelmann, 1969.

Schwartz, Baruch J. "Ezekiel's Dim View of Israel's Restoration." Pages 43–67 in Odell and Strong, *The Book of Ezekiel.*

————. "A Priest Out of Place: Reconsidering Ezekiel's Role in the History of the Israelite Priesthood." Pages 61–71 in Cook and Patton, *Ezekiel's Hierarchical World.*

Scott, James M., ed. *Exile: Old Testament, Jewish, and Christian Conceptions.* JSJSup 51. Leiden: Brill, 1997.

Sedlmeier, Franz. *Das Buch Ezechiel.* 2 vols. NSKAT. Stuttgart: Katholisches Bibelwerk, 2002–2013.

————. "'Sie werden mir zum Volk': Zur 'Bundesformel' im Ezechielbuch." Pages 211–18 in *Für immer verbündet: Studien zur Bundestheologie der Bibel.* Edited by Christoph Dohmen and Christian Frevel. SBB 211. Stuttgart: Katholisches Bibelwerk, 2011.

————. *Studien zu Komposition und Theologie von Ezechiel 20.* SBB 21. Stuttgart: Katholisches Bibelwerk, 1990.

Seeligmann, I. L. "Erkenntnis Gottes und historisches Bewußtsein im alten Israel." Pages 414–45 in *Beiträge zur alttestamentlichen Theologie: Festschrift für Walther Zimmerli zum 70. Geburtstag.* Edited by Herbert Donner et al. Göttingen: Vandenhoeck & Ruprecht, 1977.

————. "Voraussetzungen der Midraschexegese." Pages 150–81 in *Congress Volume: Copenhagen 1953.* Edited by G. W. Anderson. VTSup 1. Leiden: Brill, 1953.

Seinecke, L. Chr. F. W. *Geschichte des Volkes Israel.* 2 vols. Göttingen: Vandenhoeck & Ruprecht, 1876–1884.

Seitz, Christopher R. "The Prophet Moses and the Canonical Shape of Jeremiah." *ZAW* 101 (1989): 3–27.

Sharon, Diane M. "A Biblical Parallel to a Sumerian Temple Hymn? Ezekiel 40–48 and Gudea." *JANES* 24 (1996): 99–109.

Simon, Uriel. *Reading Prophetic Narratives.* Translated by Lenn J. Schramm. Bloomington: Indiana University Press, 1997.

Ska, J. –L. "La sortie d'Égypte (Ex 7–14) dans le récit sacerdotal (Pg) et la tradition prophétique." *Bib* 60 (1979): 191–215.

Smend, Rudolf. *Der Prophet Ezechiel.* 2nd ed. Leipzig: Hirzel, 1880.

Smith, D. L. *The Religion of the Landless: the Social Context of the Babylonian Exile.* Bloomington, IN: Meyer-Stone, 1989.

Smith, Gary V. *Isaiah.* 2 vols. NAC. Nashville: B & H, 2007–09.

Smith-Christopher, Daniel L. *A Biblical Theology of Exile.* OBT. Minneapolis: Fortress, 2002.

————. "Ezekiel in Abu Ghraib: Rereading Ezekiel 16:37–39 in the Context of Imperial Conquest." Pages 141–57 in Cook and Patton, *Ezekiel's Hierarchical World.*

————. "Ezekiel on Fanon's Couch." Pages 108–44 in *Peace and Justice Shall Embrace* (Millard Lind Festschrift). Edited by T. Grimsrud et al. Telford, PA: Pandora, 1999.

————. "Reassessing the Historical and Sociological Impact of the Babylonian Exile (597/587–539 BCE)." Pages 7–36 in Scott, *Exile.*

————. "Trauma and Old Testament: Some Problems and Prospects." Pages 223–43 in *Trauma and Traumatization in Individual and Collective Dimensions: Insights from Biblical Studies and Beyond*. Edited by Eve-Marie Becker, Jan Dochhorn, and Else K. Holt. Göttingen: Vandenhoeck & Ruprecht, 2014.

Soggin, J. Alberto. *Introduction to the Old Testament*. Translated by John Bowden. 3rd ed. OTL. Philadelphia: Westminster, 1989.

Sommer, Benjamin D. "Exegesis, Allusion and Intertextuality in the Hebrew Bible: A Response to Lyle Eslinger." *VT* 46 (1996): 479–89.

————. *A Prophet Reads Scripture: Allusion in Isaiah 40–66*. Stanford: Stanford University Press, 1998.

Spiegel, Shalom. "Ezekiel or Pseudo-Ezekiel?" *HTR* 24 (1931): 245–321.

————. "Toward Certainty in Ezekiel." *JBL* 54 (1935): 145–71.

Sprinkle, Preston. "Law and Life: Leviticus 18.5 in the Literary Framework of Ezekiel." *JSOT* 31 (2007): 275–93.

Stackert, Jeffrey. *A Prophet Like Moses: Prophecy, Law, and Israelite Religion*. Oxford: Oxford University Press, 2014.

Stevenson, Kalinda Rose. *The Vision of Transformation: The Territorial Rhetoric of Ezekiel 40–48*. SBLDS 154. Atlanta: Scholars Press, 1996.

Stiebert, Johanna. *The Construction of Shame in the Hebrew Bible*. JSOTSup 346. London: Sheffield Academic, 2002.

Stökl, Jonathan. "'I Have Rained Stones and Fiery Glow on Their Heads!' Celestial and Meteorological Prophecy in the Neo-Assyrian Empire." Pages 239–51 in *"Thus Speaks Ishtar of Arbela": Prophecy in Israel, Assyria, and Egypt in the Neo-Assyrian Period*. Edited by Robert P. Gordon and Hans M. Barstad. Winona Lake, IN: Eisenbrauns, 2013.

Strazicich, John. *Joel's Use of Scripture and Scripture's Use of Joel*. BibInt 82. Leiden: Brill, 2007.

Strine, C. A. "The Role of Repentance in the Book of Ezekiel: A Second Chance for the Second Generation." *JTS* 63 (2012): 467–91.

————. *Sworn Enemies: The Divine Oath, the Book of Ezekiel, and the Polemics of Exile*. BZAW 436. Berlin: de Gruyter, 2013.

Strong, John T. "Egypt's Shameful Death and the House of Israel's Exodus from Sheol (Ezekiel 32.17–32 and 37.1–14)." *JSOT* 34 (2010): 475–504.

————. "Ezekiel's Use of the Recognition Formula in His Oracles against the Nations." *PRSt* 22 (1995): 115–33.

————. "God's *Kābôd:* The Presence of Yahweh in the Book of Ezekiel." Pages 69–95 in Odell and Strong, *The Book of Ezekiel*.

Stuart, Douglas. *Hosea-Jonah*. WBC 31. Waco, TX: Word, 1987.

Surls, Austin. *Making Sense of the Divine Name in the Book of Exodus: From Etymology to Literary Onomastics*. BBRSup 17. Winona Lake, IN: Eisenbrauns, 2017.

Sweeney, Marvin A. "Ezekiel." Pages 1042–138 in *The Jewish Study Bible*. Edited by Adele Berlin and Marc Zvi Brettler. New York: Oxford University Press, 2004.

————. "Ezekiel's Conceptualization of the Exile in Intertextual Perspective." *HeBAI* 1 (2012): 154–72.

————. "Ezekiel: Zadokite Priest and Visionary Prophet of the Exile." Pages 728–51 in *Society of Biblical Literature, 2000 Seminar Papers*. Atlanta: Society of Biblical Literature, 2000.

———. *Prophetic Conflict: Its Effect upon Israelite Religion*. BZAW 124. Berlin: de Gruyter, 1971.

———. *TANAK: A Theological and Critical Introduction to the Jewish Bible*. Minneapolis: Fortress, 2012.

Sweeney, Marvin A., and Ehud Ben Zvi, eds. *The Changing Face of Form Criticism for the Twenty-First Century*. Grand Rapids: Eerdmans, 2003.

Talmon, Shemaryahu. "Synonymous Readings in the Textual Traditions of the Old Testament." Pages 335–83 in *Studies in the Bible*. Edited by Chaim Rabin. ScrHier 8. Jerusalem: Magnes, 1961.

Talmon, Shemaryahu, with Carol Newsom and Yigael Yadin. *Masada VI: Hebrew Fragments from Masada (the Yigael Yadin Excavations 1963–1965)*. Jerusalem: Israel Exploration Society, 1999.

Taylor, John B. *Ezekiel, An Introduction and Commentary*. TOTC. London: Tyndale, 1969.

Thackeray, H. St. John. "The Greek Translators of Ezekiel." *JTS* 4 (1903): 398–411.

———. *The Septuagint and Jewish Worship: A Study in Origins*. The Schweich Lectures 1920. 2nd ed. London: H. Milford for the British Academy, 1923.

Thiel, Winfried. "Die Erkenntnisaussage in den Elia- und Elisa-Überlieferungen." Pages 204–17 in *Gelebte Geschichte: Studien zur Sozialgeschichte und zur frühen prophetischen Geschichtsdeutung Israels*. Edited by Peter Mommer and Simone Pottmann. Neukirchen-Vluyn: Neukirchener Verlag, 2000.

———. *Könige*. BKAT 9/2. Neukirchen-Vluyn: Neukirchener Verlag, 2000–.

Thompson, Henry O. "Yahweh." *ABD*, 6:1011–12.

Toffelmire, C. M. "Form Criticism." *DOTPr*, 257–71.

Tooman, William A. "Covenant and Presence in the Composition and Theology of Ezekiel." Pages 151–82 in *Divine Presence and Absence in Exilic and Post-Exilic Judaism*. Edited by Nathan MacDonald and Izaak J. de Hulster. FAT 2.61. Tübingen: Mohr Siebeck, 2013.

———. "Ezekiel's Radical Challenge to Inviolability." *ZAW* 121 (2009): 498–514.

———. *Gog of Magog: Reuse of Scripture and Compositional Technique in Ezekiel 38–39*. FAT 2.52. Tübingen: Mohr Siebeck, 2011.

———. "On the Meaning of דבר ודם in Ezekiel (5:17; 14:19; 28:23; 38:22)." *VT* 60 (2010): 666–68.

———. "Transformation of Israel's Hope: The Reuse of Scripture in the Gog Oracles." Pages 50–110 in *Transforming Visions: Transformations of Text, Tradition, and Theology in Ezekiel*. Edited by William A. Tooman and Michael A. Lyons. PTMS. Eugene, OR: Pickwick, 2010.

Tooman, William A., and Penelope Barter, eds. *Ezekiel: Current Debates and Future Directions*. FAT 112. Tübingen: Mohr Siebeck, 2017.

Torrey, C. C. "Certainly Pseudo-Ezekiel." *JBL* 53 (1934): 291–320.

———. *Pseudo-Ezekiel and the Original Prophecy*. Repr. ed. with response by Shalom Spiegel and prolegomenon by Moshe Greenberg. New York: KTAV, 1970.

Tov, Emanuel. "Recensional Differences between the MT and LXX of Ezekiel." *ETL* 62 (1986): 89–101.

Towner, W. Sibley. *Daniel*. Interpretation. Atlanta: John Knox Press, 1984.

Trimm, Charles. "Recent Research on Warfare in the Old Testament." *CurBR* 10 (2012): 171–216.

Tucker, Gene M. "Prophecy and the Prophetic Literature." Pages 325–68 in Knight and Tucker, *The Hebrew Bible and Its Modern Interpreters*.

Tuell, Steven S. "Divine Presence and Absence in Ezekiel's Prophecy." Pages 97–116 in Odell and Strong, *The Book of Ezekiel*.

———. "The Meaning of the Mark: New Light on Ezekiel 9 from the History of Interpretation." Pages 185–202 in Mein and Joyce, *After Ezekiel*.

Tull, Patricia K. "Rhetorical Criticism and Intertextuality." Pages 156–80 in *To Each Its Own Meaning: An Introduction to Biblical Criticisms and their Application*. Revised ed. Edited by Steven L. McKenzie and Stephen R. Haynes. Louisville: Westminster John Knox, 1999.

———. "The Rhetoric of Recellection." Pages 71–78 in Lemaire and Sæbø, *Congress Volume, Oslo 1998*.

Tull [Willey], Patricia K. *Remember the Former Things: The Recollection of Previous Texts in Second Isaiah*. SBLDS 161. Atlanta: Scholars Press, 1997.

Turner, P. D. M. "The Septuagint Version of Chapters I–XXXIX of the Book of Ezekiel: The Language, the Translation Technique and the Bearing on the Hebrew Text." DPhil diss., Oxford University, 1970/1996.

Turner, Stuart W., and Caroline Gorst-Unsworth. "Psychological Sequelae of Torture: A Descriptive Model." *British Journal of Psychiatry* 157 (1990): 475–80. doi:10.1192/bjp.157.4.475.

Ulrich, Eugene, and Peter W. Flint. *Qumran Cave 1, II: The Isaiah Scrolls*. Part 1: Plates and Transcriptions. DJD 32. Oxford: Clarendon, 2010.

Vall, Gregory. "An Epistemology of Faith: The Knowledge of God in Israel's Prophetic Literature." Pages 24–42 in *The Bible and Epistemology: Biblical Soundings on the Knowledge of God*. Edited by Mary Healy and Robin Parry. Milton Keynes, UK: Paternoster, 2007.

Vanderhooft, David S. "Ezekiel in and on Babylon." *Bible et Proche-Orient, Mélanges André Lemaire III*. Edited by J. Elayi et al. *Transeuphratène* 46 (2014): 99–119.

———. *The Neo-Babylonian Empire and Babylon in the Latter Prophets*. HSM 59. Atlanta: Scholars Press, 1999.

VanGemeren, Willem A. *Interpreting the Prophetic Word*. Grand Rapids: Academie Books, 1990.

———, ed. *New International Dictionary of Old Testament Theology and Exegesis*. 5 vols. Grand Rapids: Zondervan, 1997.

Van Groningen, Gerard. *Messianic Revelation in the Old Testament*. Grand Rapids: Baker, 1990.

Van Seters, John. *Abraham in History and Tradition*. New Haven: Yale University Press, 1975.

———. "Dating the Yahwist's History: Principles and Perspectives." *Bib* 96 (2015): 1–25.

Van Winkle, D. W. "The Relationship of the Nations to Yahweh and to Israel in Isaiah XL–LV." *VT* 35 (1985): 446–58.

Veen, Peter van der. "Sixth-Century Issues: The Fall of Jerusalem, the Exile, and the Return." Pages 383–405 in *Ancient Israel's History: An Introduction to Issues and Sources*. Edited by Bill T. Arnold and Richard S. Hess. Grand Rapids: Baker Academic, 2014.

Vermes, Geza. *Scripture and Tradition in Judaism: Haggadic Studies*. Studia Post-Biblica 4. Leiden: Brill, 1961.

Vervenne, Marc. "The Phraseology of 'Knowing YHWH' in the Hebrew Bible: A Preliminary Study of Its Syntax and Function." Pages 467–92 in *Studies in the Book of Isaiah:*

Festschrift Willem A. M. Beuken. Edited by J. van Ruiten et al. BETL 132. Leuven: Leuven University Press; Peeters, 1997.

Vogels, Walter. "Restauration de l'Égypt et universalisme en Ez 29,13–16." *Bib* 53 (1972): 473–94.

Vos, Geerhardus. *Biblical Theology.* Grand Rapids: Eerdmans, 1948.

Vries, Pieter de. *The Kābôd of YHWH in the Old Testament: With Particular Reference to the Book of Ezekiel.* SSN 65. Leiden: Brill, 2016.

Vriezen, Th. C. *An Outline of Old Testament Theology.* Translated by S. Neuijen. Oxford: Blackwell, 1958.

Waller, Margaret. "An Interview with Julia Kristeva." Pages 280–94 in O'Donnell and Davis, *Intertextuality and Contemporary American Fiction.*

Walsh, Jerome T. *1 Kings.* Berit Olam. Collegeville, MN: Liturgical Press, 1996.

Waltke, Bruce K., and M. O'Connor. *An Introduction to Biblical Hebrew Syntax.* Winona Lake, IN: Eisenbrauns, 1990.

Watts, James W. Review of *The Rhetoric of Revelation in the Hebrew Bible,* by Dale Patrick, *HBT* 24 (2002): 129–31.

Weinfeld, Moshe. *Deuteronomy and the Deuteronomic School.* Oxford: Clarendon, 1972.

———. "Pentateuch." *EncJud,* 13:231–61.

———. *The Place of the Law in the Religion of Ancient Israel.* VTSup 100. Leiden: Brill, 2004.

———. "Universalism and Particularism in the Time of the Exile and Restoration." *Tarbiz* 34 (1964): 228–42 [Hebrew].

Weingreen, J. "Exposition in the Old Testament and in Rabbinical Literature." Pages 187–201 in *Promise and Fulfilment: Essays Presented to S. H. Hooke.* Edited by F. F. Bruce. Edinburgh: T&T Clark, 1963.

———. *From Bible to Mishna: The Continuity of Tradition.* Manchester: Manchester University Press, 1976.

———. "Rabbinic-Type Glosses in the Old Testament." *JSS* 2 (1957): 149–62.

Weippert, Manfred. "Aspekte israelitischer Prophetie im Lichte verwandter Erscheinungen des Alten Orients." Pages 287–319 in *Ad Bene et Fideliter Seminandum (Festgabe für Karlheinz Deller).* Edited by G. Mauer et al. AOAT 220. Neukirchen-Vluyn: Neukirchener Verlag, 1988.

———. "'Heiliger Krieg' in Israel und Assyrien: Kritische Anmerkungen zu Gerhard von Rads Konzept des 'Heiligen Krieges im alten Israel.'" *ZAW* 84 (1972): 460–93.

———. "'Ich bin Jahwe'—'Ich bin Ištar von Arbela': Deuterojesaja im Licht der neuassyrischen Prophetie." Pages 31–59 in *Prophetie und Psalmen: Festschrift für Klaus Seybold zum 65. Geburtstag.* Edited by Beat Huwyler et al. AOAT 280. Münster: Ugarit-Verlag, 2001.

Wellhausen, Julius. *Prolegomena to the History of Israel.* Translated by J. Sutherland Black and Allan Menzies. 1885. Repr., Atlanta: Scholars Press, 1994.

Wenham, Gordon J. *The Book of Leviticus.* NICOT. Grand Rapids: Eerdmans, 1979.

———. "Pondering the Pentateuch: The Search for a New Paradigm." Pages 116–44 in *The Face of Old Testament Studies: A Survey of Contemporary Approaches.* Edited by David W. Baker and Bill T. Arnold. Grand Rapids: Baker; Leicester: Apollos, 1999.

———. "The Priority of P." *VT* 49 (1999): 240–58.

Westermann, Claus. *Isaiah 40–66: A Commentary.* Translated by David M. G. Stalker. OTL. Philadelphia: Westminster, 1969.

Wevers, John. *Ezekiel.* NCBC. Greenwood, SC: Attic, 1969.

Weyde, Karl William. *Prophecy and Teaching: Prophetic Authority, Form Problems, and the Use of Traditions in the Book of Malachi.* BZAW 288. Berlin: de Gruyter, 2000.

White, Hugh C., ed. *Speech Act Theory and Biblical Criticism. Semeia* 41 (1988).

Whybray, R. N. *The Making of the Pentateuch: A Methodological Study.* JSOTSup 53. Sheffield: JSOT Press, 1987.

Wiener, Aharon. *The Prophet Elijah in the Development of Judaism: A Depth Psychological Study.* London: Routledge; Keegan Paul, 1978.

Wildberger, Hans. *Isaiah 28–39.* Translated by Thomas H. Trapp. CC. Minneapolis: Fortress, 2002.

Williams, Catrin H. *I Am He: The Interpretation of ʾAnî hûʾ in Jewish and Early Christian Literature.* WUNT 113. Tübingen: Mohr Siebeck, 2000.

Williamson, H. G. M. *The Book Called Isaiah: Deutero-Isaiah's Role in Composition and Redaction.* Oxford: Clarendon, 1994.

———. "History and Memory in the Prophets." Pages 132–48 in *The Oxford Handbook of the Prophets.* Edited by Carolyn J. Sharp. New York: Oxford University Press, 2016.

———. "Isaiah 62:4 and the Problem of Inner-Biblical Allusions," *JBL* 119 (2000): 734–39.

———. Review of *Isaiah,* by Brevard Childs. *ThTo* 59 (2002): 124.

Willis, Timothy M. *The Elders of the City: A Study of the Elders-Laws in Deuteronomy.* Atlanta: Society of Biblical Literature, 2001.

Wilson, Ian. *Out of the Midst of the Fire: Divine Presence in Deuteronomy.* SBLDS 151. Atlanta: Scholars Press, 1995.

Wilson, Robert R. "An Interpretation of Ezekiel's Dumbness." *VT* 22 (1972): 91–104.

———. "Prophecy in Crisis: The Call of Ezekiel." Pages 157–69 in *Interpreting the Prophets.* Edited by James Luther Mays and Paul J. Achtemeier. Philadelphia: Fortress, 1987.

Wiseman, D. J. *Chronicles of Chaldean Kings (626–556 B.C.) in the British Museum.* London: British Museum, 1956.

Wolde, Ellen van. "From Text via Text to Meaning: Intertextuality and Its Implications." Pages 160–99 (ch. 10) in *Words Become Worlds: Semantic Studies of Genesis 1–11.* BibInt 6. Leiden: Brill, 1994.

———. "Texts in Dialogue with Texts: Intertextuality in the Ruth and Tamar Narratives." *BibInt* 5 (1997): 1–28.

———. "Trendy Intertextuality?" Pages 43–49 in *Intertextuality in Biblical Writings: Essays in Honour of Bas van Iersel.* Edited by Sipke Draisma. Kampen: Kok, 1989.

Wolff, Hans Walter. "Erkenntnis Gottes im Alten Testament." *EvT* 15 (1955): 426–31.

———. *Hosea.* Translated by G. Stansell. Hermeneia. Philadelphia: Fortress, 1974.

———. *Joel and Amos.* Edited by S. Dean McBride Jr. Translated by Waldemar Janzen, S. Dean McBride Jr. and Charles A. Muenchow. Hermeneia. Philadelphia: Fortress, 1977.

———. "'Wissen um Gott' bei Hosea als Urform von Theologie." *EvT* 12 (1952): 533–54.

Wolters, Al. *Zechariah.* HCOT. Leuven: Peeters, 2014.

Wong, Ka Leung. *The Idea of Retribution in the Book of Ezekiel.* VTSup 87. Leiden: Brill, 2001.

World Union of Jewish Studies, eds. *Proceedings of the Eighth World Congress of Jewish Studies.* Jerusalem: Magnes, 1983.

Worton, M., and J. Still, eds. *Intertextuality: Theories and Practices.* Manchester: Manchester University Press, 1990.

Woudstra, Marten H. "Edom and Israel in Ezekiel." *CTJ* 3 (1968): 21–35.

———. "The Everlasting Covenant in Ezekiel 16:53–63." *CTJ* 6 (1971): 22–48.

Wright, A. G. "The Literary Genre Midrash." *CBQ* 28 (1966): 105–38.

Wright, Christopher J. H. *The Message of Ezekiel*. The Bible Speaks Today. Leicester: Inter-Varsity Press, 2001.

Wright, G. Ernest. *God Who Acts: Biblical Theology as Recital*. SBT. London: SCM, 1952.

Wu, Daniel Y. *Honor, Shame, and Guilt: Social-Scientific Approaches to the Book of Ezekiel*. BBRSup 14. Winona Lake, IN: Eisenbrauns, 2016.

Yoon, David I. "The Ideological Inception of Intertextuality and its Dissonance in Current Biblical Studies." *CurBR* 12 (2012): 58–76.

Young, E. J. *An Introduction to the Old Testament*. Grand Rapids: Eerdmans, 1949.

Young, Ian, ed. *Biblical Hebrew: Studies in Chronology and Typology*. JSOTSup 369. London: T&T Clark, 2003.

Zadok, Ran. *The Jews in Babylonia during the Chaldean and Achaemenian Periods According to the Babylonian Sources*. Haifa: University of Haifa Press, 1979.

Zenger, Erich. "The God of Exodus in the Message of the Prophets as Seen in Isaiah." Pages 22–33 in *Exodus: A Lasting Paradigm*. Edited by Bas van Iersel and Anton Weiler. Edinburgh: T&T Clark, 1987.

Zevit, Ziony. "Converging Lines of Evidence Bearing on the Date of P." *ZAW* 94 (1982): 481–511.

Zewi, Tamar. "Nominal Clause." *EHLL*, 2:830–39.

Ziegler, Joseph, ed. *Ezechiel*. Septuaginta: Vetus Testamentum Graecum 16.1. 3rd ed. Göttingen: Vandenhoeck & Ruprecht, 2006.

Zimmerli, Walther. "Deutero-Ezechiel?" *ZAW* 84 (1972): 501–16.

———. *Erkenntnis Gottes nach dem Buche Ezechiel: Eine theologische Studie*. ATANT 27. Zürich: Zwingli, 1954.

———. *Ezekiel 1: A Commentary on the Book of the Prophet Ezekiel, Chapters 1–24*. Translated by Ronald E. Clements. Hermeneia. Philadelphia: Fortress, 1979. Translation of *Ezechiel 1*. BKAT 13/1. Neukirchen-Vluyn: Neukirchener Verlag, 1969.

———. *Ezekiel 2: A Commentary on the Book of the Prophet Ezekiel, Chapters 25–48*. Translated by James D. Martin. Hermeneia. Philadelphia: Fortress, 1983. Translation of *Ezechiel 2*. BKAT 13/2. Neukirchen-Vluyn: Neukirchener Verlag, 1969 [with additions from the second German edition of 1979].

———. *Gottes Offenbarung: Gesammelte Aufsätze zum Alten Testament*. TB 19. Munich: Kaiser, 1963.

———. "Das Gotteswort des Ezechiel." *ZTK* 48 (1951): 249–62.

———. "The History of Israelite Religion." Pages 351–84 in *Tradition and Interpretation: Essays by Members of the Society for Old Testament Study*. Edited by G. W. Anderson. Oxford: Clarendon, 1979.

———. *I Am Yahweh*. Edited by Walter Brueggemann with introduction. Translated by Douglas W. Stott. Atlanta: John Knox, 1982.

———. "Ich bin Jahwe." Pages 179–209 in *Geschichte und Altes Testament* (Albrecht Alt Festschrift). BHT 16. Tübingen: Mohr Siebeck, 1953.

———. *The Law and the Prophets: A Study of the Meaning of the Old Testament*. Translated by R. E. Clements. Oxford: Blackwell, 1965.

———. "The Message of the Prophet Ezekiel." *Int* 23 (1969): 131–57.

———. "Le nouvel 'exode' dans le message des deux grands prophètes de l'exile." Pages 216–27 in *Maqqél shâqédh, La branche d'amandier: Hommage à Wilhelm Vischer*. Edited by Jean Cadier. Montpellier, FR: Causse, Graille, Castelnau, 1960.

———. "'Offenbarung' im Alten Testament." *EvT* 22 (1962): 15–31.

———. *Old Testament Theology in Outline*. Translated by David E. Green. Edinburgh: T&T Clark, 1978.

———. "Die Phänomen der 'Fortschreibung' im Buche Ezechiel." Pages 174–91 in *Prophecy: Essays Presented to Georg Fohrer*. Edited by J. A. Emerton. BZAW 150. Berlin: de Gruyter, 1980.

———. "Prophetic Proclamation and Reinterpretation." Pages 69–100 in Knight, *Tradition and Theology in the Old Testament*.

———. "Die Quellen der alttestamentlichen Gotteserkenntnis." Pages 226–40 in *Theologie und Wirklichkeit: Festschrift für Wolfgang Trillhaas zum 70. Geburtstag*. Edited by Hans Walter Schütte et al. Göttingen: Vandenhoeck & Ruprecht, 1974.

———. "The Special Form- and Traditio-Historical Character of Ezekiel's Prophecy." *VT* 15 (1965): 515–27.

———. "Das Wort des göttlichen Selbsterweises (Erweiswort), eine prophetische Gattung." Pages 154–64 in *Mélanges Bibliques rédigés en l'honneur de André Robert*. TICP 4. Paris: Bloud et Gay, 1957.

Zimmermann, Heinrich. "Das absolute Ἐγώ εἰμι als die neutestamentliche Offenbarungsformel." *BZ* 4 (1960): 54–69, 266–76.

Bulletin for Biblical Research Supplements